UNDERSTANDING WELL-BEING IN THE OLDEST OLD

The demographic and social structures of most industrialized and developing countries are changing rapidly as infant mortality is reduced and population life span has increased in dramatic ways. In particular, the oldest-old (85 years and older) population has grown and will continue to grow. This segment of the population tends to suffer physical and cognitive decline, and little information is available to describe how their positive and negative distal experiences, habits, and intervening proximal environmental influences affect their well-being and how social and health policies can help meet the unique challenges they face. *Understanding Well-Being in the Oldest Old* is the outcome of a four-day workshop attended by U.S. and Israeli scientists and funded by the U.S.-Israel Binational Science Foundation to examine both novel and traditional paradigms that could extend our knowledge and understanding of the well-being of the oldest old. This book engages social scientists in sharing methods of understanding and, thereby, possibly improving the quality of life of older populations, especially among the oldest old.

Leonard W. Poon is University of Georgia Distinguished Research Professor and Professor of Public Health and Psychology. He is also Director of the Institute of Gerontology and the Georgia Geriatric Education Center, Chair of the Faculty of Gerontology, and Executive Director of the International Centenarian Consortium. He was Director of the Georgia Centenarian Study, funded by the National Institutes of Health, from 1988 to 2009. Dr. Poon's primary research interests are longevity and survival of the oldest old by using a multidisciplinary approach to examine the contributors and predictors of functional capacities, life satisfaction, quality of life, personality, and ability to cope, as well as genetics, environment, and neuropathological contributions to longevity. His other research interests are normal and pathological changes in memory and learning, the impact of exercise on cognition, and clinical diagnosis of early dementia. He has received more than 33 research grants and has published more than 160 articles and books.

Jiska Cohen-Mansfield is Professor in the Department of Health Promotion at Tel Aviv University and Professor at the George Washington University Medical Center. She is also Chair of the Department of Health Promotion and Director of the Herczeg Institute on Aging at Tel Aviv University and was previously Director of the Research Institute at the Hebrew Home of Greater Washington. Her awards include the Recognition Award for Outstanding Contributions in Gerontological Research from the Maryland Gerontological Association (1994), the Barry Reisberg Award for Alzheimer's Research for advances in nonpharmacological research and clinical treatment from Hearthstone Alzheimer's Family Foundation (2003), the award in appreciation of outstanding contribution from Psychologists in Long Term Care (2007), and the M. Powell Lawton Distinguished Contribution Award in Applied Gerontology from Adult Development and Aging, American Psychological Association (2010). She has published around 300 articles and books and is the coeditor of *Satisfaction Surveys in Long-Term Care* (with F. K. Ejaz and P. Werner). She is a highly cited researcher as listed by the Institute for Scientific Information.

Understanding Well-Being in the Oldest Old

Edited by

Leonard W. Poon
University of Georgia

Jiska Cohen-Mansfield
Tel Aviv University and George Washington University

CAMBRIDGE UNIVERSITY PRESS
Cambridge, New York, Melbourne, Madrid, Cape Town,
Singapore, São Paulo, Delhi, Tokyo, Mexico City

Cambridge University Press
32 Avenue of the Americas, New York, NY 10013-2473, USA

www.cambridge.org
Information on this title: www.cambridge.org/9780521132008

First published 2011

Printed in the United States of America

A catalog record for this publication is available from the British Library.

Library of Congress Cataloging in Publication data

Understanding well-being in the oldest old /
[edited by] Leonard W. Poon, Jiska Cohen-Mansfield.
p. cm.
Includes bibliographical references and index.
ISBN 978-0-521-11391-5 (hardback) – ISBN 978-0-521-13200-8 (paperback)
1. Older people – Psychology. 2. Older people – Social conditions. 3. Aging – Psychological aspects. 4. Aging – Social aspects. 5. Quality of life. I. Poon, Leonard W., 1942–
II. Cohen-Mansfield, Jiska.
BF724.8.U53 2011
155.67–dc22 2010048222

ISBN 978-0-521-11391-5 Hardback
ISBN 978-0-521-13200-8 Paperback

CONTENTS

PART II. PARADISE LOST: BETWEEN TRAUMA AND HAPPINESS

PART III. PATHWAYS AND GATEKEEPERS: MODERATING, MEDIATING, AND PROXIMAL PROCESSES

PART IV. SIGNPOSTING PARADISE: MEASUREMENT OF WELL-BEING

TABLES

CONTRIBUTORS

ALEX J. BISHOP, PH.D. Assistant Professor, Human Development and Family Science Department, Oklahoma State University, Stillwater, Oklahoma

SARA CARMEL, PH.D. Professor of Medical Sociology and Gerontology, Center for Multidisciplinary Research in Aging, and Department of Sociology of Health, Faculty of Health Science, Ben-Gurion University of the Negev, Beer-Sheva, Israel

JINMYOUNG CHO, M.S. Gerontology Program, Iowa State University, Ames, Iowa

JISKA COHEN-MANSFIELD, PH.D. Director of the Herczeg Institute on Aging, Professor and Chair of the Department of Health Promotion at the School of Public Health, Herczeg Institute on Aging, and the Department of Health Promotion, Sackler Faculty of Medicine, Tel Aviv University, Tel Aviv, Israel

ADAM DAVEY, PH.D. Associate Professor, Department of Public Health, College of Health Professions and Social Work, Temple University, Philadelphia, Pennsylvania

NEHA DESHPANDE-KAMAT, Gerontology Program, Iowa State University, Ames, Iowa

CHRISTINE L. FRY, PH.D. Professor Emeritus, Loyola University of Chicago, Chicago, Illinois

DOROTHY HAUSMAN, PH.D. Associate Research Scientist, Department of Foods and Nutrition, University of Georgia, Athens, Georgia

HAIM HAZAN, PH.D. Professor of Social Anthropology and Sociology, Department of Sociology and Anthropology and Herczeg Institute on Aging, Tel Aviv University, Tel Aviv, Israel

LEE HYER, PH.D. Professor of Psychiatry, Georgia Neurosurgical Institute and Mercer University School of Medicine, Macon, Georgia

CHARLOTTE IKELS, PH.D. Professor of Anthropology, Department of Anthropology, Case Western Reserve University, Cleveland, Ohio

MARIA C. ISALES, M.P.H. Institute of Gerontology, University of Georgia, Athens, Georgia

MARY ANN JOHNSON, PH.D. Bill and June Flatt Professor of Foods and Nutrition, Department of Foods and Nutrition, University of Georgia, Athens, Georgia

HOWARD LITWIN, D.S.W. Professor, Paul Baerwald School of Social Work and Social Welfare, Israel Gerontological Data Center, Hebrew University of Jerusalem, Mount Scopus, Jerusalem, Israel

MAURICE MACDONALD, PH.D. Professor and Director, Family Studies and Human Services, College of Human Ecology, Kansas State University, Manhattan, Kansas

JENNIFER A. MARGRETT, PH.D. Assistant Professor, Human Development and Family Studies and the Gerontology Program, College of Human Sciences, Iowa State University, Ames, Iowa

PETER MARTIN, PH.D. Professor and Director, Gerontology Program, Iowa State University, Ames, Iowa

BENJAMIN T. MAST, PH.D. Associate Professor, Department of Psychological and Brain Sciences, University of Louisville, Louisville, Kentucky

GALIT NIMROD, PH.D. Lecturer, The Guilford Glazer School of Business and Management, Department of Hotel and Tourism Management, and the Center for Multidisciplinary Research in Aging, Ben-Gurion University of the Negev, Beer-Sheva, Israel

YUVAL PALGI, PH.D. Department of Psychology and Herczeg Institute on Aging, Tel Aviv University, Tel Aviv, Israel

LEONARD W. POON, PH.D. Distinguished Research Professor and Director of the Institute of Gerontology and the Georgia Geriatric Education Center, Institute of Gerontology, University of Georgia, Athens, Georgia

GRACE DA ROSA, M.S. Gerontology Program, Iowa State University, Ames, Iowa

ELISABETH LILIAN PIA SATTLER, B.S. PHARM. Department of Foods and Nutrition, University of Georgia, Athens, Georgia

CIERA V. SCOTT, B.A. Research Coordinator, Georgia Neurosurgical Institute, Macon, Georgia

DOV SHMOTKIN, PH.D. Associate Professor, Department of Psychology, and Senior Researcher, Herczeg Institute on Aging, Tel Aviv University, Tel Aviv, Israel

AMIT SHRIRA, PH.D. Department of Psychology and Herczeg Institute on Aging, Tel Aviv University, Tel Aviv, Israel

CATHERINE A. YEAGER, PH.D. Georgia Neurosurgical Institute and Mercer University School of Medicine, Macon, Georgia

FOREWORD

To grapple with the meaning of well-being is to seek understanding of the human condition when the glass is nearly full. Not surprisingly, this rich and challenging issue has engaged philosophers for more than 2,000 years. In our contemporary era, well-being has become a prominent focus of research that spans the scientific disciplines – it has become empirically tractable. Well-being is now studied with the same fervor once restricted to obviously objective facts, such as rates of death and disease. The field of aging was surprisingly prescient in recognizing the importance of well-being from the outset. Classic studies in social gerontology dating back to the middle of the past century were fundamentally concerned with understanding old age not simply as a process of decline and deterioration but as an experience of meaningful inner evaluations and satisfactions. These initial ideas have been extensively elaborated in subsequent decades, and entire literatures of aging and well-being have now been assembled.

This book carries the study of well-being into important new territory. By focusing on the oldest old, that historically unprecedented stretch of living, the authors address some of the most fascinating questions imaginable: Is well-being possible at the very end? For whom? What is the shape and form of positive experience when life is nearly over and the future has been swallowed by the past? Multiple chapters, crafted by notably thoughtful scholars, probe theoretical meanings of well-being and how it is possible in the face of adversity and consider the adaptation processes by which very old people draw on their distant past and their immediate resources to make lives go well. Of particular interest are excellent contributions dealing with the effects of past life trauma on the oldest old, including how such experience is integrated into one's life narrative. Variability is a persistent theme, from those whose survival is robust and vital to those who are embattled and demented.

Contemporary science affords opportunities to explore critical influences on well-being among the oldest old, and these are richly arrayed in the book. Such factors are wide ranging, from the basics of nutrition and dietary intake to the importance of cognitive vitality, social relationships, spiritual and religious connections, and leisure activities. Clearly, the pathways to well-being in the very late decades of aging are many, as are the routes away from it toward despair and suffering.

Appropriately, the book begins and ends with the central challenge – namely, how to define and measure well-being. That is the ultimate question, and as illustrated by the outstanding work in this book, there is no single right answer. There are many ways to know well-being, some of which are likely to be experienced only at the end of a long life, when much has been lost and yet there remains a powerful will to continue living. The authors and the editors of this fine collection have elevated the discourse and the science. Well-being, in their hands, with their late life focus, has never been a more penetrating subject.

Carol D. Ryff, Ph.D.
Director, Institute on Aging
Professor of Psychology
University of Wisconsin-Madison

PART I

THEORY: NEW HORIZONS IN WELL-BEING RESEARCH

1

Toward New Directions in the Study of Well-Being among the Oldest Old

LEONARD W. POON AND JISKA COHEN-MANSFIELD

ABSTRACT

This chapter provides a road map to address the dearth of information and the central theme of this volume: well-being among the oldest old. A reality among the oldest old is the increasing variability in both subjective and psychological well-being found within an individual owing to variations in cumulative experiences and differences in strategies to survive into very old age. This chapter outlines the strategies in addressing the central theme by describing four different views on well-being among the oldest old (Section I), the influence of experiences and trauma on well-being at the end stage of life (Section II), examination of moderating and mediating influences (Section III), measurement issues (Section IV), and conclusions (Section V).

INTRODUCTION

The life course is marked by individuality and diversity. An individual's life is a process that, if scrutinized at a singular instance, would yield incorrect assumptions about its trajectory. Instead, the gradual accumulation of events in a person's life provides perspective into how that person arrived at his or her present state of well-being. This chapter provides a road map of the contents in this edited volume on the well-being of the oldest old. Although the age of the oldest-old cohort is continually increasing as a result of the rectangularization of the population pyramid, this volume defines the oldest old as those individuals older than 75 years of age. This cohort deserves its own conception of well-being because of its distinctiveness in comparison with younger generations. For example, individuals in the fourth age are referred to with ethereal adjectives, such as *gerotranscendence*, *empowerment, maturation,* and *resilience* (see Chapter 2). Nonetheless, there are minimal data and discourse available on the oldest old; the lack of exploration into the well-being of individuals in the fourth age can be attributed to the large amount of individual variability within the cohort, which makes it difficult to reach generalizations for the group. Our goals for this volume were to describe (a) the conceptions of well-being among the oldest old, (b) the accumulation of trauma throughout the life span and how it affects the perception of well-being, (c) the influence of moderating, mediating, and proximal processes on well-being, and (d) issues relating to the measurement of well-being.

The understanding of well-being has both personal and psychological implications that have generated a significant volume of scientific inquiry (e.g., Kahn, 1986; Rowe & Kahn, 1997; Ryan & Deci, 2001; Ryff, 1989a, 1989b; Ryff & Singer, 2000). For example, answering the question, "How are you?" seems simple and straightforward; however, the answer is dependent on a host of inter- and intraindividual differences, as well as environmental and cultural variations. In a seminal experiment on misattribution of well-being, researchers found that people use their momentary emotional states to make judgments on how satisfied they are with their lives in general (Schwarz & Clore, 1983). Participants interviewed on sunny days reported greater well-being than participants interviewed on rainy days; however, when the interviewer mentioned the weather, the participant's attention was drawn to the source of their mood, thereby eliminating the effect of the participant's mood on overall life satisfaction. This experiment demonstrates how even the subconscious influences the perception of our lives.

There are countless theories and debates on the definition, meaning, measurement, antecedent, consequences, and impact of well-being. On one level, well-being or happiness can be defined by feelings generated by pleasure and positive reinforcement while avoiding unpleasant and negative reinforcement (Kahneman et al., 1999). On another level, well-being is defined by the actualization of one's goal (Ryff & Singer, 1998, 2000; Waterman, 1993). The literature further differentiated between subjective well-being, which is defined by the individual, and psychological well-being, which consists of components or factors defined by those who study the concept. For example, Ryff and Keyes (1995) hypothesized six pertinent components: autonomy, personal growth, self-acceptance, life purpose, mastery, and positive relatedness. Another similar and related hypothesis that defines the impact of well-being is the self-determination theory (Ryan & Deci, 2000). The self-determination theory noted that the process of self-actualization seeks to satisfy the basic needs of autonomy, competence, and relatedness, which in turn produce psychological growth, integrity, vitality, and well-being.

The different models and hypotheses of well-being produce convergent and divergent concepts and data. However, as noted by Ryff (1989b), the level and permanency of happiness and well-being are ultimately seen through the prism of the individual or through the eye of the beholder. It is notable that the literature has produced some robust findings on predictors of well-being. For example, the personality of an individual seems to influence the level of subjective well-being. DeNeve and Cooper (1998) found that individuals high on extraversion and agreeableness tend to be high on subjective well-being, whereas individuals high on neuroticism tended to be low on subjective well-being. Health status influences subjective well-being in interesting ways (Okun et al., 1984). When physical health was reported by the individual, the correlation to subjective well-being was positive. However, this correlation disappeared when using the objective report of the physician. The finding confirmed the subjective and individualized nature of well-being. Similarly, studies on quality of relationships showed that affiliation and relationship-enhancing traits are highly related to subjective well-being, whereas loneliness has the opposite effects. The quality of the relationship was found to be related to subjective well-being, whereas the quantity of relationship was not (Nezlek, 2000). Studies on the influence of wealth revealed interesting relationships with well-being and life satisfaction (Diener & Diener, 1995). Satisfaction with family, friends, and finances among college students was found to be positively correlated with overall life satisfaction in poorer countries but not in wealthier countries. People in wealthier countries tended to be happier than those in poorer countries; however, increases in wealth do not predict increases in happiness, and people who strongly desire wealth and money are unhappier than those who do not.

In summary, the concept of wellness is central to describing and comparing the quality of life of individuals and cohorts across social and cultural contexts as well as to evaluating the impact of policies and policy changes. Research in the past 4 decades has provided an improving understanding of the definitions and measurement; however, one particular paradox regarding the impact of aging on well-being remains unresolved. That is, with increasing age, humans face the certainty and reality of diminishing health, resources, and support systems. Diminishment of those factors has been found to compromise well-being. In spite of diminishing resources, the paradox is that well-being tended not to decline among older individuals (Carstenson, 1998; Mroczek & Kolarz, 1998; Ryff, 1991). In fact, perceived well-being has been shown to increase for some. We explore this phenomenon in this edited volume. Do very old individuals think of themselves differently than they did when they were young? Does being at the end stage of life change the way they perceive themselves and their environment? The probability of encountering adversities is greatest among the oldest old, and yet they have learned to survive into very old age. What types of moderating and mediating processes are operating to enhance well-being for the very old? Are some types of adaptation skills necessary and sufficient to survive and sustain a level of well-being?

This edited volume is designed to answer the foregoing questions. The volume contains nineteen chapters that are divided into four parts. Part I (Chapters 2–5) offers four different alternatives in viewing well-being among the oldest old. Chapter 2 defines the category of the very old, the fourth age, and outlines how this segment of life is different from other stages of life. The chapter questions whether traditional measures of quality of life are applicable to the fourth age and whether extant languages describing old age in terms of disengagement, disintegration, and invisibility should be applied to those who have survived into the fourth age. Chapter 3 addresses an important paradox: why do the oldest old have a high level of well-being when individuals are more affected by the bad events rather than the good? This chapter notes that objective life conditions that are related to subjective quality of life tend to explain only a small amount of variance among the very old. Negative affects tend to remain stable or decrease with advancing age, whereas positive affects tend to remain stable or increase. Chapter 4 outlines a theory to explain the relatively high level of well-being in the oldest old despite significant worsening in determinants of well-being. Both community-dwelling adults and cognitively impaired nursing-home residents are offered as examples to demonstrate the utility of the theory. Finally, Chapter 5 outlines three models – the Georgia adaptation model, the developmental adaptation model, and the resource change model – to describe adaptation and change in the fourth age. It is noted that adaptability to change rather than the process of change helps individuals attain an optimal state of well-being. This adaptability is achieved through the ability of older adults to rely on resilience dimensions, such as mental and physical health as well as life satisfaction. The goal of the four chapters is to provide multivariate models and testable hypotheses to support the phenomenon that well-being remains high among the oldest old.

Part II (Chapters 6–8) examines types of trauma accumulated during the life course and ways survivors cope and adapt in the face of such adversities. Central to these traumas is the delicate balance between the resilience of survival and the vulnerability of imminent frailty and death. Chapter 6 examines three approaches toward survival of trauma in old-old life: dementia, robust, and embattled survival. The individual's mode of survival is dependent on the coping mechanisms utilized. Holocaust survivors provide a paradigm for the challenge of long-term effects by an extreme trauma. Chapter 7 examines how stressful life events affect oldest-old survivors. The emphasis is on both distal and proximal experiences and their influences on psychosocial resources, coping, and well-being. Proximal stressors were found to increase levels of negative affect and reduce levels of positive affect; distal events enhanced the level of positive affect. Chapter 8 examines the multidimensional nature of trauma in late life, which is distinct from that of younger adults because the gains and losses of aging mix with the traumatic event(s). Posttraumatic stress disorder (PTSD) is used as a model to examine early onset of trauma, its chronic course, and trauma incurred at late life. Biological influences of PTSD are described, as are suggestions for treatment.

Part III (Chapters 9–14) outlines the moderating, mediating, and proximal processes associated with the well-being of the oldest old. The goal is to examine and describe how well-being is affected by the use or disuse of certain lifestyle factors at the end stage of life. Chapter 9 addresses the influence of resources, notably income, medical care, and caregiving services on mental health and psychological well-being. Using data from the Georgia Centenarian Study (GCS), this chapter also compares the roles of social support and proximal personal resources to adapt to the influence of distal resources such as education and primary occupation and major life events. The data showed that mental health depended primarily on income; however, neither social nor economic resource adequacy was necessary for psychological well-being or for maintaining personal independence. Chapter 10 also employs data from the GCS to examine how nutrition and dietary factors could affect well-being, particularly mental health and depression, among the oldest old. A strong association was found between depression defined by the Geriatric Depression Scale and appetite loss in the population sample. The GCS data showed that depressed centenarians were twice as likely to lose appetite and to have had more weight change than nondepressed centenarians. Chapter 11 brings forth the notion of cognitive vitality in very old age and how to use the concept to predict indicators of well-being such as subjective health and depression. Chapter 12 underscores the importance of social networks and social exchange in relation to morale and survival among older Jewish Israelis, as well as the great diversities that prevail among the oldest old. Socioemotional selectivity theory indicates that the older persons benefit from meaningful social relations, but they also tend to disassociate from ties that are not likely to provide optimal return. From this perspective, the reality is that there is a network reduction among the oldest old. The well-being of the oldest old is more dependent on the robustness of social network rather than the age of the individual. Chapter 13 describes theoretical conceptualizations and definitions of religious coping in conjunction with physical and mental well-being. Gender, health impairment, and negative affect were found to be longitudinal predictors of religious coping among centenarians. Finally, Chapter 14 examines the impact of leisure activities on well-being of the very old and notes that innovation – the addition of brand new activities – may contribute to an enhanced sense of well-being and serve as a resource for resilience.

Part IV (Chapters 15–17) presents three chapters that examine measurement issues relating to well-being among the oldest old. The central thesis of this edited volume is that the fourth age presents special challenges and losses in which the oldest old may perceive their impact in a different way through mediating and moderating processes. Hence, the measurement of well-being must be sensitive to those processes. Chapters 15 and 17 outline the strategies and needed sensitivities in measuring well-being in this population. Chapter 15 emphasizes the importance of culture in ethnographic and qualitative strategies to elicit dimensions of well-being. It is noted that well-being is heterogeneous because it is culturally mediated and self-generated. Chapter 17 emphasizes the advantages and disadvantages in the use of global, temporal-oriented, alternative, and domain-specific measurement of well-being among the oldest old. Chapter 16 introduces the will to live as a unique measurement tool for general well-being, commitment to life, and desire to continue living because of its diagnostic and prognostic values for the prolongation of life among the oldest old.

Finally, Part V (Chapters 18–19) contains two chapters that examine implications and interventions, as well as provide summary, conclusion, and future directions. Chapter 18 notes that the description of distal and proximal events is necessary but not sufficient to prescribe potential intervention. The chapter considers the biopsychosocial model as it applies to the oldest old, noting their strengths, problems, and future directions. Chapter 19 summarizes and integrates the contents of the different chapters to better understand the mechanisms associated with the aging paradox of why and how old-old adults with diminishing resources can survive with a sense of well-being.

A publication that involves authors from different countries could not be successfully executed without assistance from a variety of supporters. First, we are grateful to the U.S.-Israel Binational Science Foundation, whose grant supported a conference at Tel Aviv University, Israel, and provided the foundation for the writing of this volume. Second, the primary supporting organizations from the United States are the Institute of Gerontology at the University of Georgia and the Gerontology Program at Iowa State University. Supporting organizations from Israel are the Herczeg Institute on Aging, Tel Aviv University, the Center for Multidisciplinary Research on Aging at Ben-Gurion University, and Hebrew University. Acquisition of new knowledge on the well-being of older citizens is of special interest to scientists in both countries. The editors are grateful for the supportive organization of our copy editor, Maria C. Isales, BA, MPH, at the University of Georgia, whose persistence, perseverance, and diplomacy help all of us stay on schedule. We are also grateful to Rano Rakhimova, MD, PhD, at the University of Georgia, for her assistance in coordinating with the publisher and the formulation of the subject index.

REFERENCES

Carstensen, L. (1998). A life-span approach to social motivation. In J. Heckhausen & C. Dweck (Eds.), *Motivation and self-regulation across the life span* (pp. 341–364). New York: Cambridge University Press.

DeNeve, K.M., & Cooper, H. (1998). The happy personality: A meta-analysis of 137 personality traits and subjective well-being. *Psychological Bulletin, 124*, 197–229.

Diener, E., & Diener, M. (1995). Cross-cultural correlates of life satisfaction and self-esteem. *Journal of Personality and Social Psychology, 68*, 653–663.

Kahn, R. (1986). Renewing the commitment to oral hygiene. *Geriatric Nursing, 7*, 244–247.

Kahneman, D., Diener, E., & Schwarz, N. (Eds). (1999). *Hedonic psychology: Scientific prospective on enjoyment, suffering, and well-being.* New York: Russell Sage Foundation.

Mroczek, D.K., & Kolarz, C.M. (1998). The effect of age on positive and negative affect: A developmental perspective on happiness. *Journal of Personality and Social Psychology, 75*, 1333–1349.

Nezlek, J. B. (2000). The motivational and cognitive dynamics of day-to-day social life. In J. P. Forgas, K. Williams, & L. Wheeler (Eds.), *The social mind: Cognitive and motivational aspects of interpersonal behaviour* (pp. 92–111). New York: Cambridge University Press.

Okun, M.N., Stock, W.A., Haring, M.J., & Witter, R.A. (1984). Health and subjective well-being: Ameta-analysis. *International Journal of Aging and Human Development, 19*, 111–132.

Rowe, J., & Kahn, R. (1997). Successful aging. *The Gerontologist, 37*, 433–440. *Aging and Society, 18*, 371–378.

Ryan, R.M., & Deci, E.L. (2000). Self-determination theory and the facilitation of intrinsic motivation, social development, and well being. *The American Psychologist, 55*, 68–78.

Ryan, R.M., & Deci, E.L. (2001). On happiness and human potentials: A review of research on hedonic and eudaimonic well-being. *Annual Review of Psychology, 52*, 141–166.

Ryff, C.D. (1989a). Beyond Ponce de Leon and life satisfaction: New directions in quest of successful aging. *International Journal of Behavioral Development, 12*, 35–55.

Ryff, C.D. (1989b). Happiness is everything, or is it? Exploration on the meaning of psychological well-being. *Journal of Personality and Social Psychology, 57*, 1069–1081.

Ryff, C.D. (1991). Possible selves in adulthood and old age: A tale of shifting horizons. *Psychology and Aging, 6*, 286–295.

Ryff, C.D., & Keyes, C.L.M. (1995). The structure of psychological well-being revisited. *Journal of Personality and Social Psychology, 69*, 719–727.

Ryff, C.D., & Singer, B.H. (1998). The contours of positive human health. *Psychological Inquiry, 9*, 1–28.

Ryff, C.D., & Singer, B.H. (2000). Biopsychosocial challenges of the new millennium. *Psychotherapy and psychosomatics, 69*, 170–177.

Schwarz, N., & Clore, G.L. (1983). Mood, misattribution, and judgments of well-being: Informative and directive functions of affective states. *Journal of Personality and Social Psychology, 45*, 513–523.

Waterman, A.S. (1993). Two conceptions of happiness: Contrasts of personal expressions (eudaimonia) and hedonic enjoyment. *Journal of Personality and Social Psychology, 64*, 678–691.

2

From Ageless Self to Selfless Age: Toward a Theoretical Turn in Gerontological Understanding

HAIM HAZAN

ABSTRACT

This chapter argues that the conceptual language employed to analyze the self and its well-being in later life reflects issues and concerns pertinent to styles and anxieties relevant to midlife, such as continuity, success, and meaning, rather than the underpinnings of the end of existence. Although most populations defined as elderly are amenable to being understood in terms of cumulative attainments and corresponding aspirations, the category of the very old, otherwise known as the fourth age, occupies a distinct human territory, displaying properties of time and space quite different from those marking other phases of the life course. Any attempt at comprehending the experience of the oldest old should take into account the plausibility of a reshaped identity abandoning no-longer-relevant regulative principles of subjectivity, such as emotional and cognitive lifelong constructions.

PROLOGUE: A LOST CATEGORY

The quest to understand well-being as a gerontological aspiration can be viewed as a form of resistance to the cultural imagery of old age as formulated, for example, by the founding father of gerontology, the Nobel laureate Elie Metchnikoff, in 1905 as "an infectious, chronic disease which is manifested by a degeneration or an enfeebling of the noble elements" (p. 48). Even as a metaphoric figure of speech, such phrasing, counteracting the ethos of the modern quest for the normal and the nonpathological (Foucault, 2003), would not withstand the scrutiny of current political correctness. Hence the reluctance of mainstream gerontology to address those modes in the category of old age that seem to accord pejorative attributes to the last decline in a secular life trajectory with no prospect of sustaining the homeostatic premises and promises of well-being. It would seem that the association made in the relevant literature between well-being and life satisfaction attests to the ambivalence ingrained in treating aging as a contemporary concept. In terms of general measures of the right for modern versions of the Aristotelian concept of the good life embracing all ages, old age is no exception. However, the modern time acknowledgement of the risks involved in the deteriorating process of being at the brink of the capacity and the prerogative of accomplishing the "good life," renders it subversive to that very striving for ideal living. Stepping over that imaginary age-related existential edge presumably means entering a discrete, yet secret, category in which common measures and measurements of quality of life are no longer applicable.

The following is an invitation to critically submit that final phase to the veiled gaze of the regime of gerontological knowledge, in spite of its inbuilt resistance to incorporate this phase into its discursive fold.

RECOGNIZING AN ABSENT CATEGORY OF GERONTOLOGICAL KNOWLEDGE

Looming on the horizon of aging is the ominous cloud of an unfathomable age. That is the category marked, for want of better finely tuned terms, as "the old-old", "the oldest old," or "the fourth age." Not only is it a challenge to the analytic capacity and capability of gerontologists to contain and explain their subject matter, but also it questions the very self-justification of gerontology as an academic-professional turf in its own right, or as an "undisciplined discipline" (Katz, 1996). What Baltes and Smith (2003) call, in a somewhat disillusioned comparison with the thriving research on the third age, "the not so good scientific news: the fourth age" presents a subversive factor for undermining the tenets on which the run-of-the-mill discipline is edified. For if the conceptual tools, the theoretical paradigms, and their derived methodologies are no different from those employed in the construal of other phases of the life course, it behooves the student of old age to consider the dubiousness of any age-specific scholarly agenda, including the one pertaining to the penultimate accord of being. Falling short of undermining the rationale for constructing an exclusively designated apparatus for comprehending old age, the gerontological nomenclature devised to handle the issue at stake speaks for itself in its inherent drawbacks and inadequacies. Thus, terms such as *deculturation* (Anderson, 1972), *disengagement* (Cumming & Henry, 1961), *disintegration* (Rosow, 1974), *invisibility* (Myerhoff, 1978; Unruh, 1983), *rolelessness* (Burgess, 1950), *role exit* (Blau, 1973), *integration* (Lomranz, 1998), *subcultural aging* (Blaikie, 2002), and so forth constitute a self-evident negative language testifying to the absence of conceptual substance in the attempt to recognize old age (Hazan, 1994).

Two contradictory, yet complementary, reasons are responsible for this lacuna of affirmative framing of scientific knowledge of old age. The first is the age-centric origin of writing about old age by middle-age consciousness, extending lifestyles and desires attributed to prime years to aspired images of later years, thus reproducing the reality of old age in its own image (Hazan & Raz, 1997). This expectation of an uninterrupted continuation of prowess and standing is incarnated in the prevalent language of good adjustment and worthy living expressed in locutions such as *optimum, successful, productive,* and *meaningful aging* (Bowling, 2007). The presumed pursuit of these goals extrapolates middle-age values and norms to old age to the extent that the boundaries set between these two socially imagined categories (Shweder, 1998) are rendered blurred and untenable. Prolonged life expectancy intertwined with compressed morbidity (Fries, 1980) stretches the ageist antiaging consumerist culture embedded in the peak of wealth and power in contemporary Western society (Bytheway, 1995) to the existentially ominous brink of gerontophobic awareness of the undiscovered country of the oldest old. This unavoidable realization of prospective final decrepitude and senseless senescence leads to the second reason for the intellectual bankruptcy involved in the reluctant endeavor to identify the fourth age, that is, the adherence to the chief paradigm under which all ages are perceived, namely the modernist perspective of progress and development (Gubrium & Holstein, 2002). This discourse is subjectified in an assumed integrated selfhood driven by cumulative experience, phenomenologically edified by retention and pretension (Rogers, 1983). However, if the fourth age is indeed a quintessential phase in the aging process, as some would have it (Johnson & Barer, 1997), two core dilemmas pertaining to the very foundation of gerontology ought to be considered and elucidated. The first is the subsuming of the robust chronologically old, functionally indistinguishable from midlifers, under one academic-cum-public category denoting an indivisible human condition culturally recognized as old age. Dovetailed with, yet contrary to, this misnomer is the second dilemma of propounding an alternative language appropriate to the analysis of that exceptional state of existence dubbed "the fourth age," thus according it an analytically inaccessible status. Seductively obscure terms such as *empowerment, resistance, resilience, gerotranscendence,* and *spirituality* have been amply employed in recent gerontological discourse to serve as a vocabulary in the moral economy of aging (Mimkler & Estes, 1991), thus absolving society from practical accountability and responsibility for the unsettling category of the socially disenfranchised. This is in contrast to the activity-laden, middle-age-slanted lingo directed toward the culturally accepted old whose mind and body are still deemed fit to conform to midlife standards of production and consumption.

The following is a proposition to examine the divide between an academically prominent, albeit seemingly redundant, analytic category of old age, colloquially marked as the third age, on the one hand, and an academically deprived, nevertheless essentially vital, category constituting old age, consecutively marked as the fourth age, on the other hand. Such examination can be carried out by tracking down the interplay between the two imaginary protagonists of the modern scene – the concept of the self and the concept of the body as they transform from the third to the fourth age. It is argued that the fourth age can be recognized and identified not by chronological indices or by self-declared well-being, but according to the metamorphosis in the dialectics of self and body experienced among that population. The advent of this process spells critical changes for the economy of managing living, from stratagems of survival, temporarily suspending long-term goals, to practices of mere existence, divorced from any future orientation. Because such propositions are not empirically inferred but are mere reflections of a research agenda seeking to formulate the reality of growing old in today's late-modern world, the analysis refers mainly to discursive models of the relations between self and body in later years. From this viewpoint, it seems that the temporal premises on which knowledge of old age is constructed are rickety in accounting for the theoretically uncharted phenomena associated with the territory of the fourth age. However, should the developmentally based temporal perspective constituting the run-of-the-mill study of aging be replaced with an emphasis on the spatial organization of experience in the oldest old, a fresh map of the category of the fourth age could and should be drawn.

THE QUEST FOR AN AGELESS SELF

The social oblivion of old age juxtaposed with death in a youth-centered culture is well expressed, for instance, in the gerontophobic assertion by the French social philosopher Jean Baudrillard (1976), who describes the redundancy of old age as generating a taboo that is "a marginal and ultimately asocial slice of life – a ghetto, a reprieve and the slide into death. Old age is literally being eliminated. In proportion, as the living live longer, as they win over death, they cease to be symbolically acknowledged" (p. 163). This near-death excommunicated position designating the old as social residuals is echoed in various writings (Butler, 1975; Callahan, 1990; De Beauvoir, 1975; Fukuyama, 2003; Kaufman, 2005). It represents the demise of the two discredited protagonists of the modern spectacle of symbolic immortality (Lifton, 1977), namely the self and the body. In a pre-old-age phase, appearances of an integrated self, as depicted and sought after in modern therapeutic discourse (Illouz, 2008; Rose, 1990), embrace the socially subjugated, that is, the disciplined, culturally constructed "me," together with its counterpart, the individually autonomous quintessential "I" (Mead, 1934). These two constitutive concepts in the annals of constructionist sociological theory form the compound of dialectical selfhood that follows the life course until the onset of old age renders it analytically defunct, as amply demonstrated in writings based on constructionist approaches to the life course, in which old age is by and large amiss (Bellah, Sullivan, Tipton, & Swidler, 1985; Berger & Berger, 1976; Chamberlayne, Bornat, & Wengraf, 2000; Fivush & Haden, 2003; Gergen, 1994; Langness & Frank, 1981). Thus, the invincible body, sustained by antiaging ethos and its derived techniques, houses that self-contradictory, yet indivisible, self and is interactively regulated by its codes of rendering the corporeal subjective, and vice versa (Archer, 2000). The ravages of old age, however, often separate body from mind, because their respective trajectories are no longer effectively synchronized. This functionally related discrepancy spells a conceptual concern for gerontologists who grapple with the cultural predominance of current holistic discourses of the nexus of the social and the corporeal.

Embedded in the much-discussed term *embodiment* (i.e., the incorporation of the cultural into the symbolic fabric of the body) is the coupling of the materiality of the physical with the meaning-laden quality instilled in the self (Csordas, 1990; Weiss, 1999). The intractable unit cemented in that fusion might be challenged by a reluctant return to a dualistic opposition of withering weak flesh contrasted by resilient and willing spirit socially expected and personally invoked in old age. The socioanthropological handling of this age-dependent Cartesian dichotomy can be addressed with respect to gerontology from two diametrically opposed angles. The first dismisses the importance of the body in and of itself as an active agent of being-in-the-world. It reflects an idealistic celebration of the prevalence of the integrity, continuity, and solidity of the self, overriding any disruptive breach in its enduring experiential presence, even to the abandonment of the presence of the somatic (Hallam, Hockey, & Howarth, 1999). The second approach, however, disregards the interpretative authority of the autonomous subject, thus consigning socially oppressed selves into an assumed domain of excommunication sometimes termed *social death* (Goffman, 1961; Sudnow, 1967) or *wasted lives* (Bauman, 1991). This is the scrap heap of bio-power-processed populations, which, to use Agamben's (2000) terminology, can be killed but not sacrificed and are thus devoid of any cultural significance. Gerontology seems to be roughly torn between two contingencies of viewing old age: as first and foremost subjectively molded or primarily as somatically determined. It should be noted that the difference between the two approaches is not necessarily an offshoot of empirical observations on the state of being old but follows a divergence in the philosophical appraisal of the human condition. The former – the bodily anchored perspective – hinges on a positivist, natural cosmology, whereas the latter echoes interpretive voices of the socially constructed subject. This Cartesian split between Snow's (1998) "two cultures" of science and the humanities seems to offer two mutually exclusive gerontological narratives of aging: as a bio-sociopsychological predestined developing process versus a contingently dynamic image of an adaptive self (Gergen, 1991) capable of shifting involvements and reframing identities (Goffman, 1974). In either case, the guiding discursive principle is the assumption of the working of a sense of selfhood responsible for setting the emotional, political, and cultural scene for mapping the subject as a shifting locus of forging identities (Pile & Thrift, 1995). Notwithstanding some anthropological reservations as to the premise of the transcultural presence of the self (Ewing, 1990; Geertz, 1979), it is the logic of modern capitalism – of cumulative aggregation of wealth and investment in future enterprises – that sets that concept at its core as an imagined, predetermined, ubiquitous entity resistant to contextual conditioning, a free and independent spirit. The advent of nonbehavioristic therapeutic culture is a testimony to the ethos and operation of that conviction and the need to assert and express an unequivocal sense of autonomous self (Illouz, 2008).

For a considerable period in the annals of gerontology, the dilemma of taking a stand between the two philosophical options did not exist, as both sociology, through the rise and fall of the theory of disengagement (Cumming, 1975), and anthropology, by its observations in simple societies (Glascock & Feinman, 1981; Holmes & Holmes, 1995), synchronized self and body in a double helix of withdrawal. However, growing awareness of the ambivalences and contradictions built into the project of modernity (Bauman, 1991) prompted gerontologists to consider the option of setting discourses of self and body apart. Subsequently, the study of the experience of aging was skewed toward a dualistic explanatory model hinged on the binary of the mental and the corporeal. This was underscored by the assumption of a bifurcated identity consisting of an inner being based on lifelong self-identity, on the one hand, and socially disciplined, culturally performed appearances and modes of functioning of a changing body **formed again** by the ravages of aging on the other. Thus, starting with the principles underlying the ethos of the continuity perspective (Atchley, 1989) through the concept of the enduring, extant identity of the ageless self (Kaufman, 1986), and extending to the iron cage of the mask of aging that splits immutable self-image from age-dependent social constraints (Featherstone & Hepworth, 1991), the study of aging drives a wedge between meaning-seeking forms of identity construction, on the one hand, and survival-geared approaches to dwindling resources, on the other hand – that is, a breakup or an interface between conceptions of lifelong agency and exigencies of present-bound structural conditions. Nevertheless, lately a significant shift turning this dual discursiveness into one has been introduced into gerontology by pervasive feminist studies (Twigg, 2004), which advocates the embodied unity of the physical and the mental. Subscription to this ethos is stipulated and encouraged by the assumed familiarity between the two socially underprivileged categories, women and the old, thereby setting the scene for enacting the feminist theme – "our bodies, ourselves" – by removing the mask of aging that renders innermost selfhood and outer appearance mutually exclusive. To accomplish that embodied incongruity between desires and performance, old people often participate in what Woodward (1991, 1995) and Biggs (1999, 2004) call a masquerade of role reversals, where bodily modifications intertwined with corresponding lifestyles project externally and internally contrived images of personal choice rather than rules (Blaikie, 1999). As long as the postmodern enables and allows that carnival-like spectacle of agelessness to be staged, age boundaries continue to erode while the costumes worn by the old actors throw into relief the shunned presence of their absent backstage identity.

THE EMERGENCE OF A SELFLESS AGE

However, the analogy drawn between women and the old that furnishes the stage management of ageless identity is defied by the biologically based onset of the aging process. The acid test for the applicability and credibility of the paradigm of embodiment is thus provided by the case of Alzheimer's disease – the condition of those afflicted demonstrates, albeit in its initial stages, the unbridgeable duality of body and mind. Notwithstanding numerous attempts to decipher the phenomenology of the Alzheimerian self (Kontos, 2004; Phinney & Chesla, 2003; Sabat & Harre, 1992), the eventuality of the disease presents a crack in the mirror of the concept of embodiment supposedly compounding self and body, as the former no longer informs the latter. This chink in the armor of holistic approaches to old age is reverberated and amplified in the fear-riddled attitude toward the impact of increasing dementia on contemporary culture, described as the "Alzheimerization of society" (Gilleard & Higgs, 2000, pp. 168–187).

The growing medical awareness of dementia constitutes a discourse of a pathologically driven return to the much-maligned dualistic perspective. This spills over to the nonpathological, thus putting into question the very idea of a "normal" aging selfhood, as conventional sociological wisdom knows it. If extreme old age signifies a functional and an attitudinal departure from midlife linear temporality, then any definition of identity in terms of past-bound future orientations, prospects, and choices is patently aborted. The resulting convoluted self, therefore, is lodged no longer in the realm of temporal constructions of scripts of prospective options and opportunities but in spatial, ad hoc arrangements of making do under pressing constraints and present needs. The potential loss of a sense of self incurred by that shift from living to existing heralds critical transformations in identity to the extent that research suggests processes of forsaken gender distinctions (Silver, 2003), dissolved cross-generational bonds (Hazan, 2003; Phillipson, 2003), disappearing adaptive alternatives (de Medeiros, 2005), and silenced life-story narration (Hazan, 2006). All these do not necessarily mean that self-conception among some of the oldest old is rendered defunct, but rather that it becomes increasingly untenable as a reflectively anchored gerontological discourse. Thus, gerontologists are left with little choice but to consider the often malfunctioning, observable body as almost the only template for relating to the being-in the-world of the old subject (Gubrium & Holstein, 2002). This amounts to adopting a monistic and a minimalistic mode of understanding old age through its performed corporeality under the guise of viewing it as a holistic entity.

THE FUTILE SEARCH FOR INTERSECTION AND INTERACTION

The inaccessibility of selfhood in the fourth age to students interested in that phase of the life span is evident in the dearth of scholarly references to that phase of aging as a source of knowledge concerning self-concept among the oldest old. Aside from scant attention given in the gerontological literature to the possibility of tapping selfhood in people with dementia, albeit "through a tangled veil" (Sabat, 2001), the bulk of research into the fourth age eschews the issue of selfhood while focusing on matters of morbidity, resilience, social support, and survival (Poon, Jang, Reynolds, & McCarthy, 2005). As the underlying assumption guiding this research agenda rests on a life-course developmental perspective, the agenda is not amenable to addressing the queries concerning the existential rupture experienced in the fourth age as raised by Baltes and Smith (2003). This might attest to a critical discrepancy between the self-contingent worldview of the researcher and the seemingly selfless experience of the older persons studied. Under such a priori circumstances of incommunicability, the research act is rendered methodologically inept because it fails to translate one reality into the terms of another. It therefore calls for the relinquishing of hierarchically based temporal concepts such as role, identity, mobility, memory, story, meaning, adaptability, continuity, productivity, and the like, in favor of a surrogate spatially and selflessly generated language. Such vocabulary should consist of multidirectional, labile terms. Such terms of reference would not purport to reach experience by asking what a certain phenomenon means but by tapping how it works (Deleuze & Guariari, 1987). The blatant differences in course and content between the two research modes can be ascertained when semistructured interviews are compared with free-floating conversations. Although the former guide and regulate the encounter to fit the forward-looking outlook usually held by interviewers as embedded in their interpretive discourses, the latter allows for unleashed expressions of unadulterated being-experience. It might throw into relief the fine line discerning the false from the authentic, the forced from the genuine.

This critique of the superimposed conceptualization exercised by gerontologists as routine theorizing transforms attention from examining the epistemological adequacy of the discipline (Hazan, 2009; Katz, 1996) to proposing a positive alternative that accounts for the spatially constructed of the here-and-now qualities implicit in the intergenerational encounter between the two interlocutors engaged in that peculiar type of research situation. Rather than committing its design and purpose to a developmentally geared set of relationships, the research situation should open up to nonlinear, nonhierarchical discursive management. Be it a questionnaire, an interview, or a conversation – they all ought to be formatted in terms of a shared, pervasive experience rather than as fixated discrepant positions, thereby dissolving the built-in cultural lag separating them. The search for that other approach not only summons the gerontological endeavor of comprehending the fourth age to return to the conceptual drawing board but also mainly enables the exploration of the parameters and properties of that yet-unknown space occupied by the very old.

The ethnographic method of participant observation seems to offer the closest experiential opportunity for accomplishing this mission, but the impossibility of translation between two such distant voices doggedly foils any cogent interpretation of academically reported dialogues fractured by diverse temporalities (Fabian, 1983). However, it is the very challenge of confronting this problem of temporal incommensurability that might facilitate any attempt at addressing the crucial question of the feasibility of gaining access to that apparently unique world. Notwithstanding this failure to reconcile the two, it provides an observation point that holds a promise of recognizing the contours and the distinct otherness of that arguably selfless age category. In effect, the two parallel courses of signification do not intersect to produce the site of betweenness viewed by many anthropologists as the breeding ground that forms a joint voice of both interlocutors in the research act (Crapanzano, 2004; Stoller, 2009). This experiential and theoretical void could turn a disciplinarian bane into a refreshed knowledge boon, thus putting a new complexion on the face of old-age research by transforming the advent of compressed morbidity into an adventure in compressed gerontology. Although it might delimit its scope to a near-death category that warrants radical revision of theory and tools, the study of the fourth age is likely to deepen its self-justification as a distinguishable academic arena engaging in the hermeneutics of extracultural existential categories rather than of individuals, groups, or populations. This option of substituting the traditional gerontological preoccupation with people, problems, and images for the logics inherent in the inimitable state of being terminally old posits the understanding of that category at the forefront of the intellectual pursuit of sensing the edges of the social, the cultural, and the psychological from within and from without that categorical stage.

EPILOGUE: A PRESENT CATEGORY WITH AN ABSENT WELL-BEING

Aiming thus at the nebulous summit of the fourth age might unfold a special panoramic view of all ages and possibly all societies. To that end, and to the end of this chapter, it is appropriate to pay tribute to the living spirit and wisdom of an eminent centenarian whose pioneering work is an inspiration to most disciplines of the humanities. Born in 1908 and passed away in 2008, the anthropologist Claude Lévi-Strauss is responsible for many revolutionary ideas in the understanding of the origins of human cognition and its resulting social organization. Among them is the distinction drawn between what he termed *hot societies*, founded on the dynamics of history, cumulative memory, and a sense of continuity, and *cold societies*, based on the static nature of myth, present-bound spontaneous considerations, and a mythical sense for the eternal now (Lévi-Strauss, 1966). Put somewhat glibly, it could be argued that the image of society in the fourth age is commensurable with the cold type, whereas other ages construct their life according to the hot model – both the former and the latter view the same period of chronological time simultaneously from two diametrically opposed angles. For example, as Lévi-Strauss (2001) suggests, grandparents whose outlook on life is devoid of memory, "cold" in his locution (i.e., selfless in our terms) are diametrically opposed to their grandchildren, whose prospective on life trajectory is hot (i.e., skewed toward a progressively developed selfhood).

If this is indeed the case, is it plausible to assert that the assumption of the fourth age as effacing the temporal significance of the corporeal by virtue of the inability to control its changes (Kirkwood, 2002) is subsequently about changing bodily regulated social climate (Shilling, 2005; B. Turner, 1987) as well as somatically formulated language? Both are in need of radical revision as objects for gerontological research, possibly in the line of some anthropological enterprises in the understanding of temporality in other cultures, such as the elicitation of the nonlinear properties in temporal terminologies that prevail among certain tribal societies (Geertz, 1960; Gell, 1992; Lee, 1950) and in certain states of transition, such as the liminal stage in rites of passage (V. Turner, 1969). All these ethnographic instances offer reflections on the possible status of the temporal dimension as a stable category ephemerally impervious to forces of change. Likewise, it can even be argued that an anthropological unraveling of the temporal principles of fourth agers' language and its ensuing vocabulary might lend itself to developing a corresponding theoretical model of that category, a model that could be incorporated into discourses of the behavioral sciences and still be faithful to the quiddity of that phase of life.

In fact, the problem of translation could offer a clue as to a yet-unavailable definition of the inhabitants of the category in question: the fourth age. It therefore could be argued that wherever there occurs a nonpathologically induced breach in communication in an encounter with an elderly subject, it gives ground for considering that exit from one form of dialogue as an entry point to another mode of understanding based on a recognition of that gap as a cultural cleavage. Belonging to this state of otherness is thus not a predestined consequence of social or academic classification but an emergent property of an untoward disjuncture in a supposedly transgenerational, mutually constructed narrative. When such aborted communication no longer provides a credible source for observation and ensuing lessons, a sense of fourth age emerges. In other words, recognition of the state of fourth age hinges on the point beyond which middle age and its concomitant third age irretrievably cease to inform and manufacture knowledge and experience of some of culture of the oldest old. Hence, an irredeemable breach in dialogue could signal the onset of such awareness of this kind of unfathomable otherness. Talking of well-being in the fourth age, therefore, should rest on the realization that, even though it ought to sprout out of a dialogical communication between the actors defining an encounter with those occupying that existential territory, the encounter does not lend itself to such dialogue. Thus, a triangulation of the disparate points of view constituting situations of care, academic interview, or just an attempt to get acquainted does not necessarily produce some sound sense or understanding as to what well-being really consists of. Put bluntly, the dilemma of optional construal of the concept of well-being can be paraphrased in terms of the right to appropriate the meaning of life itself: whose or – better phrased – what kind of well-being is it anyway? A glimpse into the nebulous category of the fourth age throws that dilemma embedded in the study of the aging process into stark relief.

REFERENCES

Agamben (2000). *Homo sacer*: Sovereign power and bare life. *Substance*, *29*, 124.

Anderson, B. (1972). The process of deculturation: Its dynamics among United States aged. *Anthropological Quarterly*, *45*, 209–216.

Archer, M. S. (2000). *Being human: The problem of agency*. Cambridge: Cambridge University Press.

Atchley, R. C. (1989). A continuity theory of normal aging. *Gerontologist*, *29*, 183–190.

Baltes, B., & Smith, J. (2003). New frontiers in the future of aging: From successful aging of the young old to the dilemmas of the fourth age. *Gerontology*, *49*, 123–135.

Baudrillard, J. (1976). *Symbolic exchange and death*. London: Sage.

Bauman, Z. (1991). *Modernity and ambivalence*. Cambridge, Polity Press.

Bellah, R. N., Sullivan, W. M., Tipton, S. M., & Swidler, A. (1985). *Habits of the heart: Individualism and commitment in American life*. Berkeley: University of California Press.

Berger, P. L., & Berger, B. (1976). *Sociology: A biographical approach*. New York: Penguin.

Biggs, S. (1999). The blurring of the life course: Narrative, memory and the question of authenticity. *Journal of Aging and Identity*, *4*, 209–222.

Biggs, S. (2004). Age, gender, narratives, and masquerades. *Journal of Aging Studies*, *18*, 45–58.

Blaikie, A. (1999). *Ageing and popular culture*. Cambridge: Cambridge University Press.

Blaikie, A. (2002). The secret world of subcultural aging. In L. Anderson (Ed.), *Cultural gerontology* (pp. 96–110). Westport, CT: Auburn House.
Blau, Z. S. (1973). *Old age in a changing society.* New York: New Viewpoint.
Bowling, A.(2007). Aspirations for older age in the 21st century: What is successful aging? *International Journal of Aging and Human Development, 64*, 263–297.
Burgess, B. (1950). Personal and social adjustment in old age. In M. Deeber (Ed.), *The aged and society* (pp. 138–156). Champaign, IL: Industrial Relations Research Association.
Butler, R. (1975). *Why survive: Being old in America.* New York: Harper and Row.
Bytheway, B. (1995). *Ageism.* Buckingham: Open University Press.
Callahan, D. (1990). *What kind of life: The limits of medical progress.* New York: Simon and Schuster.
Chamberlayne, P., Bornat, J., & Wengraf, T. (Eds.). (2000). *The turn to biographical methods in social science.* London: Routledge.
Crapanzano, V. (2004). *Imaginative horizons: An essay in literary philosophical anthropology.* Chicago: University of Chicago Press.
Csordas, T. J. (1990). Embodiment as a paradigm for anthropology. *Ethos, 18*, 5–47.
Cumming, E. (1975). Engagement with an old theory. *International Journal of Aging and Human Development, 6*, 187–191.
Cumming, E., & Henry, W. E. (1961). *Growing old: The process of disengagement.* New York: Basic Books.
De Beauvoir, S. (1975). *The coming of age.* New York: Warner Communications.
Deleuze, G., & Guariari, F. (1987). *A thousand plateaus: Capitalism and schizophrenia* (B. Massumi, Trans.). Minneapolis: University of Minnesota Press.
De Medeiros, Kate, d. M. (2005). The complementary self: Multiple perspectives on the aging person. *Journal of Aging Studies, 19*, 1–14.
Ewing, K. P. (1990). The illusion of wholeness: Culture, self, and the experience of inconsistency. *Ethos, 18*(3), 251–278.
Fabian, J. (1983). *Time and the other: How anthropology makes its object.* New York: Columbia University Press.
Featherstone, M., & Hepworth, M. (1991). The mask of ageing and the postmodern life course. In M. Featherstone & B. Turner (Eds.), *The body: Social processes and cultural theory* (pp. 370–389). London: Sage.
Fivush, R., & Haden, C. A. (Eds.). (2003). *Autobiographical memory and the construction of a narrative self.* Mohawk, NJ: Erlbaum.
Foucault, M. (2003). *Abnormal: Lectures at the College de France, 1974–75.* New York: Picador.
Fries J. F. (1980). Aging, natural death, and the compression of morbidity. *New England Journal of Medicine, 303*, 130–135.
Fukuyama, F. (2003). *Our posthuman future: Consequences of the biotechnology revolution.* New York: Picador.
Geertz, C. (1960). *The religion of Java.* Glencoe: Free Press.
Geertz, C. (1979). "From the native's point of view": On the nature of anthropological understanding. In P. Rabinow & W. M. Sullivan (Eds.), *Interpretive social science: A reader* (pp. 225–241). Berkeley: University of California Press.

Gell, A. (1992). *The anthropology of time: Cultural constructions of temporal maps and images.* Oxford, UK: Berg.

Gergen, K. J. (1991). *The saturated self: Dilemmas of identity in contemporary life.* New York: Basic Books.

Gergen, K. J. (1994). *Realities and relationships.* Cambridge, MA: Harvard University Press.

Gilleard, C., & Higgs, P. (2000). *Cultures of ageing: Self citizen and the body.* Essex: Prentice Hall.

Glascock, A. P., & Feinman, S. L. (1981). Social asset or social burden: Treatment of the aged in non-industrial societies. In L. Fry (Ed.), *Dimensions: Aging, culture and health* (pp. 13–32). New York: Bergin.

Goffman, E. (1961). *Asylums.* New York: Doubleday.

Goffman, E. (1974). *Frame analysis.* New York: Harper.

Gubrium, J. F., & Holstein, J. A. (2002). Going concerns and their bodies. In L. Anderson (Ed.), *Cultural gerontology* (pp. 191–206). Westport, CT: Auburn House.

Hallam, E., Hockey, J. L., & Howarth, G. (1999). *Beyond the body: Death and social identity.* London: Routledge.

Hazan, H. (1994). *Old age: Construction and deconstructions.* Cambridge: Cambridge University Press.

Hazan, H. (2003). Disposable children: On the role of offspring in the construction of conjugal support in later life. In V. L. Bengston & A. Lowenstein (Eds.), *Global aging and challenges to families* (pp. 159–174). New York: Aldine de Gruyter.

Hazan, H. (2006). Beyond discourse: Recognizing bare life among the very old. In J. L. Powell & A. Wahidin (Eds.), *Foucault and aging* (pp. 157–170). New York: Nova Science.

Hazan, H. (2009). Beyond Dialogue: Entering the fourth space in old age. In R. Edmonson & H. J. Von Kondratowicz (Eds.), *Helping older people: A humanistic approach to aging* (pp. 91–104). Bristol, UK: Policy Press.

Hazan, H., & Raz, A. E. (1997). The authorized self: How middle age defines old age in the postmodern. *Semiotica, 113*, 257–276.

Holmes, E., & Holmes, L. D. (1995). *Other cultures, elder years.* Thousand Oaks, CA: Sage.

Illouz, E. (2008). *Saving the modern soul.* Berkeley: University of California Press.

Johnson, C., & Barer, B. M. (1997). *Life beyond 85 years: The aura of survivorship.* New York: Springer.

Katz, D. S. (1996). *Disciplining old age: The formation of gerontological knowledge.* Charlottesville: University Press of Virginia.

Kaufman, S. (1986). *The ageless self: Sources of meaning in later life.* Madison: University of Wisconsin Press.

Kaufman, S. (2005). *And a time to die: How American hospitals shape the end of life.* Chicago: University of Chicago Press.

Kirkwood (2002). Evolution of ageing. *Mechanisms of Ageing and Development, 123*, 137–145.

Kontos, P. C. (2004). Ethnographic reflections on selfhood, embodiment and Alzheimer's disease. *Ageing and Society, 24*, 829–849.

Langness, L. L., & Frank, G. (1981). *Lives: An anthropological approach to biography.* Norato, CA: Chandler and Sharp.

Lee, D. (1950). Linear and nonlinear codifications of reality. *Psychosomatic Medicine, 12*, 89–97.

Lévi-Strauss, C. (1966). *The savage mind.* Chicago: University of Chicago Press.

Lévi-Strauss, C. (2001). *Race et histoire – Race et culture.* Paris: UNESCO.

Lifton, R. J. (1977). The sense of immortality. In H. Feifel (Ed.), *New meanings of death.* New York: McGraw-Hill.

Lomranz, J. (1998). "An image of aging and the concept of integrating: Coping and Mental Health Implications." In J. Lomranz (ed.), *Handbook of Aging and Mental Health* (pp. 217–254). New York: Springer.

Mead, G. H. (1934). *Mind, self and society.* Chicago: University of Chicago Press.

Metchnikoff, E. (1905). *Old age.* Washington, DC: Smithsonian Institute.

Mimkler, M., & Estes, C. (Eds.). (1991). *Critical perspectives on aging: The political and moral economy of growing old.* New York: Baywood.

Myerhoff, B. (1978). *Number our days.* New York: Simon and Schuster.

Phillipson, C. (2003). From family groups to personal communities: Social capital and social change in the family life of older adults. In V. L. Bengsten & A. Lowenstein (Eds.), *Global aging and challenges to families* (pp. 54–74). New York: Aldine de Gruyter.

Phinney, A., & Chesla, C. A. (2003). The lived body in dementia. *Journal of Aging Studies, 17*, 283–299.

Pile, S., & Thrift, N. (Eds.). (1995). *Mapping the subject: Geographics of cultural transformation.* London: Routledge.

Poon, L., Jang, U., Reynolds, S., & McCarthy, E. (2005). Profiles of the oldest old. In L. Johnson & P. G. Coleman (Eds.), *The Cambridge handbook of age and ageing* (pp. 346–353). Cambridge: Cambridge University Press.

Rogers, M. F. (1983). *Sociology, ethnomethodology and experience: A phenomenological critique.* Cambridge: Cambridge University Press.

Rose, N. (1990). *Governing the soul: The shaping of the private self.* London: Routledge.

Rosow, I. (1974). *Socialization to old age.* Berkeley: University of California Press.

Sabat, S. (2001). *The experience of Alzheimer's disease: Life through a tangled veil.* Oxford: Oxford University Press.

Sabat, S., & Harre, R. (1992). The construction and deconstruction of self in Alzheimer's disease. *Aging and Society, 12*, 443–461.

Shilling, C. (2005). *The body in culture, technology, and society.* London: Sage.

Shweder, R. A. (1998). Introduction: Welcome to middle age! In R. A. Shweder (Ed.), *Welcome to middle age! (And other cultural fictions)* (pp. ix–xvii). Chicago: University of Chicago Press.

Silver, C. B. (2003). Gendered identities in old age: Toward (de)gendering? *Journal of Aging Studies, 17*, 379–397.

Snow, C. P. (1998). *The Two Cultures.* Cambridge: Cambridge University Press.

Stoller, P. (2009). *The power of between: An anthropological odyssey.* Chicago: University of Chicago Press.

Sudnow, D. (1967). *Passing on: The social organization of dying.* Englewood Cliffs, NJ: Prentice Hall.

Turner, B. (1987). *Medical power and social knowledge.* London: Sage.

Turner, V. (1969). *The ritual process: Structure and anti-structure.* Chicago: Aldine de Gruyter.

Twigg, J. (2004). The body, gender, and age: Feminist insights in social gerontology. *Journal of Aging Studies, 18*, 59–73.

Unruh, D. R. (1983). *Invisible lives: Social worlds of the aged.* Beverly Hills, CA: Sage.

Weiss, G. (1999). *Body images: Embodiment as intercorporeality.* London: Sage.

Woodward, K. (1991). *Aging and its discontents.* Bloomington: Indiana University Press.

Woodward, K. (1995). Tribute to the older woman: Psychoanalysis, feminism and ageism. In M. Featherstone & A. Wernick (Eds.), *Images of aging: Cultural representations of later life* (pp. 79–98). London and New York: Routledge.

3

The Pursuit of Happiness: Alternative Conceptions of Subjective Well-Being

DOV SHMOTKIN

ABSTRACT

This chapter reviews the evolvement of the concept of happiness and its derivative, subjective well-being (SWB), in the research-oriented literature. Happiness and SWB refer to self-evaluations that people make about their general life condition, basically in positive-negative terms. The abundant studies on this topic have not resolved certain puzzles which culminate in the apparent contradiction between two large bodies of empirical research. The first provides evidence that most people are happy whereas the second demonstrates that the bad is stronger than the good in human experiences. Addressing the need to advance an integrative theory in the field, this chapter presents a new conceptual model of the pursuit of happiness in the face of adversity. This model considers SWB as an active agent of adaptation, and explicates its role and activity modules vis-à-vis the hostile-world scenarios of life. The chapter then focuses on the implications of this model for old and old-old age. SWB in advanced age has a vital adaptive value when framed in relation to the particular time perspective of living close to death, as well as to the life story required to account for the long-lived life.

FROM PHILOSOPHICAL DISCOURSE TO SCIENTIFIC STUDY: THE SHIFTING FORMULATIONS OF HAPPINESS

This chapter provides a brief overview of the concept of happiness and its research-oriented companion, the concept of subjective well-being. These concepts serve in social research as most popular indicators of adaptation, quality of life, mental health, and successful aging. Overall, happiness and SWB refer to self-evaluations that people make about their general life condition, usually in terms of a judgment or affect that can be located on a positive-negative continuum. Despite abundant research, certain essential puzzles about happiness and SWB are still unresolved. Pertinent to those puzzles is the question of how SWB can be simultaneously governed by a positivity bias (people usually rate their happiness high) and a negativity bias (people are more affected by the bad, rather than the good, events in their lives). Addressing this apparent contradiction, the chapter explicates a new conceptualization of the pursuit of happiness in the face of life adversity. Old-old age, with its unique adaptational challenges, is put forward as a test case for the relevance of basic propositions in the presented outlook on SWB.

Dual Accounts of Happiness in Western Thinking

Happiness in human life has always been a cardinal concern for philosophers, who have offered rival conceptions of its definition, attainability, and worthiness (McGill, 1967; Telfer, 1980). The main dispute between schools was whether happiness is the experiential outcome of attaining a pleasant life or, rather, a meaningful life. Largely referred to as hedonism, the former approach was crudely advocated in ancient Greek philosophy by Aristippus, who believed that the art of life lies in taking pleasures as they pass. A more sober hedonistic view was voiced by Epicurus, who argued that humans basically strive for pleasure but that this may be spiritual no less than sensual and should be consumed with restraint and reason. The opposing approach was most influentially epitomized by Aristotle's concept of eudaimonia, depicted as the supreme good. It refers to the striving toward realization of one's true potential, and its achievement signifies excellence and perfection. Embodied in virtuous activity, eudaimonia is by nature a source of pleasure, but it also involves readiness to suffer for the right end. Another school advocating virtuous life was that of the Stoics, who regarded happiness as peace of mind attained only by suppressing one's desires for pleasure.

Later philosophy continued the dispute by examining the implications of happiness for social institutions and legal systems (Brunner, 2007; Tatarkiewicz, 1976). Thus, Bentham adopted a hedonistic definition of happiness and regarded the human search for pleasure over pain as a key rule of nature. His utilitarian worldview proclaims that the duty of governments is to provide the greatest happiness to the greatest number of their citizens. In contrast, formulating a view of virtuous life under the reign of reason, Kant renounced happiness as a complete good or a necessary benchmark and considered moral duty the natural imperative in human life. More broadly, Bentham and Kant respectively represented larger schools of empiricist philosophers (e.g., Hobbes, Locke) versus idealistic and teleological philosophers (e.g., Hegel, Schopenhauer), who held contrasting views as to whether the good life should be evaluated by the earthly attainment of commonly desired ends or by the laborious perfection of a virtue or ideal (Feldman, 2004; Haybron, 2008).

The Evolution of Modern Research on Happiness

Empirical research on happiness started after World War II, stirred by movements that renewed the humanistic and phenomenological focus on the individual and laid foundations for welfare and quality of life in society at large. The seminal pioneering investigations (Andrews and Withey, 1976; Bradburn, 1969; Campbell, Converse, & Rodgers, 1976; Cantril, 1965) designed simple, often single-item, self-rating measures of happiness and satisfaction, and they applied them in large-scale, nationwide surveys. These works demonstrated that the vast majority of the respondents, whether young or old, completed such measures willingly and smoothly, thus suggesting that people have a heuristic notion about what happiness is despite its philosophical complexities. These early works also established the basic dimensional composition that still underlies the operational assessment of SWB: A factor of life satisfaction, which is a basically cognitive, long-term judgment of one's life as a whole, along with immediate experiences of positive affect and negative affect whose balance induces the emotional tone that dominates one's condition (Diener, 1984).

Thorough reviews (Diener, Suh, Lucas, & Smith, 1999; Veenhoven, 1984) and compilations (Eid & Larsen, 2008; Kahneman, Diener, & Schwarz, 1999; Strack, Argyle, & Schwarz, 1991) present the prolific accumulation of research on SWB over the past decades. The main findings are that objective life conditions (e.g., education, income, marital status) are consistently related to SWB, yet they usually explain, all together, only a small proportion (10–20%) of its variance. In contrast, personality traits (e.g., neuroticism, extroversion) and self-perceptions (e.g., self-esteem, subjective health) constitute the strongest and the most stable correlates of SWB. In addition, social-cognitive processing of information, by which people exercise differential (and often biased) attributions of qualities to themselves as compared with others, yields a variety of contextual and transient effects on SWB. Furthermore, although SWB typically reflects evaluations of the personal domain, it is subjected to different cultural construals in various national or societal settings (for a further discussion of major SWB-related findings, see Shmotkin, 2005).

From a gerontological viewpoint, a remarkable finding is that SWB does not necessarily decrease with advancing age. In U.S. studies, negative affect remained stable or decreased with age, whereas positive affect remained stable or increased with age (Carstensen, Pasupathi, Mayr, & Nesseroade, 2000; Charles, Reynolds, & Gatz, 2001; Mroczek and Kolarz, 1998). Although findings in other countries reveal a more mixed picture (Diener & Suh, 1997; Kunzmann, Little, & Smith, 2000; Shmotkin, 1990), it is evident that old age per se does not lower SWB if adjustments are made to age-related adverse conditions, such as poor health and widowhood. This finding sheds light on certain modes of adaptation to old age, such as the adjustment of aspirations, the use of complimentary social comparisons, and restrained emotional reactivity (Shmotkin, 1998). In old-old age, SWB appears to be sustained by staying reasonably responsive to the will to live (Carmel, 2001; see Chapter 16) and to the positive implications of psychological traits and states (Adkins, Martin, & Poon, 1996). Nevertheless, the maintenance of SWB in old-old age cannot be taken for granted, and it requires an integrative theory about the mechanisms of well-being at large (for an exposition of such theory, see Chapter 4) as well as appropriate platforms for measuring well-being in late life (see Chapter 17). This most pertinent relation between SWB and age is revisited later in the chapter.

A significant development in well-being research has been the revival of the old philosophical distinction between hedonic well-being, mainly referring to the conventional SWB dimensions of satisfaction and affective tone, and eudaimonic well-being, mainly referring to meaningful pursuits that promote purpose and growth in life (King & Napa, 1998; Ryan & Deci, 2001; Ryff, 1989). Various frameworks in the past decade have located the construct of SWB beside various modalities of eudaimonic well-being. According to Ryff and Singer's (1998) conceptualization of psychological well-being, the effects of SWB are usually secondary to those of positive health in human life; yet SWB may help differentiate different types of positive coping with life challenges, such as mastery of one's environment and purpose in one's life (Keyes, Shmotkin, & Ryff, 2002). From a different perspective, SWB is a component of larger networks of qualities of life and arts of life, representing different modes of feelings, cognitions, and behaviors by which people attempt to optimize their essential life conditions (Veenhoven, 2000, 2003). Another, currently influential approach is known as positive psychology (Keyes & Haidt, 2003; Seligman & Csikszentmihalyi, 2000); its agenda delineates processes by which people can flourish. Although SWB is a natural ingredient of flourishing, a broader attention in this approach is given to human strengths and virtues (e.g., engagement, creativity, hope) that produce an array of meanings in life (Aspinwall & Staudinger, 2003; Peterson & Seligman, 2004).

The ample research on SWB notwithstanding, the quest for happiness is still a source of considerable perplexity. Is happiness a realistic outcome within the tangible reach of most people, or is it an elusive and treacherous experience that ultimately leaves those who seek it unhappy? Protagonists for both ideas can be readily found to argue with each other. As presented next, this confusion requires a further consideration of what we know about SWB.

CONFLICTING PRINCIPLES: "MOST PEOPLE ARE HAPPY" VERSUS "BAD IS STRONGER THAN GOOD"

The Positivity Bias in Well-Being

The authoritative assertion that "most people are happy" (Diener & Diener, 1996, p. 181) summarizes an intriguing body of research on SWB accumulated since the 1950s. Numerous surveys worldwide have shown that the vast majority of respondents report greater-than-medium levels of happiness, including people in disadvantageous conditions such as those who are old-old (i.e., older than 75), are poor, are severely disabled, or have passed an adjustment period of no more than a few months after terrible misfortunes in life. This positivity bias in well-being is rooted in pervasive mechanisms of both emotional and cognitive nature. Part of these mechanisms dwells on the general phenomenon of positivity bias in emotions (Cacioppo, Gardner, & Berntson, 1999), which enables positive emotions to facilitate behavioral options and to strengthen adaptive resources (Fredrickson, 2001; Lyubomirsky, King, & Diener, 2005). The evidence that people's SWB is largely hereditable (Lykken, 1999) and homeostatically maintained around a positive set point (Cummins & Nistico, 2002) suggests that being happy is a universally advantageous condition from an evolutionary perspective.

The Negativity Bias in Human Experience

The foregoing evidence appears to contradict not only pessimistic philosophical traditions (Tatarkiewicz, 1976) but also an empirical body of other evidence showing that "bad is stronger than good" (Baumeister,

Bratslavsky, Finkenauer, & Vohs, 2001, p. 323; Rozin & Royzman, 2001). This evidence indicates that undesirable, harmful, or unpleasant outcomes have a greater psychological impact than desirable, beneficial, or pleasant ones. Thus, although people manifest a powerful capability of adaptation to most adverse conditions, certain negative events that are relatively common (e.g., disability, unemployment, divorce) may lower SWB lastingly (Diener, Lucas, & Scollon, 2006; Lucas, 2007). Psychological trauma, which often represents ineradicable loss or suffering, may be particularly likely to perpetuate its harsh impact by shattering people's assumptive world and instigating further cycles of loss (Herman, 1992; Hobfoll, Dunahoo, & Monnier, 1995; Janoff-Bulman, 1992; see Chapter 6).

The predominant power of the bad over the good is reasonably explained by the critical implications that negative experiences may bear for one's protection and survival. These implications may be particularly acute in old and old-old age when the balance between gains and losses is strained and the reserves of resources are increasingly depleted (Baltes, 1997; Hobfoll & Wells, 1998). Hence, it is intriguing to observe the apparent contradiction whereby most people report high levels of happiness for themselves while simultaneously judging other people to be more imbued by distress than by happiness (Diener & Diener, 1996; Seligman & Csikszentmihalyi, 2000). This discrepancy cannot be dismissed as merely a defensive illusion because, as seen earlier, it genuinely reflects two conflicting principles of positivity and negativity in life. The following section proposes a conceptual framework that addresses this conflict by a newly elaborated outlook on SWB.

IN NEED OF INTEGRATION: THE MODEL OF PURSUING HAPPINESS IN THE FACE OF ADVERSITY

Rethinking SWB: The Dynamic Formulation

Shmotkin (2005; Shmotkin & Shrira, in press) has proposed a conceptual model of SWB that explicates the adaptational role of this construct on both dynamic and structural grounds. In contrast to traditional views of SWB as a psychological outcome, Shmotkin's model presents SWB as an agentic system whose principal role is to constitute a favorable psychological environment, conceived of as a positive state of mind that allows an individual to maintain ongoing activity with minimal disruption by adverse contingencies. Complementary to SWB in this model is a system termed the *hostile-world scenario* (HWS), which refers to an image of actual or potential threats to one's life or, more broadly, to one's physical and mental integrity. The HWS is nourished by beliefs about catastrophes and inflictions, such as accidents, violence, natural disasters, wars, illness, aging, and death. This image of adversity functions as a system of appraisal that scans for any potential negative condition or for an even worse condition when a negative one already prevails. When activated adaptively, the HWS helps keep people vigilant to threats in the struggle to remain safe and well, but an extreme HWS generates a sense of a precarious living in a disastrous world.

Both SWB and HWS regulate each other by various mechanisms to fulfill respective tasks of promoting pleasantness and accomplishment while ensuring safety and protection. Thus, the potent mechanism of adaptation enables people to habituate to most, albeit not all, adverse experiences, so that they can ultimately return to their original SWB baseline (Frederick & Loewenstein, 1999). By another mechanism of counteracting, SWB employs antidotes, such as positive affect, to dismantle HWS-induced negative emotions (Fredrickson, 2001). In parallel, on a cognitive track, SWB-enhancing beliefs, such as positive illusions (consistently exaggerated perceptions of one's worth and capabilities; Taylor & Brown, 1988) and a favorable assumptive world (faith in the essentially benevolent nature of the world; Janoff-Bulman, 1992), filter negative information by overstressing mastery, benefits, and prospects in life. Still another mechanism involves a dialectical coactivation of SWB and HWS. Thus, in novel or complex situations, SWB facilitates approaching behaviors, such as exploration and manipulation, whereas the HWS simultaneously ensures alertness to potential dangers (Cacioppo et al., 1999). These and other mechanisms illustrate how SWB constantly negotiates with the HWS so that life is not overridden by a nightmarish imminence of catastrophe, yet not driven to the naïveté of a fool's paradise.

Rethinking SWB: The Structural Formulation

Subjective well-being is a dynamic and flexible agent of adaptation because it operates in multiple structures, or modules, of activity. The modules enumerated by Shmotkin's (2005) model locate SWB in four contexts of psychological space and time. These modules include the private domain of self-awareness (experiential SWB), the public domain of self-reports (declarative SWB), the synchronic combinations of different dimensions in the self (differential SWB), and the diachronic trajectories of the personal life story along time (narrative SWB). This framework creates profiles of SWB across the distinctive modules. For instance, people who publicly report being happy (high declarative SWB) may belong to strikingly different SWB profiles, which possibly include private experiences of either happiness or unhappiness, differential combinations of affect by which positive affect and negative affect either coactivate or coinhibit each other, and perceived narratives of either progression or regression in happiness along a time continuum. Such configurations of SWB provide flexible options of inducing favorable psychological environments when the HWS becomes distressful or dangerously real.

The previous formulation also helps better understand the boundaries between SWB and meaning-in-life (Keyes et al., 2002). Although SWB is a system that provides self-evaluations concerning the favorableness of one's life, meaning-in-life refers to a combination of cognitive schemas (e.g., concepts and beliefs) that provide an explanation for essential aspects of one's life (e.g., its worthiness, guiding values, course, and purpose). Both are designed to deal with life adversity. Thus, in terms of the present model, SWB can regulate the HWS so that the HWS becomes manageable, whereas meaning can reconstruct the HWS so that the HWS becomes interpretable. Put otherwise, although SWB adjusts the level of HWS by inducing favorable life perceptions, meaning structures the content of the HWS by offering premises and beliefs to lean on.

OLD-OLD AGE: A TEST CASE FOR SUBJECTIVE WELL-BEING

The Particular Implications of Old-Old Age for SWB

The survival to old-old age is a dialectical achievement. People wish to defy death and thus usually do their utmost to prolong their own life and the lives of their loved ones. A long-lived life attests to constitutional and psychological fortitude, yet it simultaneously summons agonizing deterioration, frailty, and losses. Thus, the triumph over death actually makes death even more imminent. This dialectic is further complicated when coping with old-old age is challenged by the sequelae of earlier trauma in life (for discussion of trauma in late life, see Chapters 6–8) and by societal positions that disconnect old-old age from the younger parts of the life course (see Chapter 2). Hence, old-old age presents an intriguing mode for the intertwining of resilience and vulnerability.

A few theories offer some understanding of the basic processes governing old-old age. The common-cause theory (Fried & Guralnik, 1997) suggests that the decline of biological capability in old-old age overrides all the other adaptation functions. Baltes's (1997) theory of incomplete architecture of human ontology asserts that human development is not programmed to function optimally in the "fourth age" (about age 80 onward) because the compensatory role of culture-based resources (e.g., knowledge, skills) becomes less efficient to overcome the biological dysfunctions. Similarly, the gerodynamics theory (Birren & Schroots, 1996) postulates that old systems can hardly stabilize their far-from-equilibrium conditions, thus leading to lower-order transformations until the system's death.

The foregoing theories suggest that the psychological status of the old-old is forced to align with the dominating biological determinants in this age. Thus, the most consistent predictors of mortality among the old-old are advanced age, gender (being male), physical disability, and poor self-rated health (Ben-Ezra & Shmotkin, 2006). Beyond those predictors, studies on mortality still reveal significant effects of certain psychosocial predictors, such as social networks (Litwin & Shiovitz-Ezra, 2006; see Chapter 12), volunteering activity (Shmotkin, Blumstein, & Modan, 2003), and emotional support and solitary leisure activity (Walter-Ginzburg, Shmotkin, Blumstein, & Shorek, 2005). Reasonably, when the criterion for health is not strictly factual (mortality) but subjective (self-rating), the role of psychosocial factors expands (Quinn, Johnson, Poon, & Martin, 1999).

The preceding considerations bear certain implications for SWB in old-old age. First, the particular lability and unpredictability in the physical status of the old-old may make SWB more subordinate to conditions of morbidity and disability than in younger ages. Second, the temporal location of old-old age near the very end of life puts SWB within a critical frame of time perspective. This implication is now discussed in more detail.

Living under the Shadow of an Approaching End: Time Perspective and SWB in Late Life

Subjective well-being functions within a time perspective of past, present, and future. People in different ages manifest differential evaluations of the three time perspectives in a way that facilitates adaptation to their particular location in the life span (Ryff, 1991; Shmotkin, 1991). A coherent time perspective provides the individual with the sense of both consistency and change in the passage of his or her life along the time course (Shmotkin & Eyal, 2003). Thus, perceived congruence of the past, by which the individual can reconcile with negative life events and cherish good ones, is positively associated with present SWB (Bishop, Martin, & Poon, 2006).

As proposed by Shmotkin's (2005) model, people bear in mind a certain conception about their SWB trajectory, depicting how well their life has proceeded over time. Operationally, such a trajectory is defined as an imaginary line connecting SWB self-evaluations (e.g., life satisfaction) that the person attributes to his or her remembered past, currently perceived present, and anticipated future (Busseri, Choma, & Sadava, 2009; Röcke & Lachman, 2008; Shmotkin, 1991). In conceiving their individual trajectories, people may consider life adversities, threats, and daily hassles as well as successes, achievements, and happy events. Trajectories represent a certain direction (or directions) of one's change along the time course (Gergen & Gergen, 1988). Most typically, life trajectories reveal that younger adults rank their present as more satisfying than the past and the future as more satisfying than the present, whereas older adults tend to rank their past as more satisfying than the present and the future (Lachman, Röcke, Rosnick, & Ryff, 2008; Shmotkin, 1991; Staudinger, Bluck, & Herzberg, 2003). Conventional life trajectories may be destabilized by traumatic experiences, which possibly leave people psychologically stuck in their past or deprive them of hope and optimism, which are often projected into the future (Holman & Silver, 1998; Lomranz, Shmotkin, Zechovoy, & Rosenberg, 1985; see Chapter 6).

Recent studies examined the implications of SWB trajectories in late life. One study (Cohen, Lernau, & Shmotkin, 2009) analyzed trajectories derived from happiness ratings of outstandingly meaningful life periods, reported by a random sample of older Israelis (age 60–85, mean 73). Progressive trajectories (an overall upward tendency through time) were found to be related to favorable life circumstances (e.g., better subjective health, higher SWB) than were regressive trajectories (an overall downward tendency through time). Another study (Palgi & Shmotkin, 2010) analyzed trajectories derived from life satisfaction ratings of past (5 years earlier), present, and future (1 year ahead) reported by old-old Israelis (aged 86–105, mean 92) who participated in a national longitudinal study. Progressive trajectories in this age group were presented by no more than 7.3% of the participants. An equilibrated trajectory (with equal ratings of past, present, and future) exhibited the best functioning (e.g., better physical performance, fewer depressive symptoms). Regressive trajectories, which actually depicted a fairly realistic view of life in this very advanced age, presented a medium-level functioning. Those who refrained from rating any of their time perspectives fared worst in comparison with the others.

The mentioned studies point to the shift in the time perspective of old-old people, whose foreshortened future poses threats of deterioration, possible suffering, and death (Kastenbaum, 1975). People who feel close to the end of life can improve their emotional regulation by resorting to corrective mechanisms, such as a selective investment in relationships and activities that maintain a dominance of positive emotions over negative ones (Carstensen, Isaacowitz, & Charels, 1999; on leisure activities, see also Chapter 14). In this vein, our studies reveal a sizable proportion of old-old people who deliberately decline the request that they evaluate their future even though they do evaluate their past and present. These people (approximately 30% among octogenarians and nonagenarians in two different samples) may not necessarily reveal a critically poorer functioning or lower SWB (provided that they do not ignore their past and present as well) than those who provide an evaluation of their future (Palgi & Shmotkin, 2010; Shmotkin, 1992). Thus, although some of our findings suggest that avoiding one's futurity is linked with more negative attitudes toward one's aging, the regulatory function of this avoidance is nevertheless apparent. As certain remarks by our participants suggest (e.g., "At my age, how can I tell what my future will be like?" "There's no point in thinking about a time when I may not be alive"), bypassing the notion of one's future is a reasonably realistic approach for old-old people. This approach accords with the temporal optimization principle (Lawton, 1996), by which people's time perspective reflects selectively chosen time segments that maximize present SWB.

Accounting for the Evolvement in Time: The Life Story and SWB in Late Life

Narrative psychology postulates that people, storytellers by nature, continuously formulate their individual life story in ways that support their self-identity and provide them with a sense of coherence and purpose (McAdams, 1993). From another view, the life story is vital not for its coherence but for its diversity: it enables people to formulate multiple identities through alternating relationships and changing life phases (Gergen, 1994). In both views, life stories involve identifiable sequences of events and outcomes that strongly reflect SWB (Gergen & Gergen, 1988; McAdams, Reynolds, Lewis, Patten, & Bowman, 2001).

The life story supports the old-age developmental tasks by processes of life review and reminiscence (Butler, 1963; Haight & Webster, 1995). Older people employ these processes to achieve integrity, defined as a sense of coherence and wholeness about one's life while facing finitude (Erikson, 1998). Oriented to the past, life review and reminiscence benefit from the positive bias prevailing in autobiographical memory (Walker, Skowronski, & Thompson, 2003). Compared with people of younger ages, those in old age usually remember the past more positively and the past brings them more satisfaction (Fernandes, Ross, Wiegand, & Schryer, 2008; Kennedy, Mather, & Carstensen, 2004; Singer, Rexhaj, & Baddeley, 2007). Although the positive bias of autobiographical memory in old age facilitates emotional regulation in coping with age-related losses (Labouvie-Vief, 2008; Mather & Carstensen, 2005), older people may also suffer from the revival of negative memories that can be damaging to SWB (Cappeliez & O'Rourke, 2006; Wong & Watt, 1991). Traumatic experiences in one's life may further inflict a persistent distress over autobiographical memory and SWB (O'Kearney & Perrott, 2006; Porter & Peace, 2007; see also Chapter 6).

According to Shmotkin's (2005) model, the SWB trajectory described in the previous section actually portrays a narrative SWB, as it tells us the core story of how favorably one's life evolved. The narrative SWB is the nexus between SWB and the life story. This nexus is exposed in our investigations by evaluations of SWB that individuals attributed to anchor periods in their life story, which are life periods or events of outstanding meaning (e.g., "the happiest period in my life," "the most difficult period in my life"). Representing paramount experiences, anchor periods are reference points for reconstructing and evaluating other life experiences, and, practically, they supply a heuristic outlook on one's life story. The inquiry into anchor periods reveals not only SWB-related affects (e.g., happiness, suffering) but also core meanings of life. Thus, anchor periods, or the trajectory that connects their evaluations, may convey underlying messages such as growth, recovery, mastery, struggle, and renewal. Old and old-old people may stress messages of survival, the bearing of a legacy, self-preservation, loss, and decline. These messages resemble Gergen's (1994) concept of valued endpoint, which sums up the story's essence.

Our studies of old and old-old people showed that different valences of anchor periods (positive or negative) were either congruent or incongruent with the ensuing emotions (happiness or suffering). In a sample whose age range was 58–94 (mean 76), older participants differed from younger ones in the negative, "most miserable" period, which they rated lower on both suffering and happiness (Shmotkin, Berkovich, & Cohen, 2006). Moreover, the older participants differed from their younger counterparts by reporting a positive, rather than negative, relationship between suffering in the most miserable period and current life satisfaction (Shrira & Shmotkin, 2008). Although the latter study also pointed to an opposite trend among traumatized people (see Chapter 6), the findings suggest that old-old people, more than old people, resort to emotional regulatory mechanisms that attenuate, and even contrast, memories of suffering in the life story.

Besides this age differentiation, further results showed that, although past happiness weakened certain inverse relationships between past suffering and SWB indices, it paradoxically strengthened the relationship when both happiness and suffering incongruently ensued from negative and positive periods, respectively (Shmotkin & Shrira, 2010). The findings, in general, indicate that effects of life stories on the SWB of older people combine memories of both happiness and suffering in those stories. Those emotions may interact with each other or be incongruent with their anchor-period context. For example, a participant told of how he frightfully watched his house ruined in war, and yet felt happy about remaining alive; another participant told about the joy she had of having all her grandchildren united with her in a family celebration, yet acutely feeling the pain that her husband had not survived to that moment. An excessively high level of incongruence may disrupt the expectedly reinforcing impact of the life story on SWB in old age, possibly because such incongruence signals a decrease in the predictability of outcomes in this age (Birren & Schroots, 1996) or an increase in the predominance of losses over gains (Hobfoll & Wells, 1998).

CONCLUSION

Subjective well-being is essentially more dialectical than commonly assumed. Thus, positive concomitants of adaptive functioning and favorable life conditions are not unique to a high-SWB profile, whereas negative concomitants of dysfunction and unfavorable conditions are not unique to a low-SWB profile (Busseri, Sadava, Molnar, & DeCourville, 2009; Shmotkin, 1998). In line with this complexity, this chapter has presented a model that explicates the regulatory role of SWB vis-à-vis its complementary image of adversity (termed the *hostile-world scenario*). Acting in different modules of psychological space and time, SWB has multiple appearances that may be contradictory at times.

Old, and particularly old-old, age renders SWB into an even more dialectical position. On the one hand, the regulatory function of SWB, by constituting a favorable psychological environment, becomes highly imperative when scenarios of deterioration and loss are harshly realized. On the other hand, the function of SWB may be easily overwhelmed by the mounting physical forces of disablement. In this unstable condition, SWB must adapt to the unique temporal frames with which the old-old live: a foreshortened future that reshapes the personal time perspective and a prolonged past that enriches the supportive capability of the life story.

Old-old age puts forward a challenge for the study of SWB. This age constitutes an arena for exploring a labile balance between SWB, which represents the resilience with which people maintain a prevailing positive feeling, and the HWS, which represents the vulnerability people are geared to scan for. This balance may yield intriguing opposites: vital and well-lived lives of nonagenarians and centenarians (Martin, da Rosa, Siegler, Davey, MacDonald, & Poon, 2006; Poon & Perls, 2007) versus varieties of detached life plagued with dementia (Cohen-Mansfield, 2000). The special intertwining of resilience and vulnerability in old-old age bears the message that happiness should be juxtaposed with suffering, and, similarly, survival with finitude, to better understand the processes by which people negotiate with their lives.

REFERENCES

Adkins, G., Martin, P., & Poon, L. W. (1996). Personality traits and states as predictors of subjective well-being in centenarians, octogenarians, and sexagenarians. *Psychology and Aging, 11*, 408–416.

Andrews, F. M., & Withey, S. B. (1976). *Social indicators of well-being: Americans' perceptions of life quality.* New York: Plenum Press.

Aspinwall, L. G., & Staudinger, U. M. (Eds.). (2003). *A psychology of human strengths: Fundamental questions and future directions for a positive psychology.* Washington, DC: American Psychological Association.

Baltes, P. B. (1997). On the incomplete architecture of human ontogeny: Selection, optimization, and compensation as foundation of developmental theory. *American Psychologist, 52*, 366–380.

Baumeister, R. F., Bratslavsky, E., Finkenauer, C., & Vohs, K. D. (2001). Bad is stronger than good. *Review of General Psychology, 5*, 323–370.

Ben-Ezra M., & Shmotkin, D. (2006). Predictors of mortality in the old-old in Israel: The Cross-Sectional and Longitudinal Aging Study. *Journal of the American Geriatrics Society, 54*, 906–911.

Birren, J. E., & Schroots, J. J. F. (1996). History, concepts, and theory in the psychology of aging. In J. E. Birren & K. W. Schaie (Eds.), *Handbook of the psychology of aging* (4th ed., pp. 3–23). New York: Academic Press.

Bishop, A. J., Martin, P., & Poon, L. W. (2006). Happiness and congruence in older adulthood: A structural model of life satisfaction. *Aging and Mental Health, 10*, 445–453.

Bradburn, N. M. (1969). *The structure of psychological well-being.* Chicago: Aldine.

Brunner, J. (2007). Modern times: Law, temporality and happiness in Hobbes, Locke and Bentham. *Theoretical Inquiries in Law, 8*, 277–310.

Busseri, M. A., Choma, B. L., & Sadava, S. W. (2009). Functional or fantasy? Examining the implications of subjective temporal perspective "trajectories" for life satisfaction. *Personality and Social Psychology Bulletin, 35*, 295–308.

Busseri, M. A., Sadava, S. W., Molnar, D., & DeCourville, N. (2009). A person-centered approach to subjective well-being. *Journal of Happiness Studies, 10*, 161–181.
Butler, R. N. (1963). The life review: An interpretation of reminiscence in the aged. *Psychiatry, 26*, 65–76.
Cacioppo, J. T., Gardner, W. L., & Berntson, G. G. (1999). The affect system has parallel and integrative processing components: Form follows function. *Journal of Personality and Social Psychology, 76*, 839–855.
Campbell, A., Converse, P. E., & Rodgers, W. L. (1976). *The quality of American life: Perceptions, evaluations, and satisfactions.* New York: Russell Sage Foundation.
Cantril, H. (1965). *The pattern of human concerns.* New Brunswick, NJ: Rutgers University Press.
Cappeliez, P., & O'Rourke, N. (2006). Empirical validation of a model of reminiscence and health in later life. *Journal of Gerontology: Psychological Sciences, 61B*, P237–P244.
Carmel, S. (2001). The will to live: Gender differences among elderly persons. *Social Science and Medicine, 52*, 949–958.
Carstensen, L. L., Isaacowitz, D. M., & Charels, S. T. (1999). Taking time seriously: A theory of socioemotional selectivity. *American Psychologist, 54*, 165–181.
Carstensen, L. L., Pasupathi, M., Mayr, U., & Nesseroade, J. R. (2000). Emotional experience in everyday life across the adult life span. *Journal of Personality and Social Psychology, 79*, 644–655.
Charles, S. T., Reynolds, C. A., & Gatz, M. (2001). Age-related differences and change in positive and negative affect over 23 years. *Journal of Personality and Social Psychology, 79*, 644–655.
Cohen, K., Lernau, T., & Shmotkin, D. (2009). *Outlining the life story: Socio-demographic and subjective well-being correlates of life trajectories.* Unpublished paper.
Cohen-Mansfield, J. (2000). Heterogeneity in dementia: Challenges and opportunities. *Alzheimer Disease and Associated Disorders, 14*, 60–63.
Cummins, R. A., & Nistico, H. (2002). Maintaining life satisfaction: The role of positive cognitive bias. *Journal of Happiness Studies, 3*, 37–69.
Diener, E. (1984). Subjective well-being. *Psychological Bulletin, 95*, 542–575.
Diener, E., & Diener, C. (1996). Most people are happy. *Psychological Science, 7*, 181–185.
Diener, E., Lucas, R. E., & Scollon, C. N. (2006). Beyond the hedonic treadmill: Revising the adaptation theory of well-being. *American Psychologist, 61*, 305–314.
Diener, E., & Suh, M. E. (1997). Subjective well-being and age: An international analysis. *Annual Review of Gerontology and Geriatrics, 17*, 304–324.
Diener, E., Suh, E. M., Lucas, R. E., & Smith, H. L. (1999). Subjective well-being: Three decades of progress. *Psychological Bulletin, 125*, 276–302.
Eid, M., & Larsen, R. J. (Eds.). (2008). *The science of subjective well-being.* New York: Guilford Press.
Erikson, E. H. (1998). *The life cycle completed: Extended version with new chapters on the ninth stage by Joan M. Erikson.* New York: Norton.
Feldman, F. (2004). *Pleasure and the good life: Concerning the nature, varieties and plausibility of hedonism.* New York: Oxford University Press.

Fernandes, M., Ross, M., Wiegand, M., & Schryer, E. (2008). Are the memories of older adults positively biased? *Psychology and Aging, 23*, 297–306.

Frederick, S., & Loewenstein, G. (1999). Hedonic adaptation. In D. Kahneman, E. Diener, & N. Schwarz (Eds.), *Well-being: The foundations of hedonic psychology* (pp. 302–329). New York: Russell Sage Foundation.

Fredrickson, B. L. (2001). The role of positive emotions in positive psychology: The broaden-and-build theory of positive emotions. *American Psychologist, 56*, 218–226.

Fried, L. P., & Guralnik, J. M. (1997). Disability in older adults: Evidence regarding significance, etiology, and risk. *Journal of the American Geriatric Society, 45*, 92–100.

Gergen, K. J. (1994). *Realities and relationships: Soundings in social construction.* Cambridge, MA: Harvard University Press.

Gergen, K. J., & Gergen, M. M. (1988). Narratives and the self as relationship. In L. Berkowitz (Ed.), *Advances in experimental social psychology* (Vol. 21, pp. 17–56). New York: Academic Press.

Haight, B., & Webster, J. (Eds.). (1995). *The art and science of reminiscing.* Washington, DC: Taylor and Francis.

Haybron, D. M. (2008). *The pursuit of unhappiness: The elusive psychology of well-being.* Oxford: Oxford University Press.

Herman, J. L. (1992). *Trauma and recovery.* New York: Basic Books.

Hobfoll, S. E., Dunahoo, C. A., & Monnier, J. (1995). Conservation of resources and traumatic stress. In J. R. Freedy & S. E. Hobfoll (Eds.), *Traumatic stress: From theory to practice* (pp. 29–47). New York: Plenum Press.

Hobfoll, S. E., & Wells, J. D. (1998). Conservation of resources, stress, and aging: Why do some slide and some spring? In J. Lomranz (Ed.), *Handbook of aging and mental health: An integrative approach* (121–134). New York: Plenum Press.

Holman, E. A., & Silver, R. C. (1998). Getting "stuck" in the past: Temporal orientation and coping with trauma. *Journal of Personality and Social Psychology, 74*, 1146–1163.

Janoff-Bulman, R. (1992). *Shattered assumptions: Towards a new psychology of trauma.* New York: Free Press.

Kahneman, D., Diener, E., & Schwarz, N. (Eds.). (1999). *Well-being: The foundations of hedonic psychology.* New York: Sage.

Kastenbaum, R. (1975). Time, death and ritual in old age. In J. T. Fraser & N. Lawrence (Eds.), *The study of time II* (pp. 20–38). New York: Springer-Verlag.

Kennedy, Q., Mather, M., & Carstensen, L. L. (2004). The role of motivation in the age-related positivity effect in autobiographical memory. *Psychological Science, 15*, 208–214.

Keyes, C. L. M., & Haidt, J. (Eds.). (2003). *Flourishing: Positive psychology and the life well-lived.* Washington, DC: American Psychological Association.

Keyes, C. L. M., Shmotkin, D., & Ryff, C. D. (2002). Optimizing well-being: The empirical encounter of two traditions. *Journal of Personality and Social Psychology, 82*, 1007–1022.

King, L. A., & Napa, C. K. (1998). What makes a life good? *Journal of Personality and Social Psychology, 75*, 156–165.

Kunzmann, U., Little, T. D., & Smith, J. (2000). Is age-related stability of subjective well-being a paradox? Cross-sectional and longitudinal evidence from the Berlin Aging Study. *Psychology and Aging, 15*, 511–526.

Labouvie-Vief, G. (2008). Dynamic integration theory: Emotion, cognition, and equilibrium in later life. In V. L. Bengtson, D. Gans, N. M. Putney, & M. Silverstein (Eds.), *Handbook of theories of aging* (2nd ed., pp. 277–293). New York: Springer.

Lachman, M. E., Röcke, C., Rosnick, C., & Ryff, C. D. (2008). Realism and illusion in Americans' temporal views of their life satisfaction. *Psychological Science, 19*, 889–897.

Lawton, M. P. (1996). Quality of life and affect in later life. In C. Magai & S. H. McFadden (Eds.), *Handbook of emotion, adult development, and aging* (pp. 327–347). San Diego, CA: Academic Press.

Litwin, H., & Shiovitz-Ezra, S. (2006). Network type and mortality risk in later life. *Gerontologist, 46*, 735–743.

Lomranz, J., Shmotkin, D., Zechovoy, A., & Rosenberg, E. (1985). Time orientation in Nazi concentration camp survivors: Forty years after. *American Journal of Orthopsychiatry, 55*, 230–236.

Lucas, R. E. (2007). Adaptation and the set-point model of subjective well-being: Does happiness change after major life events? *Current Directions in Psychological Science, 16*, 75–80.

Lykken, D. (1999). *Happiness: What studies on twins show us about nature, nurture, and the happiness set-point.* New York: Golden Books.

Lyubomirsky, S., King, L., & Diener, E. (2005). The benefit of frequent positive affect: Does happiness lead to success? *Psychological Bulletin, 131*, 803–855.

Martin, P., da Rosa, G., Siegler, I. C., Davey, A., MacDonald, M., & Poon, L. W. (2006). Personality and longevity: Findings from the Georgia Centenarian Study. *Age, 28*, 343–352.

Mather, M., & Carstensen, L. L. (2005). Aging and motivated cognition: The positivity effect in attention and memory. *Trends in Cognitive Sciences, 10*, 496–502.

McAdams, D. P. (1993). *The stories we live by: Personal myths and making of the self.* New York: Morrow.

McAdams, D., Reynolds, J., Lewis, M., Patten, A. H., & Bowman, P. J. (2001). When bad things turn good and good things turn bad: Sequences of redemption and contamination in life narrative and their relation to psychosocial adaptation in midlife adults and in students. *Personality and Social Psychology Bulletin, 27*, 474–485.

McGill, V. J. (1967). *The idea of happiness.* New York: Praeger.

Mroczek, D. K., & Kolarz, C. M. (1998). The effect of age on positive and negative affect: A developmental perspective on happiness. *Journal of Personality and Social Psychology, 75*, 1333–1349.

O'Kearney, R., & Perrott, K. (2006). Trauma narratives in posttraumatic stress disorder: A review. *Journal of Traumatic Stress, 19*, 81–93.

Palgi, Y., & Shmotkin, D. (2010). The predicament of time near the end of life: Time perspective trajectories of life satisfaction among the old-old. *Aging and Mental Health, 14*, 577–586.

Peterson, C., & Seligman, M. E. P. (2004). *Character strengths and virtues: A handbook and classification.* New York: Oxford University Press.

Poon, L. W., & Perls, T. T. (2007). The trials and tribulations of studying the oldest old. In L. W. Poon & T. T. Perls (Eds.), *Biopsychosocial approaches to longevity* (Vol. 27 of Annual Review of Gerontology and Geriatrics, pp. 1–10). New York: Springer.

Porter, S., & Peace, K. A. (2007). The scars of memory: A prospective, longitudinal investigation of the consistency of traumatic and positive emotional memories in adulthood. *Psychological Science, 18*, 435–441.

Quinn, M. E., Johnson, M. A., Poon, L. W., & Martin, P. (1999). Psychosocial correlates of subjective health in sexagenarians, octogenarians, and centenarians. *Issues in Mental Health Nursing, 20*, 151–171.

Röcke, C., & Lachman, M. E. (2008). Perceived trajectories of life satisfaction across past, present, and future: Profiles and correlates of subjective change in young, middle-aged, and older adults. *Psychology and Aging, 23*, 833–847.

Rozin, P., & Royzman, E. B. (2001). Negativity bias, negativity dominance, and contagion. *Personality and Social Psychology Review, 5*, 296–320.

Ryan, R. M., & Deci, E. L. (2001). On happiness and human potentials: A review of research on hedonic and eudaimonic well-being. *Annual Review of Psychology, 52*, 141–166.

Ryff, C. D. (1989). Happiness is everything, or is it? Explorations on the meaning of psychological well-being. *Journal of Personality and Social Psychology, 57*, 1069–1081.

Ryff, C. D. (1991). Possible selves in adulthood and old age: A tale of shifting horizons. *Psychology and Aging, 6*, 286–295.

Ryff, C. D., & Singer, B. (1998). The contours of positive human health. *Psychological Inquiry, 9*, 1–28.

Seligman, M. E. P., & Csikszentmihalyi, M. (2000). Positive psychology: An introduction. *American Psychologist, 55*, 5–14.

Shmotkin, D. (1990). Subjective well-being as a function of age and gender: A multivariate look for differentiated trends. *Social Indicators Research, 23*, 201–230.

Shmotkin, D. (1991). The role of time orientation in life satisfaction across the life span. *Journal of Gerontology: Psychological Sciences, 46B*, P243–P250.

Shmotkin, D. (1992). The apprehensive respondent: Failing to rate future life satisfaction in older adults. *Psychology and Aging, 7*, 484–486.

Shmotkin, D. (1998). Declarative and differential aspects of subjective well-being and implications for mental health in later life. In J. Lomranz (Ed.), *Handbook of aging and mental health: An integrative approach* (pp. 15–43). New York: Plenum Press.

Shmotkin, D. (2005). Happiness in face of adversity: Reformulating the dynamic and modular bases of subjective well-being. *Review of General Psychology, 9*, 291–325.

Shmotkin, D., Berkovich, M., & Cohen, K. (2006). Combining happiness and suffering in a retrospective view of anchor periods in life: A differential approach to subjective well-being. *Social Indicators Research, 77*, 139–169.

Shmotkin, D., Blumstein, T., & Modan, B. (2003). Beyond keeping active: Concomitants of being a volunteer in old-old age. *Psychology and Aging, 18*, 602–607.

Shmotkin, D., & Eyal, N. (2003). Psychological time in later life: Implications for counseling. *Journal of Counseling and Development, 81*, 259–267.

Shmotkin, D., & Shrira, A. (in press). On the distinction between subjective well-being and meaning in life: Regulatory versus reconstructive functions in the face of a hostile world. In P. T. P. Wong (Ed.), *The human quest for meaning: A handbook of psychological research and clinical applications* (2nd ed.). New York: Routledge.

Shmotkin, D., & Shrira, A. (2010). *Happiness and suffering in the life story: An inquiry into conflicting expectations concerning the effect of perceived past on present subjective well-being in old age.* Paper submitted for publication.

Shrira, A., & Shmotkin, D. (2008). Can the past keep life pleasant even for old-old trauma survivors? *Aging and Mental Health, 12*, 807–819.

Singer, J. A., Rexhaj, B., & Baddeley, J. (2007). Older, wiser, and happier? Comparing older adults' and students' self-defining memories. *Memory, 15*, 886–898.

Staudinger, U. M., Bluck, S., & Herzberg, P. Y. (2003). Looking back and looking ahead: Adult age differences in consistency of diachronous ratings of subjective well-being. *Psychology and Aging, 18*, 13–24.

Strack, F., Argyle, M., & Schwarz, N. (Eds.). (1991). *Subjective well-being: An interdisciplinary perspective.* Oxford, UK: Pergamon.

Tatarkiewicz, W. (1976). *Analysis of happiness.* Warsaw, Poland: Polish Scientific.

Taylor, S. E., & Brown, J. D. (1988). Illusion and well-being: A social psychological perspective on mental health. *Psychological Bulletin, 103*, 193–210.

Telfer, E. (1980). *Happiness.* New York: St. Martin's Press.

Veenhoven, R. (1984). *Conditions of happiness.* Dordrecht, Holland: Reidel.

Veenhoven, R. (2000). The four qualities of life: Ordering concepts and measures of the good life. *Journal of Happiness Studies, 1*, 1–39.

Veenhoven, R. (2003). Arts-of-living. *Journal of Happiness Studies, 4*, 373–384.

Walker, W. R., Skowronski, J. J., & Thompson, C. P. (2003). Life is pleasant – and memory helps to keep it that way! *Review of General Psychology, 7*, 203–219.

Walter-Ginzburg, A., Shmotkin, D., Blumstein, T., & Shorek, A. (2005). A gender-based dynamic multidimensional longitudinal analysis of resilience and mortality in the old-old in Israel: The Cross-Sectional and Longitudinal Aging Study (CALAS). *Social Science and Medicine, 60*, 1705–1715.

Wong, P. T. P., & Watt, L. M. (1991). What types of reminiscence are associated with successful aging? *Psychology and Aging, 6*, 272–279.

4

The Shifting Baseline Theory of Well-Being: Lessons from across the Aging Spectrum

JISKA COHEN-MANSFIELD

ABSTRACT

The concept of well-being in old age is both complex and elusive. Over the course of gerontological research, numerous terminologies have emerged attempting to capture and describe this concept. In this paper, the Shifting Baseline Theory, a new theory of well-being in older persons, is presented, along with significant implications for assessment and practice, and for research of well-being across the geriatric landscape. The Shifting Baseline Theory consists of four principles: (1) Multiple levels of well-being exist at any given time, (2) Well-being is affected by both a trait and a state component, (3) People tend to return to their baseline level of well-being after changes in their baseline level of function or living conditions, and (4) There are specific exceptions to returning to the well-being baseline, such as cases in which a new functional baseline emerges that involves physical pain. This paper presents examples from the literature and research findings that support the Shifting Baseline Theory, and distinguishes it from other theories dealing with well-being in old age. Lastly, this paper examines the implications of this theory for the prioritization of policies, the assessment of quality of life, the agenda for well-being research, and the goals and practices of dementia care. This examination demonstrates the Shifting Baseline Theory's unique emphasis on the experience of daily living, rather than on the individual's objective physical state, as a determinant of well-being.

INTRODUCTION

The concept of well-being in old age is complex and elusive. Over the course of gerontological research, numerous terminologies, including life satisfaction, quality of life, positive and negative affect, happiness, and contentment, have emerged in an attempt to capture and describe the concept.

For example, well-being has been defined by Seligman (2002) as a person's positive evaluation of his or her life, including positive emotions, engagement, satisfaction, and meaning (see also Allen, Carlson, & Ham, 2007). Quality of life has been defined by the World Health Organization (1995) as "individuals' perceptions of their position in life in the context of the culture and value systems in which they live and in relation to their goals, expectations, standards and concerns. It is a broad ranging concept incorporating in a complex way the person's physical health, psychological state, level of independence, social relationships, personal beliefs and their relationships to salient features of the environment. (p. 1405)" Other concepts often used to describe well-being include subjective well-being (see Chapter 3 in this book), contentedness, peace, joy, a sense of security, morale, adjustment, pursuit of happiness (see Chapter 3), comfort, healthy relationships, resilience, and optimism (Allen et al., 2007).

This chapter proposes a theory of well-being in older persons, the shifting baseline theory, which has significant implications for assessing well-being across the geriatric landscape (Cohen, 1994). Examples from related literature and several research findings are described to clarify the theory, as are implications of this framework for setting priorities for the development and administration of programs aimed to help older persons achieve greater well-being.

The theoretical framework, the shifting baseline theory, consists of four principles:

1. *Multiple levels of well-being and a two-factor concept.* A person can experience more than one level of well-being at any given time, depending on his or her frame of mind at the time of questioning. For example, when a retired manager is asked to reflect on his retirement, he may consider his current stage of life to be a letdown, because of his loss of power, responsibility, and stature. However, in day-to-day life, this individual is concerned mainly with the daily experience of living, and it is that set of daily concerns that actually shapes his level of contentment during most hours of the day. Well-being is generally composed of both a positive and a negative component that are not highly correlated (Larsen, McGraw, & Cacioppo, 2001) and that become easier to regulate in later life (Lawton, VanHaitsma, & Klapper, 1996). This two-factor structure of affect explains the finding that positive states (pleasure, interest, and contentment) are related to one another but often not to negative states (anger, anxiety, and sadness) and that the negative states are related to one another but not to

positive states (Lawton et al., 1996). This implies that after years of life experiences, a better affect balance may be achieved through the act of choosing to be surrounded by people and situations minimizing negative emotions and maximizing positive ones (Mroczek & Kolarz, 1998; see Chapter 3 for some mechanisms that regulate this process). This process is, however, countered by the multiple losses, loneliness, and physical pain, which increase in old age and produce a poorer affect balance. Nonetheless, whether a better balance is achieved, the experience of everyday life tends to involve a mixture of both.

2. *Well-being as state versus trait.* At any age, a personal level of well-being can be conceptualized as a combination of a trait component and a state component. Rooted in genetic makeup (Lykken, 2007) and in early, lifelong, or major experiences, people have a general tendency toward a certain level of well-being, which they tend to maintain (trait well-being); there are certain ups and downs in this trait well-being level that depend on their state, or life situation, at the particular moment.
3. *Return to the baseline.* People tend to return to their baseline level of well-being (a trait level) after changes in their baseline level of function (changes in their state) or in living conditions, such as losing a spouse. Encountering life changes often results in changes in well-being that are of a limited duration. Even when people encounter the major life changes that occur in aging, such as functional or cognitive losses, they often experience a sense of loss or mourning for a limited period, after which they return to a their former baseline level in terms of their daily sense of well-being (see Figure 4.1). This return to the baseline level – a process that can be conceptualized as resilience and has also been termed *hedonic adaptation* (Frederick & Loewenstein, 1999) or the *hedonic treadmill model* (Diener, Lucas, & Scollon, 2006) – involves an active engagement with the new environment and concerns.
4. *Exceptions to the return to baseline.* There are specific exceptions to returning to a baseline level of well-being, namely situations in which a new baseline situation includes physical pain, a high level of loneliness or social isolation, significant levels of boredom, sensory isolation, or the absence of a sense of meaning (Borglin, Edberg, & Hallberg, 2005). Cases in which a person has not returned to the baseline after a traumatic event, such as widowhood, often involve one of those exceptions. For example, the person may be very lonely after the loss of the spouse, and the ongoing loneliness rather than the specific loss is the reason for negative affect.

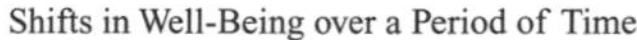

Shifts in Well-Being over a Period of Time

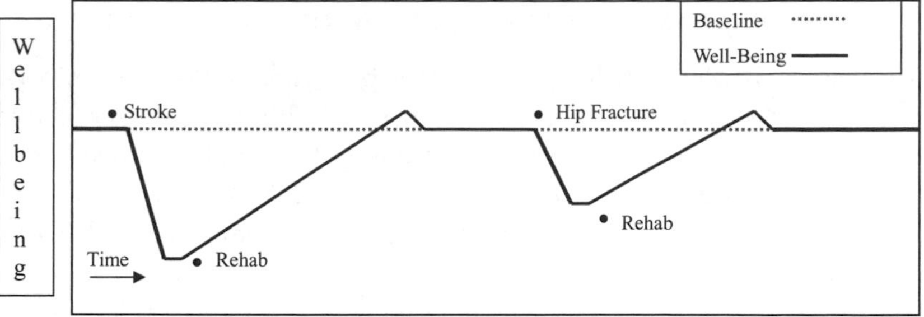

Shifts in Function over a Period of Time

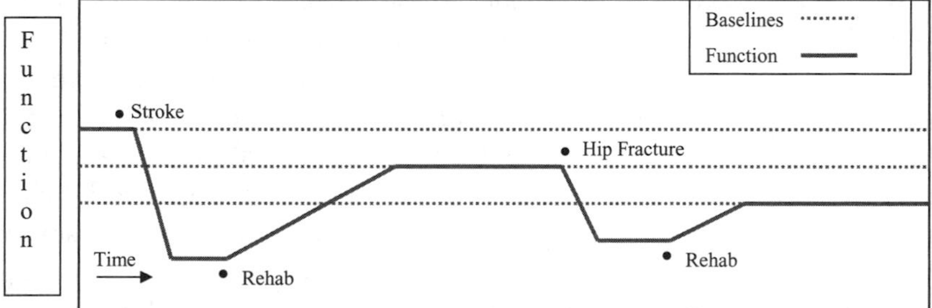

FIGURE 4.1. The shifting baseline theory – an illustration of the relationship with functional decline. When function is compromised by an illness or event (e.g., stroke, hip fracture), well-being decreases. As the person begins to adjust to a lower level of function, well-being begins to return to its baseline. Positive events, such as improvement in function, may increase well-being above the baseline level; however, well-being will return to its baseline. Whereas in old-old age function will often decline from one baseline to another, well-being can return to its original baseline, despite the new functional baselines. © Cohen-Mansfield, 2009.

This theory is not specific to older persons but applies to the entire life span. Although some of the research cited in the following descriptions of the shifting baseline theory originates from aging research, other components, such as the findings of Tversky and Kahneman and their colleagues (Dolan & Kahneman, 2005; Kahneman & Tversky, 1979), described herein, do not. The age invariance of the theory fits with the finding that age accounts for 0–1% of the variance in subjective well-being scores (Okun & Stock, 1987). Nonetheless, this chapter deals with old age because it provides a unique opportunity to explore the shifting baseline theory given the multiple losses often experienced in old age in the domains of health, function, social support, and occupational roles.

ILLUSTRATIONS OF THE SHIFTING BASELINE THEORY PRINCIPLES THROUGH EXTREME EXAMPLES FOUND IN LITERATURE

Tuesdays with Morrie (Albom, 1997) is a book about Professor Morrie Schwartz, who developed Lou Gehrig's disease in his 70s and experienced the gradual loss of neuromuscular functioning. During the relatively early stages of his disease, Morrie was interviewed by ABC-TV's *Nightline*. In the interview, Ted Koppel asked Morrie what he dreaded most about his slow decay. The answer was, "Well, Ted, one day soon, someone's gonna have to wipe my ass." Several months later, that did indeed happen. And this is the way it is described: "It took some getting used to, Morrie admitted, because it was, in a way, complete surrender to the disease.... 'Mitch, it's funny' he said, 'I'm an independent person.... I felt a little ashamed, because our culture tells us we should be ashamed if we can't wipe our own behind. But then I figured, *Forget what the culture says*.... The strangest thing. I began to *enjoy* my dependency." In other words, regardless of the explanation given, Morrie made the adjustment, and his general level of well-being appeared no worse than during the first interview. Furthermore, his ability to maintain a positive level of well-being was bolstered by his having a strong social support network and a sense of meaning in his life, and it occurred despite a totally disfiguring and disabling physical state.

Another extreme example is presented in the novel *Fateless*, by Imre Kertesz (1992). In *Fateless*, Kertesz, who himself was imprisoned in Auschwitz as a child, tells the story of a Hungarian Jewish boy's experience in German concentration camps. The novel describes devastating concentration camp experiences but also offers rays of light. For example, when the boy becomes sick and is taken to the infirmary, the caretaker says good morning and good evening to him, and the head of the adjacent ward smuggles some additional food for him. Toward the end of the novel, the narrator looks back poignantly at his experience at the camp: "It was that special hour – I recognized it now, I recognized it here – my favorite hour in the camp, and a sharp, painful, futile desire grasped my heart: homesickness.... Yes, indeed, in a certain sense, life was purer, simpler back there.... Even back there, in the shadow of the chimneys, in the breaks between pain, there was something resembling happiness. Everybody will ask me about the deprivations, the 'terrors of the camps,' but for me, the happiness there will always be the most memorable experience, perhaps." It may be that one reason why it is difficult to describe the horrors of the concentration camp is that after an initial stage of horror and denial ("this must be a mistake," "this is temporary," "it is not meant for me"), life in the camp became, at times, a new baseline in which the boy's thoughts revolved around finding food and avoiding the most difficult work or the cruelest supervisor, and not always around the larger horror of the situation. In other words, adjusting to the new life experience is associated with a return to the habitual baseline of well-being that diminishes the sense of horror associated with the new state.

RESEARCH FINDINGS

Return to the Baseline of Well-Being

People's tendency to return to a baseline level of well-being after major experiences is demonstrated in the research of Tversky and Kahneman (Dolan & Kahneman, 2005; Kahneman & Tversky, 1979). According to their findings, when a person encounters positive or negative life changes, such as winning the lottery or losing a large sum of money, those events affect his or her perception of well-being, but only for a limited duration of time (Dolan & Kahneman, 2005). After sufficient time has passed, the person returns to his or her baseline of well-being (Dolan & Kahneman, 2005). The effect of the change usually lasts longer for negative events than for positive events (Kahneman & Tversky, 1979).

In addition to Tversky and Kahneman's exploration of the individual's well-being baseline, there has been research pertaining to the stability of populations' well-being over time. For example, although the production of goods and services in the United States (as measured by the Gross National Product) increased dramatically between 1940 and 2000, levels of life satisfaction remained stable (Allen et al., 2007). Similarly, George (1994) reported that for the previous 15–20 years, the vast majority (approximately 85%) of older adults reported being satisfied or very satisfied with their lives.

Factors Associated with Well-Being in Old Age

Social support and physical pain are two examples of factors that have been shown to affect perceptions of well-being. The centrality of social support is illustrated by the work of Newsom and Schulz (1996), which demonstrates that a lack of social support is an important reason for the decrease in life satisfaction and the increase in depressed affect in older adults. This research has shown that social support mediates the relationship between functional status and quality of life. The essential role of pain in well-being can be seen in consistent research documenting the positive association between pain and depressed affect (e.g., Asghari, Ghaderi, & Ashory, 2006; Cohen-Mansfield & Marx, 1993; Parmelee, Katz, & Lawton, 1991; Zanocchi et al., 2008).

The Well-Being of Community-Dwelling Older Persons – Results from Two National Surveys in Israel

It is difficult to examine the theoretical framework described here without ongoing, continuous monitoring of the well-being of older persons and the losses and gains they encounter. Given the absence of such findings in the research literature, we used data from two random samples of the Israeli population. One cohort included participants aged 75–94 from the Cross-Sectional and Longitudinal Aging Study (CALAS; Walter-Ginzburg, Blumstein, Chetrit, & Modan, 2002), conducted around 1990. The second cohort included participants aged 65–94 from the Israeli Multidisciplinary Aging Study (IMAS; Shmotkin et al., 2010), which was conducted around 2001. For the two cohorts, we examined cross-sectional age differences in well-being and in its determinants. Findings (presented in Table 4.1) indicate significant worsening in determinants of well-being, such as loneliness and functional status, across the age groups. This is accompanied by a much less dramatic decline in the well-being measure (depressive symptoms). The use of the two cohorts, assessed a decade apart, suggests that the finding that the decline in function in old age is not accompanied by an equivalent decline in well-being is robust, thus providing partial validation of the shifting baseline theory.

Well-Being in Nursing-Home Residents with Dementia

Persons with dementia residing in nursing homes present one of the most disabled, disenfranchised segments of society. Not only do these people suffer from cognitive and physical deficits; they also reside in institutions, and their care is most often insufficient. Indeed, many consider the lot of persons with dementia in this situation to be a state worse then death (Patrick, Starks, Cain, Uhlmann, & Pearlman, 1994). We therefore examined the well-being of this population from data on the affect of 193 participants diagnosed with dementia residing in seven nursing-home buildings in Maryland. The analyses utilized baseline data from a study on engagement of nursing-home residents. Residents were observed by trained research assistants during routine life in the nursing home. On average, there were 11.6 observations per resident with a minimum of 7 observations and a maximum of 16.

TABLE 4.1. *Means and t-tests/analyses of variance and post hoc Scheffe tests examining the differences in measures of well-being between different age groups in the CALAS and IMAS random national samples of community-dwelling self-responding participants*

Variables		IMAS ($n = 721$)				CALAS ($n = 1200$)		
Age (n)	Means	Means 65–74 (300)	75–84 (268)	85+ (153)	ANOVA + Scheffe	Means 75–84 (752)	85+ (448)	t-test[a]
Depression (range: 0–3; 3 = more depressed)[b]		.65	.71	.76	$F(2, 685) = 3.27^{*}$ 65–74 ≠ 85+	.73	.77	$t(1143) = 1.28$
Loneliness (range: 0–3; 3 = more lonely)[c]		.47	.67	.90	$F(2, 685) = 9.19^{***}$ 65–74 ≠ 85+	.62	.73	$t(1145) = 1.79^{*}$
Function (ADL)[d]		.54	1.39	3.48	$F(2,718) = 40.73^{***}$ All groups diff	.96	1.93	$t(715) = 4.90^{**}$
Function (IADL)[e]		2.49	4.76	9.70	$F(2,718) = 69.07^{***}$ All groups diff	3.40	6.22	$t(775) = 7.98^{***}$

[a]One-tailed test. [b]Center for Epidemiologic Studies Depression Scale (CES-D), except for the item on loneliness (Radloff, 1977). [c]Feeling lonely in the previous month (0 = no, 1 = sometimes, 2 = most of the time, 3 = almost everyday). [d]Activities of daily living (ADL) index (Katz, Downs, Cash, & Gratz, 1970; 0 = no difficulty, 3 = much difficulty).[e]IADL included preparing meals, doing daily shopping, doing nondaily shopping (buying clothing, sweets, and presents), doing easy housework (making the bed, washing dishes), doing difficult housework (washing floors, cleaning windows), going by oneself to the nearest bus stop, and doing laundry (0 = no difficulty, 3 = much difficulty).

$^{***}p < .001$. $^{**}p < .01$. $^{*}p < .05$.

Seventy-eight percent of the participants were female, and the average age was 86 years with a range of 60–101 years. The majority were Caucasian (81%), and 19% were minorities. More than half were widowed (65%), 20% were married, 5% were never married, and 10% were separated or divorced. The average Mini-Mental State Exam (MMSE; Folstein, Folstein, & McHugh, 1975) was 7.2 (range 0–23), 37% had education beyond high school, and 63% had a level of education less than or equal to high school completion.

Evaluation of positive and negative affect was based on direct 3-minute observations by trained research assistants and assessed using Lawton's Modified Behavior Stream (LMBS; Lawton et al., 1996). Five different modes of affect were evaluated: pleasure, interest, anger, anxiety, and sadness; each was rated on a 5-point scale (1–5) with the choices: "Never," "Less than 16 seconds," "Less than half the time," "More than half the time," and "All or nearly all of the time." Interrater agreement evaluations were conducted repeatedly throughout the study and averaged 88% per emotional mode, with an average Intra-Class Correlation (ICC) of 0.82. Results indicated that the mean levels of pleasure and interest were 1.1 (SD = 0.2) and 2.3 (SD = 0.9), respectively, and that the mean of the maximum of the three negative affect states was 1.1 (SD = 0.2). As can be seen, positive affect was rare, and its frequency was the same as maximum of negative affect, including anger, anxiety, and sadness, even in this population with a high rate of severe dementia living in nursing homes. This finding suggests that even in one of the worst states of living in old-old age, instances of pleasure and of negative mood are about equal rather than completely negative. The finding may also suggest an overall affective constriction, which may stem from the disease process itself or from the assessment methodology, which is necessitated by the deficits in verbal communication, or they may indicate a defense that reduces the affect level to keep it balanced.

DISCUSSION

How Is This Theory Different from Other Theories of Well-Being in Older Persons?

Many theories have addressed the question of why, despite the multiple losses commonly experienced in old age, well-being in old age is not more severely compromised. One of the main differences between the shifting baseline theory and other theories is that the former assumes that general principles of human emotion and conduct are operating in older persons' reactions to their changed life circumstances rather than principles unique to old age. However, a specific, albeit rudimentary, examination of the different theories may further elucidate the concepts of the shifting baseline theory. Aspiration theory posits that older adults make an active rational decision to lower their aspirations to meet their new reality (Allen et al., 2007). According to the shifting baseline theory, older adults may preserve their prior aspirations, but in day-to-day consciousness, that is not what they focus on; thus, their general level of well-being is based on their daily experiences at the new functional baseline rather than on their prior baseline. Equity theory suggests that older persons judge their life conditions on the basis of principles of justice and fairness (Allen et al., 2007). Presumably, those who think that they have had their fair share in life may feel that their losses are just in the larger scheme of things. No such evaluation is presumed in the shifting baseline theory. Relative deprivation theory maintains that a sense of deprivation is based on a comparison with the average older person (Allen et al., 2007). Again, the shifting baseline theory claims that the perception of others' losses is not necessary to the return to baseline level of well-being. It has been acknowledged that these and other mechanisms (e.g., lowered ideal-self assessment, reduction in both hoped-for selves and feared selves, discounting of domains in which function is low, engagement in self-enhancing comparisons, altering goals, and lowered emotional reactivity; see Chapter 3 for some of those mechanisms) may contribute to the relatively low effect of aging-related losses on well-being. The shifting baseline theory proposes that those may simply be factors enhancing the natural process of shifting to one's baseline level of well-being or, in other words, experience living from whichever functional baseline one is at, which becomes the new basis for well-being.

Although the theoretical perspective of this theory is not unique to older persons, there may be differences across ages in its manifestation. For example, the rate of return to baseline may differ among age groups and should be explored in future research.

IMPLICATIONS

Priorities, Expectations, End-of-Life Issues, and Worse-Than-Death States

The shifting baseline theory suggests that the priority of care in old age should be to enhance well-being in the person's current state by addressing those factors which interfere with his or her well-being. This places a great emphasis on basic needs, such as pain alleviation, provision of social contact, and engagement in activities that are both meaningful and appropriate across the aging spectrum. Such an emphasis stands in contrast with a more medical approach that emphasizes end-of-life care options or proper diets. Priorities for research and policy have generally emphasized preventing or reversing changes in functional status, image, and decline in old age (see Chapter 2). With the current enhanced life expectancy that is often accompanied by irreversible chronic disease, a much greater emphasis needs to be placed on preventing conditions that preclude return to the emotional baseline of well-being. This conclusion is also supported by Kane's (2001) findings that there are 11 domains of quality of life that are important for nursing-home residents and have not been emphasized in previous work on quality of life. These domains include (a) sense of safety, security, and order; (b) physical comfort; (c) enjoyment; (d) meaningful activity; (e) relationships; (f) functional competence; (g) dignity; (h) privacy; (i) individuality; (j) autonomy/choice; and (k) spiritual well-being. These domains focus on emotional well-being rather than physical health. Although Kane (2001) does include functional competence as a domain, she clarifies that this domain does not refer to an objective level of function, but rather to the individual's personal sense of independence; "functional competence means that within the limits of the person's physical and cognitive capacities, the Long Term Care (LTC) consumer is as independent as he or she wants to be" (p. 297).

These interpretations need to be considered in an appropriate framework. Obviously, any person would rather maintain his or her function than lose it, and rehabilitation and prevention of functional decline are of great value to the well-being of older persons. Indeed, they prevent the devastating decline in well-being that can accompany decline in function. All of this is well known and documented. What is insufficiently clear is the opportunity for, and presence of, psychological well-being within states of functional deficits.

Measures of Quality of Life

According to the conceptualization described here, measures of quality of life should emphasize the psychological well-being of older persons and the presence of barriers that could prevent the return to their baseline level of well-being, such as physical discomfort or social isolation. An examination of existing measures of quality of life (see Table 4.2) reveals that psychological/emotional status is a component in all but one of the measures. However 10 of the 15 measures include physical health status, 5 include functional status, and 4 include cognitive functioning as determinants of quality of life. The respective numbers for those assessments specifically focusing on persons with dementia (last four rows in Table 4.2) are as follows: two of the four assessments of quality of life specifically designed for persons with dementia include physical health, one includes functional status, and three include cognitive abilities (Table 4.2). Although these are very important components of health and function, the tenets of the shifting baseline theory suggest that they are not essential components of quality of life and should not be included in the measure. In contrast, physical discomfort should be included and is generally not part of such assessment.

Regulation, Monitoring, and Accreditation

As shown earlier, the shifting baseline theory has implications for the design of care systems in terms of the prioritization of care activities that maximize well-being. This has implications for monitoring and regulatory activities. Current regulations often measure what is easy to measure, including the existence of written plans and records. However, much of this does not seem to relate to actual well-being in day-to-day life, and many of the quality indicators do not relate to actual care or quality of life (Hyer, Heath, & Yeager, 2006; Schnelle et al., 2003). The system needs to change to one that examines the actual day-to-day practice of care as it affects fluctuations in daily well-being, and thus focuses on constructs such as loneliness, respect, and comfort (Cohen-Mansfield & Parpura-Gill, 2007).

The Agenda of Well-Being Research

An examination of the shifting baseline theory suggests a need for a transformation in the research agenda on well-being in the oldest old. It raises a host of questions that have not been addressed in prior research. For example, what is the trajectory of decline in well-being due to different life losses, such as medical conditions, different trajectories of decline in function, or loss of a spouse or a friend? What is the variability in the pace of return to baseline, and what are the determinants of that pace? For instance, persons who have adjusted to prior life changes, such as a change in location or occupation, may be more adaptable and may shift back to baseline more quickly than

TABLE 4.2. *Quality-of-life (QOL) assessments for older persons*

Assessments	Social relationships	Cognitive abilities	Enjoyment of activities	Psychological emotional status	Physical health status	Functioning/ daily activities	Living situation	Global measure of life
*World Health Organization Quality of Life (**WHOQOL**)* (Demura, Kobayashi, & Kitabayashi, 2005; WHO, 1995)	X			X	X	X	X	
Adjusted Scale from George & Bearon (1980) (Lee, 2005)	X			X	X			
*Hong Kong Quality of Life for Older Persons Scale (**HKQoLOP**) (Chan, Cheng, Phillips, Chi, & Ho, 2004)*	X			X	X		X	
*The Quality of Life Scale for the Elderly (**QLSE**) (McKenna, 2001)*	X				X	X	X	
*Manchester Short Assessment of Quality of Life (**MANSA**) (Depla, De Graaf, & Heeren, 2006; Priebe, Huxley, Knight, & Evans, 1999)*	X			X	X		X	X
QOL measured using 100 mm visual analog scale (Ishine et al., 2006)	X			X	X		X	
Sarvimaki & Stenbock-Hult, (Sarvimaki & Stenbock-Hult, 2000)				X				

*Needs satisfaction measure of QoL in old age (**CASP-19**) (Hyde, Wiggins, Higgs, & Blane, 2003)*				*X*				
*Patrick's Perceived Quality of Life Scale (**PQL**) (Montuclard et al., 2000; Patrick, Danis, Southerland, & Hong, 1998)*	*X*	*X*		*X*	*X*	*X*	*X*	
*World Health Organization Quality of Life (**WHOQOL-OLD**) (Low & Molzahn, 2007)*	*X*			*X*	*X*	*X*	*X*	
Assessments for Persons with Dementia								
Japanese QL instrument for the elderly with dementia (**AD-HRQL-J**) (**AD-HRQ**) (Yamamoto-Mitani et al., 2000)	*X*	*X*	*X*	*X*				
Quality of Life Assessment Schedule (**QOLAS**) (Selai, Trimble, Rossor, & Harvey, 2001)	*X*	*X*		*X*	*X*	*X*		
*The Quality of Life-Alzheimer's Disease (**Qol-AD**) Scale (subjective QoL) (Logsdon, Gibbons, McCurry, & Teri, 1999; Thorgrimsen et al., 2003)*	*X*	*X*	*X*	*X*	*X*		*X*	*X*
*Dementia Quality of Life (**D-QoL**) Scale – developed through focus groups (Brod, Stewart, Sands, & Walton, 1999; Thorgrimsen et al., 2003)*				*X*				

those who have stayed in the same life situation throughout their adult lives. The trajectories of return to baseline may be influenced by age and, if so, could serve as a marker of aging processes. It is also necessary to examine the extent to which trajectories change with different measures of quality of life, including positive measures such as life satisfaction, negative measures such as depressed affect, and potentially global measures such as the will to live (see Chapter 16). At what age is the general well-being baseline formed and what are the relative contributions of heredity and life conditions to its formation? There are indications that some life experiences, such as major trauma, may change a person's baseline of well-being (see Chapter 6). These questions should be investigated within the framework of the shifting baseline theory. It is also important to define and describe those life conditions that prevent a return to baseline, such as social isolation, and examine the degree to which they are universal or, rather, interact with certain personal characteristics.

Although the proposed main research agenda focuses on changes in well-being, the trajectories experienced in function over time in old and old-old age also need to be documented and better understood. Obviously, functional trajectories have a biological component, but they are also strongly affected by the environment, especially pertaining to resources that are or are not invested in rehabilitation for subgroups of the older population (Davis, Biddison, & Cohen-Mansfield, 2007).

Goals of Dementia Care

Because the shifting baseline theory suggests that well-being is independent of a person's level of function, it provides a basis for the concept of successful dementia (Cohen-Mansfield, 1996), which is the benchmark for future dementia care. Its premise is that (1) care aims to maximize quality of life for persons with dementia, and (2) the concept of quality of life changes throughout the progression of dementia. This involves shifting baselines of quality of life, with a sense of well-being having different manifestations as dementia progresses. In early stages, occasions of active, positive affect, such as positive and meaningful engagement, and moments of laughter and pleasure can be more frequent and, though they remain a goal as dementia progresses, they are attained with more difficulty and at a lower frequency (Cohen-Mansfield, Marx, Regier, & Dakheel-Ali, 2009). Successful dementia, then, refers to the prevention of negative affect and agitation, the latter often indicating discomfort while maximizing indications of positive affect, such as contentment and pleasure.

The circumstances that promote successful dementia change over the course of the disease and may include the following: (a) preservation (or deceleration of decline) of function, especially in the early stages of the disease, if the functional ability promotes options for meaningful engagement or sense of autonomy; (b) preservation of control over some functions, for example, caring for a plant (Langer & Rodin, 1976) or having a choice of clothes to wear; (c) a sense of purpose, meaning, or spirituality, or (d) enjoyment of social contact and basic stimuli, such as sunshine or a favorite melody (Cohen-Mansfield & Werner, 1997; Gerdner, 2000). These examples demonstrate the emphasis of the shifting baseline theory on the experiences of daily living, rather than on objective states, as determinants of well-being.

The shifting baseline theory focuses on the person's affective states as the ultimate focal point of well-being. It offers a parsimonious set of principles clarifying well-being levels across the life span, with special relevance to old-old age including states of cognitive and final functional decline. Those late stages of decline provide a special opportunity to refine those mechanisms without the "noise" involved in active living in the prime of life. The implications of the shifting baseline theory direct the attention of clinicians, policy makers, and researchers from life events, conditions, and accomplishments to the fulfillment of basic needs to ensure an adequate level of well-being in daily living.

REFERENCES

Albom, M. (1997). *Tuesdays with Morrie: An old man, a young man, and life's greatest lesson.* New York: Doubleday.

Allen, D., Carlson, D., & Ham, C. (2007). Wellbeing: New paradigms of wellness – Inspiring positive health outcomes and renewing hope. *American Journal of Health Promotion, 21*, 1–9.

Asghari, A., Ghaderi, N., & Ashory, A. (2006). The prevalence of pain among residents of nursing homes and the impact of pain on their mood and quality of life. *Archives of Iranian Medicine, 9*, 368–373.

Borglin, G., Edberg, A. K., & Hallberg, I. R. (2005). The experience of quality of life among older people. *Journal of Aging Studies, 19*, 201–220.

Brod, M., Stewart, A. L., Sands, L., & Walton, P. (1999). Conceptualization and measurement of quality of life in dementia: The Dementia Quality of Life Instrument (DQoL). *Gerontologist, 39*, 25–36.

Chan, A. C. M., Cheng, S.-T., Phillips, D. R., Chi, I., & Ho, S. S. Y. (2004). Constructing a quality of life scale for older Chinese people in Hong Kong (HKQOLOCP). *Social Indicators Research, 69*, 279–301.

Cohen, G. D. (1994). The geriatric landscape – Toward a health and humanities research agenda in aging. *American Journal of Geriatric Psychiatry, 2*, 185–187.

Cohen-Mansfield, J. (1996). New ways to approach manifestations of Alzheimer's disease and to reduce caregiver burden. *International Psychogeriatrics, 8*, 91–94.
Cohen-Mansfield, J., & Marx, M. S. (1993). Pain and depression in the nursing home: Corroborating results. *Journal of Gerontology, 48*(2), P96–P97.
Cohen-Mansfield, J., Marx, M., Regier, N., & Dakheel-Ali, M. (2009). The impact of personal characteristics on engagement in nursing home residents with dementia. *International Journal of Geriatric Psychiatry, 24*, 755–763.
Cohen-Mansfield, J., & Parpura-Gill, A. (2007). Practice style in the nursing home: Dimensions for assessment and quality improvement. *International Journal of Geriatric Psychiatry, 23*, 376–386.
Cohen-Mansfield, J., & Werner, P. (1997). Management of verbally disruptive behaviors in nursing home residents. *Journals of Gerontology Series A: Biological and Medical Sciences, 52*, M369–M377.
Davis, E., Biddison, J., & Cohen-Mansfield, J. (2007). How much should we invest: Hip fracture rehabilitation in persons with dementia. *Annals of Long Term Care, 15*, 19–21.
Demura, S., Kobayashi, H., & Kitabayashi, T. (2005). QOL models constructed for the community-dwelling elderly with ikigai (purpose in life) as a composition factor, and the effect of habitual exercise. *Journal of Physiological and Anthropological Applied Human Science, 24*, 525–533.
Depla, M. F. I. A., De Graaf, R., & Heeren, T. J. (2006). The relationship between characteristics of supported housing and the quality of life of older adults with severe mental illness. *Aging & Mental Health, 10*, 592–598.
Diener, E., Lucas, R. E., & Scollon, C. N. (2006). Beyond the hedonic treadmill: Revising the adaptation theory of well-being. *American Psychologist, 61*, 305–314.
Dolan, P., & Kahneman, D. (2005). *Interpretations of utility and their implications for the valuation of health.* Paper presented at Labor Economics Workshop (April 25th, 2005, Cornell University).
Folstein, M. F., Folstein, S. E., & McHugh, P. R. (1975). Mini-Mental State: A practical method for grading the cognitive state of patients for the clinician. *Journal of Psychiatric Research, 12*, 189–198.
Frederick, S., & Loewenstein, G. (1999). Hedonic adaptation. In D. Kahneman, E. Diener, & N. Schwarz (Eds.), *Well-being: The foundations of hedonic psychology* (pp. 302–329). New York: Russell Sage Foundation.
George, L. K. (1994). Life satisfaction. In J. R. M. Copeland, M. T. Abou-Saleh, & D. C. Blazer (Eds.), *Principles and practice of geriatric psychiatry* (pp. 97–101). Chichester, UK: Wiley.
George, L. K., & Bearon, L. B. (1980). *Quality of life in older persons: Meaning and measurement.* New York: Human Sciences Press
Gerdner, L. A. (2000). Effects of individualized versus classical "relaxation" music on the frequency of agitation in elderly persons with Alzheimer's disease and related disorders. *International Psychogeriatrics, 12*, 49–65.
Hyde, M., Wiggins, R. D., Higgs, P., & Blane, D. B. (2003). A measure of quality of life in early old age: The theory, development and properties of a needs satisfaction model (CASP-19). *Aging and Mental Health, 7*, 186–194.
Hyer, L., Heath, J., & Yeager, C. A. (2006). How dare we presume to define quality of life within long term care? *PTLC Newsletter, 20*, 11–16.

Ishine, M., Wada, T., Sakagami, T., Dung, P. H., Vienh, T. D., Kawakita, T., et al. (2006). Comprehensive geriatric assessment for community-dwelling elderly in Asia compared with those in Japan: VII. Khon Khen in Thailand. *Geriatrics and Gerontology International*, *6*, 40–48.

Kahneman, D., & Tversky, A. (1979). Prospect theory: Analysis of decision under risk. *Econometrica*, *47*, 263–291.

Kane, R. A. (2001). Long-term care and a good quality of life: Bringing them closer together. *Gerontologist*, *41*, 293–304.

Katz, S., Downs, T., Cash, H., & Gratz, R. (1970). Progress in development of the index of ADL. *Gerontologist*, *10*, 20–30.

Kertesz, I. (1992). *Fateless*. Evanston, IL: Northwestern University Press.

Langer, E. J., & Rodin, J. (1976). The effects of choice and enhanced personal responsibility for the aged: A field experiment in an institutional setting. *Journal of Personality and Social Psychology*, *34*, 191–198.

Larsen, J. T., McGraw, A. P., & Cacioppo, J. T. (2001). Can people feel happy and sad at the same time? *Journal of Personality and Social Psychology*, *81*, 684–696.

Lawton, M. P., VanHaitsma, K., & Klapper, J. (1996). Observed affect in nursing home residents with Alzheimer's disease. *Journals of Gerontology Series B: Psychological Sciences and Social Sciences*, *51*, P3–P14.

Lee, J. J. (2005). An exploratory study on the quality of life of older Chinese people living alone in Hong Kong. *Social Indicators Research*, *71*, 335–361.

Logsdon, R., Gibbons, L. E., McCurry, S. M., & Teri, L. (1999). Quality of life in Alzheimer's disease: Patient and caregiver reports. *Journal of Mental Health and Aging*, *5*, 21–32.

Low, G., & Molzahn, A. E. (2007). Predictors of quality of life in old age: A cross-validation study. *Research in Nursing and Health*, *30*, 141–150.

Lykken, D. T. (2007). Comment on Diener, Lucas, and Scollon (2006): "Beyond the hedonic treadmill: revising the adaptation theory of well-being." *American Psychologist*, *62*, 611–612.

McKenna, M. C. (2001). Development and validation of the Quality of Life Scale for the Elderly (QLSE). *Dissertation Abstracts International*, *62*(11), 5383B.

Montuclard, L., Garrouste-Orgeas, M., Timsit, J. F., Misset, B., De Jonghe, B., & Carlet, J. (2000). Outcome, functional autonomy, and quality of life of elderly patients with a long-term intensive care unit stay. *Critical Care Medicine*, *28*, 3389–3395.

Mroczek, D. K., & Kolarz, C. M. (1998). The effect of age on positive and negative affect: A developmental perspective on happiness. *Journal of Personality and Social Psychology*, *75*, 1333–1349.

Newsom, J. T., & Schulz, R. (1996). Social support as a mediator in the relation between functional status and quality of life in older adults. *Psychology and Aging*, *11*, 34–44.

Okun, M. A., & Stock, W. A. J. o. A. (1987). Correlates and components of subjective well-being among the elderly. *Gerontology*, *6*, 95–112.

Parmelee, P. A., Katz, I. R., & Lawton, M. P. (1991). The relation of pain to depression among institutionalized aged. *Journals of Gerontology*, *46*, P15–P21.

Patrick, D. L., Danis, M., Southerland, L. I., & Hong, G. (1998). Quality of life following intensive care. *Journal of General Internal Medicine, 3*, 218–223.
Patrick, D. L., Starks, H. E., Cain, K. C., Uhlmann, R. F., & Pearlman, R. A. (1994). Measuring preferences for health states worse than death. *Medical Decision Making, 14*, 9–18.
Priebe, S., Huxley, P., Knight, S., & Evans, S. (1999). Application and results of the Manchester Short Assessment of Quality of Life (Mansa). *International Journal of Social Psychiatry, 45*, 7–12.
Radloff, L. S. (1977). The CES-D Scale: A self-report depression scale for research in the general population. *Applied Psychological Measurement, 1*, 385–401.
Sarvimaki, A., & Stenbock-Hult, B. (2000). Quality of life in old age described as a sense of well-being, meaning and value. *Journal of Advanced Nursing, 32*, 1025–1033.
Schnelle, J. F., Cadogan, M. P., Yoshii, J., Al-Samarrai, N. R., Osterweil, D., Bates-Jensen, B. M., et al. (2003). The minimum data set urinary incontinence quality indicators: Do they reflect differences in care processes related to incontinence? *Medical Care, 41*, 909–922.
Selai, C. E., Trimble, M. R., Rossor, M. N., & Harvey, R. J. (2001). Assessing quality of life in dementia: Preliminary psychometric testing of the Quality of Life Assessment Schedule (QOLAS). *Neuropsychological Rehabilitation, 11*, 219–243.
Seligman, M. E. P. (2002). *Authentic Happiness.* New York: Free Press.
Shmotkin, D., Lerner-Geva, L., Cohen Mansfield, J., Blumstein, T., Eyal, N., Shorek, A., et al. (2010). Profiles of functioning as predictors of mortality in old age: The advantage of a configurative approach. *Archives of Gerontology and Geriatrics, 51*, 68–75.
Thorgrimsen, L., Selwood, A., Spector, A., Royan, L., de Madariaga Lopez, M., Woods, R. T., et al. (2003). Whose quality of life is it anyway? The validity and reliability of the Quality of Life-Alzheimer's Disease (QoL-AD) scale. *Alzheimer Disease and Associated Disorders, 17*, 201–208.
Walter-Ginzburg, A., Blumstein, T., Chetrit, A., & Modan, B. (2002). Social factors and mortality in the old-old in Israel: The CALAS study. *Journals of Gerontology Series B: Psychological Sciences and Social Sciences, 57*, S308–S318.
World Health Organization. (1995). The World Health Organization Quality of Life Assessment (WHOQOL): Position paper from the World Health Organization. *Social Science and Medicine, 41*, 1403–1409.
World Health Organization. (1998). WHOQOL User Manual (Draft). Geneva: Author.
Yamamoto-Mitani, N., Abe, T., Yamada, Y., Yamazato, C., Amemiya, H., Sugishita, C., et al. (2000). Reliability and validity of a Japanese quality of life scale for the elderly with dementia. *Nursing and Health Sciences, 2*, 69–78.
Zanocchi, M., Maero, B., Nicola, E., Martinelli, E., Luppino, A., Gonella, M., et al. (2008). Chronic pain in a sample of nursing home residents: Prevalence, characteristics, influence on Quality of Life (QoL). *Archives of Gerontology and Geriatrics, 47*(1), 121–128.

5

The Model of Developmental Adaptation: Implications for Understanding Well-Being in Old-Old Age

PETER MARTIN, NEHA DESHPANDE-KAMAT, LEONARD W. POON, AND MARY ANN JOHNSON

ABSTRACT

This chapter introduces the model of developmental adaptation, an extension of the adaptation model used in the Georgia Centenarian Study. The focus of this model is to combine distal experiences and past achievements as important predictors of well-being and adaptation in later life. Modeling results suggest that distal events have a direct effect on adaptation, proximal events have a direct effect on adaptation, and that the effect of distal variables on adaptation is mediated by proximal resources. Illustrations of the developmental adaptation model will be given. For example, results suggest that education and life-time negative events (as distal variables) predict mental health with competence (a proximal resource) as a mediator. The implications for understanding well-being in old-old age will be discussed.

INTRODUCTION

Very old individuals face a number of uniquely demanding life challenges. For those persons entering the 9th, 10th, and 11th decades of life, negotiating increasingly restrictive functional limitations and rapidly shrinking social-support networks becomes a dominant life concern and activity (Martin, Poon, Kim, & Johnson, 1996). How do older adults adapt to these changes? The purpose of this chapter is to introduce a model of developmental adaptation that incorporates distal and proximal influences in the prediction of longevity and adaptation in later life. In the first section of this chapter, we review a number of common adaptation models. This section is followed by an overview of studies based on the Georgia adaptation model. We then discuss the model of developmental adaptation and show illustrative examples for this model.

MODELS OF ADAPTATION IN ADULT LIFE

The study of adult development and the adaptability to change has received considerable attention in the past few decades (Frisancho, 2009; Martin & Martin, 2002; Schlossberg, 1981). Some of the early research in adult development highlights the critical aspects of life transitions such as chronological age (Levinson, Darrow, Klein, Levinson, & McKee, 1978), individual variability (Neugarten, 1979), changing relationships (Hartup & Stevens, 1999; Vaillant, 1977), and adaptation to life events (Lowenthal, Thurnher, & Chiriboga, 1975; Martin & Martin, 2002; Ong & Bergeman, 2004). Schlossberg (1981) described adaptation as the balance of individual resources and deficits as well as differences in transition environments in her model of successful adaptation. Her model also highlighted characteristics of the particular transition (role change, affect, timing, onset, and duration), environmental characteristics (internal support systems, family, friends, and institutional support) and characteristics of the individual (age, gender, ethnicity, health status, socioeconomic status, and value orientation) as the key determinants of successful adaptation.

Complementing some of the earlier models of aging and adaptation is the life-course framework, which underscores a variable sequence of development and the pivotal role of life events in individual development throughout the life span. Successful aging is often referred to as a guiding theme for optimal adaptation to social, psychological, and physical changes and overall well-being in later life (Rowe & Kahn, 1997). The selective optimization and compensation model (Baltes & Baltes, 1990) explains the process of successful aging through effectively selecting areas of functioning, optimizing those areas as best as possible, and compensating for losses as people age. A link between gender role changes in later life, and successful adaptation has also been reported (Shimonaka, Nakazato, Kawaai, & Sato, 1997). Steverink, Lindenberg, and Ormel (1998) suggested a hierarchical and patterned change in resources and goals as a determinant of successful adaptation. Ong and Bergeman (2004) have argued that emotional resilience and adaptability to stressful life events were the key determinants of well-being in later life. This might be especially relevant for the oldest old, who witness a range of life stressors such as loss of spouse, loss of children or siblings, diminished social contact, and physical and cognitive impairments. Although a range of disciplines have attempted to study human adaptation as we age (Frisancho, 2009), there is consensus that it is not the process of change per se but adaptability to change that makes the process of aging successful and helps us attain an optimal state of well-being.

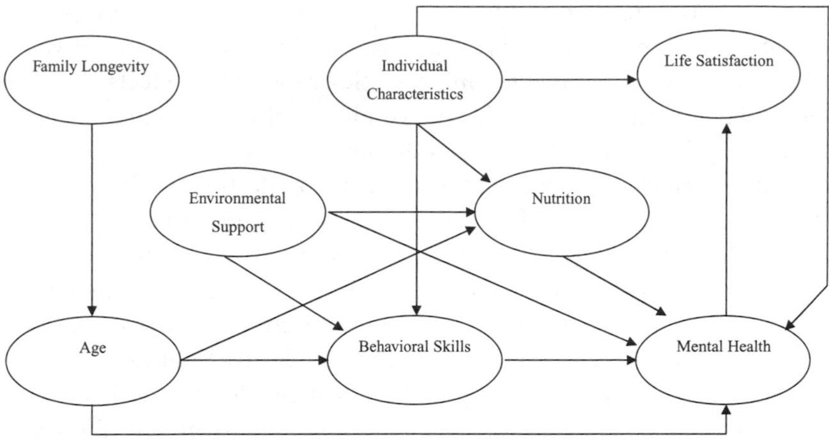

FIGURE 5.1. Georgia Adaptation Model. From Poon et al. (1992; figure 2). The Georgia Centenarian Study. Published by Baywood Publishing Company. Reproduced with permission.

THE GEORGIA ADAPTATION MODEL

The Georgia Adaptation Model (GAM; see Figure 5.1; Poon et al., 1992; Poon, Johnson, & Martin, 1997) was specifically developed to assess adaptational characteristics of long-lived individuals. The model is based on Lehr's (1982) longevity model and features seven clusters of interrelated variables that constitute a network of adaptational predictors and outcomes integral to physical and psychological well-being in extreme old age. The GAM contains the following elements: family longevity (i.e., how long family members lived), environmental support, individual characteristics, behavioral skills, nutrition, mental and physical health, and life satisfaction. Some of the model elements (e.g., biomedical), may be more important for survival in oldest-old populations, whereas other elements (psychosocial factors) may be more important among the younger-old populations (Hagberg, 2006).

The GAM is a heuristic model that has been applied in a number of our publications. For example, Martin et al. (1992) tested the relationship among personality, events, coping, and mental health and reported that anxiety was the strongest predictor of low morale and mental health, whereas extraversion and life stress were positively related to active coping. In using the GAM as a conceptual framework to predict loneliness, Martin, Hagberg, and Poon (1997) reported that low social support and low cognitive functioning were salient predictors of loneliness. Martin, Rott, Kerns, Poon, and Johnson (2000) tested several predictive models of depression and reported that the personality trait tension and hearing impairment were significant predictors of depression, but those direct associations were mediated by the way in which health was appraised to limit activities. Moderating effects were also found. For example, only under the condition of health being perceived as standing in the way of activities did low levels of social relations significantly predict depressive symptoms. Bishop, Martin, MacDonald, and Poon (2010) recently tested a model of life satisfaction for a centenarian sample. Not surprisingly, their results suggested that past satisfaction with life emerged a key predictor of happiness. However, past life satisfaction also predicted perceived economic security and subjective health, and perceived economic security had a strong influence on subjective health status.

The GAM has been extensively used as a heuristic framework in research related to health-care practices and functional health in later life (Fees, Martin, & Poon, 1999; Poon, Martin, Clayton, Messner, Noble, & Johnson, 1992). A range of literature confirms the critical role of psychosocial adaptation among very old adults as an important predictor of outcomes such as physical health and disability (Jang, Poon, & Martin, 2004; Lupien & Wan, 2004), functional status (Gondo et al., 2006), mental health (Jang et al., 2004; Fry & Debats, 2002), and autonomy (Ozaki, Uchiyama, Tagaya, Ohida, & Ogihara, 2007).

DEVELOPMENTAL ADAPTATION MODEL

Although the Georgia Adaptation Model has served as a useful framework for the study of longevity and adaptation in late life, at least one important component is missing from the model: the inclusion of distal experiences. An extension of the model was therefore introduced in our most current work (Martin & Martin, 2002), which resulted in the proposal of the Developmental Adaptation Model (Figure 5.2).

The general assumption in the Developmental Adaptation Model is that personal resources and experiential factors optimize adaptation over the life span (Fry & DeBats, 2006). The model integrates distal influences, resources, behavioral skills, and developmental outcomes. As intervening variables, individual, social and economic resources, proximal life events, and behavioral "coping" skills represent the contribution of adaptational processes to positive developmental adaptation outcomes. The exogenous variables (distal life events and past personal achievements) signify the influence(s) of distal experiences and events. The developmental outcomes (functional capacity and subjective health, cognitive impairment, mental health, economic cost and burden, psychological well-being, and longevity) reflect

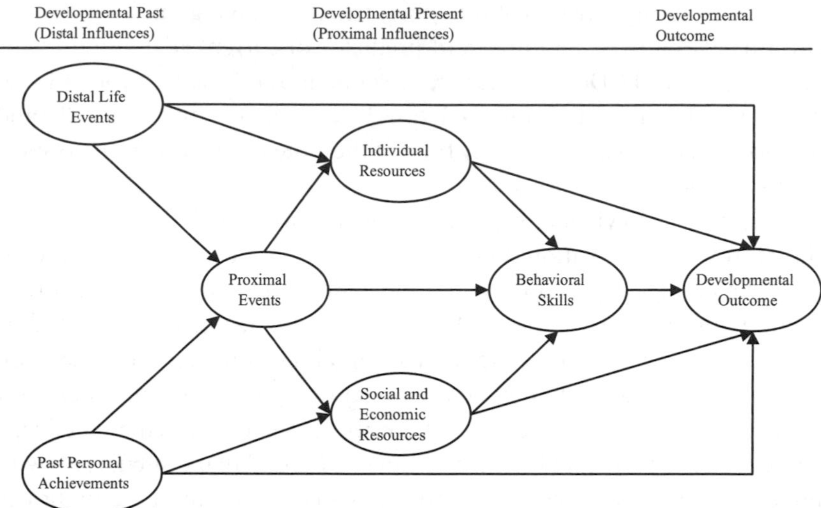

FIGURE 5.2. The Developmental Adaptation Model. Reprinted from Martin and Martin (2002), with permission from Elsevier.

fundamental quality-of-life characteristics. Recent empirical evidence underlines the importance of distal influences: childhood economic status, lifetime trauma, and children's personality traits continue to have long-lasting influences on physical functioning and health behaviors in mid- and later life (Guralnik, Butterworth, Wadsworth, & Kuh, 2006; Hampson, Goldberg, Vogt, & Dubanosk, 2006; Krause, Shaw, & Cairney, 2004). Shmotkin (Chapter 3) and Hyer (Chapter 8) also provide ample evidence that early traumatic experiences continue to exert influences on late-life adaptation. As Shmotkin points out, "trauma is a 'distal' (past) factor whose influence on developmental outcomes may be direct or indirect, depending on its interaction with 'proximal' (present or recent) resources and coping behaviors."

Our own recent studies have demonstrated that distal variables play an important role in adaptation. Hensley, Martin, MacDonald, and Poon (2010) reported that the number of children significantly predicted the ability to engage in activities of daily living and loneliness after controlling for other distal influences (e.g., childhood health, financial situation early in life). Older adults who had more children had higher scores in activities of daily living and lower scores in loneliness. In addition, childhood health significantly predicted loneliness. Poor health in childhood was associated with higher loneliness scores. The cognitive evaluation of distal experiences therefore is important for optimal adaptation and coping (Simsek, 2009).

Engaged lifestyle (e.g., volunteering, traveling, giving public speeches) also turned out to be an important predictor of current adaptation (Martin, Baenziger, MacDonald, Siegler, & Poon, 2009). Results suggested that centenarians, who had volunteered, traveled, and had given public talks and balanced their checkbooks at any time of their life were more likely to show relatively high mental status scores.

In spite of the evidence supporting the importance of distal variables, a shortcoming of adaptation models is the omission of specific change variables explaining adaptational outcomes. For example, changes in resources, rather than resources by themselves, may be responsible for rapid decline in functioning among very old adults. Initial levels of resources may also explain differential decline in adaptational outcomes. Randall (2006), for example, evaluated the relationship between resources and activities of daily living for the Georgia centenarian sample and found that centenarians with initially higher social resources showed a steeper decline in activities of daily living than centenarians with lower social resources, which suggests that high social supports do not slow down changes in activities of daily living for extremely old individuals. Other research has demonstrated that change in self-rated health is a stronger predictor of mortality than initial or later levels of self-rated health (Han et al., 2005).

In the recent literature, the developmental adaptation model has been used to study a range of proximal and distal influences, such as educational attainment (Bishop & Martin, 2007), losses related to residential status and community (Cook, Martin, Yearns, & Damhorst, 2007) and its effects on health and well-being in later life (Fry & Debats, 2006; Simsek, 2009). In addition, the model has been applied to emphasize the influence of proximal and distal events to other population groups and broader issues such as marital interactions in midlife (Schmitt, Kliegel, & Shapiro, 2007), individuals with learning disabilities (Margalit, 2003), substance abuse among adults (Schulenberg & Maggs, 2008), and parenting behaviors of adolescents' mothers (Meyers & Battistoni, 2003). The model has also been applied by Martin et al. (Chapter 7) to assess the influence of proximal and distal events on well-being; by Hyer and Yeager (Chapter 8) to address the importance of posttraumatic stress disorder and by MacDonald and Cho (Chapter 9) to assess the interplay between distal events, proximal resources, and well-being. Bishop (Chapter 13) evaluates the important model component of religious coping for well-being in late life.

Another extension of adaptation models includes the test of model equivalence across different cultural groups. Fry and Ikels (Chapter 15) underline the importance of assessing cultural differences in well-being and differences in the measurement of well-being. The domains health and body status, material security, social issues, and personhood mentioned in their chapter are consistent with our models that include individual and social resources and developmental outcome measures. These domains may manifest themselves differently in different cultures.

To what extent do the model relationships fit oldest old survivors in the United States and in European or Asian survivors? Distal experiences may be more important among cultures with more direct involvement in wars or economic depressions. Environmental support (e.g., family support) may be more important in cultures in which intergenerational family residence is the social norm. Personality traits may have different effects in cultures emphasizing self-esteem and openness to experience. Finally, functional, physical, and mental health may be culturally determined as well. An assessment of cultural invariance can easily be accomplished by conducting multiple group analyses that would allow for the systematic equivalence test of measurement models, structural models, and error variance.

One caveat in the comparison of studies across cultures is that not all studies draw from the same resource and adaptation measures. However, in those cases, parallel analyses can still be conducted. One example is the comparison of the Georgia Centenarian Study data with data from the Swedish Centenarian Study. Martin et al. (1997) demonstrated that comparative studies are meaningful even if they are based on different measures, and they reported substantial differences for the prediction of loneliness among centenarians.

ILLUSTRATIVE EXAMPLE

Potential pathways for the effect of distal and proximal variables are illustrated in Figures 5.3 and 5.4. Data for this analysis come from centenarian self reports of the Georgia Centenarian Study (Poon et al., 2007). Centenarians reported on a number of life events that had occurred during any time of their lives. We assessed overall distal events (those experiences that happened at least 20 years before our interviews) to evaluate the cumulative effect of events. Furthermore, we assessed very specific individual events and their impact on adaptation in very late life. In the first example, we included the age when centenarians had experienced the death of their parents. Experiencing the death of a parent early in life can increase resources (e.g., personality or economic resources), because individuals have to rely on their own skills. Losing a parent late in life, in turn, signifies a longer shared life. As an important distal achievement variable we included level of education.

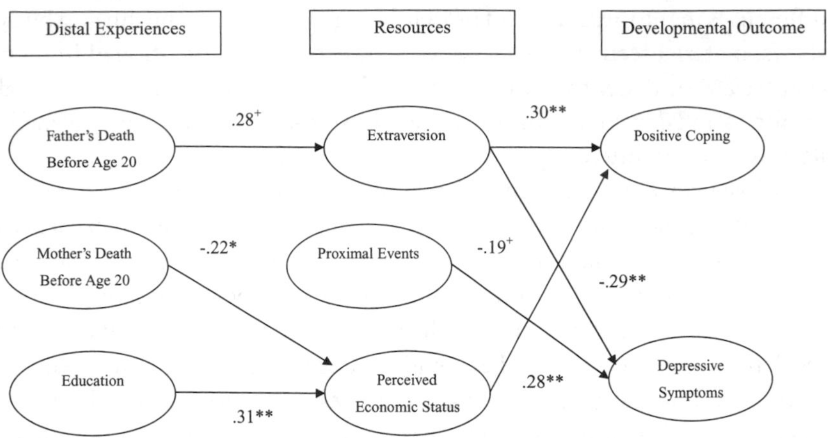

FIGURE 5.3. Parents' Death, Education, and Proximal Predictors of Depressive Symptoms ($^*p < 0.05$; $^{**}p < 0.01$).

Level of education may influence economic resources, which in turn may serve as important resources in late life. Resource variables included proximal events, extraversion as a personal resource, and perceived economic status as an economic resource. Our two dependent variables included positive coping abilities ("Saw the positive side of the situation") and depressive symptoms, as measured by the Geriatric Depression Scale.

The results of this exploratory path model suggest a significant pathway from father's age at death via extraversion to depressive symptoms. Those centenarians whose fathers had died at an older age were less extraverted,

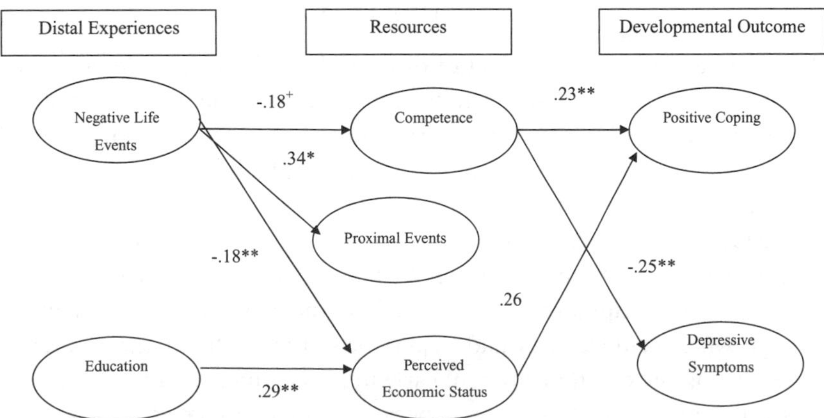

FIGURE 5.4. Cumulative Events, Education, and Proximal Predictors of Depressive Symptoms ($^*p < 0.05$; $^{**}p < 0.01$).

and extraversion in turn was significantly related to depressive symptoms. Mother's age at death did not influence centenarians' personality, but it did have a negative effect on perceived economic status in late life. Centenarians who reported to have lost their mothers in early life were less likely to view their economic status as high. A third significant pathway indicated how influential education was in predicting perceived economic status. Perceived economic status, in turn, influenced positive views of coping. Proximal events were only marginally associated with depressive symptoms.

The second example (Figure 5.4) highlights the relationship between cumulative negative life events and education (as distal influences) in relationship to resources (competence, proximal events, perceived economic status), and developmental outcomes (positive coping and depression). Lifetime (cumulative) negative events eroded the personality trait competence, which was significantly related to positive coping and lower levels of depression. Lifetime negative events were also associated with proximal events and diminished levels of perceived economic status. Higher economic status, in turn, was positively associated with positive coping.

Taken together, the models in Figures 5.3 and 5.4 exemplify that specific early events (e.g., losing a parent) and lifetime cumulative events are associated with individual and economic resources, which in turn are related to mental health and adaptation outcomes. Education is an additional important distal influence, particularly in determining economic resources in late life. These examples suggest that distal experiences and proximal resources are important correlates of adaption in very late life.

CONCLUSIONS

The models introduced have a number of important implications for studying the well-being of old and very old adults. Conceptual models force researchers and practitioners to think beyond single causes by focusing on a distinct network of variables responsible for adaptational outcomes. Multivariate models also allow for the test of mediating (indirect) and moderating (difference) effects. By including distal experiences in conceptual models, building blocks of later-life reminiscence and congruence between aspirations and achievements are posited (Bishop, Martin, & Poon, 2006). Social and economic resources provide older adults with support and help that is necessary when physical, functional, and mental health decline. Individual characteristics, such as personality and religiosity, help provide a sense of stability when challenges abound. Individual and socioeconomic resources may also explain why some older adults continue to do well and others do not. Shrira and Shmotkin (Chapter 6) report that, even after major trauma (e.g., having experienced the Holocaust) and under accelerating decline associated with old-old age, past experiences can continue to exert positive effects on well-being, but past distress also maintains its predictive power on well-being. Perhaps past pleasant or past disturbing experiences can be maintained or exacerbated when resources remain strong (i.e., positive influences) or weaken considerably (i.e., negative influences). The connection among these lifelong influences on well being, mediated through resources, is the primary proposition of the developmental adaptation model.

Behavioral skills and nutritional health behaviors allow older adults to maintain a sense of control even under difficult late-life circumstances. Finally, the maintenance and optimization of mental health, physical health, and life satisfaction are core components in the quality of life among old and very old adults. Well-being in very late life is multifaceted and multidimensional. Cohen-Mansfield's contribution in this book (see Chapter 4) points out that there is a lot to be learned from older adults who adapt to regular changes in their lives. Often seen as a static outcome variable, well-being may indeed be the baseline from which older adults shift when resources are scarce or stress is too overpowering. Because well-being contains many dimensions, older adults are able to rely on some resilience dimensions while experiencing the decline of others.

The Georgia Adaptation Model and the Developmental Adaptation Model may prove fruitful for purposes of intervention. As Hyer (Chapter 8) noted, several therapeutic interventions with older adults suffering from posttraumatic stress disorder promise to be effective: anxiety management training, cognitive behavioral approaches, exposure therapy, and reminiscence with positive and negative self-focus. These interventions attempt to alter some of the perceptions or direct components of developmental adaptation, and Hyer proposes to take a stepwise approach to therapy with patients of posttraumatic stress disorder . The first task focuses on the symptoms, perhaps best represented by the adaptational outcome variables in our models. Another step focuses on developmental factors, which for the most part are congruent with our notion of individual and social resources. The next steps described by Hyer deal directly with the distal traumatic event recalled by an older adult.

Conceptual models are often thought of as hypothesis-testing models, and sophisticated structural equation modeling programs allow us to evaluate the fit of a model to available data. Conceptual models, however, can also be helpful in identifying possible avenues of intervention and treatment that may ultimately increase the well-being of individuals who experience developmental changes and transitions. In that regard, theoretical models should be considered more or less useful in explaining phenomena and guiding therapeutic interventions.

REFERENCES

Adkins, G., Martin, P., & Poon, L.W. (1996). Personality traits and states as predictors of subjective well-being in centenarians, octogenarians, and sexagenarians. *Psychology and Aging, 11*, 408–416.

Baltes, P. B., & Baltes, M. M. (1990). *Successful aging: Perspectives from the behavioral sciences.* Cambridge: Cambridge University Press.

Bishop, A. J., & Martin, P. (2007). The indirect influence of educational attainment on loneliness among unmarried older adults. *Educational Gerontology, 33*, 897–917.

Bishop, A., Martin, P., MacDonald, M., & Poon, L. W. (2010). Predicting happiness among centenarians. *Gerontology, 56*, 88–92.

Bishop, A. J., Martin, P., & Poon, L. W. (2006). Happiness and congruence in older adulthood: A structural model of life satisfaction. *Aging and Mental Health, 10*, 1–9.

Blazer, D. (2003). Depression in late life: Review and commentary. *Journal of Gerontology: Medical Sciences, 58A*, 249–265.

Blazer, D., Burchett, B., Service, C., & George, L. K. (1991). The association of age and depression among the elderly: An epidemiological exploration. *Journal of Gerontology: Medical Sciences, 46*, 210–215.

Cook, C. C., Martin, P., Yearns, M., & Damhorst (2007). Attachment to "place" and coping with losses in changed communities: A paradox for aging population. *Family and Consumer Sciences Research Journal, 35*, 201–214.

Fees, B. S., Martin, P., & Poon, L. W. (1999). A model of loneliness in older adults. *Journal of Gerontology: Psychological Sciences, 54B*, 231–239.

Frisancho, R. A. (2009). Developmental adaptation: Where we go from here. *American Journal of Human Biology, 21*, 694–703.

Fry, P. S., & Debats, D. L. (2002). Self-efficacy beliefs as predictors of loneliness and psychological distress in older adults. *International Journal of Aging and Human Development, 55*, 233–269.

Fry, P. S., & Debats, D. L. (2006). Sources of life strengths as predictors of late-life mortality and survivorship. *International Journal of Aging and Human Development, 62*, 303–334.

Gondo, Y., Hirose, N., Arai, Y., Inagaki, H., Masui, Y., Yamamura, K., et al. (2006). Functional status of centenarians in Tokyo, Japan: Developing better phenotypes of exceptional longevity. *Journal of Gerontology: Medical Sciences, 61A*, 305–310.

Guralnik, J. M., Butterworth, S., Wadsworth, M. E. J., & Kuh, D. (2006). Childhood socioeconomic status predicts physical functioning a half century later. *Journal of Gerontology: Medical Sciences, 61A*, 694–701.

Guralnik, J. M., & Kaplan, G. A. (1989). Predictors of healthy aging: Prospective evidence from the Alameda County Study. *American Journal of Public Health, 79*, 703–708.

Hagberg, B. (2006). Survival after 100 years of age. *Global Ageing: Issues and Action, 4*, 27–33.

Hampson, S. E., Goldberg, L. R., Vogt, T. M., & Dubanosk, J. P. (2006). Forty years on: Teacher's assessments of children's personality traits predict self-reported health behavior and outcomes at midlife. *Health Psychology, 25*, 57–64.

Han, B., Phillips, C., Ferrucci, L., Bandeen-Roche, K., Jylha, M., Kasper, J., et al. (2005). Change in self-rated health and mortality among community-dwelling disabled women. *Gerontologist, 45*, 216–221.

Hartup, W. W., & Stevens, N. (1999). Friends and adaptation across the life span. *New Directions in Psychological Science, 8*(3), 76–79.

Hensley, B., Martin, P., MacDonald, M., & Poon, L. W. (2010). Family history and adaptation among centenarians and octogenarians. *Gerontology, 56*, 83–87.

Jang, Y., Haley, W. E., Small, B. J., & Mortimer, J. A. (2002). The role of mastery and social resources in the association between disability and depression in late life. *Gerontologist, 42*, 807–813.

Jang, Y., Poon, L. W., & Martin, P. (2004). Individual differences in the effects of disease and disability on depressive symptoms: The role of age and subjective health. *International Journal of Aging and Human Development, 59*, 125–137.

Johnson, C. L., & Barer, B. M. (1997). *Life beyond 85 years: The aura of survivorship.* New York: Springer.

Johnson, M. A., Brown, M. A., Poon, L. W., Martin, P., & Clayton, G. M. (1992). Nutritional patterns of centenarians. *International Journal of Aging and Human Development, 34*, 57–76.

Koenig, H. G., & Blazer, D. G. (1992). Mood disorders and suicide. In J. E. Birren, R. B. Sloane, & G. D. Cohen (Eds.), *Handbook of mental health and aging* (2nd ed., pp. 379–407). San Diego, CA: Academic Press.

Krause, N., Shaw, B. A., & Cairney, J. (2004). A descriptive epidemiology of lifetime trauma and the physical health status of older adults. *Psychology and Aging, 19*, 637–648.

Lehr, U. (1982). Social-psychological correlates of longevity. *Annual Review of Gerontology and Geriatrics, 3*, 102–147.

Levinson, D. J., Darrow, C. N., Klein, E. B., Levinson, M. H., & McKee, B. (1978). *The seasons of a man's life.* New York: Ballantine.

Li, L. W., & Liang, J. (2007). Social exchanges and subjective well-being among older Chinese: Does age make a difference? *Psychology and Aging, 22*, 386–391.

Lowenthal, M. F., Thurnher, M., & Chiriboga, D. (1975). *Four stages of life: A comparative study of women and men facing transitions.* San Francisco: Jossey-Bass.

Lupien, S. J., & Wan, N. (2004). Successful ageing: From cell to self. *Philosophical Transactions of the Royal Society B: Biological Sciences, 359*, 1413–1426.

Margalit, (2003). Resilience model among individuals with learning disabilities: Proximal and distal influences. *Learning Disabilities Research & Practice, 18*, 82–86.

Martin, P. (2007). Personality and coping among centenarians. In L. W. Poon & T. T. Perls (Eds.), *Annual review of gerontology and geriatrics. Vol. 27: Biopsychosocial approaches to longevity* (pp. 89–106). New York: Springer.

Martin, P., Baenziger, J., MacDonald, M., Siegler, I., & Poon, L. W. (2009). Engaged lifestyle, personality, and mental status among centenarians. *Adult Development, 16*, 199–208.

Martin, P., Hagberg, B., & Poon, L. W. (1997). Predictors of loneliness in centenarians: A parallel study. *Journal of Cross-Cultural Gerontology, 12*, 203–224.

Martin, P., & Martin, M. (2002). Proximal and distal influences on development: The model of developmental adaptation. *Developmental Review, 22*, 78–96.

Martin, P., Poon, L. W., Clayton, G. M., Lee, H. S., Fulks, J. S., & Johnson, M. A. (1992). Personality, life events, and coping in the oldest-old. *International Journal of Aging and Human Development, 34*, 19–30.

Martin, P., Poon, L. W., Kim, E., & Johnson, M. A. (1996). Social and psychological resources in the oldest old. *Experimental Aging Research, 22*, 121–139.

Martin, P., Rott, C., Kerns, M.-D., Poon, L. W., & Johnson, M. A. (2000) Predictors of depressive symptoms in centenarians. In P. Martin, C. Rott, B. Hagberg, & K. Morgan (Eds.), *Centenarians: Autonomy vs. dependence in the oldest old* (pp. 91–104). New York: Springer.

Masui, Y., Gondo, Y., Inagaki, M., & Hirose, N. (2006). Do personality characteristics predict longevity? Findings from the Tokyo Centenarian Study. *Age, 28*, 353–361.

Meyers, S. A., & Battistoni, J. (2003). Proximal and distal correlates of adolescent mothers' parenting attitudes. *Applied Developmental Psychology, 24*, 33–49.

Neugarten, B. L. (1979). Time, age, and the life cycle. *American Journal of Psychiatry, 136*, 887–894.

Ong, A. D., & Bergeman, C. S. (2004). Resilience and adaptation to stress in later life: Empirical perspectives and conceptual implications. *Ageing International, 29*, 219–246.

Ozaki, A., Uchiyama, M., Tagaya, H., Ohida, T., & Ogihara, R. (2007). The Japanese Centenarian Study: Autonomy was associated with health practices as well as physical status. *Journal of the American Geriatric Society, 55*, 95–101.

Poon, L., Clayton, G. M., Martin, P., Johnson, M. A., Courtenay, B. C., Sweaney, A. L., et al. (1992). *The Georgia Centenarian Study. International Journal of Aging and Human Development, 34*, 1–17.

Poon, L. W., Jazwinski, S.M., Green, R. C., Woodard, J. L., Martin, P., Rodgers, W. L., et al. (2007). Methodological considerations in studying centenarians: Lessons learned from the Georgia Centenarian Studies. In L. W. Poon & T. T. Perls (Eds.), *Annual review of gerontology and geriatrics. Vol. 27: Biopsychosocial approaches to longevity* (pp. 231–264). New York: Springer.

Poon, L. W., Johnson, M. A., & Martin, P. (1997). Looking into the crystal ball: Will we ever be able to accurately predict individual differences in longevity? In J. M. Robine, J. W. Vaupel, B. Jeune, & M. Allard (Eds.), *Longevity: To the limits and beyond* (pp. 113–119). Berlin: Springer.

Poon, L. W., Martin, P., Clayton, G. M., Messner, S., Noble, C. A., & Johnson, M. A. (1992). The influence of cognitive resources on adaptation and old age. *International Journal of Aging and Human Development, 34*, 31–46.

Randall, G. K. (2006). *A comprehensive investigation of change in self-reported resources of older adults.* Unpublished dissertation, Iowa State University.

Rowe, J. W., & Kahn, R. L. (1997). Successful aging. *Gerontologist, 37*, 433–440.

Ruskin, P. E., Blumstein, Z., Walter-Ginzburg, A., Fuchs, Z., Lusky, A., Novikov, I., et al. (1996). Depressive symptoms among community-dwelling oldest-old residents in Israel. *American Journal of Geriatric Psychiatry, 4*, 208–217.

Schlossberg, N. K. (1981). A model for analyzing human adaptation to transition. *Counseling Psychologist, 9*, 2–18.

Schmitt, M., Kliegel, M., & Shapiro, A. (2007). Marital interaction in middle and old age: A predictor of marital satisfaction. *International Journal of Aging and Human Development, 65*, 283–300.

Schulenberg, J. E., & Maggs, J. L. (2008). Destiny matters: Distal developmental influences on adult alcohol use and abuse. *Addiction, 103*, 1–6.

Shimonaka, Y., Nakazato, K., Kawaai, C., & Sato, S. (1997). Androgyny and successful adaptation across the life span among Japanese adults. *Journal of Genetic Psychology, 158*, 389–400.

Simsek, O. F. (2009). Happiness revisited: Ontological well-being as a theory-based construct of subjective health. *Journal of Happiness Studies, 10*, 505–522

Staudinger, U. M., Freund, A. M., Linden, M., & Maas, I. (1999). Self, personality, and life regulation: Facets of psychological resilience in old age. In P. B. Baltes & K. U. Mayer (Eds.), *The Berlin Aging Study: Aging from 70 to 100* (pp. 302–328). Cambridge: Cambridge University Press.

Steverink, N., Lindenberg, S., & Ormel, J. (1998). *Ageing and Society, 18*, 441–467.

Terry, D. F., Wilcox, M., McCormick, M. A., Lawler, E., & Perls, T. T. (2003). Cardiovascular advantages among the offspring of centenarians. *Journal of Gerontology: Medical Sciences, 58A*, 425–431.

Vaillant, G. E. (1977). *Adaptation to life*. Boston, MA: Little, Brown.

PART II

PARADISE LOST: BETWEEN TRAUMA AND HAPPINESS

6

Does Trauma Linger into Old-Old Age? Using the Holocaust Experience as a Paradigm

DOV SHMOTKIN, AMIT SHRIRA, AND YUVAL PALGI

ABSTRACT

Trauma that lingers from early to very late life poses a special threat to the labile conditions of adaptation while facing imminent frailty and death. This chapter examines long-term effects of trauma in three modes of survival into old-old age: (a) dementia-molded survival, which raises a question as to whether cognitive impairment sensitizes traumatic memories or blunts them, (b) embattled survival, which involves either a chronic confrontation with the past trauma or else its reactivation in the adverse conditions of late life, and (c) robust survival, which maintains the capacity to stay well in the face of age-related challenge as well as past trauma. Coping with past trauma under robust survival typically generates a delicate balance between general resilience and specific vulnerabilities. This chapter dwells on research of old and old-old Holocaust survivors, who provide a paradigm for the special challenge of long-term effects of extreme trauma.

LIFETIME TRAUMA AND SURVIVAL IN OLD-OLD AGE

A key issue that developmental models need to account for is the combined impact of distal influences, such as adverse events early in life, and proximal influences, such as recent experiences and resources (Martin & Martin, 2002; see Chapter 5). As developmental trajectories become increasingly obscured and labile in old-old age (Baltes, 1997; Poon & Perls, 2007), the interactive effects of distal trauma and proximal age-related experiences are particularly intricate or unpredictable.

Several theories and findings suggest that the long-term effects of trauma may become insurmountable when faced with the developmental demands of old-old age (for further discussions of trauma in old-old age, see

Chapters 7 and 8). Psychosocial coping mechanisms may be overpowered by the decline of biological capabilities. Accordingly, Baltes (1997) maintained that the last stage of life represents the incomplete segment in the architecture of human development, as optimal functioning is doomed to disruption by irreparable biological dysfunctions. In contrast, there is evidence that traumatic effects can be managed even in old-old age. Thus, some psychosocial resources are not overwhelmed by physical deterioration and may even gain power when congruent and meaningful perceptions of oneself and one's life are maintained in late life (Bishop, Martin, & Poon, 2006; Erikson, 1998).

The aforementioned evidence implies a heterogeneous picture of functioning in old-old traumatized people. In this chapter, we maintain that effects of trauma in old-old age can be delineated by three cardinal modes: dementia-molded survival, embattled survival, and robust survival. Next, the chapter addresses major questions pertinent to each mode, dwelling on empirical studies of Holocaust survivors, who serve as a paradigm for exceptionally extreme trauma happening early in life for whom the trauma sequelae linger to old and old-old age. Such a paradigm may help delineate both similarities and differences in the effects of severe traumas occurring in other places and circumstances.

CARDINAL SURVIVAL MODES

Parallel to increasing life expectancy, the widening prevalence of dementia and the varieties of its manifestations are essential concomitants of old-old age (Cohen-Mansfield, 2000), therefore requiring an account of dementia-molded survival. As traumatic remnants are mostly embodied in memory and symptoms of dementia mostly refer to cognitive-related impairments, there is much confusion about the way that dementia shapes traumatic memories and the way traumatic memories shape the manifestation of dementia. One viewpoint suggests that dementia-related deterioration of memory might blur, and consequently relieve, the long-lasting, agonizing experience of trauma (Kensinger, 2006). However, from a different viewpoint, traumatic stress can be intensified by dementia because regulatory mechanisms are undermined and formerly controlled traumatic memories are thus disinhibited (Cook, Ruzek, & Cassidy, 2003). This conundrum is, to date, a relatively uncharted research area, partly because the expression of inner experiences, whether positive or negative, of people with dementia is complex and elusive (Cohen-Mansfield & Lipson, 2002; see Chapter 4).

The mode of embattled survival refers to the cognitively functioning old-old for whom traumatic events in childhood and adulthood have an accumulating detrimental effect on their late-life adaptation (Kraaij & De Wilde, 2001). Sensitized by physical and mental frailty, for these old-old people, the lingering trauma may appear as a chronic condition (Averill & Beck, 2000), possibly expressed in the form of posttraumatic stress disorder (PTSD). The early trauma may also undergo a delayed reactivation of traumatic suffering catalyzed by age-related vulnerability and losses (Hyer & Sacks, 2008; Kahana, 1992).

Robust survival depicts a completely different mode of old-old who exhibit good adaptation relative to their age, despite their past trauma. This mode is compatible with evidence that older persons do not differ from younger adults in their reactions to trauma (Bleich, Gelkopf, Melamed, & Solomon, 2005) and show relatively low symptom levels even after high trauma exposure (Schnurr, Spiro, Vielhauer, Findler, & Hamblen, 2002). This potential inoculation in old age can be explained by the maturity and experience that come with age (Hyer & Sacks, 2008), as well as by underestimated reserves of resilience among traumatized old people (Ryff, Singer, Love, & Essex, 1998). Thus, with certain psychosocial conditions, long-term traumatic effects can be buffered so that a sense of satisfaction and meaning, and possibly posttraumatic growth, can be obtained even among the old-old (Jennings, Aldwin, Levenson, Spiro, & Mroczek, 2005; Krause, 2005).

In the following sections, an array of studies on Holocaust survivors illustrates the effects of the trauma among the old-old. By now, Holocaust survivors have become old. The physical and mental status of survivors is interwoven with long-term effects of the extreme trauma they experienced, extensive efforts to reconstruct their lives, and their current aging process. Research on Holocaust survivors describes a host of disturbances that lasted decades after the Holocaust, but it also points to a general resilience expressed in daily functioning (Barel, Van IJzendoorn, Sagi-Schwartz, & Bakermans-Kranenburg, 2010; Kahana, Harel, & Kahana, 2005; Shmotkin, 2003). This interplay of vulnerability and resilience provides a suitable theoretical and empirical framework for examining the three survival modes proposed herein and some of the most pertinent questions that these modes pose.

DEMENTIA-MOLDED SURVIVAL: WHAT HAPPENS TO TRAUMATIC MEMORIES IN DEMENTIA?

Dementia prevalence may be as high as 20–30% among octogenarians and even higher among nonagenarians (Ferri et al., 2005). As Holocaust survivors are moving from old to old-old age, the increasing prevalence of dementia among them calls attention to the possible manifestations of their past trauma under this latest affliction. Depictions of survivors by pioneer studies on survivor syndrome (Eitinger, 1964) delineated a trajectory moving from early manifestation of psychosomatic symptoms and personality disturbances to later manifestations of premature aging and an organic phase (Ryn, 1990). As studies dealing with this issue among Holocaust survivors are scarce, we present them together with complementary research on other old-old traumatized groups.

There is evidence suggesting that the memory of emotional information is blunted in dementia (Kensinger, 2006). Blunted emotional memory in dementia may be a result of the abundance of neuritic plaques and neurofibrillary tangles in the amygdala, which has been consistently implicated as a key regulator of emotional memory in the brain (Hamann, 2001; Vogt, Human, Van Hoesen, & Damasio, 1990). Although there are no direct findings suggesting blunted emotional memories in Holocaust survivors with dementia, a rare controlled study found that old war veterans with dementia and PTSD were not more emotionally agitated than their counterparts without PTSD, with former prisoners of war with PTSD being even less so (Verma et al., 2001). It might be, then, that dementia blunts emotional memories and thus alleviates posttraumatic distress.

Contrary to the foregoing notion, certain sources suggest that dementia is associated with heightened levels of PTSD (Johnston, 2000). Thus, some case studies report that symptoms became uncontrollable and highly disruptive following the onset of neurologic illness and dementia among Holocaust survivors (Grossman, Levin, Katzen, & Lechner, 2004). Moreover, psychogeriatric data showed more chronic hospitalizations for survivors with dementia compared with other dementia patients who were not Holocaust survivors (Terno, Barak, Hadjez, Elizur, & Szor, 1998). Golier, Harvey, Legge, and Yehuda (2006) found an accelerated cognitive decline among Holocaust survivors with PTSD but not among Holocaust survivors without PTSD.

In line with the possibility that emotional memories in dementia are intensified rather than blunted, it was found that people with dementia may vividly recall fragments of adverse life events, possibly in exaggerated flashbulb memories (Budson et al., 2004). Emotional memories may be increased as a result of the decline of brain regions in charge of emotional inhibition and regulation (Grady, Furey, Pietrini, Horwitz, & Rapoport, 2001). Dementia may also dismantle long-standing adaptive coping mechanisms, such as repression, thus releasing formerly compartmentalized traumatic memories. Furthermore, dementia may induce a retrograde memory impairment in which remote events are remembered better than more recent ones

(Butters & Delis, 1995). Holocaust survivors in early stages of dementia may well conceive of their past trauma as actually continuing in present life and further cling to inadequate reactions, such as preparing oneself for another Holocaust and confusing current somatic problems with ones at the time of the trauma (Shmotkin & Barilan, 2002).

In conclusion, it seems that there may be a noxious interplay between dementia and PTSD (Cook, Ruzek, & Cassidy, 2003). More specifically, PTSD may catalyze the process of dementia, whereas dementia, in its turn, may aggravate posttraumatic stress. Scarce evidence still points to the contradictory possibility that dementia diminishes stress among traumatized older persons by fogging traumatic memories. It is difficult to draw firm conclusions about this intriguing issue because later stages of dementia among traumatized people remain mostly unexplored. For example, we do not know the extent or the implications of losing one's identity as a trauma survivor, which may be part of a broader decline in the sense of identity as estimated from reports by persons with dementia themselves and as judged, even more strongly, by their family members (Cohen-Mansfield, Parpura-Gill, & Golander, 2006). Although the methodological access to authentic feelings is severely obstructed among people with dementia (Byrne-Davis, Bennett, & Wilcock, 2006), the high prevalence of dementia in old-old age requires that further efforts be made to trace the traumatic effects in those living with the disease.

EMBATTLED SURVIVAL: HOW DOES TRAUMA LINGER INTO OLD-OLD AGE?

Embattled survival involves a nearly constant confrontation with the past trauma or its repercussions. Normal developmental tasks of later life may become arenas of such confrontation. Most pertinent to these tasks is Erikson's (1998) concept of ego integrity, defined as a sense of coherence and wholeness about one's life in the face of finitude. An integrative outlook on life is especially difficult for traumatized old-old people who need to interweave the unresolved traumatic events with other life experiences. As exemplified in Laufer's (1988) concept of serial self, the legacy of the trauma involves a lifelong struggle in which the traumatized part of the self is encapsulated into a distinct timeless biographical segment. This segment cannot be elaborated and integrated into the adaptive parts of the self that are plausibly bound to the time before or after the trauma. Danieli (1981) proposed that a complete acceptance of, and a reconciliation with, the inevitability of all events in one's life, is often an insurmountable task for old Holocaust survivors.

Integrity is generally achieved through a life-review process, in which older people reminisce about their past and revise its interpretation (Butler, 1963). Through a congruent self-narrative, older people can achieve a sense of unity and identity (McAdams, 2001). On the basis of these theories, we have performed a series of studies to investigate how survivors constructed their life periods into a life narrative. In these investigations, we implemented a new model of anchor periods (Shmotkin, 2005), which refer to specific time segments perceived as outstandingly meaningful in one's life (i.e., the happiest period, the most miserable period). Anchor periods are markers of the most significant experiences, whether positive or negative, that help map people's life narratives.

We found that Holocaust survivors, compared to persons from comparison groups, reported less happiness and greater suffering in relation to negative anchor periods in their lives but revealed no differences in those emotions in relation to positive periods (Shmotkin, Berkovich, & Cohen, 2006; Shrira & Shmotkin, 2008). Shrira and Shmotkin (2008) also found that suffering in a negative anchor period had a stronger negative association with life satisfaction among old-old Holocaust survivors but a smaller negative, or even a positive, association with life satisfaction in the old-old comparison groups. Stated differently, old-old survivors assimilated their negative life experience in their current satisfaction, whereas old-old comparisons could contrast such experience to their present self, thereby improving their well-being.

The foregoing findings demonstrate how lingering trauma may disrupt the ability of individuals to manage their life narrative, thus leading them to inefficient links between perceptions of past and present. Such effects may originate from chronic, lifelong posttraumatic stress or otherwise reactivated traumatic suffering, both of which are typical conditions of embattled survival. Thus, chronic psychological morbidity was documented, in some of the studies, to continue among Holocaust survivors for decades after the trauma in both clinical (Brom, Durst, & Aghassy, 2002) and community (Joffe, Brodaty, Luscombe, & Ehrlich, 2003) samples (for a meta-analysis on this issue, see Barel et al., 2010). Moreover, some survivors who were exposed to ongoing extreme traumatic stress were in a high risk of developing complex PTSD, characterized by recurrent dissociative reactions and pervasive personality disturbances (Herman, 1992). Such characteristics, which typically depict a long-lasting fragmented identity, were described among Holocaust survivors mainly by clinical reports (Müller & Barash-Kishon, 1998; Shamai & Levin-Megged, 2006). As a result of lack of longitudinal data on Holocaust survivors in nonclinical settings, the evidence on lifelong chronicity of traumatic stress relies on survivors' retrospective reports or researchers' inferences (Joffe et al., 2003; Landau & Litwin, 2000).

A reactivation of traumatic stress may occur even among older persons who have been relatively free from posttraumatic symptoms for long periods since the traumatic event. In the context of the aging process, Gutmann's (1998) theory of late-onset disorders pinpoints niches of risky psychic vulnerability that were compartmentalized from regular functioning, and hence controlled, in earlier life, but had become hard to defend in older age. Thus, in young adulthood, the daily routine of family, career, and social life kept the individual busy and distracted from the traumatic past. However, in old and old-old age, the focus shifted from doing and planning to contemplating and reminiscing (Danieli, 1981). Adversities of old age also exacerbate residual effects of trauma. In that line, Holocaust survivors, relative to comparison groups of similar origin with age being adjusted for, manifested lower subjective well-being in indices based on aging-related themes, such as attitudes toward aging and congruence with one's past (Shmotkin & Lomranz, 1998).

When coping with adverse conditions, age-related stressors and major external stressors may lower the threshold for reactivation of traumatic experiences. Such reactivation was found among Holocaust survivors encountering severe medical conditions such as cancer (Hantman & Solomon, 2007; Peretz, Baider, Ever-Hadani, & Kaplan De-Nour, 1994). As another example, Holocaust survivors in Israel showed high vulnerability in response to military conflicts, such as the Gulf War (Solomon & Parger, 1992) and terrorist attacks (Dekel & Hobfoll, 2007).

ROBUST SURVIVAL: HOW DO OLD-OLD PEOPLE REGULATE THE REMNANTS OF TRAUMA?

Robust survival refers to a capacity to stay well, recover, or even improve in the face of cumulating challenge (Ryff et al., 1998). Most investigators agree that a large portion of older persons who endured trauma in early life demonstrate resilience (Schnurr et al., 2002). The question is whether this is true regarding survivors of massive trauma who have reached old-old age, such as a sizable number of Holocaust survivors still currently alive.

Whereas earlier studies on Holocaust survivors found relatively high levels of psychological and physical vulnerability, more recent studies have failed to find major differences between survivors and comparisons (Landau & Litwin, 2000; Shmotkin, Blumstein, & Modan, 2003). This is partly because the studies shifted from examining clinical samples to investigating survivors in the community. It is also plausible that feebler survivors passed away and the survivors who have survived to old-old age are a select group with a unique biopsychosocial constitution (Shanan, 1989). Moreover, the survivor group that participates in studies is part of community samples that are biased to represent old-old individuals of robust constitutional and personality makeup until their last years (Martin, da Rosa, Siegler, Davey, MacDonald, & Poon, 2006).

Old-old survivors are generally found to be physically and functionally fit, yet they manifest fragility in certain psychosocial markers of functioning (Barel et al., 2010). Specifically, old survivors usually do not show more physical morbidity or a higher mortality risk than comparison groups (Ayalon & Covinsky, 2007). In one of two nationwide random samples of the older Jewish population in Israel, old-old concentration-camp survivors even showed a lower mortality risk than that of other survivors who had not been incarcerated in such camps during the Holocaust and of other comparison groups (Shrira, Palgi, Ben-Ezra, & Shmotkin, in press). Old survivors, however, have been found in various community studies to present a higher prevalence of PTSD, weaker social support, and lower levels of enjoyable and social lifestyle activities (Landau & Litwin, 2000; Palgi & Shmotkin, 2007; Shmotkin et al., 2003). In line with these findings, Shmotkin (2003) has suggested a dialectical model of endurance and suffering, according to which survivors demonstrate a general resilience along with specific vulnerabilities.

The robust survival mode among old-old Holocaust survivors is epitomized by posttraumatic growth, which refers to a process of improvement and deepening in perceptions of the self, interpersonal relationships, and philosophy of life (Tedeschi & Calhoun, 2004). Thus, many survivors succeeded in regaining self-reliance and fortitude, and they flourished in familial and professional domains (Kahana et al., 2005). Some studies even found survivors to be better off than comparison groups in specific aspects of coping, social adjustment, and hope (Kahana et al., 2005; Shmotkin & Lomranz, 1998). A portion of the survivors managed to lead extraordinarily successful lives (Helmreich, 1992).

There are various mechanisms by which old-old Holocaust survivors remain resilient or even show better functioning than their counterparts (Shmotkin, 2003). A central aspect of resilience relates to the ability of many survivors to formulate new meanings in life. Frankl (1963) proposed that, following their traumatic experiences, survivors became painfully aware of what was precious and valuable in their lives, and thus further toiled to preserve it. Old Holocaust survivors may find meaning in the families they have created, in the careers they have built, and in the testimonies they have given (Kahana et al., 2005). Survivors may also hold a stronger sense of identity than other postwar immigrants who were not under Nazi rule – a comparative group used in some recent studies (Palgi & Shmotkin, 2007; Shmotkin & Lomranz, 1998; Shrira & Shmotkin, 2008). The latter group includes people who were indirectly affected by the Holocaust but were not recognized as Holocaust survivors and consequently were devoid of a unifying sense of identity. The availability of meaningful survivor identity may explain why Holocaust survivors were also found to be more resilient than survivors of the Soviet labor camps (Bachner, Carmel, & Sagi, 2007).

The meaning schemas, or assumptions, that old survivors hold about their self and the world, are of mixed valence: some are more negative, some are similar, and others are more positive relative to those of comparison groups (Brom et al., 2002). The mixed results seemingly attest to the complex, indeed paradoxical, process by which survivors establish renewed schemas of meaning (Shmotkin & Shrira, in press). The complex organization of meaning found among many survivors may reflect what Lomranz (2005) termed *aintegration*, which refers to the individual's ability to maintain satisfaction and competence in spite of incongruent dimensions in life.

Rather than by seeking meaning in traumatic experiences, robust survival can also be achieved by avoiding, or repressing, any engagement with those experiences. The deliberate or automatic repression of negative stimuli is often considered in a context of defense mechanisms or of coping styles. Repressive coping in late life serves a self-protective function by allowing the old to maintain a high degree of well-being in the face of decline (Erskine, Kvavilashvili, Conway, & Myers, 2007). Thus, Shmotkin and Barilan (2002) found that Holocaust survivors who compartmentalized their trauma by seeing it as a singular and demarcated event of the past (Holocaust-as-past) appeared more adapted (with fewer mental symptoms and fewer medical diagnoses) than other survivors whose daily life was still overpowered by the trauma (Holocaust-as-present). However, this study also found that Holocaust-as-past survivors were also more likely than Holocaust-as-present survivors to be rated by physicians as being in a high danger to life, thus suggesting that the repressive coping style of these survivors possibly took its toll in physiological vulnerability.

Although not without costs, modes of avoidance or repression seems beneficial for Holocaust survivors. Cohen and Shmotkin (2007), for example, found that old survivors (mostly septuagenarians) who showed flattened emotional reactions in recalling anchor periods that had taken place during the Holocaust, yet also showed high emotional reactions in recalling periods before and after the Holocaust, reported the highest well-being in the present. This study suggests that a certain level of emotional restriction was associated with the preservation of the survivors' well-being but only when it was specifically focused on the Holocaust experiences and not on other life experiences. Yet the cross-sectional data did not permit a causal conclusion as to whether repression increased well-being or whether a heightened well-being decreased the emotional impact of the Holocaust periods. Palgi and Shmotkin (2007) found that old-old survivors (mostly octogenarians) with deflated emotional reactions – being low on both positive and negative affect – had a lower mortality risk than survivors in the specifically vulnerable position of being low on positive affect and high on negative affect. Moreover, deflated emotional reactions predicted mortality among Holocaust survivors but not among comparison groups. Palgi and Shmotkin (2007) suggested that deflated emotional reactions in old age probably denote a tendency to preserve a mental equilibrium vis-à-vis adversity.

CONCLUSIONS

Surviving trauma and reaching old-old age mark a triumph over adversity and death. On the one hand, this achievement may merely indicate prolonged distress when the psychic capital of trauma survivors is depleted to the point at which it eventually fails to regulate the sequelae of past trauma. Such a failure may be lifelong or may be due to a reactivation of the trauma experiences in the face of frailty or a new trauma. On the other hand, normal adaptation to old-old life can be sustained if the effects of past trauma, as well as those of the aging-related losses, are managed by a variety of optional coping mechanisms.

Our review discussed three major modes of surviving into old-old age with a lingering trauma. First, traumatic effects may mingle with an age-related dementia. The findings suggest that traumatic symptoms are intensified in a dementia-molded survival, although there is some information suggesting that an opposite process that blurs the traumatic memories may also take place. Knowledge about these kinds of dementia-molded survival is still deficient. Second, old-old people may be diverted into an embattled survival by chronic posttraumatic effects or by a reactivated traumatic experience, whether because of age-related stressors (e.g., frailty) or because of external forces (e.g., war). Third, despite the combined burden of trauma- and age-related stressors, a large portion of traumatized people reaching old-old age may present a robust survival whereby they manage to lead a relatively normal life, thus sustaining a delicate balance between a general resilience and specific vulnerabilities. Although the first two modes of survival – dementia molded and embattled – are described mainly in clinical studies, the robust survival mode and the various mechanisms that facilitate it are observed in community studies. An obvious reason is that large community studies on the old-old predominantly sample better-functioning people who are more likely to present a robust survival. Future research should try to obtain a more balanced picture.

To corroborate the three survival modes in old-old age, we presented a body of evidence, mainly from studies on Holocaust survivors. These survivors, when reaching old or old-old age, provide a paradigmatic perspective on the lifelong repercussions of massive trauma. Further investigations should examine whether the conclusions drawn from this body of evidence can be generalized to older survivors of other devastating traumas and catastrophic events, such as war, massacre, terrorist attack, torture, forced migration, persistent hunger, and other kinds of severe victimization and deprivation. Accumulation of data from different trauma-stricken populations is expected to facilitate the formulation of an overarching conceptualization on the role of trauma in late life.

The foregoing survival modes attest to the heterogeneity of response and functioning among traumatized old-old individuals. In this respect, the fourth age of people that endured trauma should not be viewed exclusively in a frame of inescapable deterioration (Baltes, 1997) but as a life phase in which frailty and robustness may coreside. Hence, although researchers and practitioners are required to better understand how trauma may doom people to lifelong anguish, some comfort may be derived from the fortunate option of maintaining successful aging even by old-old trauma survivors.

REFERENCES

Averill, P. M., & Beck, J. G. (2000). Posttraumatic stress disorder in older adults: A conceptual review. *Journal of Anxiety Disorders, 14*, 133–156.

Ayalon, L., & Covinsky, K. E. (2007). Late-life mortality in older Jews exposed to the Nazi regime. *Journal of the American Geriatrics Society, 55*, 1380–1386.

Bachner, Y. G., Carmel, S., & Sagi, D. (2007). Physical health and psychological resources: A comparison between Holocaust survivors under the Nazi regime and survivors of the Soviet labor camps. *Gerontology: Journal of Aging Studies, 34*, 63–77 (in Hebrew).

Baltes, P. B. (1997). On the incomplete architecture of human ontogeny: Selection, optimization, and compensation as foundation of developmental theory. *American Psychologist, 52*, 366–380.

Barel, E., Van IJzendoorn, M. H., Sagi-Schwartz, A., & Bakermans-Kranenburg, M. J. (2010). Surviving the Holocaust: A meta-analysis of the long-term sequelae of a genocide. *Psychological Bulletin, 136*, 677-698.

Bishop, A. J., Martin, P., & Poon, L. W. (2006). Happiness and congruence in older adulthood: A structural model of life satisfaction. *Aging and Mental Health, 10*, 445–453.

Bleich, A., Gelkopf, M., Melamed, Y., & Solomon, Z. (2005). Emotional impact of exposure to terrorism among young-old and old-old Israeli citizens. *American Journal of Geriatric Psychiatry, 13*, 705–712.

Brom, D., Durst, N., & Aghassy, G. (2002). The phenomenology of posttraumatic distress in older adult Holocaust survivors. *Journal of Clinical Geropsychology, 8*, 189–201.

Budson, A. E., Simons, J. S., Sullivan, A. L., Beier, J. S., Solomon, P. R., Scinto, L., et al. (2004). Memory and emotions for the September 11, 2001, terrorist attack in patients with Alzheimer's disease, patients with mild cognitive impairment, and healthy older adults. *Neuropsychology, 18*, 315–327.

Butler, R. N. (1963). The life review: An interpretation of reminiscence in the aged. *Psychiatry, 26*, 65–76.

Butters, N., & Delis, D. C. (1995). Clinical assessment of memory disorders in amnesia and dementia. *Annual Review of Psychology, 46*, 493–523.

Byrne-Davis, L. M. T., Bennett, P. D., & Wilcock, G. K. (2006). How are quality of life ratings made? Toward a model of quality of life in people with dementia. *Quality of Life Research, 15*, 855–865.

Cohen, K., & Shmotkin, D. (2007). Emotional ratings of anchor periods in life and their relation to subjective well-being among Holocaust survivors. *Personality and Individual Differences, 43*, 495–506.

Cohen-Mansfield, J. (2000). Heterogeneity in dementia: Challenges and opportunities. *Alzheimer Disease and Associated Disorders, 14*, 60–63.

Cohen-Mansfield, J., & Lipson, S. (2002). Pain in cognitively impaired nursing home residents: How well are physicians diagnosing it? *Journal of the American Geriatrics Society, 50*, 1039–1044.

Cohen-Mansfield, J., Parpura-Gill, A., & Golander, H. (2006). Salience of self-identity roles in persons with dementia: Differences in perceptions among elderly persons, family members and caregivers. *Social Science and Medicine, 62*, 745–757.

Cook, J. M., Ruzek, J. I., & Cassidy, E. (2003). Possible association of posttraumatic stress disorder with cognitive impairment among older adults. *Psychiatric Services, 54*, 1223–1225.

Danieli, Y. (1981). On the achievement of integration in aging survivors of the Nazi Holocaust. *Journal of Geriatric Psychiatry, 14*, 191–210.

Dekel, R., & Hobfoll, S. E. (2007). The impact of resource loss on Holocaust survivors facing war and terrorism in Israel. *Aging and Mental Health, 11*, 159–167.

Eitinger, L. (1964). *Concentration camp survivors in Norway and Israel.* Oslo: Oslo University Press.

Erikson, E. H. (1998). *The life cycle completed: Extended version with new chapters on the ninth stage by Joan M. Erikson.* New York: Norton.

Erskine, J. A. K., Kvavilashvili, L., Conway, M. A., & Myers, L. (2007). The effects of age on psychopathology, well-being, and repressive coping. *Aging and Mental Health, 11*, 394–404.

Ferri, C. P., Prince, M., Brayne, C., Brodaty, H., Fratiglioni, L., Ganguli, M., et al. (2005). Global prevalence of dementia: A Delphi consensus study. *Lancet, 366*, 2112–2117.

Frankl, V. E. (1963). *Man's search for meaning: An introduction to logotherapy.* New York: Washington Square Press.

Golier, J. A., Harvey, P. D., Legge, J., & Yehuda, R. (2006). Memory performance in older trauma survivors: Implications for the longitudinal course of PTSD. *Annals of the New York Academy of Sciences, 1071*, 54–66.

Grady, C. L., Furey, M. L., Pietrini, P., Horwitz, B., & Rapoport, S. I. (2001). Altered brain connectivity and impaired short-term memory in Alzheimer's disease. *Brain, 124*, 739–756.

Grossman, A. B., Levin, B. E., Katzen, H. L., & Lechner, S. (2004). PTSD symptoms and onset of neurologic disease in elderly trauma survivors. *Journal of Clinical and Experimental Neuropsychology, 26*, 698–705.

Gutmann, D. (1998). The psychoimmune system in later life: The problem of the late-onset disorders. In J. Lomranz (Ed.), *Handbook of aging and mental health* (pp. 281–295). New York: Plenum Press.

Hamann, S. (2001). Cognitive and neural mechanisms of emotional memory. *Trends in Cognitive Science, 5*, 394–400.

Hantman, S., & Solomon, Z. (2007). Recurrent trauma: Holocaust survivors cope with aging and cancer. *Social Psychiatry and Psychiatric Epidemiology, 42*, 396–402.

Helmreich, W. B. (1992). *Against all odds: Holocaust survivors and the successful lives they made in America.* New York: Simon and Schuster.

Herman, J. L. (1992). Complex PTSD: A syndrome in survivors of prolonged and repeated trauma. *Journal of Traumatic Stress, 5*, 377–391.

Hyer, L., & Sacks, A. (2008). PTSD (post-traumatic stress disorders) in later life. In D. Gallagher-Thompson, A. M. Steffen, & L. W. Thompson (Eds.), *Handbook of behavioral and cognitive therapies with older adults* (pp. 278–294). New York: Springer.

Jennings, P. A., Aldwin, C. M., Levenson, M. R., Spiro, A., & Mroczek, D. K. (2006). Combat exposure, perceived benefits of military service, and wisdom in later life. *Research on Aging, 28*, 115–134.

Joffe, C., Brodaty, H., Luscombe, G., & Ehrlich, F. (2003). The Sydney Holocaust study: Posttraumatic stress disorder and other psychosocial morbidity in an aged community sample. *Journal of Traumatic Stress, 16*, 39–47.

Johnston, D. (2000). A series of cases of dementia presenting with PTSD symptoms in World War II combat veterans. *Journal of the American Geriatrics Society, 48*, 70–72.

Kahana, B. (1992). Late-life adaptation in the aftermath of extreme stress. In M. L. Wykle, E. Kahana, & J. Kowal (Eds.), *Stress and health among the elderly* (pp. 151–171). New York: Springer.

Kahana, B., Harel, Z., & Kahana, E. (2005). *Holocaust survivors and immigrants: Late life adaptations.* New York: Springer.

Kensinger, E. A. (2006). Remembering emotional information: Effects of aging and Alzheimer's disease. In E. M. Welsh (Ed.), *Frontiers in Alzheimer's disease research* (pp. 213–226). Hauppauge, NY: Nova Science.

Kraaij, V., & De Wilde, E. J. (2001). Negative life events and depressive symptoms in the elderly: A life span perspective. *Aging and Mental Health, 5,* 84–91.

Krause, N. (2005). Traumatic events and meaning in life: Exploring variations in three age cohorts. *Aging and Society, 25,* 501–524.

Landau, R., & Litwin, H. (2000). The effects of extreme early stress in very old age. *Journal of Traumatic Stress, 13,* 473–487.

Laufer, R. S. (1988). The serial self: War trauma, identity, and adult development. In J. P. Wilson, Z. Harel, & B. Kahana (Eds.), *Human adaptation to extreme stress: From the Holocaust to Vietnam* (pp. 33–53). New York: Plenum.

Lomranz, J. (2005). Amplified comment: The triangular relationships between the Holocaust, aging, and narrative gerontology. *International Journal of Aging and Human Development, 60,* 255–267.

Martin, P., da Rosa, G., Siegler, I. C., Davey, A., MacDonald, M., & Poon, L. W. (2006). Personality and longevity: Findings from the Georgia Centenarian Study. *Age, 28,* 343–352.

Martin, P., & Martin, M. (2002). Proximal and distal influences on development: The model of developmental adaptation. *Developmental Review, 22,* 78–96.

McAdams, D. P. (2001). The psychology of life stories. *Review of General Psychology, 5,* 100–122.

Müller, U., & Barash-Kishon, R. (1998). Psychodynamic-supportive group therapy model for elderly Holocaust survivors. *International Journal of Group Psychotherapy, 48,* 461–475.

Palgi, Y., & Shmotkin, D. (2007). The relations of experiences in World War II and affect types of subjective well-being with functioning and mortality at old-old age. *Gerontology: Journal of Aging Studies, 34,* 35–62 (in Hebrew).

Peretz, T., Baider, L., Ever-Hadani, P., & Kaplan De-Nour, A. (1994). Psychological distress in female cancer patients with Holocaust experience. *General Hospital Psychiatry, 16,* 413–418.

Poon, L. W., & Perls, T. T. (2007). The trials and tribulations of studying the oldest old. In L. W. Poon & T. T. Perls (Eds.), *Biopsychosocial approaches to longevity. Vol. 27: Annual Review of Gerontology and Geriatrics* (pp. 1–10). New York: Springer.

Ryff, C. D., Singer, B., Love, G. D., & Essex, M. J. (1998). Resilience in adulthood and later life: Defining features and dynamic processes. In J. Lomranz (Ed.), *Handbook of aging and mental health: An integrative approach* (pp. 69–99). New York: Plenum Press.

Ryn, Z. (1990). The evolution of mental disturbances in the concentration camp syndrome (KZ-syndrome). *Genetic, Social, and General Psychology Monographs, 116,* 21–36.

Schnurr, P. P., Spiro, A., Vielhauer, M. J., Findler, M. N., & Hamblen, J. L. (2002). Trauma in the lives of older men: Findings from the Normative Aging Study. *Journal of Clinical Geropsychology, 8,* 175–187.

Shamai, M., & Levin-Megged, O. (2006). The myth of creating an integrative story: The therapeutic experience of Holocaust survivors. *Qualitative Health Research, 16*, 692–712.

Shanan, J. (1989). Surviving the survivors: Late personality development of Jewish Holocaust survivors. *International Journal of Mental Health, 17*, 42–71.

Shmotkin, D. (2003). Vulnerability and resilience intertwined: A review of research on Holocaust survivors. In R. Jacoby & G. Keinan (Eds.), *Between stress and hope: From a disease-centered to a health-centered perspective* (pp. 213–233). Westport, CT: Praeger.

Shmotkin, D. (2005). Happiness in face of adversity: Reformulating the dynamic and modular bases of subjective well-being. *Review of General Psychology, 9*, 291–325.

Shmotkin, D., & Barilan, Y. M. (2002). Expressions of Holocaust experience and their relationship to mental symptoms and physical morbidity among Holocaust survivor patients. *Journal of Behavioral Medicine, 25*, 115–134.

Shmotkin, D., Berkovich, M., & Cohen, K. (2006). Combining happiness and suffering in a retrospective view of anchor periods in life: A differential approach to subjective well-being. *Social Indicators Research, 77*, 139–169.

Shmotkin, D., Blumstein, T., & Modan, B. (2003). Tracing long-term effects of early trauma: A broad-scope view of Holocaust survivors in late life. *Journal of Consulting and Clinical Psychology, 71*, 223–234.

Shmotkin, D., & Lomranz, J. (1998). Subjective well-being among Holocaust survivors: An examination of overlooked differentiations. *Journal of Personality and Social Psychology, 75*, 141–155.

Shmotkin, D., & Shrira, A. (in press). On the distinction between subjective well-being and meaning in life: Regulatory versus reconstructive functions in the face of a hostile world. In P. T. P. Wong (Ed.), *The human quest for meaning: A handbook of psychological research and clinical applications* (2nd ed.). New York: Routledge.

Shrira, A., Palgi, Y., Ben-Ezra, M., & Shmotkin, D. (in press). Functioning and mortality of Holocaust survivors: Physical resilience and psychosocial vulnerabilities. *Journal of Loss and Trauma.*

Shrira, A., & Shmotkin, D. (2008). Can past keep life pleasant even for old-old trauma survivors? *Aging and Mental Health, 12*, 807–819.

Solomon, Z., & Prager, E. (1992). Elderly Israeli Holocaust survivors during the Persian Gulf War: A study of psychological distress. *American Journal of Psychiatry, 149*, 1707–1710.

Tedeschi, R. G., & Calhoun, L. G. (2004). Posttraumatic growth: Conceptual foundations and empirical evidence. *Psychological Inquiry, 15*, 1–18.

Terno, P., Barak, Y., Hadjez, J., Elizur, A., & Szor, H. (1998). Holocaust survivors hospitalized for life: The Israeli experience. *Comprehensive Psychiatry, 39*, 364–367.

Verma, S., Orengo, C. A., Maxwell, R., Kunik, M. E., Molinari, V. A., Vasterling, J. J., et al. (2001). Contribution of PTSD/POW history to behavioral disturbances in dementia. *International Journal of Geriatric Psychiatry, 16*, 356–360.

Vogt, L. J. K., Human, B. T., Van Hoesen, G. W., & Damasio, A. R. (1990). Pathological alterations in the amygdala in Alzheimer's disease. *Neuroscience, 37*, 377–385.

7

The Impact of Life Events on the Oldest Old

PETER MARTIN, GRACE DA ROSA, AND LEONARD W. POON

ABSTRACT

Very old adults have experienced many events in their lives, some many years ago, some more recently. This chapter highlights events perceived as the most important ones in the lives of centenarians. Domain-specific events are also considered in this chapter, including health events, family events, and work events. Finally, the impact of life events on the overall well-being of the oldest-old adults is considered. The evidence suggests that positive cumulative ("lifetime") events reduce levels of negative affect, whereas cumulative ("lifetime") negative events promote negative affect. When proximal events (i.e., those experienced in the past 20 years) and distal events (i.e., those experienced more than 20 years ago) are considered, proximal events are more likely to reduce levels of positive affect and enhance levels of negative affect. Distal events, on the other hand, are more likely to enhance overall feelings of positive affect.

INTRODUCTION

Individuals who have lived for a long time can look back on a life filled with many experiences. Formative life events can go back as far as early childhood, spread over the adolescent and adult years, and continue to occur very late in life. The effect of these events on physical and mental health, as well as on ways of coping and adaptation has been demonstrated in many studies. For example, a meta-analysis of 25 studies (Kraaij, Arensman, & Spinhoven, 2002) suggested that older adults in general may be at greater risk of depression because they have experienced an accumulation of many stressful events and daily hassles. This study concluded that life events and the total number of daily hassles strongly related to depression in older adults. Cumulative life events affect not only depressive symptom levels but also changes in depressive symptoms (Glass, Kasl, & Berkman, 1997).

The assessment of life events is particularly important when considering the oldest-old population. Centenarians and nonagenarians most likely have lost their spouses, they may have lost children and most of their contemporaries, they may have moved to long-term-care facilities, and they perhaps see their economic resources dwindle. By all accounts, these can be considered stressful experiences. In contrast, these oldest-old adults can also look back on many event-related accomplishments and achievements: work success and family formation; residential moves that brought more comfort; and historical changes, such as purchasing the first automobile, traveling, and accumulating personal wealth. All these events are part of the biography of older adults and reflect gains and losses experienced over the life span (Baltes & Baltes, 1993).

In this chapter, we outline the importance of life events in the lives of oldest-old adults. In addition, we assess what types of life events are commonly experienced, and we assess the impact of life events on the well-being of older adults. Throughout the chapter, we incorporate some words of wisdom from expert survivors, Mrs. Mary Sims Elliott (aged 105 at death) and Mrs. Ann Cooper (aged 107 at death).

PROXIMAL AND DISTAL LIFE EVENTS IN VERY OLD LIFE

As indicated in Martin et al. (Chapter 5), proximal and distal (lifetime) events are important for optimal well-being in later life. What type of life events have oldest-old adults experienced? Commonly, life-event research summarizes family events, work-related events, financial events, residence events, social events, and health-related experiences. Johnson and Troll (1996) discussed three major transitions for people in very late life: the end of marriage, living alone, and the loss of independence or the need for help.

Most of the major transitions or events in very late life appear to be negative in nature and refer to loss events. This suggests that the last years and decades of life pose some of the most stressful challenges any individual could experience. One might wonder whether centenarians and other late-life survivors continue to feel "happy in a hostile world," as Shmotkin (see Chapter 3) suggests for adults who have survived trauma. The hostile-world scenario, referred to as an "image of actual or potential threats to one's life or, more broadly, to one's physical and mental integrity" (see Chapter 3), broadly applies to older adults who survive into very old age: the older one becomes, the more likely one is challenged by stressful events, and changes in physical and mental well-being could be upsetting. Cohen-Mansfield's theory of shifting baseline (Chapter 4) can also help to understand why many very old individuals adapt seemingly well even if they have encountered increasing losses. Oldest-old adults have learned over many years that after grieving loss events they will return to a baseline level of well-being. The two proverbs "After rain comes sunshine" and "Dawn follows every night" reflect this form of adaptation. Mrs. Ann Cooper, an African American centenarian born in 1902, just one generation past slavery, has outlived her husband and three of her four children. When asked about her secret to longevity, she replied: "I don't know how it happened, but being cheerful had a lot to do with it. I've always been a happy person, a giggling person – a wide-mouthed person!"

In contrast, we also wonder whether life events lists typically used in the stress and coping literature (see Holmes & Rahe, 1967), disregard positive experiences occurring in very late life. Certainly, the hundredth birthday in itself is often considered a positive event. Very old people continue to make new friends and enjoy gaining members in their families through the birth of great-grandchildren and marriages of their grandchildren. At the end of life, older adults may still take special trips or be recognized in the community. Some write their own family biography or poetry (Poon, Clayton, & Martin, 1991). Mrs. Mary Sims Elliott, an accomplished artist, musician, and writer throughout her lifetime, published her autobiography, *My First One Hundred Years*, at the age of 105. Rarely are those events the focus of life event analyses.

Cappeliez, Beaupré, and Robitaille (2008) investigated the characteristics and impact of changes in trajectories among older adults (60–87 years) and concluded that health (of the adults and of their significant others) and family domains are considered main turning points by women. Work and family experiences were more common life transitions reported by men. Hardy, Concato, and Gill (2002) investigated life events that older adults identified as the most stressful experience and their perceptions of the consequences of them. Among those who reported a stressful life event, 42% identified the death of a family member or a friend; 23%, the illness of a family member or a friend; 18%, a personal illness; and 17%, a nonmedical event.

In our most recent centenarian study, we asked participants about "the most important event" in their lives. One hundred thirty-seven centenarians, participants of the Georgia Centenarian Study (Poon et al., 2007), were asked about these events. The specific question we posed was, "Could you tell me what the most important experience was that you had in your life?" The

TABLE 7.1. *Most important events*

Event	Frequency
Marriage	105
Children/birth of child	78
Work and retirement	24
Religion/relationship with God	22
Death of a family member	22
Education	20
Residential events	16
Family	15
Travel	14
Social events/activities	11
Health events	8
Surviving accidents	6
Hobbies	6
Historical events	4
Miscellaneous	14

participants were then probed for two additional important experiences. We collapsed these three questions and noted a total of 365 life experiences. Table 7.1 summarizes the results.

Most of the events listed in Table 7.1 can be considered expectable, normative life events. Marriage was listed most often as the most important life event for centenarians followed by events related to their children. Events related to work and retirement were the third most important events in the lives of centenarians, followed by religious or spiritual events.

Some centenarians, however, also mentioned unique events. Among them were survival of an automobile accident, falling in water and almost drowning, getting shot, singing in church, a husband's alcohol problem, playing music, and "washing walls of the tallest building." Mrs. Elliott's lifelong passion for music inspired her to serve as organist for her grandson's wedding at the age of 86. Only a few centenarians mentioned historical events. Among them were the Great Depression ("surviving the Hoover years") and a hurricane.

In the following section, we report our findings concerning the number of domain-specific experiences, beginning with health events. These events were part of our overall assessment of centenarians. Participants were asked whether they had experienced 23 specific events, how often these events had occurred, whether they were negative or positive experiences, and how old centenarians were at the time of the occurrence. Events included death of father, death of mother, parents' divorce or separation, marriage, divorce, death of spouse, death of siblings, death of a close friend, birth of children, loss of children, birth of grandchildren, loss of grandchildren, first job, change of employment, retirement, serious financial problems, residential change, institutionalization, major decrease of activities, hospitalization, injury or illness, worsening relationship to child, being burglarized, and institutionalization of spouse.

HEALTH EVENTS

Among the most important events experienced by oldest-old adults are health-related events. Aldwin, Sutton, Chiara, and Spiro (1996) reported that adults 75 years and older were more likely to report health problems than were their younger counterparts. Likewise, Moos, Schütte, Brennan, and Moos (2005) noted that health-related stressors had increased in a 10-year follow-up of older adults. Smith, Borchelt, Maier, and Jopp (2002) reported that chronic illness and functional impairments (e.g., vision, hearing, mobility, strength) limited the well-being of oldest-old adults compared to young-old adults.

A number of studies have indicated that centenarians almost always live with health-related impairments. A Japanese study, for example, reported that 95% of study participants had chronic diseases, including hypertension, heart disease, stroke, fractures, and cataracts (Takayama et al., 2007).

Much discussion in centenarian research has been conducted around the fact that some centenarians appear to "escape" health problems for their entire life. Evert, Lawler, Bogan, and Perls (2003), for example, reported that 32% of all male centenarians and 15% of all female centenarians had escaped a major health event. In contrast, 24% of all male centenarians and 43% of female centenarians had survived a health-related event. The remaining centenarians (i.e., 44% of male and 42% of female centenarians) had delayed the experience of a health event until at least age 80. For supercentenarians (those 110 years and older), D. C. Willcox et al. (2008) reported that none of their Okinawa supercentenarians had a history of cancer or diabetes, and other clinical diseases, if at all prevalent, did not occur until late in life. It seems as though not experiencing health events can facilitate survivorship.

Functional impairment can be considered a life stressor as well. The rate of impairment for common activities of daily living increases dramatically as individuals reach the 9th, 10th, and 11th decade of their lives (Martin, Poon, Kim, & Johnson, 1996). Among centenarians, one study estimated that only 20% of women and 44% of men were able to perform all

TABLE 7.2. *Family events in the lives of centenarians*

Family event	Frequency	Percentage	Mean age	Range
Marriage	126	93.3	27.59	16–84
Death of siblings	123	90.4	65.22	0–100
Death of spouse	117	87.3	70.71	25–100
Birth of children	102	74.5	27.57	18–49
Loss of children	44	32.1	71.51	21–100
Loss of grandchildren	24	17.8	84.24	45–99
Divorce	15	10.9	43.36	19–69
Parents' divorce	11	8.1	9.60	0–20
Institutionalization of spouse	11	8.1	78.80	33–96
Worsening relationship	8	5.9	68.50	16–98

activities of daily living independently (Andersen-Ranberg et al., 1999). These numbers correspond to a Japanese study reporting that about 24% of centenarians showed independence in activities of daily living (ADLs; Gondo et al., 2006). A recent study by Engberg, Christensen, Andersen-Ranberg, Vaupel, and Jeune (2008), however, noted that more recent cohorts of centenarians showed better self-reported ADLs compared to a previous cohort, even though the effect was found only for women and not for men. Mrs. Ann Cooper describes functional issues that prevent her from taking full advantage of her longevity: "I realize that I am older than I ever expected to be and I realize now why I can't do a lot of the things that I thought if I ever got back into my health I would do them. Now I can't do anything because I've got to hold onto something with both hands."

Regardless of study and prevalence, many very old people face challenging health events that compromise their daily living. Does this translate into an overall lower quality of life? Not necessarily, because centenarians (as any other age group) may have multiple levels of well-being (see Chapter 4) and draw a sense of quality of life from their distal and proximal experiences concerning family and work. When Mrs. Elliott's sight became limited, she said, "It was a catastrophe.... I didn't let it really get me down. I don't let things upset me.... I have the Lord with me, and if he wants to do something different, that's his way."

FAMILY AND WORK EVENTS

Family events are among the most predominant experiences in the lives of individuals. Table 7.2 summarizes the frequency of the most often occurring family events in our centenarian study. Table 7.2 suggests that marriage is the most often occurring family event in the lives of centenarians, followed by death of siblings and spouse. Birth of children is the fourth event most commonly experienced by centenarians. Mean age at marriage was about 28 years, and the birth of children on average occurred at 28 years. A few centenarians had seen their parents' divorce during their childhood, but for those who were divorced themselves (17 centenarians), the divorce did not occur on average until age 43. Events occurring relatively late in life included the death of a spouse (on average at age 73), the loss of children (on average at 72), and even the loss of grandchildren (on average at age 84). Finally, several centenarians experienced the institutionalization of a spouse (on average at age 79) and the temporary or permanent worsening of a relationship to a family member (on average at age 69). These events remind us that there are large individual differences for when these events occurred.

It is a bit disheartening that the death of children becomes more likely with advanced age (Johnson & Troll, 1996). One third of centenarians had lost a child and more than 16% a grandchild. These numbers correspond to the ones mentioned by Johnson and Troll (1996).

Longevity does not only make it likely that certain family events will occur; family events may also predict longevity. For example, the literature supports a direct relation between childbirth and longevity (McArdle et al., 2006). Müller, Chiou, Carey, and Wang (2002), for example, reported enhanced longevity for highly fertile women and women with late births. The relationship between late age at birth and longevity for women and increased longevity associated with a larger number of children was also reported by McArdle et al. (2006).

Divorce and widowhood are also related to longevity. For example, children of divorced parents face a one third greater mortality risk than individuals whose parents remained married at least until they reached age 21 (Friedman et al., 1995), and there is substantial evidence that marriage is correlated with longer life, whereas inconsistently married people are at higher risk for premature mortality (Friedman et al., 1995). Perhaps marriage provides opportunities that directly relate to longer life, but it is also possible that factors related to getting married and staying married contribute to the survivorship effect. In our study, a small but noticeable number of centenarians had experienced the divorce of parents early in life. Some participants had experienced their own divorce.

Work-related events are summarized in Table 7.3, which suggests that most centenarians had a first job at some point in their lives and that three fourths had changed employment at least once in their lifetime. More

TABLE 7.3. *Work, retirement, and financial events*

Work event	Frequency	Percent	Mean age	Range
First job	128	94.8	18.75	4–62
Change of employment	99	74.4	25.93	8–89
Retirement	83	62.9	67.10	32–96
Serious financial problems	25	18.8	31.00	7–74

than 60% had retired from a job, and almost 20% had a serious financial problem at some point in their lives. The average age at which centenarians had a first job was at 19, and a major change of employment occurred on average at age 26. Average retirement age was at 67, and for those reporting a serious financial problem, an average age of 31 was reported. It is noteworthy that no centenarian reported a serious financial problem later than age 74. As noted previously, there is tremendous variability among centenarians. Mrs. Cooper became a socialite after her husband established himself as a prominent dentist in Atlanta. Although Mrs. Cooper was not formally employed, she occupied her time with public work, serving for more than 50 years on the board of the Gate City Nursery Association and helping found the Girls Club for African-American Youth in Atlanta.

MISCELLANEOUS EVENTS

Additional miscellaneous events mentioned by centenarians are summarized in Table 7.4. This list of events indicates that some experiences are very common, such as residential change and decrease of activities, whereas others occurred to only a few centenarians. The mean age of when centenarians experienced a residential change was around 19 years, and 89% of centenarians experienced a decrease in activity around the age 90. Only 27% of centenarians experienced institutionalization, and the mean age for that

TABLE 7.4. *Miscellaneous events*

Events	Frequency	Percent	Mean age	Range
Residential change	131	99.2	19.20	0–99
Personal injury	120	89.6	84.10	0–105
Decrease in activity	116	89.9	90.13	55–101
Being burglarized	65	47.8	74.57	23–103
Hospitalization	133	97.8	76.11	10–105
Institutionalization	39	28.7	95.19	69–101

event was around the age of 96 years. These results are based on self-reports by centenarians who were not cognitively impaired. When including centenarians with cognitive impairments, the results for any of the events might be different.

LIFE EVENTS AND WELL-BEING

A number of studies show substantial evidence that there is a relationship between life stressors and the vulnerability to physical and psychological problems. A study by Cairney and Krause (2008) investigated the effects of life events exposure on age-related decline of mastery. This study concluded that exposure to life events was associated with lower levels of perceived control at any age. But the impact of stress was found to be greater among older adults. Loss of personal and social resources could be the reason older adults were more susceptible to the negative effects of stress (Cairney & Krause, 2008). There is evidence, however, of great individual differences, which suggests that a significant proportion of very old adults continue to maintain diverse social ties and actively engage in these relations (Chapter 12).

The relationship between life stressors and depression appears to be reciprocal. Moos et al. (2005) reported that more life stressors were associated with subsequent increases in depressive symptoms, in support of the social causation hypothesis. At the same time, more depressive symptoms were associated with subsequent increases in stressors, in support of the social selection or stress-generating hypothesis. Mrs. Elliott still speaks vividly about when her mother died. But now she is missing her daughter Josephine especially. Almost stubbornly, however, Mrs. Elliott doesn't let the pain intrude on her daily life. She copes with loss, the researchers believe, by talking about it with those who will listen. "I'm beginning to thaw," she says. "I was so stunned by her death. I'm just beginning to melt enough to let the natural tears come." And slowly, one tear spills from her eye and rolls down her cheek.

Recently experienced life events may not be as important in predicting well-being as is the inclusion of lifetime trauma. Krause (2004) provided evidence that greater lifetime trauma defined as sexual or physical abuse or premature loss of parents and participation in combat was associated with lower levels of life satisfaction. Emotional support, however, can offset the effects of trauma among oldest-old adults.

In our own studies of oldest-old adults, we reported that cumulative life stress was negatively associated with morale and mental health (Martin et al., 1992). In the same study, we reported that life stress also promoted active coping with health-related events in late life. Hensley, Martin, MacDonald, and Poon (2010) found that health events in childhood had a lasting impact on centenarians' loneliness.

To what extent do positive and negative experiences over one's lifetime affect overall well-being among centenarians? On the basis of our earlier work with centenarians, we reported that adverse lifetime events reduced both social and economic resources, and that those cumulative events also had a direct negative effect on mental health (Martin, 2002). MacDonald and Cho (see Chapter 9) found no effects of distal life events influencing perceived economic resources.

We analyzed data from the 137 participants of the Georgia Centenarian Study who provided information about the life events mentioned earlier in the chapter. On the basis of a conceptualization introduced by Ingersoll-Dayton, Morgan, and Antonucci (1997), we then tested alternative models of life events and positive and negative affect as measured by Bradburn's (1969) Affect Balance Scale. The models first suggest that positive events are positively associated with positive affect and negatively associated with negative affect (positivity hypothesis). The second alternative hypothesis suggests that negative events are negatively associated with positive affect and positively associated with negative affect (negativity hypothesis). The third hypothesis states that positive events affect only positive affect and negative events affect only negative affect (domain-specific hypothesis). Finally, the last hypothesis suggests that positive events both influence negative and positive affect and that negative events both influence positive and negative affect (combined-effect hypothesis). The model variations are summarized in Figure 7.1.

In our study, centenarians rated each event as a positive or negative event. Figure 7.2 summarizes the results. We found partial support for the positivity and negativity hypotheses. Positive events reduced the level of negative affect but were only marginally related to positive affect. Negative events were associated only with negative affect but not with positive affect. The stronger effects of negative events support the assumption that bad is stronger than good (Baumeister, Bratslavsky, Finkenauer, & Vohs, 2001), as discussed by Shrira and Shmotkin (Chapter 6). Even though our participants did not survive a traumatic event such as the Holocaust or other posttraumatic stress disorders (see Chapter 11), negative cumulative events appear to affect the subjective well-being among our survivors. An alternative explanation for the direct relationship between events and well-being may be a third variable, such as neuroticism, that is the cause of negative events and negative affect.

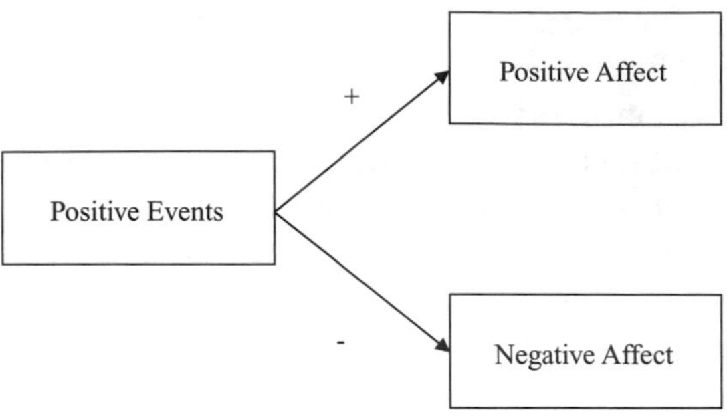

Positivity Hypothesis

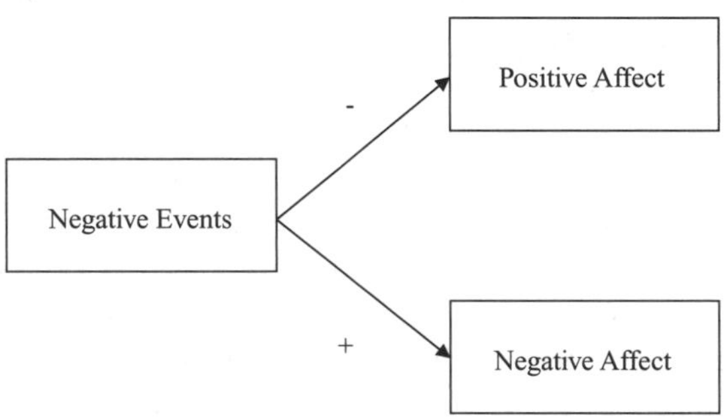

Negativity Hypothesis

FIGURE 7.1. Four Models of Life Events and Well-Being.

Because positive events were not significantly associated with positive affect (although there was a statistical trend, $\beta = .16$, $p = .07$), the third hypothesis received only weak support. The final hypothesis of a combined effect received the strongest support. Positive and negative events were

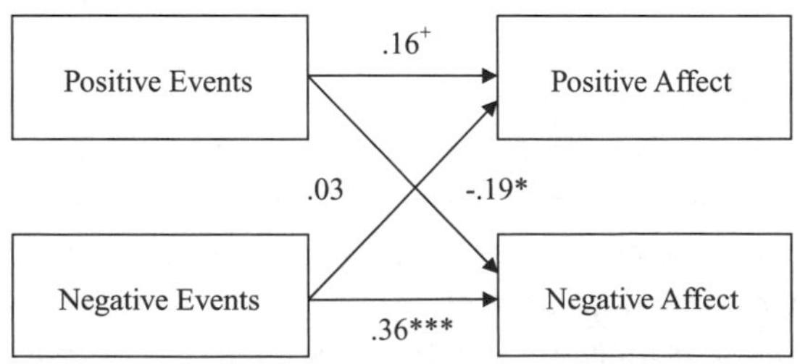

FIGURE 7.2. The Effect of Positive and Negative Events on Positive and Negative Affect ($^{*}p < 0.05$; $^{***}p < 0.001$).

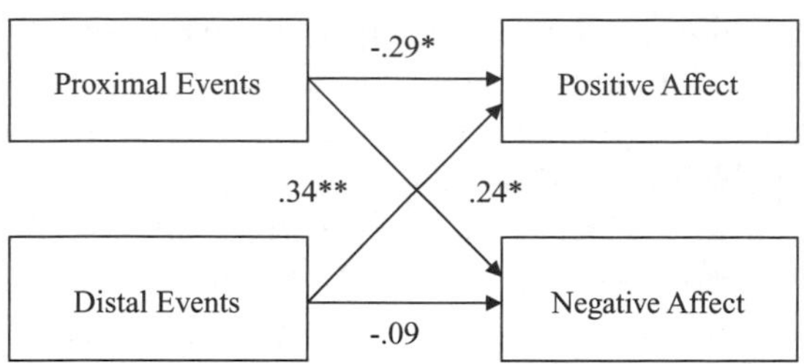

FIGURE 7.3. The Effect of Proximal and Distal Events on Positive and Negative Affect (*$p < 0.05$; **$p < 0.01$).

associated with negative affect, but less support was found for negative or positive events predicting positive affect. The results suggest that cumulative negative life events promote negative affect and that cumulative positive experiences reduce the level of negative affect in very late life.

Our final analysis step assessed the relationship between proximal and distal events and well-being. Distal events were defined as those experiences that had occurred at least 20 years before testing. Proximal events were defined as those events that had occurred during the past 20 years (i.e., during the old-old years). The combined model is depicted in Figure 7.3. The results suggest that proximal events (perhaps more often negative in nature) reduce the level of positive affect and enhance the level of negative affect, whereas distal events, regardless of whether they are positive or negative, enhance the level of positive affect. Taken together, these results suggest that more recent stressors are responsible for negative affect, whereas distal experiences enhance feelings of positive affect. The results provide evidence for the importance of proximal and distal events as outlined in the developmental adaptation model (Chapter 5).

IMPLICATIONS

What are the lives of older adults like and what experiences have shaped these individuals? When considering the well-being of older adults, it would be a mistake to look only at the current level of life satisfaction or subjective well-being. Much of the general outlook in late life may be determined by a long series of events, starting with lasting influences that date back to childhood experiences and finishing with recent events that affect old and very old adults. Events shaping one's life story may be traumatic, as noted by Shmotkin (see Chapter 3), thus leaving older adults in a hostile world with little additional time perspective, or events may be ordinary and pleasant to reminisce about, thus leading oldest-old adults to the conclusion that they have lived a full and meaningful life.

Centenarians are a special group of older adults who at first sight may be most vulnerable to stressful events. They typically have lost a spouse, perhaps even children. Their functional health has often declined. Financial resources may be running low, and a residential change to a long-term-care facility may be imminent. By all stress measures, these experiences would make centenarians most vulnerable to mental and physical health changes. In spite of these major life changes, many survivors do not seem to be depressed as a result of these traumatic events.

How can this be? A number of explanations may help understand the paradox that very old adults experience many losses, yet seem quite content and satisfied. First, perhaps it is simply the will to live that carries survivors on to the next challenge in life. Carmel (Chapter 16) pointed out that the will to live is a strong predictor of long-term survival. Second, perhaps long-lived individuals relish their special status as long-lived survivors. Third, positive family events may compensate for the loss of function and ability. Fourth, religious faith may keep many centenarians in relatively good spirits (see Chapter 13). Finally, continued support from family, friends, and the community may buffer the effect of stress on well-being (see Chapter 12). The strength taken from one's own past, from the will to live, and from ample social support may explain why so often survivors into very old age are seen as robust. This late-in-life robustness or resilience may be real rather than a false comparison of later life to midlife (Chapter 2).

Not all events have the same effect on well-being. Our analyses suggest that cumulative (lifetime) negative events have a direct impact on negative affect. Positive events, however, can reduce levels of negative affect. Furthermore, proximal and distal variables appear to have differential effects on well-being. Proximal stressors are more likely to increase levels of negative affect and reduce levels of positive affect. Distal events, in contrast, appear to enhance the level of positive affect.

Life events play an important role for the well-being of older adults. They cause concern, redirect development, and move adults at any age out of their regular comfort zone. As illustrated in Chapter 5, early experiences may increase individual and socioeconomic resources and they may also influence levels of affect. Events arguably play the most important role in causing developmental change, and though change is not always positive, change can serve as a new developmental challenge, even in very old age. Survivors into very late life celebrate age, in spite of physical decline. In that sense, oldest-old adults appear to overcome a false dichotomy of physical and mental state (Chapter 2). Perhaps moving toward the second century of life means overcoming the temptations of the ageless self to take pride in the aged self. Mrs. Elliott insists, "No matter how awful things get sometimes, there's a good side. I have a life filled with love because I have always tried to love others. It's been a wonderful saga, a wonderful life. Just marvelous!"

REFERENCES

Aldwin, C. M., Sutton, K. J., Chiara, G., & Spiro, A., III. (1996). Age differences in stress, coping, and appraisal: Findings from the Normative Aging Study. *Journal of Gerontology: Psychological Sciences, 51B*, P179–P188.

Andersen-Ranberg, K., Christensen, K., Jeune, B., Skytthe, A., Vasegaard, L., & Vaupel, J. W. (1999). Declining physical abilities with age: A cross-sectional study of older twins and centenarians in Denmark. *Age and Ageing, 28*, 373–377.

Baltes, P. B., & Baltes, M. (1993). Psychological perspectives on successful aging: The model of selective optimization with compensation. In P. B. Baltes & M. Baltes (Eds.), *Successful aging: Perspectives from the behavioral sciences* (pp. 1–34). Cambridge: Cambridge University Press.

Baumeister, R. F., Bratslavsky, E., Finkenauer, C., & Vohs, K. D. (2001). Bad is stronger than good. *Review of General Psychology, 5*, 323–370.

Bradburn, N. M. (1969). *The structure of psychological well-being.* Chicago: Aldine.

Cairney, J., & Krause, N. (2008). Negative life events and age-related decline in mastery: Are older adults more vulnerable to the control-eroding effect of stress? *Journal of Gerontology: Social Sciences, 63B*, S162–S170.

Cappeliez, P., Beaupré, M., & Robitaille, A. (2008). Characteristics and impact of life turning points for older adults. *Aging International, 32*, 54–64.

Engberg, H., Christensen, K., Andersen-Ranberg, K., Vaupel, J. W., & Jeune, B. (2008). Improving activities of daily living in Danish centenarians – but only in women: A comparative study of two birth cohorts born in 1895 and 1905. *Journal of Gerontology: Medical Sciences, 63A*, 1186–1192.

Evert, J., Lawler, E., Bogan, H., & Perls, T. (2003). Morbidity profiles of centenarians: Survivors, delayers, and escapers. *Journal of Gerontology: Medical Sciences, 58A*, 232–237.

Friedman, H. S., Tucker, J. S., Schwartz, J. E., Tomlinson-Keasey, C., Martin, L. R., Wingard, D. C., et al. (1995). Psychosocial and behavioral predictors of longevity: The aging and death of the "Termites." *American Psychologist, 50*, 69–78.

Glass, T. A., Kasl, S. V., & Berkman, L. F. (1997). Stressful life events and depressive symptoms among the elderly. *Journal of Aging and Health, 9*, 70–89.

Gondo, Y. Hirose, N., Arai, U. Y., Inagaki, H., Masui, Y., Yamamura, K., et al. (2006). Functional status of centenarians in Tokyo, Japan: Developing better phenotypes of exceptional longevity. *Journal of Gerontology: Medical Sciences, 61A*, 305–310.

Hardy, S. E., Concato, J., & Gill, T. M. (2002). Stressful life events among community-living older persons. *Journal of General Internal Medicine, 17*, 841–847.

Hensley, B., Martin, P., MacDonald, M., & Poon, L. W. (2010). Family history and adaptation among centenarians and octogenarians. *Gerontology, 56*, 83–87.

Holmes, T. H., & Rahe, R. H. (1967). The Social Readjustment Rating Scale. *Journal of Psychosomatic Research, 11*, 213–218.

Ingersoll-Dayton, B., Morgan, D., & Antonucci, T. (1997). The effects of positive and negative social exchanges on aging adults. *Journal of Gerontology: Social Sciences, 52B*, S190–S199.

Johnson, C. L., & Troll, L. (1996). Family structure and the timing of transition from 70 to 103 years of age. *Journal of Marriage and the Family, 58*, 178–187.

Kraaij, V., Arensman, E., & Spinhoven, P. (2002). Negative life events and depression in elderly persons: A meta-analysis. *Journal of Gerontology: Psychological Sciences, 57B*, P87–P94.

Krause, N. (2004). Lifetime trauma, emotional support, and life satisfaction among older adults. *Gerontologist, 44*, 615–623.

Martin, P. (2002). Individual and social resources predicting well-being and functioning in later years: Conceptual models, research, and practice. *Ageing International, 27*, 3–29.

Martin, P., Poon, L. W., Clayton, G. M., Lee, H. S., Fulks, J. S., & Johnson, M. A. (1992). Personality, life events, and coping in the oldest-old. *International Journal of Aging and Human Development, 34*, 19–30.

Martin, P., Poon, L. W., Kim, E., & Johnson, M. A. (1996). Social and psychological resources in the oldest old. *Experimental Aging Research, 22*, 121–139.

McArdle, P. F., Pollin, T. I., O'Connell, J. R., Sorkin, J. D., Agarwala, R., Schäffer, A. A., et al. (2006). Does having children extend life span? A genealogical study of parity and longevity in the Amish. *Journal of Gerontology: Biological Sciences and Medical Sciences, 61A*, 190–195.

Moos, R. H., Schütte, K. K., Brennan, P. L., & Moos, B. S. (2005). The interplay between life stressors and depressive symptoms among older adults. *Journal of Gerontology: Psychological Sciences, 60B*, P199–P206.

Müller, H.-G., Chiou, J.-M., Carey, J. R., & Wang, J.-L. (2002). Fertility and lifespan: Late children enhance female longevity. *Journal of Gerontology: Biological Sciences, 57A*, B202–B206.

Poon, L. W., Clayton, G. M., & Martin, P. (1991). In her own words: Cecilia Payne Grove, 1889–1990. *Generations, 15*, 67–68.

Poon, L. W., Jazwinski, S. M., Green, R. C., Woodard, J. L., Martin, P., Rodgers, W. L., et al. (2007). Methodological considerations in studying centenarians: Lessons learned from the Georgia Centenarian Studies. In L. W. Poon & T. T. Perls (Eds.), *Annual Review of Gerontology and Geriatrics: Vol. 27. Biopsychosocial approaches to longevity* (pp. 231–264). New York: Springer.

Smith, J., Borchelt, M., Maier, H., & Jopp, D. (2002). Health and well-being in the young old and oldest-old. *Journal of Social Issues, 58*, 715–732.

Takayama, M., Hirose, N., Arai, Y., Gondo, Y., Shimizu, K., Ebihara, Y., et al. (2007). Morbidity of Tokyo-area centenarians and its relationship to functional status. *Journal of Gerontology: Medical Sciences, 62A*, 774–782.

Willcox, D. C., Willcox, B. J., Wang, N.-C., He, Q., Rosenbaum, M., & Suzuki, M. (2008). Life at the extreme limit: Phenotypic characteristic of supercentenarians in Okinawa. *Journal of Gerontology: Medical Sciences, 63A*, M1201–1208.

8

Posttraumatic Stress Disorder and Its Treatment at Late Life

LEE HYER AND CATHERINE A. YEAGER

ABSTRACT

We discuss psychological trauma, notably Posttraumatic Stress Disorder (PTSD), at late life, paying special attention to what is distinctive at advanced ages. PTSD is fundamentally a diathesis-stress disorder. The role of aging as a mediating or moderating influence in the expression of psychological trauma is highlighted, especially as it applies to the oldest old. As a general position, older victims tend to be no more or less vulnerable or reactive to trauma than younger victims despite increasing stress rates at older ages. That said, older age presents differences in both the experience of life and in the integration of trauma into one's life narrative. In examining aging as it relates to trauma, we first discuss the biological sequelae of trauma in PTSD, as well as the effects of a biological core feature of aging: memory impairment and overall cognitive decline. PTSD is then considered as it relates to the understanding of the self in aging. Later, we elaborate on relevant PTSD models, especially the Developmental Adaptation and Changes of Adaptation models. We end with an examination of PTSD interventions originally developed for younger age groups and review the empirical support for older adults.

INTRODUCTION

Our understanding of the very long-term effects of trauma has grown rapidly in the past two decades or so, in great measure because of knowledge gained from studying war trauma, both combat veterans and victims of war. Before this, apart from a few notable exceptions, it was thought that any problems arising from war experience were either low in prevalence or would be relatively short lived. We can now confidently say that exposure to trauma when younger poses the significant possibility that the psychological consequences of that traumatic event(s) will affect one for the rest of his or her life. In contrast, although there is now a great deal of evidence relating to the longer-term sequelae associated with war experience, we are unsure of the mechanisms by which trauma effects persist over the life span. This occurs in part because the study of trauma in older people is methodologically difficult and theoretically complex. In the relatively recent past, the social sciences have addressed trauma and its effects from the clinical perspective, examining the "disorder" of the construct. The diagnosis, posttraumatic stress disorder (PTSD; American Psychiatric Association, 2000), has taken hold for almost three decades now. It is characterized by three clusters of signs and symptoms – reexperiencing the trauma, avoidance and/or numbing, and hyperarousal – all of which must manifest at least 1 month post-trauma to qualify for the diagnosis. The diathesis-stress model of PTSD is commonly accepted: extreme psychological trauma is necessary but not sufficient for PTSD to develop. As in other psychiatric disorders that have a kindling effect, older adults with multiple episodes of posttraumatic symptoms, including depression, become increasingly susceptible to repeat episodes. This kindling is underpinned by internal processes, such as ruminative thinking cycles, which are reactivated by minor stresses or dysphoric mood (Ma & Teasdale, 2004).

As such, the trauma response in aging individuals is complex. Although a spate of studies and meta-analyses on the assessment and treatment of PTSD have appeared in recent years, in truth, little data exist regarding the role of age as a mediating or moderating influence in the expression of trauma. We do not yet fully know the importance of a life lived, one's life perspective, and how the long view affects reactions to contemporary trauma or how past trauma is experienced through the lens of aging. We can, however, make some general statements about long-term adaptation to trauma. Prevalence data suggest low rates of full blown PTSD in older adults who have experienced early trauma, but there also is evidence that (a) subclinical or partial PTSD in this group is common and that (b) subclinical symptoms do cause suffering but are frequently overlooked or misconstrued by health-care providers (Summers & Hyer 1991; Weiss et al., 1992). Holocaust survivors appear to have adapted positively in the daily activities of life, whereas traumatized combat veterans tend to experience lower functional adaptation. Persistent symptoms in all war-trauma groups include sleep disruptions and nightmares, intrusive memories, mistrustfulness, avoidance of stress, and increased vulnerability to various types of age-associated retraumatization. Intergenerational research on trauma points to a similar prevalence in the development of PTSD in younger and older victims of a contemporary traumatic event (Hyer & Sohnle, 2001).

There are, however, differences in the manifestation of PTSD symptoms in older individuals, especially in the domains of emotion and cognition. For example, we now know that older adults in general are more vulnerable to source-monitoring problems and false-memory effects (e.g., Roediger & Gereaci, 2007) and are less likely to apply executive functioning strategies to disambiguate source misattributions (Mohlman, 2008). How do such deficits impact memory for past trauma or the processing of contemporary trauma? Developmentally, age-related declines no doubt play an important role in the ongoing processing of trauma, but can these presumed deficits be indicative of growth processes as well?

In this chapter, we attempt to clarify some important mediators and moderators in the manifestation of posttraumatic symptoms in aging. First, we discuss problems in the diagnosis of PTSD. We then consider the biological response in PTSD and the disorder's impact on health. We also consider how core features of aging, namely cognitive and memory decline, interact with trauma symptom expression, as well as the effects of current stress on aging in the context of PTSD. Third, we elaborate on the idea that PTSD is, above all, a disorder of self. Fourth, we present a model of PTSD in the context of aging (a companion to the Developmental Adaptation and Changes of Adaptation models described in Chapter 1). Here, we highlight key proximal and distal linkages to well-being in the face of a trauma history. Finally, at the chapter's close, we address therapy with the older adult who suffers from PTSD. Although clinical data regarding person-treatment interactions are lacking in this age group, we have apt models of treatment for younger age groups that, we believe, can reasonably be exported to provide empirically supported principles for older adults.

TRAUMA IDENTIFICATION AND DIAGNOSIS

Lifetime exposure to at least one major stressor event sums to 69% and is slightly higher (as expected) for older adults (Norris, 1992). Older victims tend to be no more vulnerable or reactive than younger individuals, despite increased rates of stressful events (Hyer & Sohnle, 2001). Current rates of PTSD in younger adults exposed to traumatic events range from about 5% to 11% (Kessler, Sonnega, Bromet, Hughes, & Nelson, 1995); rates are about the same for older adults (Hyer & Sohnle, 2001). In later life, PTSD has been linked to suicide, adverse reactions to medical events, smoking and alcohol abuse, more outpatient visits and primary-care use, and behavioral disturbances in long-term care (Cook, O'Donnell, Moltzen, Ruzek, & Sheikh, 2005; Davidson, Hughes, Blazer, & George, 1991; Frueh et al., 2003; Hyer & Stanger, 1997; Schnurr & Spiro, 1999; Spiro, Schnurr, & Aldwin, 1994).

Although there may be agreement on how to define a PTSD stressor, it is really a highly subjective experience, and traumatic stress is considered a complex blend of objectively identified experience and one's subjective interpretation of and response to it (Sutker, Uddo-Carne, & Allain, 1991). We also know that PTSD symptoms generally increase in a direct relationship to the intensity of the trauma, but this, too, is not always so. Furthermore, we know that the core phenomenology of a trauma involves an event plus the perception that the event is sudden and that there is little control over its outcome. Fundamentally, however, trauma is the loss of faith in one's safety and order in life *and* the feeling of helplessness. Posttrauma variables are equally important in determining emerging psychopathology, especially the presence of other stressors (e.g., ill health, social losses, financial hardship) and the degree of social support. Once the symptom complex emerges, the disorder can become chronic and highly resistant to change. Finally, just as trauma may result in PTSD symptoms, the associated problems with this diagnosis are not always the result of the trauma.

Research is reasonably confirmatory that people are strongly affected even when experiencing "normal" distress, like illness, divorce, bereavement, or job loss. In fact, older adults who become depressed for the first time have likely experienced just such a stressor 60% of the time. And older adults develop symptoms to life's vicissitudes at rates similar to those who undergo traumatic stress (Gold, Marx, Soler-Baillo, & Sloan, 2005). In this sense, the impact of a distressing event is similar whether the (trauma) stressor is big or small. Small traumas can appear negligible on the outside, as they are the small slights that result in a perception (of the event) and a response (coping). But this slight, a small humiliation perhaps, can result in a reaction and lasting effect that is puzzling when seen from afar. If one is humiliated, then a whole series of internal and external actions occur to handle this. This may be perceived as being unloved, abandoned, a failure. It means further that this event and all like it can be translated into a prototype of danger. The person reacts with feeling, cognition, and/or physiological modes. The past is repeated in the present. The person develops methods of operation to handle this – overly detached, excessively dependent, aggressive, or ambivalent. These become staple responses in the person's life. They become, in fact, the personality. For most, these are occult markers of the person, unearthed only at rare times or in therapy. These coping patterns, however, are epigenetic – a stress sensitization process where a recurrence of the problem is asserted after some exacerbation that triggers the initial episode. Over time, kindling occurs (Post, 1992), and even minor perturbations become irritating enough to initiate a recurrence of PTSD symptoms (see Monroe & Harkness, 2005).

All that said, PTSD is conceptually less complicated than the diagnostic criteria listed in the *Diagnostic and Statistical Manual of Mental Disorders* (e.g., DSM-IV-TR; American Psychiatric Association, 2000). A study by Broman-Fulks et al. (2006) articulated this. The authors applied taxometric analyses to PTSD in two samples: a large sample of women and a group of adolescents. Results provided evidence for a dimensional PTSD solution across samples and statistical procedures. This contrasts with earlier research (e.g., Kessler et al., 1995) suggesting that age may moderate the frequency and intensity of PTSD symptoms and that adolescents especially may exhibit symptom patterns different from those of children and adults. Conceptually, the good news is that human reactions to extreme stressors are relatively stable across the life span; the bad news is that PTSD is best construed as a spectrum disorder, the manifestation of which is modulated by person-specific factors. These factors are important in predicting the intensity and duration of an individual's trauma reactions and therefore should be addressed uniquely in assessment and therapy. Trauma can evoke heterogeneity of psychological symptoms. In fact, Herman (1992) suggested that responses to trauma are best understood as a spectrum of conditions rather than as a single disorder. Those in the field of geropsychology must become cognizant that, although the prevalence of full diagnostic criteria for PTSD is relatively low in older adults, there are other long-term psychological and medical effects of traumatic exposure that require assessment and treatment.

Despite the DSM, the question "what is trauma?" is undefined in any real sense. Perhaps the existing model of PTSD is not well anchored because it does not take into account the vulnerabilities of a given developmental stage when psychological trauma is encountered. Pynoos et al. (1995) raise this issue:

> The diagnosis of PTSD is being construed as a type of Platonic form; as a result, the intimate relationship of these symptoms to a particular and complex experience of an individual child is in danger of being lost. We speak of intrusive images as if they are reproductions of the original photograph negatives of a gruesome scene. In so doing we are missing the clinical and experiential picture of the child's mind. Of special

importance is that these many memory markers also indicate injury to a developmental expectation that have serious developmental consequences. (p. 98)

HEALTH, BIOLOGY, AND TRAUMA

Two neuroendocrine stress response systems operate in relation to trauma exposure. The first is the immediate biological reaction to the traumatic event, which is driven by the adrenergic (catecholamine) system and produces increased blood flow, heart rate, heart-rate variability, blood pressure, and glucose availability to muscles to enable fight or flight in response to the threatening situation. The second neuroendocrine system, modulated by the hypothalamic-pituitary-adrenal (HPA) axis, involves the production of corticosteroids in response to stress. Indeed, circulating cortisol levels can provide a window onto the ongoing impact of trauma on the brain and body. There have been numerous studies during the past 10 years examining trauma's impact on these two systems. In the best known of those studies, Yehuda, Morris, Labinsky, Zemelman, and Schmeidler (2007) investigated the longitudinal course of mean 24-hour urinary cortisol excretion in PTSD. The authors evaluated 24-hour cortisol excretion in 28 Holocaust survivors 10 years after obtaining an initial estimate. Cortisol levels increased in participants whose PTSD had remitted ($n = 3$) but diminished in participants who developed PTSD during the study period ($n = 3$) or whose PTSD status did not change over time (PTSD+: $n = 14$, PTSD–: $n = 8$). Cortisol levels at Time 1 predicted change in diagnostic status better than psychological variables, including exposure to other traumatic events between assessments. The authors concluded that cortisol levels are affected by change in PTSD status and age. Over time, cortisol levels become lower and perpetuate the PTSD process; thus, the consequences of low cortisol at some point in the aftermath of a trauma are a problem. In summary, trauma disregulates these neurophysiologic processes. This appears to be the case with immune and inflammatory responses as well (Yehuda, Golier, & Kaufman, 2005).

Psychophysiological responses to a trauma continue over time, apparently on all exposed individuals, whether or not they develop post-trauma symptoms. Pole et al. (2007), for example, performed an emotion-modulated startle experiment with different levels of threat regarding a forthcoming finger shock. They measured physiological activation and self-reported psychological activation in two groups of community-dwelling adults, with and without trauma histories. Compared to the no-trauma group, the trauma group (childhood trauma) had fewer positive emotions, more negative emotions, greater eye-blink response, and greater skin conductance. These were adults without PTSD. Such results support the idea that prolonged psychophysiological changes do occur after traumatic stress and therefore confer risk for mood and anxiety disorders many years after the trauma was in play.

The genetic makeup of some individuals appears to render them more vulnerable than others to develop PTSD, anxiety, and depressive symptoms. A unique study (Goenjian et al., 2008) that tracked individuals from 12 multigenerational families exposed to a massive earthquake in Armenia in 1988 found that 41% of the variation of PTSD symptoms was due to genetic factors. Furthermore, 61% of the variation of depressive symptoms and 66% of anxiety symptoms in the cohort also were attributable to genetics. The investigators also noted that the high heritability rates for anxiety (61%) and depressive symptoms (66%) in adjusted analyses extend earlier findings for these phenotypes. In addition to showing that the genetic makeup of some individuals makes them more vulnerable to PTSD, anxiety, and depression, the authors noted that their data also indicate that a substantial portion of genetic vulnerabilities among the three phenotypes are shared and that these genetic factors may be a more important cause of comorbidity than environmental factors. The study's findings also suggest that PTSD, anxiety, and depression belong to the same diagnostic spectrum of disorders.

Several studies have shown that a variety of health problems, disability, and suicidal ideation are more common in men and women with PTSD than in their peers without PTSD. Sareen et al. (2007) surveyed 36,984 community-dwelling individuals, of which 478 had PTSD (1%). Although the prevalence of the disorder was exceedingly low in this sample, PTSD was associated with significantly greater odds of asthma, chronic obstructive pulmonary disorder, chronic fatigue syndrome, arthritis, fibromyalgia, migraines, cancer, cardiovascular disease, gastrointestinal disorders, and pain disorders. Individuals with PTSD also had elevated levels of distress and a much greater prevalence of mood and/or anxiety disorders, alcohol or drug problems, suicide attempts, and more disability days because of mental illness. Similarly, Rauch, Morales, Zubritsky, Knott, and Oslin (2006) noted that, in their sample, PTSD and depression were related to negative health behaviors (smoking, alcohol use) and perceptions in older adults. Krause, Shaw, and Cairney (2004) assessed whether lifetime trauma exposure moderated the relationship between health and aging. Data from their nationwide survey of people ages 65 years and older ($N = 1518$) showed that the effects of trauma over a lifetime were related to worse health in late life. Individuals at ages 65–74 years were at greatest risk for health declines, whereas the oldest old (85+) were at greatest risk for functional declines. The authors also found that trauma exposure specifically between the ages of 18–31 years had the greatest negative impact on health status at old age. A path analysis by Schnurr and Spiro (1999) supports the previous findings in that it revealed PTSD to be a strong predictor of poor health outcomes in old age, over and above negative health behaviors such as smoking and alcohol consumption.

WORKING MEMORY IN AGING AND TRAUMA

It is now well documented that neuropsychological deficits can occur in PTSD regardless of age (Bremner, 2002). Reviews on the structural and functional anatomy of PTSD (e.g., Bremner, 2002; Elzinga & Bremner, 2002; Hull, 2002) note compromised neurocognitive functioning, which is thought to impede a person's ability to cope with future traumatic stressors (see Brewin, Andrews, & Valentine, 2000). On the one hand, there appears to be a cognitive preferential bias or hypervigilance associated with the presentation of threat-related stimuli in individuals with PTSD (see Hyer & Sohnle, 2001). On the other hand, cognitive deficits in several domains are due to PTSD: memory (Bremner, Southwick, Johnson, Yehuda, & Charney, 1993; Elzinga & Bremner, 2002; Sutker, Uddo-Carne, & Allain, 1991; Vasterling, Brailey, Constans, Borges, & Sutker, 1997), attention (Vasterling et al., 2002), executive functioning (Beckham, Crawford, & Feldman, 1998), and global intellectual functioning (Sutker, Uddo-Carne, & Allain, 1991; Vasterling et al., 2002). The coexistence of neuropsychological impairment and PTSD symptoms suggests a poorer prognosis and is likely reflective of problems regarding chronicity of PTSD symptoms (Vasterling & Braily, 2005), again regardless of age.

Cognitive decline occurs in aging, and especially in older adults with PTSD. Memory is composed of distinct systems, the content of which alters throughout life. Understanding memory processes, however, is anything but simple. Working memory (WM), the soul of a person's cognition, has been modeled by Baddeley (2000), Tulving (1995), Conway (2001), Schacter (1996), and more recently by Eustache and Desgranges (2008). Whether WM ultimately consists of few or many units, it is necessary for all complex tasks – learning, comprehension, and reasoning – as well as for integrating episodic and semantic memory systems independently. What is known to date is that WM has a limited capacity and naturally degrades with age. As one example, Yehuda et al. (2005) administered the California Verbal Learning Test (CVLT) to examine learning and memory performance in aging combat veterans with ($n = 30$) and without ($n = 20$) PTSD, and in veterans unexposed to combat ($n = 15$). After correcting for vocabulary and block-design performances on the Wechsler Adult Intelligence Scale, combat veterans with PTSD showed a variety of memory impairments compared with non-exposed veterans, but only long-delay free recall consistently discriminated the PTSD group from combat-exposed subjects without PTSD. Moreover, differences in total learning scores also were associated with PTSD after controlling for substance abuse and depression. Indeed, impairments in total learning were similar to what has been observed in Holocaust survivors (see Yehuda et al., 2007). Two contrast measures, proactive interference and recognition hits, also distinguished combat from noncombat veterans, and this was hypothesized to be related to trauma exposure. Most noteworthy for the aging brain, however, was the finding that increased severity of rapid forgetting appears to be a specific alteration in older combat veterans, which likely reflects aspects of both combat exposure and aging. This is working memory.

The neuropsychological status of older trauma victims has been examined for the past decade at least. Several investigators have suggested that severe or prolonged trauma, or a history of such exposure, places the aging individual at increased risk for cognitive decline or dementia (Cook, Ruzek, & Cassedy, 2003). Most older adults, unlike younger groups, develop deficits in binding and retrieval access to recollective information. This deficit demands additional executive functioning strategies to overcome recall deficits. Given the role of executive functioning in aiding memory, then, older adults with poorer frontal functioning are at heightened risk of cognitive failures and memory illusions in everyday acts. Kane, Conway, Miura, and Colflesh (2007) showed that adults with poorer working memories had a difficult time concentrating on effortful tasks during a normal week of activities. This occurred throughout the day and was a problem only for more challenging tasks. It is a good bet that this faulty cognitive process also affects how traumatic experiences are recollected, partially and incompletely. For trauma victims, this can translate into a rekindling of trauma experiences (see Hyer & Sohnle, 2001).

The unfolding of cognitive decline is not trivial. Grossman, Levin, Katzen, and Lechner (2004) presented a case study of two Holocaust survivors who appeared to have adapted well post-trauma but to have developed severe PTSD symptomatology following the onset of neurologic illness in later life. Neuropsychological evaluations revealed cognitive problems related to memory, executive functioning, and attention. Such case studies demonstrate the need for systematic research to better elucidate the relationship among aging, degenerative disease, and PTSD symptoms in elderly trauma survivors.

PTSD AND COPING IN LATER LIFE

At its root, PTSD is an anxiety disorder, and anxiety disorders are associated with increased disability, diminished well-being, and excessive and inappropriate use of medical services at older ages (Wetherell, Gatz, & Craske, 2003). As stated previously, PTSD is characterized by signs and symptoms of reexperiencing, avoidance and/or numbing, and hyperarousal. A recent meta-analysis identified the following variables as the best predictors of the development of PTSD post-trauma: trauma history, prior psychological maladjustment, family history of psychopathology, perceived life threat during the event, lack of social support, peritraumatic emotional response, and peritraumatic dissociation (Ozer, Best, Lipsey, & Weiss, 2003). Ehring, Ehlers, and Glucksman (2008) also noted that cognitive predictors of PTSD are important. These involved the nature of the trauma memory and problematic appraisals of the trauma and/or its aftermath.

At its base, stress is experienced when there is an inadequate match between the person's coping ability and environmental demands (whether exogenous or endogenous). Posttraumatic stress disorder further alters perception, thereby heightening distress. As Seyle (1974) noted, "It is not what happens that counts: It is how you take it" (p. 258). Individuals suffering from PTSD have a lower threshold for perceiving situations as threatening; the perception of threat activates a biologically predisposed survival mode that includes fear and anger (Chemtob, Novaco, Hamada, Gross, & Smith, 1997). Riggs, Dancu, Gershuny, Greenberg, and Foa (1992) hypothesized that individuals with PTSD are motivated to avoid feelings of fear and anger. Mausbach et al. (2006) additionally showed that avoidant coping was a key mediator in the association between problem behaviors and depression among older adults. In addition, many older individuals with PTSD ruminate about the traumatic event and how it could have been prevented (Ehlers, Mayou, & Bryant, 1998), often lowering the threshold for negative affect and reactive anger (Nolen-Hoeksema & Morrow, 1991).

The initial brunt of the PTSD symptoms may be predictive of later problems. Zatzick et al. (2002), for example, assessed 101 randomly selected hospitalized survivors of vehicular accidents or assaults and then assessed them 1, 4 and 12 months after inpatient care. At the hospital, 73% screened positive for high levels of distress; at 1, 4, and 12 months, the initial reported symptom levels were the most parsimonious predictors of persistent symptoms over the course of a year. Also, greater levels of postinjury emotional distress and physical pain were associated with increased risk of symptoms indicative of a PTSD diagnosis. Notably, approximately 70% of trauma survivors who had acute stress disorder (ASD; American Psychiatric Association, 2000), a condition that is ostensibly PTSD, which emerges in the first month after exposure, go on to develop chronic PTSD. However, approximately 40% of individuals who have chronic PTSD do not initially show ASD (e.g., Bryant, 2004). In the current Iraq and Afghanistan conflicts, there is an 18% prevalence rate of PTSD (Hoge et al., 2004), and although this is alarmingly high (this study suggests that approximately 2 of every 10 soldiers are very significantly impaired), they evaluated PTSD cross-sectionally, while soldiers were still on active duty. We can glean from these kinds of findings on maladaptive reactions to trauma that the symptom trajectory is fluid and that, more likely than not, the PTSD prevalence rate will change over time. Ultimately, many factors moderate one's response to trauma over the life course; some will maintain a chronic level of PTSD symptoms and functional impairment, some will recover their preexposure level of homeostasis, and some will grow and mature from their experiences.

Factors that initiate distress-related psychopathology are generally not the same as those that maintain its persistence. At least six studies of trauma survivors support the finding that early reexperience of symptoms significantly predicts later PTSD, whereas early avoidance does not (see Mineka & Zinbarg, 2006). However, over time, avoidance does seem to maintain the disorder. Perceptions of uncontrollability and unpredictability also play a significant role in the development and course of PTSD. The traumatic event is thought to be poorly elaborated and poorly integrated into the autobiographical memory base. Poor elaboration or integration can lead to easy triggering and ineffective inhibition of memories that lack awareness of the self-in-the-past. The persisting trauma memory, then, is thought to be the result of problematic cognitive processing during the trauma, especially data-driven processing (i.e., sensory data processing absent the meaning of the situation), and a lack of self-referential processing (insufficient linking of the event to the self), these latter two overlapping with dissociation (Halligan, Michael, Clark, & Ehlers, 2003). There also are data to suggest that certain cognitive factors significantly improve the prediction of PTSD symptom severity, factors that are common in aging (Halligan et al., 2003). Furthermore, other psychological disorders are known to cohabit with PTSD or exist in place of it: depression, substance abuse, and other anxiety disorders; and those can effectively reactivate PTSD symptoms when vulnerable individuals encounter stressful situations or experience a decline in mood (Ehring et al., 2008).

UNDERSTANDING SELF AND TRAUMA

Blazer (2003) posits a dilemma: What allows us to understand how an 85-year-old man with an arthritic arm, declining energy, and loneliness can answer the question, "How are you feeling today?" He actually may be living a full and meaningful life in spite of pain, fatigue, and isolation. Yet if he parrots how most of us respond in 21st-century America, he is likely to say, "Great, just great!" Feeling great has almost become the expected response to inquiries about how we are feeling or doing. In fact, most older adults do feel good about life but not great. Similarly, when someone states that they would not change anything in their life, this could be construed as a positive and good perspective on life, as a lack of ego complexity, as denial, or as a lack of sophistication (Loevinger, 1976). What all of this says is that the intermingling of the nuanced perspective provided by the constructs of ego development and well-being change the meaning and very quality of happiness (King & Hicks, 2007). Happiness in an individual who is high in ego development differs qualitatively from that of one whose ego development is low. Such happiness may be based on a realistic perception of one's life and, as such, may be more resilient in the face of life's difficulties. Happiness is, then, more bittersweet, involving the recognition of loss and the fragility of human intention. It is also, therefore, problematic to find accurate representations of well-being in aging. Posttraumatic stress disorder and its sequelae at late life are no less intricate given the ways in which the self unfolds in old age. Understanding PTSD at later life, then, may be a problem.

As mentioned earlier, most models of trauma hypothesize that the experience of the event violates an individual's basic sense of self and of the world (Herman, 1992). At some point, meaning making or cognitive processing reconstructs those beliefs, thus resulting in maladaptation (e.g., PTSD) or growth (Park & Helgeson, 2006). Memory is encoded in excitatory, distressing, and state-dependent ways; the original perceptions also can continue to be triggered by a variety of internal and external stimuli, thus resulting in inappropriate emotional, cognitive, and behavioral reactions, as well as in overt psychiatric symptoms. In PTSD, aberrantly stored memories are understood to lay a foundation for future maladaptive responses, because perceptions of current situations are automatically linked through associative memory networks with the original trauma. Negative behaviors and even negative personality characteristics evolve from this aberrantly stored information. At the same time, a belief (e.g., "I am no good") is not accepted so much as a cause of the present problem as an effect of an unprocessed earlier experience containing intense negative affect and dysfunctional perspective. Preexisting attitudes and personality also influence the formation of new negative beliefs. Another way of saying this is that attitudes, emotions, and beliefs have to be viewed not strictly as reactions to past events but as manifestations of the physiologically stored perceptions linked in memory that then direct the formation of new dysfunctional beliefs. Knowing this can influence how therapy with the older adult is construed, as in whether changes in toxic memories occur as a result of habituation and extinction (Foa & Kozak, 1986) or because of adaptive information processing (Solomon & Shapiro, 2008).

How can the processes involved in finding meaning in life in the context PTSD be best understood? One way is related to aging research; it involves the struggle for change, best explained by the dual process model of coping (Brandtstädter & Rothermund, 2002). It bases self-regulation on two developmental processes: the offensive process of assimilation and the defensive process of accommodation (see Brandtstädter, 1999). Assimilation helps individuals manage life experiences in ways that are beneficial to the self through coping efforts that involve direct action, problem solving, and active modification of the environment. In contrast, accommodation shapes the self to correspond to the realities of life experience and is often invoked when assimilation fails. Parsing this further, Heckhausen and Schulz (1995) articulate the processes through which individuals strive to maximize control over the external world. One process is termed primary control, which is directed at the external world. Secondary control refers to an internal process evoked to minimize developmental losses and increase one's primary control. With age, the presence of secondary control increases.

Another way of understanding this involves the drive for well-being. Shmotkin (2005) aptly describes well-being and the needs of older adults: "The well-being of the older adult is best discovered in the pursuit of happiness in a hostile world" (p. 295). Shmotkin (2005) argues that subjective well-being (SWB) stands as an agentic system, the principal role of which is to establish a favorable psychological environment, conceived of as a positive state of mind that allows an individual to maintain ongoing activity with minimal disruption by adverse contingencies. Complementary to SWB in Shmotkin's model is the hostile-world scenario (HWS), which refers to an image of actual or potential threats to one's life or, more broadly, to one's physical and mental integrity. The HWS is nourished by beliefs about catastrophes and inflictions, such as accidents, violence, natural disasters, wars, illness, aging, and death. The SWB and HWS regulate each other to fulfill respective tasks of promoting pleasantness and accomplishment while ensuring safety and protection. A potent homeostatic mechanism in all this is adaptation, by which people habituate to even the most adverse experiences and ultimately return to their original SWB baseline (Diener, Lucas, & Scollon, 2006).

Shmotkin's (2005) model also draws attention to the restrictions that old age imposes on the regulatory function of SWB and on the complexity involved in HWS in conditions that combine past trauma with present frailty and impending death. Elaborating, Shmotkin advocates for four arenas regarding subjective well-being. The experiential occurs in the private context of one's introspection and is the person's own account of his or her current degree of well-being. The declarative occurs in the public face, which can become rather complex depending on context and motivation. The differential occurs in the synchronic context of relations among concurrent representations of the self (i.e., a dynamic formation of well-being based on self-constructs as positive and negative affect, life satisfaction, and time orientation). Finally, the narrative relates to the temporal pattern of well-being that characterizes the person's life story. In essence, Shmotkin's (2005) model transforms a real person (personality and all) into a dynamic interplay of well-being elements that are mostly stable and that assist in the organization of the biographical and external influences of the person.

The search for meaning at late life in the context of trauma is more understandable with this as background. However, at later life, it is a double-edged sword. On the negative side, older adults who have trauma histories or who are depressed develop an overgeneralized memory (OGM) bias, seeing past events as especially positive (Williams et al., 2007). This is construed as a way to regulate negative affect (affect-regulation hypothesis) after stressful events. This is also thought to be a harbinger of an increased vulnerability to PTSD or depression (Van Minnen, Wessel, Verhaak, & Smeenk, 2005). Relatedly, trauma survivors with PTSD show less specific autobiographical memory retrieval than those without PTSD (Schönfeld & Ehlers, 2006). This effect is reasonably specific to PTSD and depression. Rumination and positive abstract tendencies do not allow for a correction of negative self-schemas, as they provide a means of ready avoidance.

On the positive side, Carstensen, Fung, and Charles (2003) contend that selective information processing plays a constructive role in well-being at late life. When life expectancy is considered finite, older adults shift their goals to regulating emotional states to improve mood and optimize well-being. They essentially avoid negative memories simply as a function of aging. This also has been labeled the "positivity bias," which may influence cognitive load (Mather & Knight, 2005).

In general, older adults experience less choice than younger adults (Reed, Mikels, & Simon, 2008); they suffer from considerable proactive interference with memories (Emery, Hale, & Myerson, 2008); they monitor reality less well than younger adults (McDaniel, Lyle, Butler, & Dornburg, 2008); and broadly, they have memory and speed-of-processing problems in relation to younger adults. As a result, older adults, whether stressed or not, tend to compensate by viewing past events as general and positive.

Interestingly, trauma also has been construed as benefit finding in several areas: from medical problems such as cancer (Antoni et al., 2001), HIV (Milam, 2006), influenzas (Cheng, Wong, & Tsang, 2006), and motor vehicle accidents (Rabe, Zöllner, Maercker, & Karl, 2006) to psychiatric disorders (Helgeson, Reynolds, & Tomich, 2006). Variables that mediate self-views involve constructs such as optimism, positive reframing, religious coping (Lechner, Carver, Antoni, Weaver, & Phillips, 2006), social support, and changes in life priorities (Tedeschi & Calhoun, 1995), ability to forgive (McCullough, Root, & Cohen, 2006), ability to preserve resources (Hobfall et al., 2006), as well as gender and ethnicity (see Helgeson et al., 2006). Recently, Bonanno (2004) argued that resilience is more common after trauma than not. Some variables related to resilience include hardiness (being committed to finding meaningful purpose in life), self-enhancement (excessive positive bias), repressive coping, and positive emotion and laughter.

Clearly, the trauma response at late life is complex. The internal processes of an older adult, compromised by aging, can become even more deficient as a result of trauma and its costs. The internal path to accommodation is, therefore, indirect and circuitous. We now explore one more minefield: cognition.

MEMORY AND A MODEL OF PTSD

The conventional view is that people develop PTSD in the wake of exposure to a traumatic event as the imprint of that trauma comes to dominate how they organize their perceptions and experience of the world (Van der Kolk, 2002). From a biological perspective, it is argued that, when trauma occurs, a distinct neural circuit develops that is later triggered by minimal imaginal or sensory processes, thereby creating the perception that the traumatic event is occurring again. Symptoms of PTSD emerge from a complex relationship between brain and immune and nervous systems that is mediated through a disregulated HPA axis. At some point, the sheer act of imagination, powered by cognition (or by a simple external stimulus such as a telephone ringing), wreaks havoc on day-to-day behavior. The trauma, remaining resident in memory, is triggered by subsequent experiences (e.g., sounds, textures, stress) and leads to a restatement, recovery, or rapid reacquisition.

Several theories of trauma-related memory posit that memories are stuck in intermediate storage and are not properly assimilated, thereby bringing about PTSD (see Hyer & Sohnle, 2001). Assimilation into long-term memory is prevented by automatic thoughts that are fear-based or incongruent with extant metacognitions; the intermediate memory system becomes blocked as a result. Conceptually, this system is thought to operate in a continuous feedback loop in implicit memory (i.e., out of conscious awareness), and a trauma-related fault in the system guarantees the periodic activation of frightening recollections. The solution to this aversive feedback process involves a secondary process: going through a narrative review at moderate levels of arousal to settle the trauma, desensitize it, and consolidate it into long-term memory. In effect, in PTSD, trauma memories are not assimilated into prior schemas, are not part of explicit memory, and are not made into a self-narrative and consolidated in the cortex. Rather, its inadvertent storage in implicit memory produces a reexperiencing of the trauma seemingly out of the blue, with emotions, bodily sensations, and fight-flight-freeze cognitions and behaviors that are not sensed as self-in-the-past.

The differential activation model of cognitive reactivity (Resick, 2003) suggests that PTSD symptoms arise as a feature of negative thinking during posttrauma depressive episodes. At such times, an association is formed between self-states focused on PTSD symptoms, such that PTSD states, however caused, activate specific negative patterns of thinking that trigger PTSD reactions. In this way, reexperiencing, avoidance, and hyperarousal become part of a configuration of associations, actions, and feedback loops in the cognitive system. As such, they become a rehearsal pool activated with each subsequent PTSD episode similar to pairings of conditioned stimulus and conditioned response in animal conditioning (Bouton, 2002). The problem, then, is exacerbated not while in a resting state but in a pattern of thinking or behaving that is activated by a cue. Furthermore, if the system is already primed by a negative mood, the PTSD victim will react. We also know that this state-dependent process becomes reified organically, as there is a reversion to lower brain functioning as the stress level increases, cognition falters, and coping becomes stuck in primitive modes (McCranie & Hyer, 2000). In summary, trauma memories are encoded uniquely, thus enabling emotional and perceptual patterns as well as coping behaviors to become rigid.

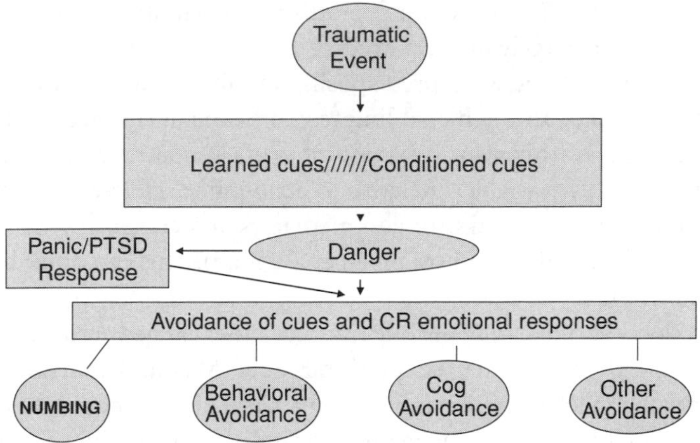

FIGURE 8.1. PTSD Model for Older Adults.

Figure 8.1 presents a simple model of the immediate development of ASD and PTSD symptoms. The model is based on a learning model in which the individual experiences a trauma, undergoes conditioning with trauma cues, encodes the experiences as "danger," and develops a panic or fight-flight-freeze response. The conditioned responses, in turn, give way to a series of avoidant behaviors that inadvertently ensure that the trauma response continues. Memory and action patterns are thus shaped and the resulting symptoms are simply the phenomenology of the person's trauma reaction.

In this way, PTSD is "encouraged" to continue. It is also fostered and fed by negative self-related schemas and ruminations (Foa, Tolin, Ehlers, Clark, & Orsillo, 1999). Kleim and Ehlers (2008) showed that reduced memory specificity at 2 weeks post-trauma predicted subsequent PTSD and depression at 6 months over and above what could be predicted from initial symptom severity. Their analyses suggested that rumination (i.e., rehearsal) partly mediated perceived permanent change and fully mediated the effects of low memory specificity on posttrauma psychopathology at follow-up. In short, as memory deteriorates in aging, recollections may transform, intensify, or fade.

A MODEL OF PTSD AND AGING

There are several general models of trauma assimilation or accommodation that shed some light on the interplay of PTSD and aging. For more than 30 years, models have outlined the relationships among predisposing, enabling, need, and utilization variables (see Hyer & Sohnle, 2001).

For Vietnam veterans, for example, predisposing variables (e.g., age, combat exposure) are largely indirect predictors of health-care utilization, such that the relationship between predisposing variables and service utilization is mostly explained through enabling (e.g., income, insurance availability) and need (e.g., posttraumatic stress, number of psychiatric diagnoses, physical comorbidities) variables. Relative to enabling variables, need variables are the most consistent and strongest mediators of predisposing variables in predicting service utilization (Maguen et al., 2007). This can differ between men and women.

How does the older adult encode trauma, either carried across time or de novo? In the Developmental Adaptation Model (Martin & Martin, 2002), a multivariate model, trauma is most often a distal factor whose influence on developmental outcomes may be direct or indirect, depending on its interaction with proximal resources and coping behaviors. The Developmental Adaptation Model enables the exploration of mediators and moderators in PTSD and aging. For instance, it allows for the fact that social and economic resources provide older adults with support that becomes necessary when physical, functional, and mental health decline. Individual characteristics, such as personality and religiosity, help provide a sense of stability when challenges abound. Behavioral skills and nutritional health behaviors allow older adults to maintain a sense of control even under difficult late-life circumstances. Finally, the maintenance and optimization of well-being through mental and physical health, resilience, and life satisfaction are core components in the quality of life among old and very old adults. Well-being in very late life is multifaceted and multidimensional. Because well-being contains many important dimensions, older adults are able to rely on some resilience dimensions when experiencing the decline of others.

Related is Mineka and Zinbarg's (2006) model of fear learning. They argue that relevant differences in life experiences may occur before, during, and after the fear conditioning experience and act singly or in combination to affect how much fear is initially experienced and maintained (i.e., resistance to extinction) over time. In addition, certain fears are more likely to resist extinction (Ohman & Mineka, 2001). For example, initial panic attacks associated with a fear-inducing event set the stage for conditioning of a generalized panic response to internal and external cues associated with the event and its initial sequelae, thus setting in motion a cascade of cues that kindle and sensitize the person to further anticipatory anxiety and fear.

Based on the foregoing models, Figure 8.2 identifies the distal and proximate elements in the expression of the trauma response. It suggests that there are distal vulnerabilities and present-focused person variables that

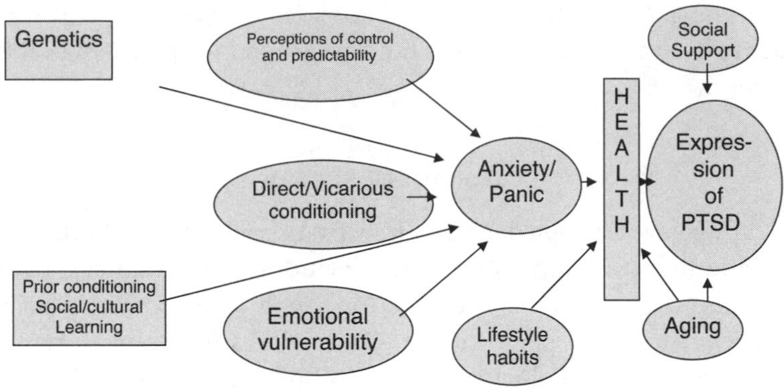

FIGURE 8.2. Core Features of the Development of PTSD.

enable a trauma response to take form. Genetics, a clearly distal variable, accounts for more than 40% of the variance of the trauma response (True et al., 1993). Importantly, this model is mediated by the influence of prior conditioning and social and cultural history (both direct and vicarious) as these relate to perceptions of controllability and uncontrollability. These learnings are established as early patterns; as a result, the person comes to view life in distinctive, potentially fearful ways. When a trauma does occur, the direct intensity of the stimulus has an impact, as does the person's perception of control over and predictability of the event, as well as the vicarious conditioning involved in the event.

Resiliency from having grown older is also a factor. For years, the paradox of well-being at later life involved positive coping (e.g., Heidrich & Ryff, 1996), savoring emotional regulation through selectively engaging in close relationships (Carstensen, 1995), and enjoying the actuarial uncoupling of positive and negative affect (Hyer & Sohnle, 2001). It is also true that the psychological status of aging aligns with the dominating biological determinants at this developmental stage. There are many components of aging that subtly or otherwise influence adjustment at late life. These include health-related variables (where health fosters better adjustment), as well as psychological constructs (e.g., positive affect; Ostir, Ottenbacher, & Markides, 2004). Further, degree of brain reserve before a new stressor becomes a good predictor of recovery to function as well as of quality of life. Beyond biopsychological predictors, studies on mortality also have revealed significant effects of psychosocial predictors, such as social networks (Litwin & Shiovitz-Ezra, 2006), volunteerism (Shmotkin, Blumstein, & Modan, 2003), emotional support and leisure activities (Walter-Ginzburg, Shmotkin, Blumstein, & Shorek, 2005), and good cognitive health (Hyer &

Sohnle, 2001). As Adkins, Martin, and Poon (1996) assert, the battle to live or die with advanced age stands as the background for psychological traits and states.

TREATMENT REVIEW

Thus far we have attempted to show how trauma at late life is both brought on by and fostered by many variables, including small traumas, kindling effects, and conditioning effects (Bouton, 2000), and how it is balanced by resiliency and well-being factors. Older adults often fail to recognize the link between psychological symptoms and mental illness. In general, older adults perceive less need for psychological treatment (Klap, Unroe, & Unützer, 2003). Somatic symptoms related to PTSD also are quite simply more noticed than psychiatric symptoms, which leads the older adult to consult primary care for symptom relief (Karlin, Duffy, & Gleaves, 2008). Indeed, if an older adult makes a connection to a mental health clinic, it is most likely driven by physical health problems rather than mental health symptoms.

This section reviews the evidence-based therapies relevant to the psychological treatment of older adults with posttraumatic symptoms. During the past 20 years, the use of cognitive behavioral therapy (CBT) has proved effective with the elderly, especially with later-life depression (Beutler et al., 1987; Gallagher & Thompson, 1981, 1982; Hyer, Swanson, & Lefkowitz, 1990; McCarthy, Katz, & Foa, 1991; Miller, Frank, Cornes, Houck, & Reynolds, 2003; Thompson, Gallagher, & Breckenridge, 1987) and anxiety (Arean, 1993; Scogin, Rickard, Keith, Wilson, & McElreath, 1992; Stanley et al., 2003). Moreover, treatment gains with older adults have been maintained over time (Gallagher-Thompson, Hanley-Peterson, & Thompson, 1990; Reynolds et al., 1999). These findings, as well as the efficacy of CBT in treating other pathological complaints, have been supported by early research studies (Garfield, 1992; Smith, Glass, & Miller, 1980) and more recent reviews (e.g., Gallagher-Thompson & Thompson, 1995; Gatz, 1994; Gatz, Popkin, Pino, & VandenBos, 1985; Knight, 1996; Niederehe & Schneider, 1998; Schramke, 1997; Teri, Curtis, Gallagher-Thompson, & Thompson, 1994). Psychotherapy with older adults has been shown to be efficacious when combined with medication (Gerson, Belin, Kaufman, Mintz, & Jarvik, 1999; Thompson, Gallagher, Hansen, Gantz, & Steffen, 1991; Reynolds et al., 1999), when applied to more difficult psychological problems (Hanley-Peterson et al., 1990; Thompson, Gallagher, & Czirr, 1988), and when applied to older adults with cognitive decline (Powers & Snow, 1999; Snow, 1999). At about the same time that CBT was proving itself efficacious, interpersonal psychotherapy (IPT) was starting to show success in evaluation studies of older adults (Hinrichsen & Clougherty, 2006).

Most studies on treatment outcome for PTSD at all ages have used variants of CBT protocols, which include exposure therapy, anxiety management, or cognitive therapy (see Hyer & Sohnle, 2001). Exposure therapy remains the best empirically supported intervention, followed by cognitive restructuring and Selective Serotonin Reuptake Inhibitor antidepressants.

The efficacy of exposure, however, is less apparent when negative self-appraisal is evident, or problematic thoughts and extreme anger are in play. In general, when cognitions are considered primary to the etiology of the PTSD, cognitive therapy plays the central role in the therapy. Cognitive therapy is especially optimal when the problem to be addressed is guilt, somatic complaints, emotional numbness, and in long-term-care promotion. So the competition between behaviorally based therapies for the treatment of PTSD is largely a matter of clinical preference and efficiency or theoretical allegiance rather than a fundamental conflict between paradigms. Cognitive processing therapy (Resick 2003) itself is a cross between cognitive and exposure based therapies. Treatments addressing the disregulation of the body's stress systems are often related but can be conceived of as independent. Ford (2010), for example, held that the core symptoms of PTSD (recollections, flashbacks, nightmares) are really by-products of psychobiological stress reactivity.

Unfortunately, few evaluative studies have been applied to older trauma victims. In general, older victims find the exposure treatments distressing (Hyer & Sohnle, 2001). Although there are many benefits to the use of prolonged exposure to treat young adults, older patients generally respond poorly to this intervention. Thorp and Stein (2005) conducted one of the few studies that successfully applied exposure, adapted for late life, to an older group of adults with PTSD. The study consisted of 12 sessions of modified exposure therapy over 6 weeks. Results indicated that participants were able to tolerate exposure conditions. In one of the few case studies of exposure therapy with a patient, Russo, Hersen, and Van Hasselt (2001) assessed the effects of imaginal exposure in a 57-year-old female suffering from current and reactivated PTSD following a transient ischemic attack. A positive outcome was noted.

Reminiscence, or the act of recollecting a memory in one's past for various purposes, has been used with some efficacy with older adults (see

Hyer & Sohnle, 2001). It has been applied in older adults for purposes of a positive self-focus (e.g., identity, death preparation, problem solving) and a negative self-focus (e.g., boredom reduction, intimacy maintenance) (Cappeliez & O'Rourke, 2006). In addition, there have been a few combined studies of medication and reminiscence therapy, but these have not been evaluated specifically for older adults (see Hyer & Sohnle, 2001).

Cognitive behavioral therapy and cognitive restructuring outcome studies with older adults with PSTD have been modest (small studies or case analyses; Boehnlein & Sparr, 1993; Hyer, Swanson et al., 1990; Lipton & Shaffer, 1986; Molinari & Williams, 1995; Snell & Padin-Rivera, 1997). Cook et al. (2005) applied a CBT group intervention to eight older veterans and found changes in clinician-rated measures in severity of PTSD. The methods applied reflect those of Hyer, Swanson et al. (1990) and Boehnlein and Sparr (1993), who used anxiety management, rational thinking, self-reward, mastery, relaxation, and psychoeducation. Absent in all cases was trauma processing via exposure.

Psychiatric medication has been used with marginal success for the treatment of PTSD (Lee & Schubert, 2009). Although a range of medications have been applied to PTSD care, including antidepressants, antipsychotics, anticonvulsants, benzodiazepines, and adrenergic modulators, most patients do not achieve full remission. This may be a result of poor methodology, complexity of patients, and poorly identified theories for change. Although there is optimism for future research in pharmacogenomics to alter the corticotrophin releasing factor (CRF) – as it mobilizes the HPA axis and locus coeruleus and norepinephrine system – as well as the application of newer agents (d-cyclocerine) in the treatment of PTSD, these efforts do not address the needs of older adults.

Existing therapies that address trauma and older adults also lack a focus that trumpets a key element in later life, well-being. Aspinwall and Staudinger (2003), however, have articulated a psychology of human strengths. They argued convincingly that adulthood remains a state of continued "becoming." Several well-being therapies are noted which integrate life satisfaction with techniques of therapy. The therapies are especially meaningful to older adults, as some of the components incorporated elements of well-being related to older ages, optimizing environmental mastery, personal growth, autonomy, self-acceptance, and positive relations with others (Ryff & Singer, 1998). Similarly, Seligman (2002) developed positive psychotherapy (PPT) with older adults in mind, which is based on signature strengths of a person and addressing an individualized care plan for meaning, pleasure, and integration.

TABLE 8.1. *Treatment model*

1. Stabilize symptoms → Treat comorbid disorders or stressors (including health).
2. Relationship building → Build trust, the ability to confront trauma with a trusted therapist. Apply the client-rated Working Alliance Inventory (WAI).
3. Attend to necessary developmental, treatment, and education (normalization) factors → Assure social supports, daily coping, social skills, and treatment compliance.
4. Apply cognitive restructuring (CR) → Teach the five-step program of CR and consider tactics of personality style as therapy-guided treatment.
5. Elicit positive core memories (PCM) → Foster a renarration of self with core memories that can generalize to current life situations.
6. Decondition trauma memories → Apply AMT.

HYER AND SOHNLE'S MODEL

Researchers can respond to uncertainty with abstraction and curiosity; clinicians must respond to uncertainty with action. Four therapies have special merit for the treatment of PTSD symptoms but none has been validated with older adults: (a) anxiety management training (AMT); (b) stress inoculation training (SIT), which is a coping model (Meichenbaum, 1993); (c) eye movement and reprocessing (EMDR), which involves titrating a dosed exposure that targets state-specific information related to the trauma, which has applicability with older victims (Hyer & Kushner, 2007); and (d) cognitive processing therapy, which involves applying gradual and multiple exposures to the trauma and consists largely of rescripting and altering distortions (Resick 2003). A related treatment that may be more applicable to older adults who have intense and continued trauma symptoms is multimodal therapy (Falsetti, Erwin, Resick, Davis, & Combs-Lane, 2003; Hyer & Sohnle, 2001).

Two mechanisms seem responsible for efficacious treatment of PTSD: (a) improvement occurs through emotional processing of and habituation to the trauma memory by repeated exposure (Foa, Rothbaum, Riggs, & Murdock, 1991), and (b) improvement occurs because the meaning of the event changes (Resick et al., 2008). Training clients to access memories in a controlled way helps them break through the rumination cycle and put the memory in perspective (Williams et al., 2007). It is also possible to reduce overgeneralized memory (OGM) bias and poor trauma adaptation by targeting rumination. Ehlers and Clark (2000) have done this in claiming-your-life experiments.

Hyer and Sohnle (2001) examined treatment components of PTSD (Table 8.1) and defined a six-step model of PTSD treatment for older adults.

In general, the greater the intensity of perturbation in the client, the more therapeutic tasks should relate to the beginning parts of this treatment model. The less the client is affected by the trauma, the more the therapist can focus on the latter parts of the model and achieve lasting change. The rationale for ordering these tasks as presented is to keep people committed to therapy, to encourage experimentation, and to create cognitive change.

The first task in this treatment model is to stabilize symptoms, including the treatment of comorbid disorders and current stressors (including health). Some symptoms are more equal than others. Up front, the astute therapist will address sleep problems, panic, anxiety, depression, substance abuse, and psychotic symptoms. These symptoms are often functionally autonomous. As reviewed in this chapter, PTSD also involves abnormalities in a number of other intraindividual domains, such as memory, mood, bodily experience, interpersonal relatedness, emotion, and behavior. In addition, medical issues require an interface with the primary-care physician. The therapist's role, then, is initially as a therapy manager, foremost in managing trauma symptoms. Often, the operative tasks of the therapy are basic: keep the trauma victim in treatment, be supportive during difficult periods, maintain appropriate arousal levels, and encourage commitment to the goals of therapy.

Second, the working alliance between client and therapist is critical. For some, the relationship is the therapy. The therapist must do three relationship tasks: (a) be liked and/or respected, (b) be believable (with a plan), and (c) initiate some early changes in the treatment. We recommend that the client-rated Working Alliance Inventory (WAI; Horvath & Greenberg, 1989) be used as a feedback tool in therapy. In several studies, the WAI mediated the success in therapy (Hyer, Carpenter, Bishmann, & Wu, 2005).

The third task is to attend to developmental factors, ensure social supports, reinforce daily coping and social skills practice, and encourage treatment compliance. Self-management skills must be in place for the therapy to be successful. The clinician also must be assured that the client's lifestyle is reasonably healthy and not interfering with life or (later) narrative repair. This includes sleep, diet, exercise, treating physical illnesses, and use of appropriate medications. Assistive behavioral interventions include standard CBT interventions (Martell, Addis, & Jacobson, 2001), especially scheduling positive events, social interaction, general activity scheduling, assertiveness training, and bibliotherapy.

Fourth, the therapeutic use of cognitive restructuring (CR) is warranted. This is the main therapeutic element that is applicable to PTSD in older

TABLE 8.2. *The five steps of cognitive restructuring*

1. SITUATION
Ask yourself, "What happened that made me upset?" Write down a brief description of the situation.

2. FEELING
Circle your strongest feeling (if more than one, use a separate sheet for each feeling):
Fear/Anxiety/Sadness/Depression/Guilt/Shame/Anger

3. THOUGHT
Ask yourself, "What am I thinking that is leading me to feel this way?" Write down your thought below.
Circle your Common Style of Thinking:
All-or-Nothing Overgeneralizing Must/Should/Never
Catastrophizing Emotional Reasoning Overestimation of Risk Self-Blame

4. CHALLENGE YOUR THOUGHT:
Rewrite your thought from Step 3:
Things that DO support my thought:______________________
Things that DO NOT support my thought:______________________

5. TAKE ACTION!
Next, ask yourself, "Do things mostly support my thought or do things mostly NOT support my thought?"
☐ NO, the evidence does *not* support my thought.
☐ YES, the evidence *does* support my thought.
Action
Plan____

adults. Cognitive restructuring is critical for enhancing the efficacy of prolonged exposure. In fact, it has merit absent the use of exposure and has been applied in several studies to good effect with trauma (Mueser, 2006). Cognitive restructuring may involve multiple curative factors, including habituation to anxiety, distinguishing between remembering and reencountering, differentiating trauma from similar but safe events, experiencing mastery, and assisting in the organization of trauma narratives. We apply a five-step CR process. This is a variant of the dysfunctional thought record (DTR) used in CBT (Beck, 1995; Hamlin, Mueser, Rosenberg, & Rosenberg, 2004), in which the client is requested to apply five specific steps to everyday challenges related to trauma as well as to other problems (Table 8.2).

The fifth component involves eliciting self-representational stories or positive core memories (PCM), including written or taped autobiographies with feedback that may involve listening to tapes, making pilgrimages or reunions, developing a genealogy, making a scrapbook or photo albums, looking at old letters and memorabilia, summarizing one's lifework, and exercising the preservation of ethno-cultural identity (Lewis & Butler, 1974). Rybarczyk and Bellg (1997) and Hyer, Swanson et al. (1990) applied PCMs alone with older adults to good effect. The application of PCMs involves a simple recounting of a positive event, reinforcing the reasonable positive interpretations, reengaging hope, reframing better worldviews, and supporting competence (see Hyer & Sohnle, 2001).

The last component involves the trauma memory. As the last step, the therapist takes time to assess whether the client is a candidate for this therapy stage by analyzing whether the client will allow access to the trauma memory and whether he or she has the requisite skills to unearth the content and embark on exposure (see Hyer & Sohnle, 2001). This therapeutic task intends to bring implicit memory into awareness as self-as-past by putting the memory into language in the form of a narrative. The more the trauma memory is organized, modified into a narrative, and placed into explicit memory as it is disclosed, elaborated, and validated, the more likely general improvement will occur (Foa, Tolin, Ehlers, Clark, & Orsillo, 1999; Pennebaker, 1989). These memories will now be retrieved with some neutrality and reduced arousal.

Anxiety management training (AMT) is recommended for this task. This is a soft exposure technique that involves a variety of procedures, including relaxation, biofeedback, and cognitive restructuring. Conceptually, trauma psychotherapy is a continual retelling of the self by shifting from previous negative narratives to more positive ones (Van der Kolk, 2002). With the combination, then, of assimilation (CBT and narrative work) and exposure work (AMT and exposure), trauma cues can become habituated (desensitized) and assimilated.

With AMT, use of exposure is done empathically and with relaxation as a lead-in (see Hyer & Sohnle, 2001). Procedurally, the sequence of memory work is straightforward (see Table 8.3). After the therapist has assessed client skills, willingness, and safety concerns, the therapist obtains the facts of the trauma memory (i.e., a "clean" rendition of events). Confusion, misattribution, fears, and gaps are highlighted and gently challenged. The objective is not to elicit an exacting account of the trauma, as there is little evidence that this helps in therapy. Normalization and education regarding the reasons for unearthing the memory are critical. A model of PTSD can be provided at this time, as well as explanations for the relaxation and exposure interchange (the therapy). Listening for fears also is therapeutically important. Use of handouts and self-report measures (e.g., Impact of Events Scale, Beck Depression Inventory) is helpful for monitoring change. Safety and suicide assessments are regularly performed.

TABLE 8.3. *Therapist tasks in trauma exposure*

Psychoeducation		
Go over symptoms		
Model of PTSD		
Go over therapy		
Go over patient's fears (loss of control, etc)		
Use handouts		
Obtain a fear hierarchy		
Use IES or BDI		
Prepare for therapy		
Safety and crisis plan		
Suicide issues/SA		
Teach Relaxation		
Exposure		
Instructions on coping		
Apply interoceptive exposure		
Apply self-control desensitization		
Therapist presents	**Client's anxiety signaled**	
a. Hierarchy	With cue	After 20″ Go to b
b. Coping image	Signal drops	
c. Postanxiety cue; Postimage relaxation	Hold	
d. Incorporate cognitive coping statements and perspective shifts		
e. If problems, use systematic desensitization for difficult images		

Relaxation is taught first for eventual use of self-controlled desensitization (Borkovec, 2005) – a gentle calming procedure according to the therapist's taste. This is performed according to AMT principles (hierarchal, gradual, repetitive, and persistent until desensitization). This is done for several sessions. Once the memory has been obtained, two added features are employed to assist with self-desensitization: (a) a simple fear hierarchy is obtained for use with exposure (often bits and pieces of the memory) and (b) the memory itself from beginning to end.

The therapist then applies AMT procedures (see Hyer & Sohnle, 2001). When AMT exposure is performed, it may be preceded by interoceptive exposure (identifying sensations that are uncomfortable) and instructions on coping or use of imagery. Regardless, a simple AMT procedure allows for the stimulus to be recognized, to be held in consciousness for a short period, for anxiety to be experienced, and then for coping to follow. The process involves interchanging relaxation and fear initially at a subjective units of disturbance (SUDS) rating of 4–6 for several minutes until remission (SUDS 0–2). On reaching this goal, additional fears can also become targets. This is done until the complete memory is desensitized.

Finally, as therapy concludes, relapse awareness is helpful for the client. The therapist anticipates the need for continuance of care, discusses issues of a change in treatment, and the importance of booster sessions. The client is taught how to recognize early warning signs, to anticipate high-risk situations, and to develop an emergency plan in the case of relapse. This includes self-help strategies and involves significant others.

CONCLUSION

Trauma at late life is most often carried across the years and is conceptually distinctive. In general, data from the past two decades have not suggested that older adults are at greater risk than younger adults for poor psychosocial outcomes following exposure to trauma. There is simply insufficient evidence to conclude that trauma causes more negative psychosocial consequences in older adults. Empirically supported therapies that apply to younger groups have more applicability to older groups than not.

We have argued that trauma at late life is multidimensional but understandable. The positive (e.g., selective emotional regulation) and negative (e.g., cognitive decline) features of aging mix with the nature of trauma to provide a complex but treatable person who is the victim of trauma. The five-step treatment model proposed here, which incorporates key elements of traditional cognitive and behavioral therapies but also expands them to have a trauma focus, is a comprehensive therapy for acute or chronic PTSD. The model treats the whole person with PTSD problems. Because older adults are less tolerant of traditional exposure techniques, memories are modified or transformed directly only as a last optional step. Throughout, the model integrates factors related specifically to aging, culture, mourning for losses, giving meaning to experiences, reestablishing self-coherence and self-continuity, and social support.

REFERENCES

Adkins, G., Martin, P., & Poon, L. W. (1996). Personality traits and states as predictors of subjective well-being in centenarians, octogenarians, and sexagenarians. *Psychology and Aging, 11*, 408–416.

American Psychiatric Association. (2000). *Diagnostic and statistical manual-IV-TR.* Washington, DC: American Psychiatric Association.

Antoni, M. H., Lehman, J. M., Kilbourn, K. M., Boyers, A. E., Culver, J. L., Alferi, S. M., et al. (2001). Cognitive-behavioral stress management intervention decreases the prevalence of depression and enhances benefit finding among women under treatment for early-stage breast cancer. *Health Psychology, 20,* 20–32.

Arean, P. (1993). Cognitive behavioral therapy with older adults. *Behavior Therapist, 16,* 236–239.

Aspinwall, L. & Staudinger, U. (2003). A psychology of human strengths: Fundamental questions and future directions for a positive psychology. Washington, DC.: APA press.

Baddeley, A. (2000). The episodic buffer: A new component of working memory? *Trends in Cognitive Sciences, 4,* 417–423.

Beck, J. (1995). *Cognitive therapy: Basics and beyond.* New York: Guilford Press.

Beckham, J. C., Crawford, A. L., & Feldman, M.E. (1998). Trail Making Test performance in Vietnam combat veterans with and without posttraumatic stress disorder. *Journal of Traumatic Stress, 11,* 811–819.

Beutler, L. E., Scogin, F., Kirkish, P., Schretlen, D., Corbishley, A., Hamblin, D., et al. (1987). Group cognitive therapy and alprazolam in the treatment of depression in older adults. *Journal of Consulting and Clinical Psychology, 55,* 550–557.

Blazer, D. G. (2003). Depression in late life: Review and commentary. *Journal of Gerontology: MEDICAL SCIENCES, 58A,* 249–265.

Boehnlein, J., & Sparr, L. (1993). Group therapy with World War II ex-POWs: Longterm adjustment in a geriatric population. *American Journal of Psychotherapy, 47,* 273–282.

Bonanno, G. A. (2004). Loss, trauma, and human resilience: Have we underestimated the human capacity to thrive after extremely adverse events? *American Psychologist, 59,* 20–28.

Borkovec, T. (2005). "GAD in the Real World." Symposium given at NJ-ACT, Westfield, NJ.

Bouton, M. E. (2000). A learning theory perspective on lapse, relapse, and the maintenance of behavior change. *Health Psychology, 19,* 57–63.

Bouton, M. E. (2002). Context, ambiguity, and unlearning: Sources of relapse after behavioral extinction. *Biological Psychiatry, 52,* 976–986.

Brandtstädter, J. (1999). Sources of resilience in the aging self: Toward integrating perspectives. T. M. Hess & F. Blanchard-Fields (Eds.), *Social cognition and aging* (pp. 123–141). San Diego, CA: Academic Press.

Brandtstädter, J., & Rothermund, K. (2002). The life-course dynamics of goal pursuit and goal adjustment: A two-process framework. *Developmental Review, 22,* 117–150.

Bremner, J. D. (2002). Neuroimaging studies in post-traumatic stress disorder. *Current Psychiatry Reports, 4,* 254–263.

Bremner, J. D., Southwick, S. M., Johnson, D. R., Yehuda, R., & Charney, D. S. (1993). Childhood physical abuse and combat-related posttraumatic stress disorder in Vietnam veterans. *American Journal of Psychiatry, 150,* 235–239.

Brewin, C. R., Andrews, B., & Valentine, J. D. (2000). Meta-analysis of risk factors for posttraumatic stress disorder in trauma-exposed adults. *Journal of Consulting and Clinical Psychology, 68,* 748–766.

Broman-Fulks, J. J., Ruggiero, K. J., Green, B. A., Kilpatrick, D. G., Danielson, C. K., Resick, H. S., et al. (2006). Taxometric investigation of PTSD: Data from two nationally representative samples. *Behavior Therapy, 37*, 364–380.

Bryant, R. A. (2004). *Assessing psychological trauma and PTSD*. New York: Guilford Press.

Cappeliez, P., & O'Rourke, N. (2006). Empirical validation of a model of reminiscence and health at later life. *Journal of Gerontology, 61B*, 237–244.

Carstensen, L. L. (1995). Evidence for a life-span theory of socioemotional selectivity. *Current Directions in Psychological Science, 4*, 151–156.

Carstensen, L. L., Fung, H. H., & Charles, S. T. (2003). Socioemotional selectivity theory and the regulation of emotion in the second half of life. *Motivation and Emotion, 27*, 103–123.

Chemtob, C. M., Novaco, R. W., Hamada, R. S., Gross, D. M., & Smith, G. (1997). Anger regulation deficits in combat-related posttraumatic stress disorder. *Journal of Traumatic Stress, 10*, 17–36.

Cheng, C., Wong, W. M., & Tsang, K. W. (2006). Perception of benefits and costs during SARS outbreak: An 18-month prospective study. *Journal of Consulting and Clinical Psychology, 74*, 870–879.

Conway, M. A. (2001). Sensory-perceptual episodic memory and its context: Autobiographical memory. *Philosophical Transactions: Biological Sciences, 356*, 1375–1384.

Cook, J., O'Donnell, C., Moltzen, J., Ruzek, J., & Sheikh, J. (2005). Clinical observations in the treatment of World War II and Korean War veterans with combat-related PTSD. *Clinical Geropsychologist, 29*, 82–94.

Cook, J. M., Ruzek, J. I., & Cassidy, E. (2003). Practical geriatrics: Possible association of posttraumatic stress disorder with cognitive impairment among older adults. *Psychiatric Services, 54*, 1223–1225.

Davidson, J. R., Hughes, D., Blazer, D. G., & George, L. (1991). PTSD in the community: An epidemiological study. *Psychological Medicine, 21*, 713–721.

Diener, E., Lucas, R. E., & Scollon, C. N. (2006). Beyond the hedonic treadmill: Revising the adaptation theory of well-being. *American Psychologist, 61*, 305–314.

Ehlers, A., & Clark, D. M. (2000). A cognitive model of posttraumatic stress disorder. *Behaviour Research and Therapy, 38*, 319–345.

Ehlers, A., Mayou, R. A., & Bryant, B. (1998). Psychological predictors of chronic posttraumatic stress disorder after motor vehicle accidents. *Journal of Abnormal Psychology, 107*, 508–519.

Ehring, T., Ehlers, A., & Glucksman, E. (2008). Do cognitive models help in predicting the severity of posttraumatic stress disorder, phobia, and depression after motor vehicle accidents? A prospective longitudinal study. *Journal of Consulting and Clinical Psychology, 76*, 219–230.

Elzinga, B. M., & Bremner, J. D. (2002) Are the neural substrates of memory the final common pathway in posttraumatic stress disorder (PTSD)? *Journal of Affective Disorders, 70*, 1–17.

Emery, L., Hale, S., & Myerson, J. (2008). Age differences in proactive interference, working memory, and abstract reasoning. *Psychology and Aging, 23*, 634–645.

Eustache, F., & Desgranges, B. (2008). MNESIS: Towards the integration of current multisystem models of memory. *Neuropsychology Review, 18*, 53–69.

Falsetti, S. A., Erwin, B. A., Resick, H. S., Davis, J. & Combs-Lane, A. M. (2003). Multiple channel exposure therapy of PTSD: Impact of treatment on functioning and resources. *Behavior Modification, 29*, 70–94.

Foa, E. B., & Kozak, M. J. (1986). Emotional processing of fear: Exposure to corrective information. *Psychological Bulletin, 99*, 20–35.

Foa,, E. B., Rothbaum, B. O., Riggs, D. S., & Murdock, T. (1991). Treatment of posttraumatic stress disorder in rape victims: A comparison between cognitive behavioral procedures and counseling. *Journal of Consulting and Clinical Psychology, 59*, 715–723.

Foa, E. B., Tolin, D. F., Ehlers, A., Clark, D. M., & Orsillo, S. M. (1999). The Posttraumatic Cognitions Inventory (PTCI): Development and validation. *Psychological Assessment, 11*, 303–314.

Ford, J. D. (2010). Just think about it: How can cognitive therapy contribute to the treatment of posttraumatic stress disorder? *Clinical Psychology: Science and Practice, 7*, 128–133.

Frisch, M. B. (2006). *Quality of life therapy: Applying a life satisfaction approach to positive psychology and cognitive therapy*. Hoboken, NJ: Wiley.

Frueh, C., Elhai, J., Gold, P., Monnier, J., Magruder, K., Keane, T., et al. (2003). Disability compensation seeking among veterans evaluated for posttraumatic stress disorder. *Psychiatric Services, 54*, 84–91.

Gallagher, D., & Thompson, L. W. (1981). *Depression in the elderly: A behavioral treatment manual.* Los Angeles: University of Southern California Press.

Gallagher, D., & Thompson, L.W. (1982). Treatment of major depressive disorder in older adult outpatients with brief psychotherapies. *Psychotherapy: Theory, Research, and Practice, 19*, 482–490.

Gallagher-Thompson, D., Hanley-Peterson, P., & Thompson, L.W. (1990). Maintenance of gains versus relapse following brief psychotherapy for depression. *Journal of Counseling and Clinical Psychology, 58*, 371–374.

Gallagher-Thompson, D., & Thompson, L.W. (1995). Psychotherapy with older adults in theory and practice. In B. Boner & L. Beutler (Eds.), *Comprehensive textbook of psychotherapy* (pp. 357–379). New York: Oxford University Press.

Garfield, S. (1992). Major issues in psychotherapy research. In D. Freedheim (Ed.), *History of psychotherapy: A century of change* (pp. 335–359). Washington, DC: American Psychological Association.

Gatz, M. (1994). Application of assessment to therapy and intervention with older adults. In M. Storandt & G. R. VandenBos, (Eds.), *Neuropsychological assessment of dementia and depression in older adults: A clinician's guide.* Washington, DC: American Psychological Association.

Gatz, M., Popkin, S. J., Pino, C. D., & VandenBos, G. R. (1985). Psychological interventions with older adults. In J. E. Birren & K. W. Schaie (Eds.), *Handbook of the psychology of aging* (2nd ed., pp. 755–785). New York: Van Nostrand Reinhold.

Gerson, S., Belin, T. R., Kaufman, A., Mintz, J., & Jarvik, L. (1999). Pharmacological and psychological treatments for depressed older patients: A meta-analysis and overview of recent findings. *Harvard Review of Psychiatry, 7*, 1–28.

Goenjian, A. K., Noble, E. P., Walling, D. P., Goenjian, H. A., Karayan, I. S., Ritchie, T., et al. (2008). Heritabilities of symptoms of posttraumatic stress disorder, anxiety, and depression in earthquake exposed Armenian families. *Psychiatric Genetics, 18*, 261–266.

Gold, S. D., Marx, B. P., Soler-Baillo, J. M., & Sloan, D. M. (2005). Is life stress more traumatic than traumatic stress? *Journal of Anxiety Disorders, 19*, 687–698.

Grossman, A. B., Levin, B. E., Katzen, H. L., & Lechner, S. (2004). PTSD symptoms and onset of neurologic disease in elderly trauma survivors. *Journal of Clinical and Experimental Neuropsychology, 26*, 698–706.

Halligan, S. L., Michael, T., Clark, D. M., & Ehlers, A. (2003). Posttraumatic stress disorder following assault: The role of cognitive processing, trauma memory, and appraisals. *Journal of Consulting and Clinical Psychology, 71*, 419–431.

Hamlin, J., Mueser, K., Rosenberg, S., & Rosenberg, H. (2004). *Brief cognitive therapy for PTSD.* New Hanover, NH: Dartmouth University Medical School Press.

Hanley-Peterson, P., Futterman, A., Thompson, L., Zeiss, A. M., Gallagher, D., & Ironson, G. (1990). Endogenous depression and psychotherapy outcome in an elderly population [abstract]. *Gerontologist, 30*, 51A.

Heckhausen, J., & Schulz, R. (1995). A life-span theory of control. *Psychological Review, 102*, 284–304.

Heidrich, S. M., & Ryff, C. D. (1996). The self in later years of life: Perspectives on psychological well being. In L. Sperry & H. Prosen (Eds.), *Aging in the 21st century: The future of gerontology and geropsychiatry* (pp. 73–102). New York: Garland.

Helgeson, V. S., Reynolds, K. A., & Tomich, P. L. (2006). A meta-analytic review of benefit finding and growth. *Journal of Consulting and Clinical Psychology, 74*, 797–816.

Herman, J. L. (1992). Complex PTSD: A syndrome in survivors of prolonged and repeated trauma. *Journal of Traumatic Stress, 5*, 377–391.

Hinrichsen, G. A., & Clougherty, K. F. (2006). *Interpersonal psychotherapy for depressed older adults.* Washington, DC: American Psychological Association.

Hobfall, S., Tracy, M., & Galea, S. (2006). The impact of resource loss and traumatic growth on probable PTSD and depression following terrorist attacks. *Journal of Traumatic Stress, 19*, 867–878.

Hoge, C. W., Castro, C. A., Messer, S. C., McGurk, D., Cotting, D. I., & Koffman, R. L. (2004). Combat duty in Iraq and Afghanistan, mental health problems, and barriers to care. *New England Journal of Medicine, 351*, 13–22.

Horvath, A., & Greenberg, L. (1989). Development and validation of the Working Alliance Inventory. *Journal of Counseling Psychology, 36*, 223–233.

Hull, A. M. (2002). Neuroimaging findings in post-traumatic stress disorder. *British Journal of Psychiatry, 181*, 102–110.

Hyer, L., Carpenter, B., Bishmann, D., & Wu, H. S. (2005). Depression in long-term care. *Clinical Psychology: Science and Practice, 12*, 280–299.

Hyer, L., & Kushner, B. (2007). Eye movement desensitization and reprocessing and stress: Research, theory and practical suggestions. In P. M. Lehrer, R. L. Woolfolk, & W. Sime (Eds.), *Principles of Stress Management* (3rd edition, pp. 545–578). New York: Guilford Press.

Hyer, L., & Sohnle, S. (2001). *Trauma among older people: Issues and treatment.* Philadelphia: Brunner-Routledge.

Hyer, L., & Stanger, E. (1997). The interaction of posttraumatic stress disorder and depression among older combat veterans. *Psychological Reports, 80*, 785–786.

Hyer, L., Swanson, G., & Lefkowitz, R. (1990). Cognitive schema model with stress groups at later life. *Clinical Gerontologist*, *9*, 145–190.

Kane, M. J., Conway, A. R. A., Miura, T. K., & Colflesh, G. J. H. (2007). Working memory, attention control, and the n-back task: A question of construct validity. *Journal of Experimental Psychology: Learning, Memory, and Cognition*, *33*, 615–622.

Karlin, B., Duffy, M., & Gleaves, D. (2008). Patterns and predictors of mental health service use and mental illness among older and younger adults in the United States. *Psychological Services*, *5*, 275–294.

Kessler, R., Sonnega, A., Bromet, E., Hughes, M., & Nelson, C. (1995). Posttraumatic stress disorder in the National Comorbidity Survey. *Archives of General Psychiatry*, *52*, 1048–1060.

King, L. A., & Hicks, J. A. (2007). Whatever happened to "what might have been"? Regrets, happiness, and maturity. *American Psychologist*, *62*, 625–636.

Klap, R., Unroe, K. T., & Unützer, J. (2003). Caring for mental illness in the United States: A focus on older adults. *American Journal of Geriatric Psychiatry*, *11*, 517–524.

Kleim, B., & Ehlers, A. (2008). Reduced autobiographical memory specificity predicts depression and posttraumatic stress disorder after recent trauma. *Journal of Consulting and Clinical Psychology*, *76*, 231–242.

Knight, B. G. (1996). *Psychotherapy with older adults* (2nd ed.). Newbury Park, CA: Sage.

Krause, N., Shaw, B. A., & Cairney, J. (2004). A descriptive epidemiology of lifetime trauma and the physical health status of older adults. *Psychology and Aging*, *19*, 637–648.

Lechner, S. C., Carver, C. S., Antoni, M. H., Weaver, K. E., & Phillips, K. M. (2006). Curvilinear associations between benefit finding and psychosocial adjustment to breast cancer. *Journal of Consulting and Clinical Psychology*, *74*, 828–840.

Lee, C. W., & Schubert, S. (2009). Omissions and errors in the Institute of Medicine's report on scientific evidence of treatment for posttraumatic stress disorder. *Journal of EMDR Practice and Research*, *3*, 32–38.

Lewis, M., & Butler, R. (1974). Life review therapy: Putting memories to work in individual and group therapy. *Geriatrics*, *29*, 165–173.

Lipton, M., & Schaffer, W. (1986). Posttraumatic stress disorder in the older veteran. *Military Medicine*, *151*, 522–524.

Litwin, H., & Shiovitz-Ezra, S. (2006). The association between activity and well-being in later life: What really matters? *Ageing and Society*, *26*, 225–242.

Loevinger, J. (1976). *Ego development: Conception and theories.* San Francisco: Jossey-Bass.

Ma, S. H., & Teasdale, J. D. (2004). Mindfulness-based cognitive therapy for depression: Replication and exploration of differential relapse prevention effects. *Journal of Consulting and Clinical Psychology*, *72*, 31–40.

Maguen, S., Schumm, J. A., Norris, R. L., Taft, C., King, L. A., King, D. W., et al. (2007). Predictors of mental and physical health service utilization among Vietnam veterans. *Psychological Services*, *4*, 168–180.

Martell, C., Addis, M., & Jacobson, N. (2001). *Depression in context: Strategies for guided action.* New York: Norton.

Martin, P., & Martin, M. (2002). Proximal and distal influences on development: The model of developmental adaptation. *Developmental Review, 22*, 78–96.

Mather, M., & Knight, M. (2005). Goal-directed memory: The role of cognitive control in older adults' emotional memory. *Psychology and Aging, 20*, 554–570.

Mausbach, B. T., Aschbacher, K., Patterson, T. L., Ancoli-Israel, S., von Känel, R., Mills, P. et al. (2006). Avoidant coping partially mediates the relationship between patient problem behaviors and depressive symptoms in spousal Alzheimer caregivers. *American Journal of Geriatric Psychiatry, 14*, 299–306.

McCarthy, P., Katz, I., & Foa, E. (1991). Cognitive-behavioral treatment of anxiety in the elderly: A proposal model. In C. Saltzman & B. Lebowitz (Eds.), *Anxiety in the elderly: Treatment and research* (pp. 197–214). New York: Springer.

McCranie, E. W., & Hyer, L. A. (2000). Posttraumatic stress disorder symptoms in Korean conflict and World War II combat veterans seeking outpatient treatment. *Journal of Traumatic Stress, 13*, 427–439.

McCullough, M. E., Root, L. M., & Cohen, A. D. (2006). Writing about the benefits of an interpersonal transgression facilitates forgiveness. *Journal of Consulting and Clinical Psychology, 74*, 887–897.

McDaniel, M. A., Lyle, K. B., Butler, K. M., & Dornburg, C. C. (2008). Age-related deficits in reality monitoring of action memories. *Psychology and Aging, 23*, 646–656.

Meichenbaum, D. (1993). Stress inoculation training: A 20-year update. In P. Lehrer & R. Woolfolk (Eds.), *Principles and practice of stress management* (pp. 373–406). New York: Guilford Press.

Milam, J. (2006). Posttraumatic growth and HIV disease progression. *Journal of Consulting and Clinical Psychology, 74*, 817–827.

Miller, M., Frank, E., Cornes, C., Houck, P., & Reynolds, C. (2003). The value of maintenance interpersonal psychotherapy (IPT) in older adults with different IPT foci. *American Journal of Geriatric Psychiatry, 11*, 97–107.

Mineka, S., & Zinbarg, R. (2006). A contemporary learning theory perspective on the etiology of anxiety disorders: It's not what you thought it was. *American Psychologist, 61*, 10–26.

Mohlman, J. (2008). More power to the executive? A preliminary test of CBT plus executive skills training for treatment of late-life GAD. *Cognitive and Behavioral Practice, 15*, 306–316.

Molinari, V., & Williams, W. (1995). An analysis of aging World war II POWs with PTSD: Implication for practice and research. *Journal of Geriatric Psychiatry, 28*, 99–114.

Monroe, S. M., & Harkness, K. L. (2005). Life stress, the "kindling" hypothesis, and the recurrence of depression: Considerations from a life stress perspective. *Psychological Review, 112*, 417–445.

Mueser, K. (2006). Cognitive-behavioral treatment of PTSD in severe mental illness: Pilot study in an ethnically diverse population. NIMH Grant. Washington, DC: National Mental Health.

Niederehe, G., & Schneider, L. (1998). Treatment of depression and anxiety in the aged. In P. Nathan & J. Gorman (Eds.), *A guide to treatments that work* (pp. 270–287). New York: Oxford University Press.

Nolen-Hoeksema, S., & Morrow, J. (1991). A prospective study of depression and posttraumatic stress symptoms after a natural disaster: The 1989 Loma Prieta earthquake. *Journal of Personality and Social Psychology, 61*, 115–121.

Norris, F. H. (1992). Epidemiology of trauma: Frequency and impact of different potentially traumatic events on difficult demographic groups. *Journal of Consulting Clinical Psychology, 60*, 409–418.

Ohman, A., & Mineka, S. (2001). Fears, phobias, and preparedness: Toward an evolved module of fear and fear learning. *Psychological Review, 108*, 483–522.

Ostir, G. V., Ottenbacher, K. J., & Markides, K. S. (2004). Onset of frailty in older adults and the protective role of positive affect. *Psychology and Aging, 19*, 402–408.

Ozer, E. J., Best, S. R., Lipsey, T. L., & Weiss, D. S. (2003). Predictors of posttraumatic stress disorder and symptoms in adults: A meta-analysis. *Psychological Bulletin, 129*, 52–73.

Park, C. L., & Helgeson, V. S. (2006). Introduction to the special section: Growth following highly stressful life events – current status and future directions. *Journal of Consulting and Clinical Psychology, 74*, 791–796.

Pennebaker, J. W. (1989). Confession, inhibition, and disease. In L. Berkowitz (Ed.), *Advances in experimental social psychology* (Vol. 22, pp. 211–244). Orlando, FL: Academic Press.

Pole, N., Neylan, T. C., Otte, C., Metzler, T. J., Best, S. R., Henn-Haase, C., et al. (2007). Associations between childhood trauma and emotion-modulated psychophysiological responses to startling sounds: A study of police cadets. *Journal of Abnormal Psychology, 116*, 352–361.

Post, R. M. (1992). Transduction of psychosocial stress into the neurobiology of recurrent affective disorder. *American Journal of Psychiatry, 149*, 999–1010.

Powers, D., & Snow, L. (August 1999). *Cognitive behavioral therapy in older patients with cognitive impairment.* Presentation at the Annual Meeting of the American Psychological Association, San Francisco, CA.

Pynoos, R. S., Goenjian, A., & Steinberg, A. M. (1995). Strategies of disaster intervention for children and adolescents. In S. E. Hobfoll & M. deVries (Eds.), *Extreme stress and communities: Impact and intervention* (pp. 445–471). Dordrecht, The Netherlands: Kluwer.

Rabe, S., Zöllner, T., Maercker, A., & Karl, A. (2006). Neural correlates of posttraumatic growth after severe motor vehicle accidents. *Journal of Consulting and Clinical Psychology, 74*, 880–886.

Rauch, S. A. M., Morales, K. H., Zubritsky, C., Knott, K., & Oslin, D. (2006). Posttraumatic stress, depression, and health among older adults in primary care. *American Journal of Geriatric Psychiatry, 14*, 316–324.

Reed, A. E., Mikels, J. A., & Simon, K. I. (2008). Older adults prefer less choice than young adults. *Psychology and Aging, 23*, 671–675.

Resick, P. A. (2003). Cognitive therapy for posttraumatic stress disorder. *Journal of Cognitive Psychotherapy, 15*, 321–330.

Resick, P. A., Galovski, T. E., O'Brien, U. M., Scher, C. D., Clum, G. A., & Young-Xu, Y. (2008). A randomized clinical trial to dismantle components of cognitive processing therapy for posttraumatic stress disorder in female victims of interpersonal violence. *Journal of Consulting and Clinical Psychology, 76*, 243–258.

Reynolds, C., Miller, M., Pasternak, R., Frank, E., Perel, J., Cornes, C., et al. (1999). Treatment of bereavement-related major depressive episodes in later life: A controlled study of acute and continuation treatment with nortriptyline and interpersonal psychotherapy. *American Journal of Psychiatry, 156*, 202–208.

Riggs, D. S., Dancu, C. V., Gershuny, B. S., Greenberg, D., & Foa, E. B. (1992). Anger and post-traumatic stress disorder in female crime victims. *Journal of Traumatic Stress, 5*, 613–625.

Roediger, H. L., & Geraci, L. (2007). Aging and the misinformation effect: A neuropsychological analysis. *Journal of Experimental Psychology: Learning, Memory and Cognition, 33*, 321–334.

Russo, S. A., Hersen, M., & Van Hasselt, V. B. (2001). Treatment of reactivated post-traumatic stress disorder: Imaginal exposure in an older adult with multiple traumas. *Behavior Modification, 25*, 94–115.

Rybarczyk, B., & Bellg, A. (1997). *Listening to life stories: A new approach to stress intervention in health care.* New York: Springer.

Ryff, C. D., & Singer, B. (1998). The contours of positive human health. *Psychological Inquiry: An International Journal for the Advancement of Psychological Theory, 9*, 1–28.

Sareen, J., Cox, B. J., Stein, M. B., Afifi, T. O., Fleet, C., & Asmundson, G. J. (2007). Physical and mental comorbidity, disability, and suicidal behavior associated with posttraumatic stress disorder in a large community sample. *Psychosomatic Medicine, 69*, 242–248.

Schacter, D. L. (1996). *Searching for memory: The brain, the mind, and the past.* New York: Basic Books.

Schnurr, P., & Spiro, A. (1999). Combat exposure, posttraumatic stress disorder symptoms, and health behaviors as predictors of self-reported physical health in older veterans. *Journal of Nervous and Mental Disease, 187*, 353–359.

Schnurr, P. P., Spiro, A., & Paris, A. H. (2000). Physician-diagnosed medical disorders in relation to PTSD symptoms in older male military veterans. *Health Psychology, 19*, 91–98.

Schönfeld, S., & Ehlers, A. (2006). Overgeneral memory extends to pictorial retrieval cues and correlates with cognitive features in posttraumatic stress disorder. *Emotion, 6*, 611–621.

Schramke, C. (1997). Anxiety disorders. In P. Nussbaum (Ed.), *Handbook of neuropsychology and aging* (pp. 80–97). New York: Plenum.

Scogin, F., Rickard, H. C., Keith, S., Wilson, J., & McElreath, L. (1992). Progressive and imaginal relaxation training for elderly persons with subjective anxiety. *Psychology and Aging, 7*, 419–424.

Seligman, M. E. P. (2002). Positive psychology, positive prevention, and positive therapy. In C. R. Snyder & S. J. Lopez (Eds.), *Handbook of positive psychology* (pp. 1–7). New York: Oxford University Press.

Seyle, H. (1974). *Stress without distress.* Philadelphia: Lippincott.

Shmotkin, D. (2005). Happiness in the face of adversity: Reformulating the dynamic and modular bases of subjective well-being. *Review of General Psychology, 9*, 291–325.

Shmotkin, D., Blumstein, T., & Modan, B. (2003). Beyond keeping active: Concomitants of being a volunteer in old-old age. *Psychology and Aging, 18*, 602–607.

Smith, M. H., Glass, G. V., & Miller, T. I. (1980). *The benefits of psychotherapy.* Baltimore: Johns Hopkins University Press.

Snell, F. I., & Padin-Rivera, E. (1997). Group treatment for older veterans with post-traumatic stress disorder. *Journal of Psychosocial Nursing and Mental Health Services, 35*, 10–16.

Snow, K. (1999, November). *Cognitive behavioral therapy with compromised older adults.* Presentation at the 52nd Annual Scientific Meeting of the Gerontological Society of America, San Francisco.

Solomon, R. M., & Shapiro, F. (2008). EMDR and the adaptive information processing model: Potential mechanisms of change. *Journal of EMDR Practice and Research, 2*, 315–325.

Spiro, R., Schnurr, P., & Aldwin, C. (1994). Combat related posttraumatic stress disorder symptoms in older men. *Psychology and Aging, 9*, 17–26.

Stanley, M., Hopko, D., Diefenbacj, G., Bourland, S., Rodriquez, G., & Wagener, P. (2003). Cognitive behavioral therapy for late life generalized anxiety disorder in primary care: Preliminary findings. *American Journal of Geriatric Psychiatry, 11*, 92–97.

Stern, Y. (2007). *Cognitive reserve: Theory and applications.* Philadelphia: Taylor and Francis.

Summers, M. & Hyer, L. (1991). Measurement of PTSD among older combat veterans. VA Merit Review Grant.

Sutker, P. B., Uddo-Carne, M., & Allain, A. N. (1991). Clinical and research assessment of posttraumatic stress disorder: A conceptual overview. *Psychological Assessment, 3*, 520–530.

Tedeschi, R. G., & Calhoun, L. G. (1995). *Trauma and transformation: Growing in the aftermath of suffering.* Thousand Oaks, CA: Sage.

Teri, L., Curtis, J., Gallagher-Thompson, D., & Thompson L. (1994). Cognitive-behavioral therapy with depressed older adults. In L. S. Schneider, C. F. Reynolds, B. D. Lebowitz, & A. J. Friedhoff (Eds.), *Diagnosis and treatment of depression in late life: Results of the NIH consensus development conference* (pp. 279–291). Washington, DC: American Psychiatric Press.

Thompson, L. W., Gallagher, D., & Breckenridge, J. S. (1987). Comparative effectiveness of psychotherapies for depressed elders. *Journal of Consulting and Clinical Psychology, 55*, 385–390.

Thompson, I. W., Gallagher, D., & Czirr, R. (1988). Personality disorder and outcome in the treatment of late-life depression. *Journal of Geriatric Psychiatry, 21*, 133–153.

Thompson, L. W., Gallagher, D., Hansen S., Gantz, F., & Steffen, A. (November 1991). *Comparison of desipramine and cognitive/behavioral therapy in the treatment of late-life depression.* Paper presented at the meeting of Gerontological Society of America, San Francisco.

Thorp, S. R., & Stein, M. B. (2005). Posttraumatic stress disorder and functioning. *PTSD Research Quarterly, 16*, 1–7.

True, W. R., Rice, J., Eisen, S. A., Heath, A. C., Goldberg, J., Lyons, M. J., et al. (1993). A twin study of genetic and environmental contributions to liability for posttraumatic tress symptoms. *Archives of General Psychiatry, 51*, 838–839.

Tulving, E. (1995). Organization of memory: Quo vadis? In M. S. Gazzaniga (Ed.), *The cognitive neurosciences* (pp. 839–853). Cambridge: Massachusetts Institute of Technology Press.

Van Der Kolk, B. A. (2002). Posttraumatic therapy in the age of neuroscience. *Psychoanalytic Dialogues, 12*, 381–392.

Van Minnen, A., Wessel, I., Verhaak, C., & Smeenk, J. (2005). The relationship between autobiographical memory specificity and depressed mood following a stressful life event: A prospective study. *British Journal of Clinical Psychology, 44*, 405–415.

Vasterling, J., & Braily, K. (2005). Neuropsychological findings in adults with PTSD. In J. Vasterling & C. Brewin (Eds.), *Neuropsychology of PTSD: Biological, cognitive and clinical perspectives* (pp. 178–207). New York: Guilford Press.

Vasterling, J. J., Brailey, K., Constans, J. I., Borges, A., & Sutker, P. B. (1997). Assessment of intellectual resources in Gulf War veterans: Relationship to PTSD. *Assessment, 4*, 51–59.

Vasterling, J. J., Duke, L. M., Brailey, K., Constans, J. I., Allain, A. N., Jr., & Sutker, P. B. (2002). Attention, learning, and memory performances and intellectual resources in Vietnam veterans: PTSD and no disorder comparisons. *Neuropsychology, 16*, 5–14.

Walter-Ginzburg, A., Shmotkin, D., Blumstein, T., & Shorek, A. (2005). A gender-based dynamic multidimensional longitudinal analysis of resilience and mortality in the old-old in Israel: The cross-sectional and longitudinal aging study (CALAS). *Social Science and Medicine, 60*, 1705–1715.

Weiss, D., Marmar, C., Schlenger, J., Jordan, K., Hough, R., & Kulka R. (1992). The prevalence of lifetime and partial posttraumatic stress disorder in Vietnam theater veterans. *Journal of Traumatic Stress, 5*, 365–375.

Wetherell, J. L., Gatz, M., & Craske, M. G. (2003). Treatment of generalized anxiety disorder in older adults. *Journal of Consulting and Clinical Psychology, 71*, 31–40.

Williams, J. M., Barnhofer, T., Crane, C., Herman, D., Raes, F., Watkins, E., et al. (2007). Autobiographical memory specificity and emotional disorder. *Psychological Bulletin, 133*, 122–148.

Yehuda, R., Golier, J. A., & Kaufman, S. (2005). Circadian rhythm of salivary cortisol in Holocaust survivors with and without PTSD. *American Journal of Psychiatry, 162*, 998–1000.

Yehuda, R., Morris, A., Labinsky, E., Zemelman, S., & Schmeidler, J. (2007). Ten-year follow-up study of cortisol levels in aging Holocaust survivors with and without PTSD. *Journal of Traumatic Stress, 20*, 757–762.

Zatzick, D. F., Kang, S. M., Müller, H. G., Russo, J. E., Rivara, F. P., Katon, W., et al. (2002). Predicting posttraumatic distress in hospitalization trauma survivors with acute injuries. *The American Journal of Psychiatry, 159*, 941–946.

Zeiss, R. A., & Steffen, A. M. (1996). Interdisciplinary health care teams: The basic unit of geriatric care. In L. L. Carstensen, B. A. Edelstein, & L. Dornbrand (Eds.), *The handbook of clinical gerontology* (pp. 423–450). Newbury Park, CA: Sage.

PART III

PATHWAYS AND GATEKEEPERS: MODERATING, MEDIATING, AND PROXIMAL PROCESSES

9

Impact of Resources on Successful Adaptation among the Oldest Old

MAURICE MacDONALD AND JINMYOUNG CHO

ABSTRACT

This chapter analyzes the influences of resources on Georgia centenarians' well-being, considering social interactions, caregiving services, and economic resource adequacy in context of other resources and constraints such as personality, cognitive ability, and functional limitations. We compare the well-being effects of proximal resources to those for distal resources and major life events. Both subjective (hedonic) and psychological (eudaimonia) well-being are analyzed. Subjective mental health is primarily related to perceived economic resources that are associated with distal resource indicators (education, ethnicity) so that centenarians can maintain a positive mental outlook despite functional limitations because their resources buffer economic anxiety. Their social interactions enhance the social provisions dimension of subjective well-being. However neither social nor economic resource adequacy influences the autonomy and growth aspects of psychological well-being, whereas personality resources are critical for that kind of adaptation.

INTRODUCTION

Previous research on the social and economic resources of centenarians and other very old individuals has demonstrated that oldest-old adults manage to maintain a fair to good level of well-being despite deficits in their functional health, cognition, and the threat of depleting personal economic resources as a result of extreme longevity (Pinquart & Sörenson, 2000); see Chapter 3 for further discussion of evidence that subjective well-being does not necessarily decrease in extreme age. Although studies have often reported protective influences of support via social interactions with friends and family on the well-being of oldest-old adults (Landau & Litwin, 2001; MacDonald, 2007), only a few studies have found that personal resource adequacy supports their mental well-being (Martin, 2002; Smith, Fleeson, Geiselmann, Settersten, & Kunzmann, 1999). In addition, investigators have used the 1988–1992 Georgia Centenarian Study of community-dwelling participants (Phase 1) to describe and assess the social and economic resources of centenarians compared to sexagenarians and octogenarians (Goetting, Martin, Poon, & Johnson, 1996; Martin, Poon, Kim, & Johnson, 1996). However, the most recent study of Georgia centenarians and octogenarians (Phase 3) provides a population-based sample that includes institutionalized participants and the study collected more comprehensive data about social and economic resources from them and proxy informants. The goals for this chapter are to analyze the antecedents of Phase 3 centenarians' social and economic resources and their association with resource adequacy and well-being, and thus to provide a more complete understanding of which resources are most critical for well-being to guide policies and practices for better support of extremely old individuals. Toward that end, we have adapted the essential features of the life-span Developmental Adaptation Model (Martin & Martin, 2002) to examine how well distal (e.g., life events, educational achievement) and proximal resources (e.g., income, caregiving services) contribute to centenarians' self-assessments of their well-being.

The first part of our analysis describes the social and economic resources of our Phase 3 Georgia study participants and contrasts findings with an earlier description of centenarians from Phase 1. Second, we explain our multivariate analysis procedures and summarize results from analyzing how social and economic resources influence resource adequacy and developmental adaptation with respect to subjective well-being (SWB, for social provisions, and mental health) and psychological well-being (PWB, for growth, and autonomy). In the concluding section, we identify social and personal economic resource deficits that could be ameliorated via social support practices for better SWB, as well as personal habits and attitudes to promote PWB in extreme age.

Phase 3 of the Georgia Centenarian Study recruited participants in a 44-county area of northern Georgia from lists of nursing facilities and personal-care homes and for registered voters with date-of-birth information, which resulted in an 83% response rate for a population-based sample of 239 community-dwelling and institutionalized centenarians and near centenarians. To participate in the interview section about resources and SWB, centenarians needed to score 17 or higher on the Mini-Mental Status

Examination (MMSE; Folstein, Folstein, & McHugh, 1975). After that restriction, the sample included 137 centenarians and near centenarians (mean age of 99.7 years; age range from 98 to 108). Although 71.8% of centenarians reported that their overall physical health was good or excellent, 44.9% lived in either a skilled nursing facility (23.5%) or in assisted-living residences (20.4%), and the remaining 56.2% lived in their private home or apartment. Most of the participants were women (78.8%). By ethnicity, 83.2% were White and the other 16.8% of the participants were African American. Only 3.6% were married; 6.6% were divorced, and 84.7% were widowed. For this chapter, we relied on proxy informants' reports to obtain measures of the centenarians' personal economic resource variables. Including those variables permits a test of whether economic resources have effects on mental health separate from that for the centenarians' perceptions about resource adequacy. Proxy informants were nominated by the centenarians to obtain a close family member first and then other relatives, or if no relatives were available another knowledgeable person (e.g., neighbors, nurses); 61.1% of proxies were adult children.

GEORGIA CENTENARIANS' SOCIAL AND ECONOMIC RESOURCES

Table 9.1 provides a description of the social and economic resources of the Georgia centenarians and the octogenarian comparison group, including chi-square tests for differences in the frequency distribution of the resource variables. In addition to describing the types and levels of various resources for the centenarians, the age-group comparisons provide cross-section evidence about the extent to which resources may appear to be more constrained for centenarians, as would be expected if their survival is associated with depleting their own personal resources or because they have few relatives and friends who have survived to provide income assistance, time help, or support for access to community agency or government benefits.

For social resources, the descriptive variables include indicators of the study participants' social network (actual visits, whether they have a confidant, and whether there is someone to provide help if needed in an emergency), use of instrumental support (for personal care, household chores, and meal preparation, as well as who provided any help of that kind), and income assistance from family members or in the form of means-tested Supplemental Security Income (SSI) from the federal government. The chi-square statistics for visits, confidant, and someone to help indicate that there was no significant difference between the centenarians' and the octogenarians' social network functioning. For both age groups, nearly all participants

TABLE 9.1. *Social and economic resources of Georgia octogenarians and centenarians*

Variable	80–89	100+	Chi-Square
Social Resources			
Actual visits	$n = 72$	$n = 139$	
None	6.9%	8.6%	0.51
1 time/week	13.9%	12.9%	
2–6 times/week	66.7%	63.3%	
Daily	12.5%	15.1%	
Confidant	$n = 71$	$n = 142$	
Yes	100.0%	98.6%	1.01
No	0.0%	1.4%	
Someone to help	$n = 72$	$n = 141$	
Yes	100.0%	97.9%	1.55
No	0.0%	2.1%	
Personal-care help	$n = 71$	$n = 114$	
Yes	11.3%	45.6%	23.55***
No	88.7%	54.4%	
Household chores help	$n = 71$	$n = 114$	
Yes	42.3%	86.8%	41.21***
No	57.7%	13.2%	
Meal preparation help	$n = 71$	$n = 116$	
Yes	15.5%	73.3%	58.86***
No	84.5%	26.7%	
Who gave any help	$n = 60$	$n = 127$	
Nursing-home staff	27.1%	51.1%	
Hired help	37.5%	23.6%	
Daughter or son	14.6%	12.7%	
Other kin	12.5%	5.7%	
Community agency	6.4%	4.7%	
Friend	0.3%	2.2%	0.93*
Income assistance from family members	$n = 59$	$n = 199$	
Yes	11.9%	14.1%	0.19
No	88.1%	85.9%	
SSI	$n = 56$	$n = 197$	
Yes	16.1%	13.7%	
No	83.9%	86.3%	0.20
Economic Resources			
Social Security	$n = 59$	$n = 199$	
Yes	89.8%	89.1%	0.03
No	10.2%	10.9%	
Pension	$n = 59$	$n = 199$	
Yes	54.8%	35.6%	7.33**
No	45.2%	64.4%	

Variable	80–89	100+	Chi-Square
Investments	$n = 54$	$n = 194$	
Yes	59.3%	50.5%	1.30
No	40.7%	49.5%	
Yearly income (dollars)	$n = 59$	$n = 199$	
<1,000–2,999	3.8%	4.4%	27.00**
3,000–3,999	1.9%	1.6%	
4,000–4,999	1.9%	1.1%	
5,000–6,999	5.8%	4.4%	
7,000–9,999	7.7%	20.9%	
10,000–14,999	9.6%	22.5%	
15,000–19,999	3.8%	9.9%	
20,000–29,999	9.6%	11.0%	
30,000–39,999	11.5%	9.9%	
40,000+	44.2%	14.3%	
Finances to meet emergency	$n = 66$	$n = 219$	
Yes	83.3%	67.1%	6.46**
No	16.7%	32.9%	

***$p < .001$. **$p < .01$. *$p < .05$.

had a confidant or reported there was someone to provide help if needed, whereas more than 75% had visitors at least two times per week. (By contrast, Table 12.2, in Chapter 12, reports that 35% of veteran Jewish Israelis age 80 and older had restricted social networks with virtually no friends or neighbors with whom they were in contact.) However, Georgia centenarians were significantly different from octogenarians on receiving instrumental support. For example, although only 11.3% of octogenarians received personal care help, 45.6% of centenarians reported that kind of help. Centenarians also received help with household chores and meal preparation at much higher rates than octogenarians (respectively, 86.8% to 42.3%, and 73.3% to 15.5%). Centenarians were also more likely than octogenarians to receive instrumental support from staff in a nursing home (either skilled nursing facility or assisted-living facility) or through hired help than from relatives, a community agency, or friend (chi-square 0.93, $p < .05$). Nearly three quarters (74.7%) of centenarians had instrumental support from their nursing home or hired help, compared with 64.6% for octogenarians. Centenarians were less likely to rely on a relative or community agency than octogenarians but more likely to rely on a friend to help them. Hence, it appears that centenarians' longevity is associated with a shift from family members as helpers toward paid staff or hired help. It could be that family members provide financial help for nursing-home costs and to pay for hired help more often for centenarians. However, on the basis of the proxy reports about income assistance from family members, there was no significant difference between the two Georgia age groups (11.9% for octogenarians, 14.1% for centenarians). Furthermore, for centenarians, the percentage who received SSI (13.7%) was about the same as for income assistance from family members, and again there was no significant difference of SSI income as a source between the two age groups.

Overall, centenarians have fairly robust social networks, and the measures for that aspect of social resources were not significantly different from octogenarians' reports. About 15% of centenarians received income assistance from either their family or SSI, and that rate was not significantly different from octogenarians'. However, a near majority of centenarians received instrumental support for personal care, and three quarters or more of centenarians had help with household chores or meal preparation, whereas for octogenarians, less than 12% reported getting help for personal care, less than 50% had help with household chores, and only about 15% received meal preparation help. Thus, it is quite evident that instrumental support received by centenarians is more critical to their well-being than for octogenarians. Our age comparisons also revealed that centenarians rely less on family members for instrumental support than octogenarians. Still, most of the instrumental support for both centenarians and octogenarians was provided by nursing-home staff or hired help.

The variables describing centenarians' personal economic resources included whether the proxy informant reported that the participants received Social Security retirement income, had income from a pension, had income from investments, their annual income bracket, and whether the participants had finances sufficient to meet an emergency. There were no significant differences between centenarians and octogenarians with respect to whether they had income from social security (about 90% did) or investments (around 50% for centenarians, and nearly 60% for octogenarians). Octogenarians were much more likely to have a pension (55%, compared with 36% of centenarians). For annual total incomes less than $7,000, the percentage for octogenarians (13.7%) was not that different from centenarians (11.5%). Centenarians were much more likely to have between $7,000 and $10,000 in annual income (43.4%) than octogenarians (17.3%). Also, there was a very large difference in the percentage of octogenarians reported to have $40,000 or more in annual income (44.2% versus 14.3% for centenarians). Apparently, those octogenarians who are fortunate enough to have incomes exceeding $7,000 are much better off than centenarians above that same income threshold, which could be attributed to the substantially greater frequency of octogenarians who had income from pensions. If pensions are an important reason for those very different middle- to upper-income distributions, it follows that Georgia centenarians' had the disadvantage of entering the workforce before pensions became either widespread or as generous as Georgia octogenarians experienced. In contrast, centenarians have apparently benefited from the development of the U.S. old-age social safety net as much as octogenarians, in that there were no age group differences with respect to Social Security or SSI income support. Nevertheless, roughly one in eight centenarians had annual incomes less than $7,000, which indicates they are below the official U.S. poverty line and therefore at risk with respect to nutritional well-being and highly likely to have other unmet consumption needs. Thus, it is not surprising that nearly one third of proxy informants reported that the centenarians did not have sufficient finances to meet emergency needs (compared with only 16.7% for octogenarians, a statistically significant difference).

In brief summary for both social resources and personal economic resources, a main result is that as few as one eighth to as many as one third of centenarians are at risk with respect to income insecurity despite assistance they receive from their family or the government, and more than 40% require instrumental support that is primarily provided by nursing-home staff or hired help. In contrast, another substantial fraction of centenarians do not appear to be that much different from octogenarians on a variety of social and economic resource measures, such as having investment income or social security benefits, as well as the social interaction they obtain from a fairly active support network and their widespread availability of confidants or someone to help them if needed. Such great variety suggests that there are differences in centenarians' sources and amounts of social and economic resources that may be linked to substantial variation in their subjective and psychological well-being.

The descriptive statistics for the Phase 3 population-based sample also provide insights that are quite different from the findings for social and economic resources of community-dwelling centenarians in the first Georgia Centenarian Study by Martin et al. (1996). For example, centenarians in the current study are much more likely to obtain help from nursing-home staff or hired help than from their family members or community agencies. By contrast, Martin et al. (1996) reported that 63% of Phase 1 centenarians' primary care was provided by sons or daughters. Turning to social interactions, Martin et al.'s (1996) comparisons across sexagenarians, octogenarians, and centenarians revealed that the latter had significantly fewer visitors and talked less on the phone. In the current study, there was no difference between octogenarians' and centenarians' visits, which seem surprising, as we would expect that a sampling to include nursing-home residents could reveal a situation in which visits are inhibited more than when considering only community-dwelling participants. Similarly, the percentage of the current study sample who reported they had a confidant or had someone to help (99% and 98%) was very high and roughly the same as in the earlier study (94% and 96%). Another comparison showed that about 75% of centenarians in the first study had help with food from family or friends, which appears quite similar to our finding that 74% of centenarians had meal preparation help. Comparisons about income sources, annual income, and finances sufficient to meet emergencies in this study with Phase 1 results (see Martin et al., 1996) were also informative to some extent. However, those comparisons are confounded because we preferred the proxy informants' reports about the centenarians' economic resources. (By comparing proxy and centenarian responses to the Older Adult Resources and Services [OARS] questions about income sources and amounts for Phase 3, we found that the proxies tended to report more income sources and greater income amounts than centenarians themselves.) One large difference was that the centenarian community dwellers from Phase 1 reported that only 21% had pensions, whereas our proxy informants for the entire centenarian population reported that 35% had a pension. In addition to the different informants, the greater percentage with pensions in Phase 3 may be a period effect from the expansion of pensions over time. Community-dwelling centenarians were more likely to report they received SSI (23%) than were the current study proxy informants (14%). However, there was no appreciable difference between the Phase 1 and Phase 3 studies for whether Social Security was an income source, and that was also the case for income assistance from family members. Although the general shape of the annual income distributions was similar for the two studies, the modal income-bracket categories were quite different. For Phase 1, the modal category was $4,000–$4,999 and included 21% of centenarians, whereas in Phase 3, the modal category was 23% for the $10,000–$14,999 bracket. Part of that difference could be attributed to income growth – social security and SSI benefits are indexed, and investments are more valuable currently than they were 20 years ago; most of it probably resulted from our use of proxy informants. Turning next to the lowest-income groups, the proxy informants reported that only about 12% of centenarians had incomes less than $7,000, whereas more than one third of the centenarians in Phase 1 reported incomes that low. Nevertheless, the proxy informants reported a greater percentage of centenarians were without finances sufficient for an emergency (33%) than

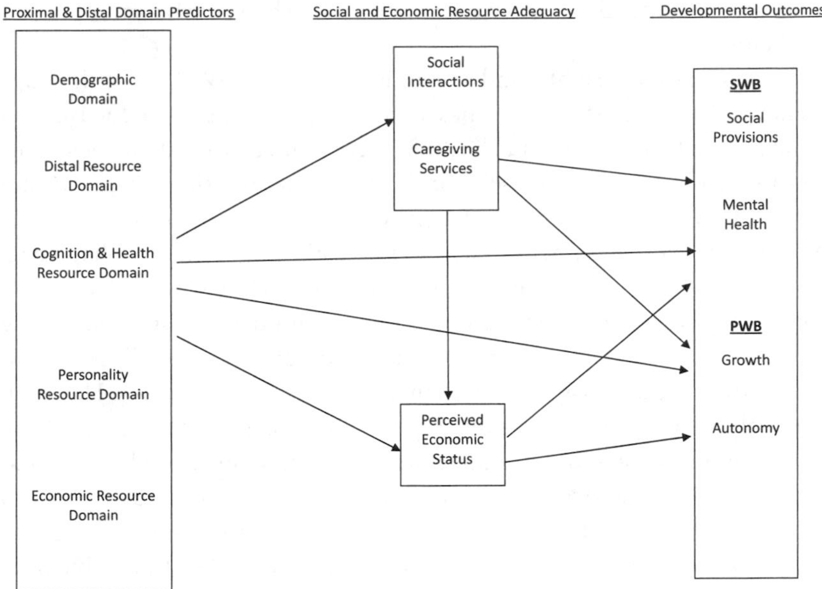

FIGURE 9.1. Theoretical Framework and Model Specification for Analysis of Social and Economic Resource Adequacy Influences on Centenarians' SWB and PWB.

was found for Phase 1 (24%). This is a very surprising difference that probably results from including nursing-home residents in the current study. Hence, our general conclusion is that, despite some growth in incomes and other factors such as increased longevity that may have helped preserve participants' family and social networks better than 20 years ago, present-day Georgia centenarians' economic resources are more inadequate then would be expected from earlier research. In contrast, Chapter 7 reported that Georgia centenarians' major life events do not include experiencing financial crises after age 70, so further research on trends in centenarians' economic well-being is warranted.

THEORETICAL FRAMEWORK AND MULTIVARIATE ANALYSIS STRATEGY

Figure 9.1 illustrates the application of a theoretical framework based on the developmental adaptation model that guided our analysis of the role of social and economic resource adequacy variables as influences on SWB and PWB. With respect to the models of adaptation for longevity considered in Chapter 5, our framework is based on that chapter's second model, to include distal experiences and past achievements as important predictors.

As shown on the right-hand side of Figure 9.1, for SWB, those developmental outcome constructs are measured by an OARS question focusing on the emotional aspect of mental health (Fillenbaum, 1988) and the social provisions scale (Cutrona & Russell, 1987). The social provisions scale includes various aspects of social relationships quality and thus can be seen as a measure of well-being, per the discussion at the beginning of Chapter 12; in particular, it is worth noting that the scale includes items for feeling "personally responsible for the well-being of another person" and having "relationships where my competence and skill are recognized" so that to some extent the scale captures exchange aspects of relationships. However, the analysis reported in Chapter 12 provides an explicit treatment of the influence of giving and receiving time and money on mental health and thus is much more focused on social exchange than our study. For PWB measurement, we used Ryff's (1989) growth and autonomy subscales; Chapter 17 provides a comprehensive discussion of Ryff's PWB scales and includes results from Bishop (2006) for old and very old men and women residing in monasteries.

Thus, we follow Keyes, Shmotkin, and Ryff (2002) to distinguish between hedonic SWB measures (e.g., mental health), which have often been found to be associated with the levels of resource variables such as education and economic status, and PWB measures, which are intended to measure aspects of life's meaning and purpose or attitudes to life's challenges (or, eudaimonia). The introduction to Chapter 3 provides a more complete discussion contrasting the hedonic SWB approach to understanding well-being with the PWB eudaimonia concept concerning striving for excellence and perfection in life. Although our study considers both SWB and PWB in their positive dimensions, Chapter 3 innovates by considering the negativity bias of human experience and how that may be integrated specifically for considering the SWB and PWB of oldest-old individuals.

For SWB, the social provisions scale is based on questions that ask the centenarian to assess the nature and quality of their social interactions, which may be dependent on the size of their social network (a resource constraint), and as discussed earlier, research on centenarians has demonstrated that their perceptions about economic resource adequacy are associated with their mental health. The Ryff (1989) growth scale includes questions about the extent to which the centenarians were "trying to make big improvements" or whether "life has been a continuing process of learning," which are attitudes that need not be constrained or supported by social and economic resources. It is less clear whether the autonomy scale, which was intended to measure ability to resist social pressures to think and act in certain ways (measured by items such as whether the participants agreed or disagreed that they "are concerned about what other people think about the choices I have made in my life"), would depend on social and economic resources. There is some evidence that autonomy appears to be stable across old age groups (Clarke, Marshall, Ryff, & Rosenthal, 2000), whereas growth declines after age 65 (Pudrovska, Springer, & Hauser, 2005). Also in their study of Canadian seniors, Clarke et al. (2000) found that autonomy was not associated with self-rated health status, whereas growth was negatively related to self-reported health. Our multivariate analysis was intended to reveal whether the two types of well-being are differentially influenced by social and economic resources and to provide a more comprehensive assessment with respect to developmental outcomes for centenarians than heretofore.

Following the developmental adaptation model, the specification of our multivariate analysis includes a distinction between the proximal and distal aspects of resource influences. As the left-hand side of Figure 9.1 displays, we also separated those exogenous variables into domains. The variables in the demographics domain are age, as determined by birth date of centenarians; gender; ethnicity; and residence type. Distal resources include an engaged lifestyle scale (Martin, Baenziger, MacDonald, Siegler, & Poon, 2009) based on affirmative responses to questions about challenging and developmental experiences such as a new career or continued education; the separate number of other important life events occurring at least 20 years before interview; total years of schooling; and a 10-point scale coding primary occupations as more or less skilled. The other domains are cognition and health (ADL ability to perform activities of daily living, and cognitive ability from the Mini-Mental Status Exam), personality (four "big five" traits, plus a scale for trust), and economic resources (income bracket level; whether they had any wealth in the form of pensions/investments or received social security benefits; and the size of the social network, based on the number of people they could visit in that person's home). We tested for whether variables in all of the proximal and distal predictor domains had statistically significant associations with resource adequacy, as well as for any associations with the SWB and PWB outcomes. In preliminary analysis, we also explored associations of those outcomes with measures indicating stress and coping behaviors (number of critical life events during the past 2 years, plus reports on the extent to which coping was based on seeking support or through religion), but there were few direct effects. (See Chapter 13 for a theoretical discussion of the potentially complex relationships among religious coping, stress, and negative affect with empirical results for Georgia centenarians.)

We were particularly interested in the direct relationships between the social and economic resource adequacy variables and the developmental outcomes, while accounting for the extent of ADL functional health and the likely critical role of cognitive ability. Chapter 11 emphasized that cognitive ability is important for problem solving in the face of everyday challenges, whereas dementia certainly hinders adaptation and resilience in extreme age. By restricting our analysis sample to participants with MMSE scores greater than 17, the scope for dementia confounds is limited to that extent. Chapter 12 demonstrates that degrees of disability and social networks are closely related to depressive symptoms in very old age.

Figure 9.1 illustrates the relationships we expected. Social interactions, instrumental support from caregiving services, and perceived economic status were specified as intervening resource adequacy variables associated with the proximal and distal domain resources and that have direct associations with each of the outcomes. Our measure of social interaction was a scale that counts the number of people the centenarian could visit in another person's home, as well as the number of recent phone calls and actual visits in the centenarians' home. Caregiving services were the total number of five different types of care services received during the previous 6 months, including nursing care, personal care, checking on their well-being, household chores, and meal preparation. Because social interactions and instrumental support presumably contribute to the centenarians' sense of economic well-being, we specified those social resources as potential influences on perceived economic status, as well as the developmental outcomes. Perceived economic status was reported by the centenarians in response to five items from the OARS that capture the present and expected future dimensions of economic resource adequacy (e.g., financial resources sufficient to "meet emergencies," "buy small luxuries," and whether "you feel you will have enough for your needs in the future"). The centenarians' perceptions of resource adequacy were conceptually and practically distinct from the economic resource domain measures of income and wealth obtained from the proxy informants, because the centenarians' basic consumption and health-care-related needs could vary greatly in any income or wealth grouping.

Because our intent was to provide a comprehensive, albeit exploratory, analysis of the influence of all the resource domains and resource adequacy measures on each developmental outcome, the number of explanatory variables is large so that we were constrained by sample size and had to develop a process for preliminary and then stage-wise analysis. A first preliminary analysis involved one-way analyses of variance with selected measures of resource adequacy predicting perceived economic status and the developmental outcomes. That analysis established that there were statistically significant ($p < .05$) bivariate relationships between social interactions and mental health (but not social provisions); social interactions and growth (but not autonomy); economic resources (income, education) and mental health (but not social provisions); and economic resources and growth (but not autonomy). We found, as expected, that perceived economic status was associated with income and education, but that kind of resource adequacy was not associated with social network size or the number of care services received. The second part of the preliminary analysis obtained separate, within-domain regressions predicting social interactions, caregiving services, perceived economic status, and each of the four developmental outcome variables. In other words, we regressed the dependent variables on age, gender, residence type, and ethnicity for the demographics domain, and so on separately for all of the other domains (e.g., regressing perceived economic status on income, wealth, and social network size for the economic resource domain predictors of that resource adequacy measure). In that fashion, we were able to identify which variables in each domain had a significant ($p < .05$) association with the intervening resource adequacy variables, as well as the SWB and PWB outcomes.

Trimming out the variables that were not significant in the proximal and distal resource domains reduced the number of variables available for use in a final set of stage-wise regressions to predict the developmental outcomes first without and then with the social and economic resource adequacy variables. When the second-stage models that included the resource adequacy variables produced significant relationships to a developmental outcome, we selected that augmented model as the final regression for our main findings. Otherwise, the first-stage model without the resource adequacy variables was selected, and in that case, our final results are for the direct influences of distal and proximal resources on the developmental outcomes. For example, we found that only the personality traits of neuroticism and competence were significant predictors for autonomy (i.e., none of the other predictors for any of the other domains was significant), so those two traits entered the first-stage regression to predict autonomy. When we added all the resource adequacy variables in the second stage, none of them was significant. Therefore, our main findings for autonomy are about the direct effects of the two

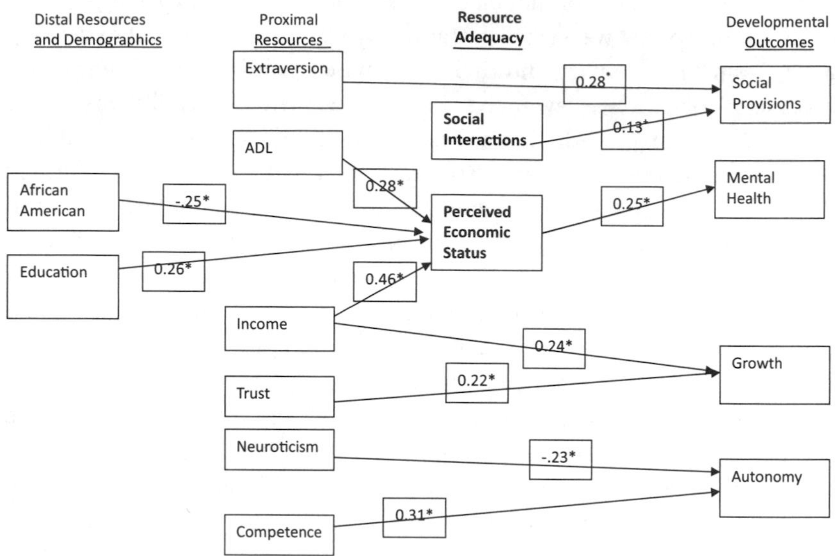

FIGURE 9.2. Heuristic Model: Combining Results for Regressions on Intervening Resource Adequacy Variables and Stage-wise Regressions on Developmental Outcomes (*$p < 0.05$).

personality domain variables, as depicted at the bottom of Figure 9.2. By contrast, the top of Figure 9.2 shows that the social interactions resource adequacy measure was marginally associated with social provisions ($p < .10$) in the second-stage regression; and in that final regression, extraversion also had a significant, direct effect.

INFLUENCES OF DISTAL AND PROXIMAL RESOURCES AND RESOURCE ADEQUACY ON SWB AND PWB

Figure 9.2 summarizes the results of multiple regression analysis with the relevant standardized regression coefficients. For those resource adequacy variables that were associated with a developmental outcome (i.e., social interaction influence on social provisions, perceived economic status influence on mental health), the coefficients are from the second part of the stage-wise analysis. Figure 9.2 also displays the results of the final regressions predicting those same resource adequacy variables, and the significant ($p < .05$) or marginally significant ($p < .10$) direct effects of the proximal and distal resource variables on the developmental outcomes.

It is apparent from Figure 9.2 that the structure of the associations found for the predictor variables with the developmental outcomes is quite different for SWB than for PWB. Some of the intervening resource adequacy variables are related to SWB (e.g., social provisions, mental health), but that was not the case for either measure of PWB. For SWB, social provisions were marginally associated with the social interactions resource adequacy measure. However, that kind of resource adequacy was not related to mental health SWB. Instead, economic resource adequacy was related to mental health. We have already noted that autonomy was positively related to competence as a personality trait and negatively related to neuroticism, which are proximal resources. Hence, one of our main conclusions is that centenarians' SWB, but not their PWB, depends critically on the adequacy of their social interactions and personal economic resources. Although income was directly associated with PWB growth, and the size of that effect (0.24) was about the same as for the trust aspect of personality (0.22) with growth, centenarians' income adequacy was not related to growth. (Our discussion here considers how that discrepancy may arise.)

Our analysis was also designed to discover whether there are any indirect effects of the proximal and distal resource variables operating via their relationships to the intervening resource adequacy variables. In Figure 9.2, such indirect effects connect variables on the left-hand side to the developmental outcomes through the resource adequacy variables in the middle of that diagram. That is the case only for mental health. The centenarians' functional health (ADL), income, African American ethnicity, and education were all related to perceived economic status, and that resource adequacy measure was positively related to mental health. Furthermore, in the second, stage-wise regression for mental health, only perceived economic status had a significant effect (although ADL was marginally significant at $p < .10$). Thus, there is some evidence that perceptions of economic resource adequacy entirely mediate whatever influence African American ethnicity, education, and income would otherwise have for mental health.

With respect to the potential importance of functional health decline on SWB, the near nonsignificance of the ADL variable highlights the value of the economic resources obtained from current income, as well as the economic advantage of more education and the disadvantage of African American ethnicity. Thus, it is quite evident that many centenarians manage to maintain a positive mental outlook because their resources are adequate enough to buffer the economic anxiety that would be associated with serious functional health limitations. However, there was no multivariate evidence that social interactions contribute to perceived economic status or mental health. Perhaps detecting such relationships requires measures that separate receiving from giving support as implemented in Chapter 12's analysis of depression among veteran Jewish Israelis.

In our initial analysis of variance for mental health and other outcomes, the number of caregiving services was negatively associated with mental health, which undoubtedly mirrors the nearly significant association we found between ADL and mental health. In another multivariate analysis that focused on the relationship of the number of hours of care received by centenarians with their mental health status, we found that there was a positive association when ADL was excluded. From that additional analysis, one can infer that instrumental social support has a positive influence on SWB for mental health, albeit it ignores the influence of ADL itself. Still, the relationship of instrumental support to SWB may not be so simple. To illustrate, the analysis of veteran Jewish Israelis' depressive symptoms in very late life reported in Table 12.4 of Chapter 12 shows that receiving help increased those symptoms when IADL disability and age were included as a predictors (however, those Israeli participants who gave help had fewer depressive symptoms). It may be that receiving more types of care or more care-hours serves as an indicator of the severity of functional limitations so that the caregiving variable is negatively associated with SWB even while controlling for ADL status.

We can obtain additional insights about factors that are critical for centenarians' adaptation for longevity by considering how prominently personality characteristics are featured in Figure 9.2's analysis summary. There were six proximal resource variables that had either direct associations with one of the SWB or PWB outcomes or that were associated with perceived economic status. Four of those were personality traits, and their effect sizes were as large or larger than for most of the other significant predictors. Extraversion ($\beta = 0.28$) was more important for social provisions SWB than for social interactions (0.13), whereas the competence-autonomy coefficient (0.31) was the largest single influence we found for any of the developmental outcomes. Also, the effect for trust (0.22) was nearly as large as for income level (0.24) on growth. In fact, the only outcome that was not associated with personality was mental health. In summary, centenarians with personalities favoring extraversion, trust, and competence, and the least neuroticism, have adapted better to their extreme age.

To put our main multivariate findings in context and to consider their contribution to knowledge about the correlates of centenarians' well-being requires some brief comparison to a few prior studies of the influence of psychosocial resources on developmental adaptation and outcomes for SWB. (There were no prior studies of growth and autonomy among centenarians.) As discussed in greater detail by MacDonald (2007), Martin (2000) found that both economic resource adequacy and social resources (ratings by the interviewer) were positively related to the centenarians' mental health in the first phase of the Georgia Centenarian Study. As a specific example, Martin (2000) reported that there was a strong positive correlation between the interviewers' rating of the quality of the centenarians' social interactions and mental health. Using more predictors, we found no relationship between social interactions and mental health, although social interaction was a tolerably good predictor of better social provisions. In contrast, Martin's measure of economic resource adequacy is conceptually quite similar to this study's perceived economic status variable, which we also found to be positively related to mental health. When Adkins, Martin, and Poon (1996) analyzed the sources of association with community-dwelling centenarians' morale, they found that extraversion was an important predictor, but we found no mental health effect of that kind. Also in contrast to our results, Martin (2000) found that adverse cumulative life events reduced both social and economic resources, and those same events had a direct, negative effect on mental health. We found no effects of distal life events (although we did not restrict our events measure to adverse events) but instead found that ethnicity and education influenced perceived economic resource adequacy. More generally, our use of social provisions for SWB and growth and autonomy as PWB outcomes has extended the range of developmental outcome measures and identified their correlates.

IMPLICATIONS FOR SOCIAL SUPPORT AND SUCCESSFUL AGING AMONG THE OLDEST OLD

In our population-based sample of centenarians, mental health depended primarily on economic resource adequacy and its correlates other than personality. Social interactions influenced social provisions, but neither social nor economic resource adequacy was associated with PWB. The one socioeconomic resource that was related to PWB was income, and it was positively associated with growth. A caveat is that the income-growth relationship may not result from current income per se and instead may capture a long-term association between positive developmental attitudes and activities or behaviors that also led to greater income attainment. Yet in the case of mental health, we also found that education was positively related to perceived economic status, which suggests that income per se contributes more to mental health than its prior association with productive behavior. Thus, at the least, we can confidently recommend that increased income support for the oldest old is associated with SWB gains for mental health. There is also potential to enhance centenarians' quality of life via social support to ensure that they have better social provisions. For PWB, our findings identify specific aspects of personality that are favorable, which may suggest attitudes and related behaviors to emulate for adaptation in extreme age.

Our description of Georgia centenarians' social and economic resources found that from one eighth to one third of them are economically insecure; an even greater fraction depends on nursing-home staff or paid help for instrumental support. On the basis of multivariate results, we found that increasing income support from government or family members would increase resource adequacy for better mental health. A related analysis we have not discussed in detail found that mental health was positively associated with greater numbers of care hours received. An additional social practice recommendation from our analysis is that efforts to keep centenarians socially engaged with their friends and relatives will enhance their well-being in the sense of better social provisions. To the extent that social interactions promote additional caregiving hours, there would be side benefits for mental health.

Our findings concerning PWB are relevant to practical advice for successful aging among oldest-old adults, whatever their resources may be. We have found that neither social nor economic resource adequacy are necessary for maintaining an independent attitude and a belief that personal development can continue in very old age. Maintaining a high level of autonomy and related personal independence requires the trait of competence, and that trait probably has to be established habitually over a long period. Perhaps the same can be said for avoiding neurotic tendencies that undermine autonomy. Trust that there will be opportunities to continue to have faith in human nature appears to help maintain growth so that interacting with people who are also interested in adaptational development would seem wise.

REFERENCES

Adkins, G., Martin, P., & Poon, L.W. (1996). Personality traits and states as predictors of subjective well-being in centenarians/octogenarians and sexagenarians. *Psychology and Aging, 11*, 408–416.

Bishop, A. J. (2006). Age and gender differences in adaptation and subjective well-being of older adults residing in monastic religious communities. *Pastoral Psychology, 55*, 131–144.

Clarke, P., Marshall, V., Ryff, D., & Rosenthal, C. (2000). Well-being in Canadian seniors: Findings from the Canadian Study of Health and Aging. *Canadian Journal on Aging, 19*, 140–159.

Costa, P. T., & McCrae, R. R. (1994). Stability and change in personality from adolescence through adulthood. In C. F. Halverson, G. A. Kohnstamm, & R. P. Martin (Eds.), *The developing structure of temperament and personality from infancy to adulthood.* (pp. 139–150). Hillsdale, NJ: Erlbaum.

Cutrona, C. E., & Russell, D. (1987). The provisions of social relationships and adaptation to stress. In W. H. Jones & D. Perlman (Eds.), *Advances in personal relationships*, (Vol. 1, pp. 37–67). Greenwich, CT: JAI Press.

Fillenbaum, G. G. (1988). *Multidimensional functional assessment of older adults: The Duke Older Americans Resources and Services Procedures.* Hillsdale, NJ: Erlbaum.

Folstein, M.F., Folstein, S. E., & McHugh, P. R. (1975). Mini-Mental State: A practical method for grading the cognitive state of patients for the clinician. *Journal of Psychiatric Research, 12*, 189–198.

Goetting, M., Martin, P., Poon, L. W., & Johnson, M. (1996). The economic well-being of community-dwelling centenarians. *Journal of Aging Studies, 10*, 43–55.

Keyes, C., Shmotkin, D., & Ryff, D. 2002. Optimizing well-being: The empirical encounter of two traditions. *Journal of Personality and Social Psychology, 82*, 1007–1022.

Landau, R., & Litwin, H. (2001). Subjective well-being among the old-old: The role of health, personality, and social support. *International Journal of Aging and Human Development, 54*, 265–280.

MacDonald, M. (2007). Social support for centenarians' health, psychological well-being and longevity. In L. W. Poon & T. T. Perls (Eds.), *Annual review of gerontology and geriatrics: Vol. 27. Biopsychosocial approaches to longevity* (pp. 107–127). New York: Springer.

Martin, P. (2000). Individual and social resources predicting well-being and functioning in later years: Conceptual models, research, and practice. *Ageing International, 27*, 3–29.

Martin, P., Baenziger, J., MacDonald, M., Siegler, I., & Poon, L.W. (2009). Engaged lifestyle, personality, and mental status among centenarians. *Journal of Adult Development, 16*, 199–208.

Martin, P., & Martin, M. (2002). Proximal and distal influences on development: The model of developmental adaptation. *Developmental Review, 22*, 78–96.

Martin, P., Poon, L., Kim, E., & Johnson, M. A. (1996). Social and psychological resources in the oldest old. *Experimental Aging Research, 22*, 121–139.

Pinquart, M., & Sörenson, S. (2000). Influences of socioeconomic status, social network, and competence on subjective well-being in later life: A meta-analysis. *Psychology and Aging, 15*, 187–207.

Pudrovska, T., Springer, K., & Hauser, R. (2005). *Does psychological well-being change with age?* Unpublished manuscript, University of Wisconsin–Madison, Center for Demography and Ecology.

Ryff, C. D. (1989). Happiness is everything, or is it? Explorations on the meaning of psychological well-being. *Journal of Personality and Social Psychology*, *57*, 1069–1081.

Smith, J., Fleeson, W., Geiselmann, B., Settersten, R., Jr., & Kunzmann, U. (1999). Sources of well-being in very old age. In P. B. Baltes & K. U. Mayer (Eds.), *The Berlin Aging Study: Aging from 70 to 100* (pp. 450–471). New York: Cambridge University Press.

10

Nutrition and Well-Being

MARY ANN JOHNSON, DOROTHY HAUSMAN, PETER MARTIN, LEONARD W. POON, ELISABETH LILIAN PIA SATTLER, AND ADAM DAVEY

ABSTRACT

The relationship of nutrition-related factors with well-being in people 80 and older has received little attention. Therefore, this chapter explores the relationships of depression and depressive symptoms, as a measure of well-being, with appetite, body weight changes, underweight, and obesity as measures of nutritional status. The sample is from the Georgia Centenarian Study (aged 80 to 89 and 98+ years, see Chapter 9). In bivariate analyses, centenarians with depression consistently had the highest prevalence of underweight when compared to centenarians without depression and all octogenarians (23% to 33% vs. 0% to 16%). When controlled for other demographic factors, clinically relevant depressive symptomatology was associated with appetite loss, while a current diagnosis of depression was associated with recent changes in body weight. However, taking antidepressant medications was not associated with any of the nutrition-related measures. Demographic factors emerged as important predictors of nutritional status. Living in a skilled nursing facility compared to living in the community was associated with a lower risk of appetite loss and higher risk of weight gain; being a centenarian or being female was associated with underweight; and being Black (vs. White) was associated with obesity. Thus, risk factors for poor nutritional status in the oldest may be related to depression as well as to specific demographic factors including age, gender, race, and residence in a skilled nursing facility.

INTRODUCTION

The World Health Organization (WHO) defines health as a state of complete physical, mental, and social well-being and not merely the absence of disease or infirmity (Preamble to the Constitution, 1948). The WHO considers depression, which affects 121 million people worldwide, to be a major factor affecting the well-being (see Chapters 7, 8, and 11). Depression is a leading cause of disability, and it is projected that it will be the second most important cause of disability worldwide in 2020 (Murray & Lopez, 1997). Depression in the elderly not only is associated with increased morbidity and mortality but also has implications on physical, mental, social, and family functioning (United States Department of Health and Human Services [USDHHS], 1999; USDHHS Healthy People 2010; National Alliance on Mental Illness, 2009). In the United States, in older adults, depressive symptoms occur in 8–20% of community dwellers (Blazer, 2003) and in up to 44% of nursing-home residents (Teresi , Abrams, Holmes, Ramirez, & Eimicke, 2001), while major depression occurs in 1–4% of older adults (Alexopoulos, 2005), and 11% of adults 65 and older had a lifetime diagnosis of depression (Centers for Disease Control and Prevention and National Association of Chronic Disease Directors, 2008). Previous studies with centenarians have shown high prevalence rates of depressive symptoms (Martin, Rott, Kerns, Poon, & Johnson, 2000; Martin & da Rosa, 2006).

The WHO (2002) also emphasizes the importance of nutrition to help prevent and reduce disability, chronic disease, and premature mortality in older adults, and the relationship of nutrition with chronic conditions is of concern to dietitians and nutritionists (Johnson et al., 2008). Body weight, body mass index (BMI), weight loss, weight gain, and changes in appetite are often used as indices of nutritional status in older adults (Hughes, Frontera, Roubenoff, Evans, & Fiatarone Singh, 2002; Johnson et al., 2008; Vellas et al., 1999; Wallace & Schwartz, 2002), including those residing in nursing homes (Morley & Silver, 1995), and have been associated with poor well-being as defined by adverse health outcomes (Lee et al., 2006; Somes, Kritchevsky, Shorr, Pahor, & Applegate, 2002). Depression is a risk factor for nutrition-related problems in older adults (as reviewed by Brownie, 2006; Forman-Hoffman, Yankey, Hillis, Wallace, & Wolinsky, 2007; Robbins, 1989), but little is known about the relationship of depression with appetite, weight changes, and body mass index in those aged in their 80s and 100s. Thus, the purpose of this chapter is to explore these relationships in the oldest old. The primary goals are to determine the relationship of age, gender, race, nursing-home residence in a skilled nursing facility (e.g., nursing home), and depression with the nutrition-related factors. As shown in our conceptual model

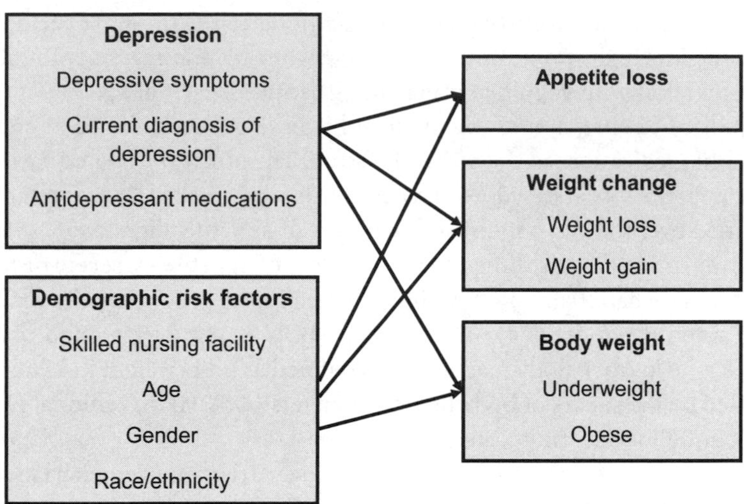

FIGURE 10.1. Nutrition and Depression Conceptual Model. It was hypothesized that depression and demographic risk factors adversely influence appetite, weight change, and body weight.

(Figure 10.1), it was hypothesized that advanced age, residence in a skilled nursing facility, and all measures of depression would be consistently associated with appetite loss, weight change, and body mass index (underweight and obesity).

METHODOLOGY

Participants were part of the Georgia Centenarian Study and included 244 centenarians (defined in this study as age 98 and older) and 80 octogenarians recruited from the community, personal-care homes, and skilled nursing facilities (Poon et al., 2007; Chapter 9). Participants were interviewed by trained personnel in their place of residence. Participants (or the caregivers of cognitively impaired participants) provided information about age, gender, race/ethnicity, living arrangements (community or skilled nursing facility), and other characteristics (e.g., depression- and nutrition-related variables). Three measures related to depression and depressive symptoms were used: clinically relevant depressive symptomatology (a score of 5 or more from the 15-item Geriatric Depression Scale [GDS]; Yesavage et al., 1982–1983; Bijl, van Marwijk, Ader, Beekman, & de Haan, 2006) in the subset of individuals with Mini-Mental State Examination (MMSE; Folstein, Folstein, & McHugh, 1975) scores of 16 or higher to minimize confounding of depression with cognitive impairment (Jongenelis et al., 2005); current diagnosis of depression in the medical history; and current use of antidepressant medications in the medical history. The nutrition-related variables were appetite loss assessed from a decline in food intake ("Has food intake declined over the past 3 months due to loss of appetite, digestive problems, chewing or swallowing difficulties?" – no loss of appetite vs. severe or moderate loss; Vellas et al., 1999), weight change in the past 3 months (gain or loss, amount not defined), underweight (BMI < 18.5 kg/m^2), and obesity (BMI ≥ 30 kg/m^2). Body mass index is defined as body weight in kilograms divided by the square of body height in meters (USDHHS, National Heart, Lung and Blood Institute, 2000).

Because of the unique nature of the octogenarian and centenarian samples, bivariate analyses of the relationships of the depression- and nutrition-related variables were conducted separately (Table 10.1).

Group differences were assessed with Student's *t*-test for continuous variables and with the chi-square test for categorical variables. Multivariate logistic regression analyses were used to explore the relationship of the nutrition-related variables in two models. Model 1 was with depression alone, and Model 2 added demographic factors that may be related to nutrition (age group, gender, race/ethnicity, and living arrangements) (Table 10.2). Analyses were conducted with the SAS statistical software (version 9.1, SAS Institute, Cary, NC). The Type I error rate was set at .05.

RESULTS

Octogenarians had an average age of 84 ($\pm$ 3) and were predominately female (66%), White (82% White, 18% Black), and resided in the community (85% community, 15% skilled nursing facility). Centenarians had an average age of 101 ($\pm$ 2) and were predominately female (85%), White (79% White, 21% Black), and resided in the community (57% community, 43% skilled nursing facility).

Table 10.1 summarizes the bivariate relationships of the nutrition-related variables with the depression-related variables in the two age groups. In octogenarians, weight change was significantly associated with a current diagnosis of depression, whereas weight gain was associated with two measures of depression (current diagnosis, antidepressant medications). In centenarians, most of the significant relationships of nutrition were with a current diagnosis of depression, which was associated with

TABLE 10.1. *Depression, appetite, weight change, underweight, and obesity in octogenarians and centenarians: Georgia Centenarian Study*

Clinically relevant depressive symptomatology[a]	Octogenarians		Centenarians	
	GDS < 5	GDS ≥ 5	GDS < 5	GDS ≥ 5
Has food intake declined over the past 3 months due to loss of appetite, digestive problems, chewing or swallowing difficulties? (n)	*60*	*7*	*112*	*22*
Appetite loss (%)	6.7	28.6+	7.1	22.7*
Change in body weight in the past 3 months? (n)	*60*	*7*	*110*	*20*
Weight change: gain or loss (%)	28.3	57.1	28.2	30.0
Weight gain (%)	13.3	14.3	10.0	5.0
Weight loss (%)	15.0	42.9+	18.2	25.0
BMI (kg/m²) (n)	*57*	*7*	*112*	*22*
Underweight BMI < 18.5 (%)	5.3	0	10.7	22.7
Obesity BMI ≥ 30 (%)	12.3	0	4.5	0
Current diagnosis of depression (from medical history)	**No**	**Yes**	**No**	**Yes**
Has food intake declined over the past 3 months due to loss of appetite, digestive problems, chewing or swallowing difficulties? (n)	*68*	*10*	*204*	*34*
Appetite loss (%)	7.4	20.0	13.2	0.0*
Change in body weight in the past 3 months? (n)	*67*	*10*	*197*	*32*
Weight change: gain or loss (%)	28.4	70.0**	32.5	56.3**
Weight gain (%)	11.9	40.0*	12.2	25.0+
Weight loss (%)	16.4	30.0	20.3	31.3
BMI (kg/m²) (n)	*65*	*10*	*197*	*33*
Underweight BMI < 18.5 (%)	3.1	10.0	15.2	33.3*
Obesity BMI ≥ 30 (%)	12.3	0	5.6	3.0
Antidepressant medications taken currently	**No**	**Yes**	**No**	**Yes**
Has food intake declined over the past three months due to loss of appetite, digestive problems, chewing or swallowing difficulties? (n)	*68*	*12*	*195*	*49*
Appetite loss (%)	11.8	0.0	12.8	6.1
Change in body weight in the past 3 months? (n)	*67*	*12*	*188*	*47*
Weight change: gain or loss (%)	31.3	50.0	33.5	40.4
Weight gain (%)	10.5	41.7**	13.3	14.9
Weight loss (%)	20.9	8.3	20.2	25.5
BMI (kg/m²) (n)	*65*	*12*	*187*	*49*
Underweight BMI < 18.5 (%)	3.1	8.3	16.0	24.5
Obesity BMI ≥ 30 (%)	12.3	8.3	4.8	6.1

[a]Defined as a score of 5 or more on the Geriatric Depression Scale (GDS) in those with MMSE ≥ 16.
*$p < 0.05$. **$p < 0.01$. ***$p < 0.001$. $^{+}p > 0.05$ and < 0.10.

TABLE 10.2. *Logistic regression analyses of depression, appetite, weight loss, underweight, and obesity: Georgia Centenarian Study*

	Appetite loss (moderate or severe vs. no loss) OR (95% CI)	Weight change (weight gain or loss vs. no change) OR (95% CI)	Weight gain (weight gain vs. loss or no change) OR (95% CI)	Weight loss (weight loss vs. gain or no change) OR (95% CI)	Underweight (BMI <18.5 vs. ≥18.5) OR (95% CI)	Obesity (BMI ≥30 vs. <30) OR (95% CI)
Depressive symptoms[a]	201	197	197	197	198	-[e]
1) Depression[b]	4.24 (1.51, 11.92)**	1.50 (0.64, 3.50)	0.64 (0.14, 2.90)	2.05 (0.82, 5.13)	2.14 (0.71, 6.42)	
2) Depression	4.25 (1.49, 12.11)**	1.43 (0.59, 3.48)	0.46 (0.09, 2.39)	2.01 (0.79, 5.08)	1.99 (0.64, 6.18)	
Age (98+ vs. 80s)	0.98 (0.34, 2.79)	0.66 (0.32, 1.35)	0.32 (0.10, 1.08)	0.98 (0.44, 2.22)	2.03 (0.54, 7.63)	
Female vs. male	0.89 (0.29, 2.69)	0.69 (0.34, 1.42)	0.47 (0.17, 1.30)	0.98 (0.42, 2.30)	6.51 (0.83, 51.01)	
Black vs. White	0.88 (0.19, 4.20)	1.18 (0.47, 2.97)	1.13 (0.29, 4.49)	1.12 (0.39, 3.22)	-[d]	
Skilled nursing facility vs. community	-[c]	3.02 (1.37, 6.65)**	7.82 (2.22, 27.50)**	1.32 (0.54, 3.27)	2.31 (0.84, 6.40)	
Current diagnosis of depression (n)	316	306	306	306	305	305
1) Depression	0.36 (0.08, 1.55)	3.21 (1.64, 6.26)***	2.90 (1.35, 6.23)**	1.87 (0.91, 3.85)	2.78 (1.30, 5.96)**	0.31 (0.04, 2.34)
2) Depression	0.55 (0.11, 2.61)	2.30*(1.09, 4.82)	1.99 (0.84, 4.74)	1.60 (0.72, 3.57)	1.70 (0.71, 4.07)	0.31 (0.04, 2.59)
Age (98+ vs. 80s)	1.52 (0.61, 3.79)	0.82 (0.45, 1.51)	0.54 (0.24, 1.25)	1.14 (0.56, 2.30)	3.84 (1.11, 13.27)*	0.39 (0.14, 1.06)
Female vs. male	1.66 (0.60, 4.63)	0.70 (0.37, 1.33)	0.73 (0.30, 1.74)	0.80 (0.39, 1.64)	4.37 (1.00, 19.05)*	2.83 (0.61, 13.13)
Black vs. White	0.67 (0.24, 1.86)	1.70 (0.93, 3.11)	2.10 (0.98, 4.47)	1.12 (0.56, 2.24)	0.62 (0.25, 1.54)	2.80 (1.05, 7.45)*
Skilled nursing facility vs. community	0.35 (0.13, 0.95)*	2.79 (1.60, 4.89)***	3.74 (1.72, 8.17)***	1.55 (0.82, 2.93)	1.96 (0.93, 4.12)	0.89 (0.30, 2.63)

Medications (n)	324	314	314	314	313	313
1) Depression	0.36 (0.11, 1.22)	1.50 (0.84, 2.67)	1.78 (0.85, 3.71)	1.10 (0.56, 2.19)	1.86 (0.91, 3.81)	0.97 (0.31, 2.99)
2) Depression	0.45 (0.13, 1.57)	1.06 (0.56, 2.00)	1.20 (0.54, 2.68)	0.91 (0.44, 1.87)	1.24 (0.58, 2.68)	1.25 (0.37, 4.21)
Age (98+ vs. 80s)	1.47 (0.62, 3.48)	0.70 (0.39, 1.28)	0.51 (0.22, 1.16)	0.98 (0.49, 1.94)	3.73 (1.09, 12.76)*	0.38 (0.14, 1.00)
Female vs. male	1.46 (0.56, 3.78)	0.83 (0.44, 1.55)	0.83 (0.35, 1.95)	0.91 (0.45, 1.84)	4.72 (1.09, 20.45)*	1.75 (0.48, 6.42)
Black vs. White	0.62 (0.23, 1.71)	1.52 (0.84, 2.76)	1.92 (0.91, 4.02)	1.03 (0.52, 2.04)	0.59 (0.24, 1.44)	3.00 (1.14, 7.86)*
Skilled nursing facility vs. community	0.34 (0.13, 0.88)*	3.48 (2.03, 5.99)***	4.45 (2.07, 9.54)***	1.84 (1.002, 3.37)*	2.14 (1.07, 4.27)*	0.69 (0.23, 2.05)

[a] Clinically relevant depressive symptomatology, defined as a score of 5 or more on the Geriatric Depression Scale (GDS) in those with MMSE $\geq$ 16.

[b] Two models were analyzed for each measure of depression: 1) depression only and 2) depression and demographic factors (centenarians vs. octogenarians; female vs. male; Black vs. White; and skilled nursing facility vs. community). Statistical significance indicated by $^{*}p < 0.05$, $^{**}p < 0.01$, and $^{***}p < 0.001$.

[c] Odds ratio could not be calculated because appetite loss was not reported in any nursing home residents.

[d] Odds ratio could not be calculated because no Blacks were underweight.

[e] Odds ratio could not be calculated because no participants with GDS $\geq$ 5 and MMSE $\geq$ 16 were obese.

significantly less appetite loss, more weight change, and more underweight. Appetite loss was more common in centenarians with clinically relevant depressive symptomatology (GDS $\geq$ 5) compared with those with GDS < 5.

Table 10.2 summarizes the logistic regression analyses and odds ratios (OR) and 95% confidence intervals (CI) are reported. Depressive symptoms, but not other measures of depression, were associated with a threefold greater risk of appetite loss, even when controlled for other factors. Current diagnosis of depression was associated with a two- to threefold greater risk of weight change, even when controlled for other factors. The association with weight gain was attenuated when controlled for other factors. Although current diagnosis of depression was associated with a higher risk of underweight, this effect was attenuated in the multivariate model. No measure of depression was associated significantly with weight loss or with obesity. Compared with the other demographic factors, residence in a skilled nursing facility was the most likely variable to be associated significantly with nutrition; residing in a skilled nursing facility (vs. the community) generally protected against appetite loss, but increased the risk of weight change or weight gain. In the models with antidepressant medications, residence in a skilled nursing facility was also associated with a highest risk of weight loss or underweight.

DISCUSSION

The nature of the relationship of nutrition with depression and depressive symptoms differed markedly across each of these measures. As illustrated in Figure 10.2, four distinct relationships were identified in the final regression models: none of the nutrition-related measures was associated with taking antidepressant medications; appetite loss was associated with having depressive symptoms (GDS of 5 or more) but not with the other depression measures; weight change was associated with a current diagnosis of depression but not with the other depression measures; and underweight and obesity were not robustly associated with any depression measure. It is also noteworthy that there was a lower likelihood of appetite loss and higher likelihood of weight gain associated with residing in a skilled nursing facility. Last, underweight was associated with being a centenarian (vs. octogenarian) or being female, whereas obesity was associated with being Black (vs. White). The significance and implications of these findings are discussed herein.

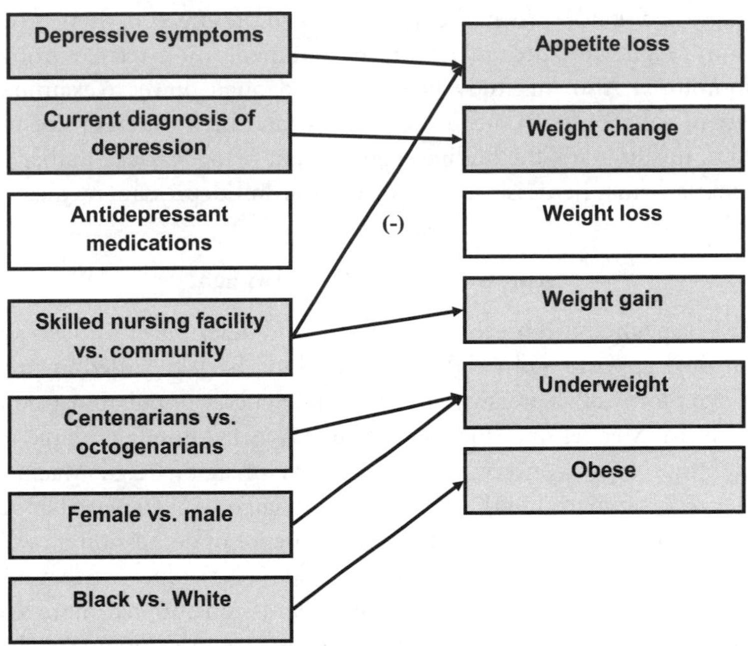

FIGURE 10.2. Nutrition and Depression in the Georgia Centenarian Study. Observed relationships of multiple measures of depression, place of residence, age, gender, and race/ethnicity with appetite loss, weight loss, weight gain, underweight, and obesity (from multivariate regression modeling).

Antidepressant Medications and Nutrition-Related Variables

Depression is a highly treatable disorder. Once diagnosed, depression can be treated in a number of ways, including with medications. Antidepressant medications normalize endogenous levels of the neurotransmitters serotonin and norepinephrine in the brain, whose levels are thought to be diminished in depressed patients. Through this mechanism, a variety of medications have been developed to help patients regain their quality of life. Some of these are known to cause weight gain (tricyclic antidepressants, the selective serotonin reuptake inhibitor [SSRI] paroxetine, mirtazapine; Zimmermann, Kraus, Himmerich, Schuld, & Pollmaecher, 2003). In the multivariate regression modeling, weight gain was not associated with taking antidepressant medications. However, in the bivariate analyses, weight gain was associated with taking antidepressant medications in the octogenarians but not the centenarians. Perhaps for many centenarians, their residence in a skilled nursing facility attenuated the effects of these medications on weight gain, because nutrition- and medication-related problems are monitored. Also, this study did not have adequate power to examine the variety of antidepressant medications in use and their different side effect profiles. In summary, the findings suggest that octogenarians, rather than centenarians, may be at risk of weight gain from antidepressant medications.

Depression, Appetite, and Weight

Since Kraepelin and Johnstone's (1904) classic description of depression, diminished appetite and weight loss have long been regarded as prominent symptoms of depressive illness in the general population (see also Beck, Ward, Mendelson, Mock, & Erbaugh, 1961). Although a large body of literature exists concerning the anorexia of aging (e.g., Macintosh, Morley, & Chapman, 2000) and factors associated with impaired appetite in older adults, little is known about the influence of depression on weight and appetite in the oldest old. Brodaty et al. (1997) reported that adults older than age 60 diagnosed with major depression suffered more severe appetite loss than did adults younger than age 60. Lee et al. (2006) concluded that symptomatic depression in older adults aged 70–79 years was significantly related to impaired appetite. Weight changes and appetite loss can be behavioral symptoms indicating depressive symptoms or major depressive disorder as defined by the American Psychiatric Association's (2000) *Diagnostic and Statistical Manual of Mental Disorders* (DSM-IV, 4th ed.). Weight or appetite changes, however, are not required for a depression diagnosis. The link between depression and weight change and appetite loss may be due to one condition causing the other because of psychological or biological mechanisms or due to a third condition or consequence related to weight change, appetite change, and depression (as reviewed by Forman-Hoffman et al., 2007). Our consistent finding of appetite loss in those with depressive symptoms extends the observations of Lee et al. (2006) in younger elders (70–79 years) to those in their 80s and beyond.

Appetite and Weight Loss in Skilled Nursing Facilities

A lower likelihood of appetite loss and a higher likelihood of weight gain were consistently seen in those residing in skilled nursing facilities than in community-dwelling participants. The reason for this may be that skilled nursing facilities in Georgia and the United States as a whole are strictly regulated by the state and federal government to be licensed or to receive

Medicare or Medicaid reimbursement for services (Code of Federal Regulations, 2005). These regulations are designed to promote and protect the health, safety, and well-being of the residents. Part of the requirement is to monitor nutritional status and to provide adequate nutrition. Consequently, residents of skilled nursing facilities may be more likely to gain weight than community-dwelling older adults. We have also reported that the dietary quality of these centenarians is higher among those residing in skilled nursing facilities rather than in the community (Johnson, Davey, Hausman, Park, & Poon, 2006).

Underweight

Although underweight was higher in centenarians with depression than in those without depression and the octogenarians, depression did not emerge as risk factors for underweight in the multivariate regression models. However, underweight was about four times more prevalent in centenarians (than in octogenarians) and women (than in men). Underweight is a risk factor for morbidity and mortality (Miller et al., 2009), so it is important to monitor weight status in older adults. Elucidating other underlying reasons for underweight, it has been proposed by Roubenoff (1999) that weight loss in older adults can be divided into three distinct types. First, wasting is an involuntary loss of weight, which is primarily caused by inadequate dietary intake. This may be attributable to both disease and psychosocial factors, and it may occur with a background of cachexia or sarcopenia, or both. Second, cachexia is an involuntary loss of fat free mass or body cell mass, which is caused by catabolism and results in changes in body composition but in which weight loss may not be initially present. It is characterized by an elevated metabolic rate and increased protein degradation. Last, sarcopenia is an involuntary loss of muscle mass, which may be an intrinsic part of the aging process rather than the effect of age associated with disease (Roubenoff, 1999; 2003). So even though depression was not associated with underweight in this study, it is important to monitor weight status in the oldest old because of its many associations with other indices of well-being.

Obesity

The prevalence of obesity in this sample of the oldest old was very low and was not associated with depression. However, the risk of being obese was about three-fold higher in Blacks compared to Whites. Thus, the high risk of obesity in Blacks in the United States (Wang, Colditz, & Kuntz, 2007) extends even into the oldest age groups. Obesity throughout the life cycle is associated with increased morbidity from a variety of chronic conditions, such as disability and impaired mobility, diabetes, hypertension, and heart disease (USDHHS, NHLBI, 2000; Penn, Fischer, Lee, Hausman, & Johnson, 2009).

CONCLUSION

Some limitations of this study are the relatively small number of participants and the cross-sectional nature of the study. Longitudinal studies are needed to ascertain the causal and temporal relationships of nutrition and depression over time. Also, our measure of appetite was rather broad, so future studies should define this measure more specifically.

In conclusion, the findings suggest that the nature of the relationships between nutrition and depression depends on how each domain is conceptualized and measured. Importantly, residence in a skilled nursing facility was protective against appetite loss and was associated with weight gain (rather than weight loss), which supports our earlier findings of higher dietary quality in residents of skilled nursing facilities than of those in the community (Johnson et al., 2006). Depressive symptoms were strongly predictive of appetite loss, whereas advanced age and being female was associated with underweight. By any measure of depression, depressed centenarians seemed to be at the highest risk for an impaired nutritional status, because they had the highest prevalence of underweight compared to nondepressed centenarians as well as octogenarians (depressed or nondepressed). As a consequence, this may call for more awareness of the detection and treatment of depression to maintain well-being in the oldest old.

REFERENCES

Alexopoulos, G. S. (2005). Depression in the elderly. *Lancet, 365*, 1961–1970.

American Psychiatric Association (2000). *Diagnostic and statistical manual of mental disorders* (4th ed.). Washington, DC: American Psychiatric Association.

Beck, A. T., Ward, C. H., Mendelson M., Mock J., & Erbaugh J. (1961). An inventory for measuring depression. *Archives of General Psychiatry, 4*, 561–571.

Bijl, D., van Marwijk, H. W. J., Adér, H. J., Beekman, A. T. F., & de Haan, M. (2006). Test-characteristics of the GDS-15 in screening for major depression in elderly patients in general practice. *Clinical Gerontologist, 29*, 1–19.

Blazer, D. G. (2003). Depression in late life: Review and commentary. *Journal of Gerontology, 58*, 249–265.

Brodaty, H., Luscombe, G., Parker, G., Hickie, W. I., Austin, M. P., & Mitchell, P. (1997). Increased rate of psychosis and psychomotor change in depression with age. *Psychological Medicine, 27*, 1205–1213.

Brownie, S. (2006). Why are elderly individuals at risk of nutritional deficiency? *International Journal of Nursing Practice, 12*, 110–118.

Centers for Disease Control and Prevention and National Association of Chronic Disease Directors (2008). The state of mental health and aging in America issue brief 1: What do the data tell us? Atlanta: National Association of Chronic Disease Directors. http://www.cdc.gov/aging/pdf/mental_health.pdf.

Code of Federal Regulations (2005). Requirements for States and Long Term Care Facilities, CFR Title 42, Chapter IV, Part 483.5–483.75. http://www.access.gpo.gov/nara/cfr/waisidx_06/42cfr483_06.html.

Folstein, M. F., Folstein, S. E., & McHugh, P. R. (1975). Mini-Mental State: A practical method for grading the cognitive state of patients for the clinician. *Journal of Psychiatric Research, 12*, 189–198.

Forman-Hoffman, V. L., Yankey, J. W., Hillis, S. L., Wallace, R. B., & Wolinsky F. D. (2007). Weight and depressive symptoms in older adults: Direction of influence? *Journal of Gerontology: Social Sciences, 62B*, S43–S51.

Himes, C. L. (2001). *Elderly Americans. Population Reference Bureau, Population Bulletin, 56*(4). Available at http://prb.org/Source/ACFD30.pdf.

Hughes, V. A., Frontera, W. R., Roubenoff, R., Evans, W. J., & Fiatarone Singh, M. A. (2002). Longitudinal changes in body composition in older men and women: Role of body weight change and physical activity. *American Journal of Clinical Nutrition, 76*, 473–481.

Johnson, M. A., Davey, A., Hausman, D. B., Park, S., & Poon, L. W. (2006). Dietary differences between centenarians residing in communities and in skilled nursing facilities: The Georgia Centenarian Study. *Age, 28*, 333–341.

Johnson, M. A., Park, S., Penn, D., McClelland, J. W., Brown, K., & Adler, A. (2008). Nutrition Education issues for older adults. *Forum for Family and Consumer Issues, 13*(3). http://ncsu.edu/ffci/publications/2008/v13-n3–2008-winter/index-v13-n3-winter-2008.php.

Jongenelis, K., Pot, A. M., Eisses, A. M., Gerritsen, D. L., Derksen, M., Beekman, A. T., et al. (2005). Diagnostic accuracy of the original 30-item and shortened versions of the Geriatric Depression Scale in nursing home patients. *International Journal of Geriatric Psychiatry, 20*, 1067–1074.

Kraepelin, E., & Johnstone, T. (1904). *Lectures on clinical psychiatry*. William Wood, New York, NY.

Lee, J. S., Kritchevsky, S. B., Tylavsky, F., Harris, T. B., Ayonayon, H. N., & Newman, A. B. (2006). Factors associated with impaired appetite in well-functioning community-dwelling older adults. *Journal of Nutrition for the Elderly, 26*, 27–43.

Macintosh, C., Morley, J. E., & Chapman, I. M. (2000). The anorexia of aging. *Nutrition, 16*, 983–995.

Martin, P., & da Rosa, G. (2006). Age differences in depressive symptoms and morale among the oldest old. *Global Ageing, 4*, 42–51.

Martin, P., Rott, C., Kerns, M. D., Poon, L. W., & Johnson, M. A. (2000). Predictors of depressive symptoms in centenarians. In P. Martin, C. Rott, B. Hagberg,

& K. Morgan (Eds.), *Centenarians: Autonomy versus dependence in the oldest old* (pp. 91–104). New York: Springer.

Miller, M. D., Thomas, J. M., Cameron, I. D., Chen, J. S., Sambrook, P. N., March, L. M., et al. (2009). BMI: A simple, rapid and clinically meaningful index of under-nutrition in the oldest old? *British Journal of Nutrition, 101*, 1300–1305.

Morley, J. E., & Silver, A. J. (1995). Nutritional issues in nursing home care. *Annals of Internal Medicine, 123*, 850–859.

Murray, J. L., & Lopez, A. D. (1997). Alternative projections of mortality and disability by cause 1990–2020: Global Burden of Disease Study. *Lancet, 349*, 1498–1504.

National Alliance on Mental Illness. (2009). Depression in Older Persons Fact Sheet. http://www.nami.org/Template.cfm?Section=by_illness&template=/ContentManagement/ContentDisplay.cfm&ContentID=17624.

Penn, D. M., Fischer, J. G., Lee, J. S., Hausman, D. B., & Johnson, M. A. (2009). High BMI and waist circumference are associated with a high prevalence of comorbidities in Older Americans Act programs in Georgia senior centers. *Journal of Nutrition, Aging, and Health 13*, 827–832.

Poon, L. W., Jazwinski, S. M., Green, R. C., Woodard, J. L., Martin, P., Rodgers, W. L., et al. (2007). Methodological considerations in studying centenarians: Lessons learned from the Georgia centenarian studies. *Annual Review of Gerontology and Geriatrics, 27*, 213–264.

Robbins, L. J. (1989). Evaluation of weight loss in the elderly. *Geriatrics, 44*, 31–37.

Roubenoff, R. (1999). The pathophysiology of wasting in the elderly. *Journal of Nutrition, 129*, S256–S259.

Roubenoff, R. (2003). Sarcopenia: Effects on body composition and function. *J Gerontol A Biol Sci Med Sci, 58*, 1012–1017.

Somes, G. W., Kritchevsky, S. B., Shorr, R. I., Pahor, M., & Applegate, W. B. (2002). Body mass index, weight change, and death in older adults. *The Systolic Hypertension in the Elderly Program: American Journal of Epidemiology, 156*, 132–138.

Teresi, J., Abrams, R., Holmes, D., Ramirez, M., & Eimicke, J. (2001). Prevalence of depression and depression recognition in nursing homes. *Social Psychiatry and Psychiatric Epidemiology, 36*, 613–620.

U.S. Department of Health and Human Services. (2000). *Healthy people 2010*. http://www.healthypeople.gov/Document/html/uih/uih_bw/uih_4.htm#mentalhealth.

U.S. Department of Health and Human Services. (1999). *Older adults and mental health: A report of the Surgeon General.* Rockville, MD: National Institutes of Health, National Institute of Mental Health. http://www.surgeongeneral.gov/library/mentalhealth/summary.html.

U.S. Department of Health and Human Services, National Institutes of Health (NIH), National Institute of Mental Health (NIMH) (2009). http://www.nimh.nih.gov/health/topics/depression/index.shtml.

U.S. Department of Health and Human Services, Public Health Service, National Institutes of Health, National Heart, Lung and Blood Institute Health Information Center. (2000). *Practical guide to the identification, evaluation and treatment of overweight and obesity in adults.* http://www.nhlbi.nih.gov.

Vellas, B., Guigoz, Y., Garry, P. J., Nourhashemi, F., Bennahum, D., Lauque, S., et al. (1999). The Mini Nutritional Assessment (MNA) and its use in grading the nutritional state of elderly patients. *Nutrition, 15*, 116–122.

Wallace, J. I., & Schwartz, R. S. (2002). Epidemiology of weight loss in humans with special reference to wasting in the elderly. *International Journal of Cardiology, 85*, 15–21.

Wang, Y. C., Colditz, G. A., & Kuntz, K. M. (2007). Forecasting the obesity epidemic in the aging U.S. population. *Obesity, 15*, 2855–2865.

World Health Organization. (1948). *Constitution of the World Health Organization.* http://www.who.int/governance/eb/who_constitution_en.pdf.

World Health Organization. (2000). *Non Communicable Diseases and Mental Health Cluster, Department of Non Communicable Disease Prevention and Health Promotion, Ageing and Life Course Unit: Men ageing and health.* http://whqlibdoc.who.int/hq/2001/WHO_NMH_NPH_01.2.

World Health Organization. (2002). *Keep fit for life. Meeting the nutritional needs of older persons.* http://www.who.int/nutrition/publications/olderpersons/en/index.html.

Yesavage, J. A., Brink, T. L., Rose, T. L., Lum, O., Huang, V., Adey, M., et al. (1982–1983). Development and validation of a geriatric depression screening scale: A preliminary report. *Journal of Psychiatric Research, 17*, 37–49.

Zimmermann, U., Kraus, T., Himmerich, H., Schuld, A., & Pollmaecher, T. (2003). Epidemiology, implications and mechanisms underlying drug-induced weight gain in psychiatric patients. *Journal of Psychiatric Research, 37*, 193–220.

11

Cognitive Functioning and Vitality among the Oldest Old: Implications for Well-Being

JENNIFER A. MARGRETT, BENJAMIN T. MAST, MARIA C. ISALES, LEONARD W. POON, AND JISKA COHEN-MANSFIELD

ABSTRACT

This chapter clarifies and differentiates changes in cognitive functioning among the oldest old at the group and individual levels. Cross-sectionally, the oldest old demonstrate normative differences of being more physically and cognitively frail compared to younger groups. More variation and successful aging is observed at the individual level. Some oldest-old individuals can perform at the same levels as adults 20 to 40 years younger. Recent literature has recognized that the concept of cognitive vitality transcends the absence of dementia or dementing processes. We seek to clarify the concept of cognitive vitality because it has not been well defined in the literature either theoretically or operationally. This chapter addresses the following questions: 1) What is cognitive vitality and how does it contribute to the well-being of older adults? 2) What factors or resources contribute to cognitive vitality among the oldest old? and 3) What new directions can be identified for future research?

COGNITIVE FUNCTIONING AND VITALITY AMONG THE OLDEST OLD: IMPLICATIONS FOR WELL-BEING

Lay people and professionals alike fall prey to aging stereotypes and myths (Ory, Hoffman, Hawkins, Sanner, & Mockenhaupt, 2003), namely that cognitive decline is inevitable and there is nothing we can do about it. Empirical research has focused on comparing the cognitive performance of younger and older adults, often noting "deficits" in older adults' abilities without taking into account context and potentially meaningful qualitative differences in older adults' approaches to cognitive problems (e.g., Marsiske & Margrett, 2006). The tendency to focus on the negative aspects of cognitive aging does not provide a comprehensive picture of normative aging and prevents the promotion of cognitive health and vitality in older adulthood. The increased heterogeneity in the functioning of the oldest old and the increasing prevalence of dementia in very late life provide challenges as well as opportunities to study successful aging and resiliency. In this chapter, we address the following questions: (a) What is cognitive vitality, and how does cognitive vitality contribute to the well-being of older adults? (b) What factors or resources contribute to cognitive vitality among the oldest old? and (c) What new directions can be identified for future research?

CONCEPTUALIZING COGNITIVE HEALTH AND VITALITY IN LATER LIFE

To clarify terms used throughout this chapter, we differentiate several related concepts. First, we refer to *cognitive functioning* as performance-based indicators of cognitive ability or skill. *Cognitive aging* refers to documented changes in cognitive functioning that occur throughout adult development and aging. Normative, or typical, changes are distinguished from nonnormative changes such as dementia. *Cognitive health* is used as a more global term to describe the spectrum of aggregate cognitive functioning, which can range from no impairment to mild cognitive impairment and more severe impairment evident with dementia. Finally, *cognitive vitality* is a construct that incorporates both cognitive functioning and other skills and disposition and is related to the successful application of cognitive skills in one's everyday environment. In the following section, we further differentiate the terms.

COGNITIVE VITALITY: EXPANDING COGNITIVE HEALTH

Cognitive health is used as a global term to describe an individual's collective cognitive functioning. Parallels can be made between definitions of physical and cognitive health. For instance, the World Health Organization (1948) defined health as "a state of complete physical, mental, and social well-being, not merely the absence of disease or infirmity." Following similar logic, Walter-Ginzburg, Shmotkin, Eyal, & Guralnik (2008) proposed that cognitive health among older people should be defined as a state of mental well-being and vitality, not merely the absence of dementia or dementing processes. A definition of cognitive health proposed by the Critical Evaluation Study Committee of the National Institutes of Health Cognitive and Emotional Health Project is also consistent with this philosophy (Hendrie et al., 2006). Both groups propose moving beyond dichotomous distinctions (e.g., absence or presence of dementia) to an expanded conceptualization of cognitive health.

Cognitive vitality extends the concept of cognitive health by considering the application of cognitive skills and resources to day-to-day living. Walter-Ginzburg et al. (2008) argue that cognitive vitality is a construct separate from dementia and can be distinguished as "the ability to exploit cognitive resources for active information processing and interaction with the environment in practical everyday activities" (p. 7). Hendrie et al. (2006) defined cognitive health in later life "as the development and preservation of the multidimensional cognitive structure that allows the older adult to maintain social connectedness, an ongoing sense of purpose, and the abilities to function independently, to permit functional recovery from illness or injury, and to cope with residual functional deficits" (p. 13). In the latter definition, adaptation and competence can be inferred, as well as maintenance of psychosocial functioning and well-being. Also implied in this definition is resilience or the ability to achieve a "good outcome in spite of serious threats to adaptation or development" (Masten, 2001, p. 227). The oldest old certainly face their share of adversities (e.g., loss of family and friends to disease and death, role loss through retirement and ageism) and threats (e.g., trauma, socioeconomic challenges, presence of genetic and environmental dementia risk factors) to well-being and functioning. Many of the oldest old achieve and maintain physical and cognitive vitality despite varying levels of adversity and the presence of risk factors.

The concept of cognitive vitality in late life has the potential to help researchers frame the analysis of the full spectrum of cognitive health in later life (Walter-Ginzburg, Shmotkin, Blumstein, & Shorek, 2005). However, the notion of vitality, and cognitive vitality in particular, has not been well explicated in the literature either theoretically or operationally. This premise underlying the concept of cognitive vitality is consistent with the components of successful aging outlined by Rowe and Kahn (1998), who suggested that being disease-free may be an advantageous precursor but not a sufficient indicator of successful aging. Explicit in the definition of cognitive vitality is a focus on the real-world application of cognitive skills, which fits well with the framework of the everyday-cognition approach. The everyday approach is thought to add value to the study of cognitive aging (Allaire & Marsiske, 2002), as it emphasizes the ecological validity of assessment strategies and the identification of the higher-order cognitive skills needed to navigate the actual day-to-day life of an older adult (for recent reviews, see Marsiske & Margrett, 2006; Thornton & Dumke, 2005). What is not clear from the literature is which benchmark to use to determine success in an everyday setting (Marsiske & Margrett, 2006). Perhaps this is the most difficult issue surrounding cognitive vitality, particularly in very late life, given altered goals and expectations and range of cognitive functioning. Is cognitive vitality possible across the spectrum of cognitive health (i.e., age-related cognitive aging with no impairment through dementia)?

We propose that cognitive vitality be viewed as a construct that incorporates both cognitive functioning and other skills and disposition and is related to successful application of cognitive skills in an individual's unique everyday environment. Although it is sometimes difficult to tease apart antecedent from consequence, as we discuss later in the chapter, cognitive vitality is related to multiple dimensions of well-being and the overall ability of older adults to adapt, achieve competence, and be resilient. As such, an individual is not limited to one static category of cognitive vitality. Cognitive vitality may fluctuate on the basis of changing individual (e.g., physical health, affect) and environmental (e.g., social support) factors. In our view, cognitive vitality is related to but does not totally overlap with other indicators of functioning and well-being. For example, an individual may exhibit poor physical functioning, yet be cognitively vital.

In this chapter, we focus primarily on cognitive vitality as the day-to-day successful application of cognitive functioning, primarily in the framework of normative cognitive aging. From this perspective, a cognitively vital individual is one who has sufficient cognitive functioning to perform the tasks required by the person's age group in the context of his or her unique living conditions. However, among the oldest old, the spectrum of cognitive health encompasses cognitive functioning, which reflects no impairment as well as varying levels of impairment ranging from mild impairment to dementia. In this book, Cohen-Mansfield discusses the concept of successful aging in the context of dementia. In Chapter 4, she describes "successful" dementia as the lack of physical or mental discomfort with some sense of contentment and well-being despite decreased cognitive function. From Cohen-Mansfield's perspective, it can be inferred that vitality in general is the totality of functions that the person manifests, including social capabilities and initiative, which allow him or her to function beyond what could be expected by his or her level of cognitive functioning alone (J. Cohen-Mansfield, personal communication, November, 12, 2009). For instance, cognitive vitality speaks to the fact that, with cognitive deficits, one may be able to navigate vitality in social and other activities, through social graces, overlearned skills, and even newly learned skills usually involving procedural memory (J. Cohen-Mansfield, personal communication, November,

TABLE 11.1. *Theoretical relation between cognitive health and vitality*

Cognitive health	Cognitive vitality: Low	Cognitive vitality: High
Low	"Vulnerable" (A) Low cognitive functioning Decreased well-being	"Successful Dementia" (B) Low cognitive functioning but more successful navigation within their environment Higher well-being than Group A Vitality may buffer future decline
High	"At Risk" (C) Individual likely performs satisfactorily in their particular environment, however, he or she may be at risk and potentially less able to adapt	"Cognitively Vital" (D) Likely to be highly engaged Individual is likely to be more adaptable Vitality may buffer future changes

12, 2009). From this perspective, cognitive vitality can be achieved in the context of dementia.

Table 11.1 depicts the theoretical juxtaposition of cognitive health status and cognitive vitality and builds on a previous discussion of resilience (Martin, MacDonald, Margrett, & Poon, 2010). As depicted in Table 11.1, the four groups are expected to vary in functional level and well-being, as well as in their ability to adapt to future changes. In general, cognitive vitality may serve as a protective or compensatory mechanism, potentially buffering against further decline for individuals experiencing either normative or nonnormative cognitive changes (i.e., Groups B and D, those achieving successful dementia or cognitive vitality, respectively). Conversely, low cognitive vitality may be as a risk factor for decline among both groups as well (Groups A and C, those groups described as vulnerable and at risk, respectively).

We believe that cognitive vitality in the context of both normative and nonnormative cognitive age changes falls under the umbrella of successful aging. As discussed in the following section, normative and nonnormative cognitive changes in very late life each present unique theoretical, assessment, and prevention and/or intervention challenges. As we consider cognitive vitality among the oldest old, questions arise to how this concept fits in the context of normative (i.e., typical, age-related changes) and nonnormative (i.e., impairment and dementia-related) cognitive aging.

NORMATIVE COGNITIVE AGING AND VITALITY

Although increased variation in normative cognitive functioning is observed in older adulthood (Morse, 1993; Nelson & Dannefer, 1992; Ylikoski et al., 1999), typical patterns of age-related changes in cognitive abilities are well documented. For instance, intellectual skills that are most related to culture and rely on accumulated knowledge and experience (e.g., verbal comprehension) tend to demonstrate growth through middle age and maintenance into the 70s (Schaie, 2005). In contrast, fluid abilities, considered more innate and biologically driven skills (e.g., memory, inductive reasoning), generally peak in the early 20s, followed by a gradual decline throughout adulthood (Schaie, 2005). Findings from a study conducted by Hagberg, Alfredson, Poon, and Homma (2001) suggest that such distinctions among cognitive abilities appear to remain important through very late life. In their study, centenarians' performance on fluid measures tended to be more homogeneous, thereby suggesting a possible floor effect with respect to these more age-sensitive abilities; however, centenarians demonstrated a greater range of performance on crystallized measures (Hagberg et al., 2001). Additional work examining the underlying structure of cognitive abilities in very late life (e.g., dedifferentiation of cognitive abilities; de Frias, Lövdén, Lindenberger, & Nilsson, 2007) is needed; however, we can expect that the nature of the cognitive task and the corresponding requisite cognitive abilities affect cognitive vitality among the oldest old. Differential patterns of cognitive aging may be evident on the basis of levels of prior functioning. One possibility is that cognitively vital older adults may demonstrate differential patterns of change in cognitive abilities as well as in the underlying cognitive structure. In addition, we can expect variation in cognitive task performance across cultural contexts as a result of the often experience-related nature of intellectual skills needed to navigate everyday life and achieve vitality. Thus, the operational definition and corresponding assessments of cognitive vitality need to be responsive to cultural context.

A second issue related to normative cognitive aging and vitality is the tendency toward accelerated cognitive decline close to death. There is empirical support suggesting terminal decline (evident approximately 3 years before death) and a more precipitous drop (evident within 1 year of death; see Bäckman, Small, & Wahlin, 2001; Berg, 1996), although some debate continues. Tendency toward accelerated cognitive decline before death likely contributes to the higher rate of cognitive impairment evident among the oldest old. As observed in some studies, the rates of terminal decline among initially nonimpaired older adults are highly variable (Wilson, Beckett, Bienias, Evans, & Bennett, 2003). Additional empirical studies of cognitively vital oldest-old individuals may reveal differential rates of terminal decline and drop and shed light on the mechanisms underlying cognitive decline.

NONNORMATIVE COGNITIVE AGING AND VITALITY

One challenge when considering cognitive vitality concerns the borderline between normative and nonnormative aging, as well as their potential overlap and transition. Most models of cognitive vitality are focused on normal aging, often defined as the absence of significant cognitive decline such as that observed in dementia syndromes. Typically, the dementias of aging are defined as a significant decline in cognitive functioning from levels of premorbid functioning such that the decline is sufficiently severe to interfere with the person's ability to function in his or her daily life (e.g., work, household tasks, relationships). Most individuals assessed for dementia have not had prior testing; thus, the determination of significant decline often relies on comparison to statistical norms of the person's age; education; and for some tests, ethnicity or culture. In this approach, those older adults who have unusually low scores relative to matched norms (typically 1.5–2.0 standard deviations below the group mean) are considered impaired, particularly if this occurs in the context of limitations in daily functioning. Using this approach, many investigators seek to differentiate those individuals who are aging normally from those with nonnormative cognitive change (i.e., cognitive impairment). However, this simple dichotomy is challenged by apparent transition periods in which a person may be moving from normal aging cognition toward more significant nonnormative changes, which creates a problematic gray area. The most prominent of these proposed states is mild cognitive impairment (MCI), which is conceptualized as a mild, isolated deficit in one cognitive ability (or very mild impairment in multiple abilities) in the context of otherwise-normal functioning (Morris et al., 2001; Petersen et al., 2001; Petersen & Morris, 2005; Storandt, Grant, Miller, & Morris, 2002). Many view this as a transition state, a significant risk factor for more severe changes (e.g., Alzheimer's disease), and possibly even an early form of Alzheimer's disease (AD; Morris et al., 2001) on the basis of findings that MCI reflects AD pathology in many cases (Markesbery et al., 2006; Petersen et al., 2006).

The borderline and/or overlap between normative and nonnormative states is complicated by two additional findings. First, it has long been suspected (and now supported by empirical data) that the underlying neuropathology of AD begins long before the first cognitive changes emerge at a level that would warrant clinical attention (Collie & Maruff, 2000). Second, cerebrovascular risk factors that are highly prevalent in the oldest old, including hypertension, diabetes, and heart disease, have been linked to subclinical cerebrovascular changes, which are also quite common in later life (Campbell & Coffey, 2001; O'Brien, 2006; O'Brien et al., 2003). Perhaps more important for our purposes, both of these underlying processes have been shown to affect cognitive functioning (Galvin et al., 2005; Gunning-Dixon & Raz, 2000; Schmitt et al., 2000). Neuroimaging studies have demonstrated that normally aging adults demonstrate changes in many brain regions, particularly in the prefrontal cortex and medial temporal lobe structures, and therefore the inclusion of individuals who have cerebrovascular risk factors such as hypertension or preclinical AD can magnify the level of change observed (Raz, 2005; Raz & Rodrigue, 2006; Raz, Rodrigue, & Acker, 2003).

Because of the issues presented in this section, such as the theory of terminal decline and the overlap between normative and nonnormative aging, the prevalence of dementia varies across studies. Age is the predominant risk for dementia; the prevalence rate of dementia among adults aged 71 and older is estimated to be 1 in 7 persons, increasing to approximately 37% among those aged 90 and older (Plassman et al., 2007). However, it is important to note that the prevalence of dementia is lower than society would lead us to believe. A study by Poon et al. (2010) found that 22.5% of centenarians had no dementia, another 16% had no dementia but did report some memory complaints, and 25.3% had mild cognitive impairment. About 25% of centenarians were estimated to be cognitively intact and functioning well in everyday life; they were not cognitively frail by any definition and should not be included in the general stereotype.

Clinico-pathological studies of preclinical AD have demonstrated that a substantial number of older persons display the pathological changes of AD (i.e., amyloid plaques and neurofibrillary tangles) but maintain relatively normal functioning (cognition and everyday functioning). Bennett, Schneider, Arvanitakis, et al. (2006) examined 134 older adults without cognitive impairment and observed that 37% had pathology consistent with AD and demonstrated poorer episodic memory than older adults without significant AD pathology (Bennett, Schneider, Arvanitakis, et al., 2006). An earlier study by Schmitt et al. (2000) yielded similar findings in that a substantial number of nondemented older adults had AD pathology on autopsy (11–49% met pathological criteria for AD, depending on classification system used) and demonstrated poorer immediate and delayed recall at their last clinical evaluation when compared with those who did not have AD pathology (Schmitt et al., 2000). Galvin et al. (2005) studied 41 community-dwelling older persons without clinical evidence of dementia before death (i.e., normal cognitive functioning over repeated longitudinal neuropsychological assessments) and found that 34% had pathological evidence of AD on autopsy.

These findings raise two possibilities. First, if the participants had lived longer, they may have developed the cognitive changes reflecting the underlying dementia-related brain changes. Age is known to be the strongest risk factor for AD and other dementias, and therefore greater longevity among these samples may have led to the full expression of dementia. Second, as Schmitt et al. (2000) suggest, these findings may indicate that, for some older persons, the brain may be able to withstand or compensate for these underlying brain changes and thereby avoid significant cognitive impairment. The latter hypothesis could be linked to cognitive vitality.

These issues raise several questions. First, does the definition and measurement of cognitive vitality differ on the basis of normative versus nonnormative status? Given that age is the strongest risk factor for dementia, how should we consider normative versus nonnormative change in centenarians? Specifically, what levels of cognitive decline should be considered normative for centenarians? Second, if we consider cognitive vitality in the broad spectrum of cognitive health, what does cognitive vitality look like among the nonnormative older persons (see Chapter 4 for relevant discussion)? Third, what pathways lead to cognitive vitality among older adults experiencing normative and nonnormative cognitive changes? Furthermore, given that cognitive vitality is not simply avoidance of impairment and disease, how can persons with dementia best exploit and apply their remaining cognitive resources to their everyday settings and challenges? In the following section, we highlight challenges to the conceptualization and measurement of functioning and vitality among very old individuals.

ASSESSING OF FUNCTIONING AND VITALITY AMONG THE OLDEST OLD

Methodological Limitations

Stereotypical assumptions regarding cognitive aging are fostered by three tendencies within the field. First, most studies focus on cross-sectional findings that highlight age-group differences in cognitive performance. Such studies exacerbate age-related differences as compared with longitudinal investigations, which focus on intraindividual (within-person) change and reveal a much more diverse array of cognitive outcomes in later life (Schaie, 1989). Second is the tendency to consider older adults' cognitive performance in an acontextual fashion without considering factors such as the older adult's environment, social partners, life experience, and motivation. A third limitation is that insufficient attention is paid to understanding successful cognitive aging and how it fits in the spectrum of cognitive health. Studies of very old individuals, who are likely to provide prime examples of successful development and adaptation, are rare. Recent studies suggest that the full range of cognitive functioning, even variation within the range of "normal," should be considered in gerontological work. The meaning of variation in cognitive functioning is relevant to this chapter for two reasons. First, as a group, the oldest old demonstrate greater heterogeneity in cognitive functioning. Second, within-person cognitive variability (i.e., fluctuation in performance and/or functioning) is believed to be an important indicator of underlying neural functioning and cognitive integrity (Hilborn, Strauss, Hultsch, & Hunter, 2009; Hultsch, MacDonald, Hunter, Levy-Bencheton, & Strauss, 2000).

Classifications of Functioning in the Oldest Old

Heterogeneity of functioning must be kept in mind when investigating functioning among the oldest old. Contrary to the stereotypic impression that cognitive and physical frailty is true for all individuals in older age, reality can be different at the individual level. Consider, for example, the distribution of cognitive functions among 60-, 80-, and 100-year-olds. These distributions show considerable overlaps in the range of observed scores (Hagberg et al., 2001). That is, some 60-, 80-, and 100-year-olds perform at the same levels, whereas individuals in the two older age groups may outperform their younger counterparts. In the literature focusing on the oldest old, we highlight two examples of classification techniques.

In one approach focusing on physical conditions, centenarians in the New England Centenarian Study were categorized as "survivors," "delayers," or "escapers," depending on when they experienced chronic disease (early in life [0–80], late in life [80–100], or near the end of life [after 100 years of age], respectively) (Evert, Lawler, Bogan, & Perls, 2003). Although more than 80% of centenarians had escaped or delayed the most serious of physical conditions such as stroke, fewer men (76%) and women (57%) demonstrated escape or delay of more common age-associated illnesses such as diabetes and hypertension. Research suggests that some centenarians have the means to cope with diseases that would have otherwise caused premature mortality. Building on the utility of such classifications, Gondo et al. (2006) identified phenotypes of exceptional longevity among Japanese centenarians using a multidimensional approach. In their study, three domains of functioning were characterized (i.e., cognitive, sensory, and physical) and subsequently contributed to an overall status designation. Cognitive functioning was assessed via the Clinical Dementia Rating scale (CDR; Burke et al., 1988) and the Mini-Mental Status Examination (MMSE; Folstein, Folstein, & McHugh, 1975). Hearing and visual acuity were used as indicators of sensory functioning and the Barthel Activities of Daily Living (ADL) index (Wade & Collin, 1988) assessed physical functioning. A continuum was developed to represent centenarians' overall functional status across the three domains and descriptors of the broad designator included "fragile" (physical and cognitive deterioration), "frail" (either physical or cognitive impairment), "normal" physical and cognitive abilities, and "exceptional" physical and cognitive functioning. The majority of centenarians in this study were described as frail (55%) or fragile (25%), with a smaller number classified as normal (18%) and very few achieving exceptional status in both cognitive and physical functioning (2%). Relevant to the current discussion are individuals in the categories of normal (CDR $\leq .5$, probably no dementia) and exceptional (CDR $= 0$, no dementia, and MMSE ≥ 21) who would likely be described as cognitively vital. As evidenced in these studies, rates of vitality depend on the operational definitions employed. We suggest that the concept of cognitive vitality be further delineated in three major ways, each of which affects assessment as well as promotion prevention and intervention efforts.

The first step is to expand the definition of cognitive vitality beyond neurobiological changes in the brain or cognitive function to include additional factors that influence cognitive health, such as social interactions, physical and functional status, cognitive and physical activity, mental health, and nutrition (e.g., Butler, Forette, & Greengrass, 2004; Fillit et al., 2002; Yevchak, Loeb, & Fick, 2008). These factors are all intricately linked to an individual's cognitive functioning on a daily basis and ultimately to cognitive vitality. The next step in measuring cognitive vitality is accounting for normative changes associated with aging. Beginning when adults are in their 20s, continuous age-related declines have been found in regional brain volume, myelin integrity, cortical thickness, serotonin receptor binding, striatal dopamine binding, accumulation of fibrillary tangles, and concentration of brain metabolites (Salthouse, 2009). Still, there are neurobiological and behavioral mechanisms that compensate for those declines, which will be discussed in further detail. Finally, the concept of cognitive vitality itself needs to be individualized to the personal circumstances of the older person. For example, cognitive vitality in a 100-year-old likely carries a different meaning than in a 60-year-old.

RELATION OF COGNITIVE FUNCTIONING AND VITALITY TO WELL-BEING AMONG THE OLDEST OLD

Previous chapters in this book have recognized that well-being is a complex concept that has a variety of definitions (see Chapter 4). However, it can be generally agreed on that well-being is a subjective measure that refers to optimal psychological experience and functioning, and that can include engagement, satisfaction, adjustment, and other attributes (Deci & Ryan, 2008). Because cognitive vitality is necessary for awareness of actions and appropriate interaction with one's surroundings, it is an integral component in the achievement of well-being. Indeed, as discussed in this chapter, cognitive vitality is the successful application of cognitive skills within one's own environment. Although cognitive vitality has not been explicitly examined in relation to well-being, the construct is akin to everyday, or applied, cognitive abilities that are discussed in the extant literature. Prior research has demonstrated that everyday measures of cognitive functioning (which are purported to be more contextual and ecologically sensitive) are related to important real-world outcomes, including ADL ability, cognitive decline, and mortality (for a discussion, see Margrett, Allaire, Johnson, Daugherty, & Weatherbee, 2010). Cognitive vitality can be considered both an important contributor to well-being and an important outcome (Martin et al., 2010). In the subsequent section, we highlight several resources that can promote cognitive health and vitality among the oldest old. As evident in this discussion, there is likely a synergistic relation between cognitive vitality and these factors.

WHAT FACTORS OR RESOURCES CONTRIBUTE TO COGNITIVE VITALITY AMONG THE OLDEST OLD?

The Georgia Adaptation Model (see Chapters 5 and 17) is used in this chapter as a framework for cognitive vitality. This model constitutes a network of adaptational predictors and outcomes integral to physical and psychological well-being in the oldest old. Among the various contributing factors, we believe that five factors are particularly germane to cognitive vitality: social support, personality, mental and physical health, and nutrition. What is not defined in the model is the pattern of factors that is appropriate for each person. In other words, what is necessary and sufficient to be classified as cognitively vital? Rather than identifying a concrete Mini-Mental Status Exam or Global Deterioration Rating Scale cutoff point above which an individual would be considered cognitively vital, we propose that cognitive vitality can be encountered at any stage of cognitive functioning given the appropriate combination of mediating factors. For example, an individual can be physically impaired and still be considered cognitively vital. The degree of functional impairment would not affect the classification of cognitive vitality, which should be considered a continuous rather than a discrete variable. This caveat is also expressed by Kahn (2002) in response to criticism of the successful aging concept (Rowe & Kahn, 1998). Investigation of mediating factors, such as those described here, can inform prevention and intervention efforts.

Social support is a fundamental resource in the attainment and maintenance of cognitive vitality for the oldest old. A lack of engagement has been found to be an independent risk factor for cognitive decline among older adults. Data from animal studies demonstrate this pattern through increased synaptogenesis, neurogenesis, and capillary formation with environmental stimulation (Eriksson et al., 1998; Sirevaag, Black, Shafron, & Greenough, 1988). For individuals with Alzheimer's disease, social support modifies the relationship between some measures of disease pathology, such as neurofibrillary tangles, to level of cognitive vitality. This provides evidence that maintaining social networks could provide a protective effect against Alzheimer's disease (Bennett, Schneider, Tang, Arnold, & Wilson, 2006). Close relationships, in which partners spend significant time together, offer opportunities for (a) cognitive stimulation via interaction and activity participation, (b) the development and use of compensatory mechanisms beneficial to cognitive performance, and (c) provision of support. For married older adults, spouses influence each other's cognitive functioning and vitality over time (Gruber-Baldini, Schaie, & Willis, 1995; Walter-Ginzburg et al., 2008). However, the social support received by the oldest old differs from that of younger cohorts in that it is reduced and primarily includes family members (see Chapter 12). It is almost normative that centenarians have lost their romantic partners and children; therefore, a reduction in social support is expected (Martin, Kliegel, Rott, Poon, & Johnson, 2008; see Chapter 12). Nonetheless, it is imperative that the oldest old maintain strong social networks because of the demonstrated risk related to cognitive decline and likely risk of decreased cognitive vitality.

Personality factors affect cognitive functioning, and ultimately cognitive vitality, among the oldest old via several mechanisms, including (a) interpersonal relations and the resulting ability to enlist social support, (b) openness to experience and thus novel situations and cognitive stimulation, (c) perseverance and preferred approaches to cognitive problems which may both be differentially effective, and (d) impact of personality on mental health (e.g., ability to cope with stress). These mechanisms are likely to vary across age group and context. For example, a study comparing personality predictors of cognitive performance among younger and older adults yielded differential results according to age and level of cognitive skill. For average-skilled younger (mean age = 34) and older adults (mean age = 69), extraversion and openness were predictive of selected cognitive abilities, albeit skill type and nature of the predictor varied across age group (Baker & Bischel, 2006). For older adults with exceptional cognitive skills (mean age = 71), openness was predictive of visual-spatial abilities, agreeableness was a negative predictor of crystallized (i.e., culturally reinforced) knowledge, and conscientiousness predicted short-term memory and auditory processing (Baker & Bischel, 2006). Relatively low neuroticism, high competence, and high extraversion have been found to be common in centenarians (Martin, da Rosa, et al., 2006). One study found that, in older adults, higher neuroticism was associated with poor decision making (Denburg et al., 2009). Recent studies conducted by Wilson and colleagues suggest that high conscientiousness may help protect older adults from cognitive decline and impairment (Wilson, Schneider, Arnold, Bienias, & Bennett, 2007), whereas chronic psychological distress associated with increased neuroticism may be detrimental to cognitive health (Wilson, Schneider, Boyle, et al., 2007). Coping mechanisms are also related to these personality factors among community-dwelling, cognitively intact persons. Centenarians were more likely to use cognitive coping mechanisms, such as creating a plan to reduce stress, than octogenarians but less likely to use active behavioral coping, such as formulating a plan and following it (Martin, Poon, et al., 1992). Centenarians were more likely to acknowledge problems than individuals in other age groups but less likely to seek social support as a coping strategy (Martin, Rott, Poon, Courtenay, & Lehr, 2001).

Mental health is another important factor related to cognitive vitality among the oldest old, although the relation between the two is likely complex and difficult to tease apart from synergistic effects with other influences such as personality, interpersonal relations, and engagement and/or activity. At the behavioral level, diminished mental health may lead to decreased social interactions and thus opportunities for cognitive engagement and monitoring of cognitive health by social partners. Poor mental health, particularly depression, may also lead to lack of motivation and decreased processing speed. Indeed, previous research has shown that depressed older adults are at increased risk for cognitive impairment and dementia. Amnesic and executive deficits as well as neurocognitive impairment are trademarks of late-life depression. Using a neuropsychological assessment, Sheline et al. (2006) found that reduced processing speed led to deficits in episodic memory, language processing, working memory, and executive functioning. In Phases I and II (1988–1998) of the Georgia Centenarian Study, compared to younger, community-dwelling cohorts, centenarians reported more somatic but not affective symptoms. No clinical depression was found among the sample of cognitively intact, community-dwelling centenarians.

Fourth, according to the common cause hypothesis, physical and cognitive capabilities are highly interrelated among older adults (e.g., Anstey, Dear, Christensen, & Jorm, 2005; Lindenberger & Baltes, 1997). Beginning in young adulthood, suboptimal health and neurological risk factors affect cognitive health (Houx, Vreeling, & Jolles, 1991). These findings have been replicated in the oldest old; data from the Georgia Centenarian Study suggest that there is significant variability in the cognitive abilities of centenarians and that these cognitive differences are related to functional capacity (Mitchell et al., in press). Chronic conditions including cardiovascular disease and diabetes are linked to decreased cognitive functioning and increased risk of cognitive decline (e.g., Gorelick, 2005; Roberts et al., 2008). In addition, polypharmacy and the use of particular prescription medications can place older adults at greater cognitive risk (e.g., Starr et al., 2004). Health disparities in the prevalence and treatment of chronic conditions among ethnically and socioeconomically diverse groups can exacerbate these effects. Finally, intervention studies demonstrate the potentially beneficial effects of physical activity on cognitive functioning, although more work is needed to discern the specific mechanisms underlying this relationship and the most amenable cognitive skills (e.g., Poon & Harrington, 2006; Tomporowski, 2006).

Finally, adequate nutritional intake affects both longevity and proper functioning of the brain. Okinawa, Japan, which has the highest prevalence of exceptionally long-lived individuals in the world, has a traditional diet consisting of low-calorie, plant-based, and mainly low-caloric-density foods such as green and yellow vegetables, soy, fish, and limited amounts of boiled red meat (Willcox, Willcox, He, Curb, & Suzuki, 2006). Studies have found that vitamins, lipids, and trace minerals can affect the risk of cognitive decline. Replicated studies have found that a high intake of polyunsaturated and monounsaturated fats and fish were associated with lower risk of Alzheimer's disease. Epidemiological data show a protective role of the B vitamins, particularly B9 and B12, against cognitive decline. Data are still conflicting on the effect of antioxidant nutrients on cognitive functioning (Gillette-Guyonnet et al., 2007). A recent study indicated that oral administration of levocarnitine produces a reduction of total fat mass, increases total muscular mass, and facilitates an increased capacity for physical and cognitive activity by reducing fatigue and improving cognitive functioning (Malaguarnera et al., 2007).

The five resources mentioned here can function in concert only if older adults become active agents in their own cognitive aging. As proposed, a cognitively vital individual is one who exploits cognitive resources and interacts with the environment (Walter-Ginzburg et al., 2008). This assertion is consistent with Stine-Morrow's (2007) description of the active older adult who shapes his or her cognitive aging via the interactive effects of life experience, cultural context (e.g., societal stereotypes and expectations regarding cognitive aging), and learner choice and self-regulation (e.g., attentional allocation, activity selection). Emphasis on a highly active older adult highlights a principle from Rowe and Kahn's (1998) theory of successful aging in that high-level cognitive functioning is thought to be key to engagement in life and ultimately to successful aging. Indeed, prior empirical work supports the premise that a synergistic relationship exists between cognitive vitality and engagement (e.g., Bosma et al., 2002; Fratiglioni, Paillard-Borg, & Winblad, 2004).

WHAT CONCLUSIONS AND NEW DIRECTIONS CAN BE IDENTIFIED FOR FUTURE RESEARCH?

As we consider cognitive health in older age, several issues come to the forefront. First, the impact of ageist stereotypes is a poignant concern affecting later-life cognitive health (Stine-Morrow, 2007), where often the focus is on anticipated deterioration and the threat of dementia. Dementia is feared and typically viewed as an eventuality of old age (Ballenger, 2006; Cutler & Hodgson, 1996; Hodgson & Cutler, 2003, 2004). On an individual (personal) level, the tendency to focus on the negative aspects of cognitive aging may lead to diminished well-being; decreased propensity to engage in healthful behaviors; and as a result, ultimately poorer outcomes (Ory et al., 2003). As noted by Fillit et al. (2002), stereotypes and ageism reach beyond the individual and prevent promotion of cognitive health as a high-priority public policy initiative.

As a result, large-scale outreach efforts tend not to focus on prevention, instead directing efforts toward post hoc intervention, such as care for individuals with Alzheimer's disease (see Kovacich, Garrett, & Forti, 2006). This leads to the second point: promotion of cognitive health must become a public policy priority that encompasses the entire spectrum of cognitive functioning, including both prevention and intervention efforts. Prior studies of older adults with normative age-related changes in cognition have demonstrated that cognitive training improves performance for both older adults who had previously demonstrated a decline as well as for individuals who had not declined (Kramer & Willis, 2002). Research is needed to understand the transition from normative cognitive aging to impairment and the efficacy of training along this spectrum. Insufficient empirical research has addressed training applications for individuals with mild cognitive impairment (Belleville, Bherer, Lepage, Chertkow, & Gauthier 2008). In general, theoretical and methodological hurdles must be overcome to further formal methods of promoting cognitive vitality (Kramer et al., 2004) and develop best practices. Methods of prevention and intervention that are multimodal (Kramer & Willis, 2002) and that incorporate aspects of social, mental, and physical functioning are likely to be most efficacious (Park, Gutchess, Meade, & Stine-Morrow, 2007; Studenski et al., 2006). Furthermore, prevention and intervention efforts must start earlier in the life span. For example, in terms of cardiovascular risk factors predictive of cognitive decline, midlife matters (Gorelick, 2005). Techniques need not be formal or direct to enhance cognitive health. Cognitive health among the oldest old can be promoted through informal means by building on and enhancing existing social networks (e.g., cognitive collaboration; Marsiske & Margrett, 2006) and activity participation (e.g., volunteerism, hobbies, church or synagogue attendance; Walter-Ginzburg et al., 2008).

A third unresolved issue is the assessment of cognitive vitality and how it can build on assessments of cognitive functioning. Relevant to the conceptualization of cognitive vitality among the oldest old is how competency, or successful cognitive functioning, is deemed in normative and nonnormative frameworks. Two overarching difficulties exist, namely distinguishing degrees of cognitive functioning and understanding the transition between normative and nonnormative cognition. Tests of normative cognitive aging often lack norms, thus making it difficult to assess cognitive performance relative to peers matched on important contributing characteristics such as age and education. In addition, multiple assessments are rare until a problem has been identified. In the absence of multiple assessments and appropriate norms, meaningful within-person change can be difficult to detect, and the statistical methods to do so are debated. The meaning of performance change on a particular test is difficult to determine. For example, does a two-point decrease from pretest to posttest assessment constitute a reliable and valid (e.g., clinically or practically significant) change? What about when we consider the interval between assessments (e.g., 2 months vs. 2 years) and individuals' baseline performance? Additional attention must be given to the meaning and consequences of intraindividual variability or change in cognitive functioning (e.g., Allaire & Marsiske, 2005). As mentioned herein, an individual's degree of cognitive vitality likely fluctuates as well.

Clinical assessments of nonnormative cognitive functioning and impairment have several advantages over tests of normative functioning. One clear advantage is the presence of norms that position individuals' performance in context. Second, tests that distinguish the presence or absence of dementia are well documented. For example, the Mini-Mental Status Examination (MMSE) developed by Folstein et al. (1975) is a commonly used screening test that assesses several aspects of cognitive performance and provides a summary score reflecting overall mental status. Tests such as the MMSE may be useful in determining whether an older adult's performance is above or below a cutoff, thereby suggesting whether or not the person is likely to have dementia. However, care must be taken when employing dichotomous distinctions. Sensitivity to degrees of variations and changes in the normative range may be lost. Brief batteries of tests such as the Consortium to Establish a Registry for Alzheimer's Disease (CERAD) or Repeatable Battery for the Assessment of Neuropsychological Status (RBANS) allow for evaluation of multiple cognitive abilities across a range of abilities while maintaining the advantage of age- and education-matched norms (Beeri et al., 2006; Duff et al., 2003; Randolph, Tierney, Mohr, & Chase, 1998).

As emphasized in this chapter, we believe that cognitive vitality is best viewed as a continuous variable based on multiple dimensions and that fluctuates over the short term on the basis of an individual's available reserves and resources. Operational definitions may need to differ across age groups, and we might also add personal and cultural relevance, denoting that cognitive vitality encompasses the tasks an individual needs to accomplish in his or her context. It seems clear that, to move beyond assessment of cognitive functioning, we must encompass other features (e.g., social, dispositional, activity), not just purely cognitive functions. Conceptually, the framework of everyday competence (Willis, 1991, 1996), in which multiple antecedents and consequences of cognitive functioning are considered, provides a foundation from which to build. From the assessment perspective, activities of daily living (ADLs) or similar multidimensional assessments of one's ability to navigate day-to-day life might be a good starting point. Walter-Ginzburg et al. (2008) describe a self-reported index of cognitive vitality for individuals without dementia that was developed in Israel. The index assesses abilities akin to higher-level instrumental activities of daily living. Their index comprised seven dichotomous (yes-no) items: "no problem identifying people," "can write or use small objects," "reads newspaper often," "attends movies, restaurants, concerts, or theater often," "writes letters often," "has no difficulty managing finances," and "has no difficulty using telephone." Individuals scoring low on the cognitive vitality scale had significantly more difficulty with ADLs at the second assessment. The correlation between the cognitive vitality scale and a measure used to assess cognitive impairment (i.e., a orientation-memory-concentration test by Katzman et al., 1983) was evaluated. Although significantly related, Walter-Ginzburg et al. (2008) argue that the two measures exhibited distinctiveness to be considered separate constructs. Using a sample of Japanese nursing-home and hospital residents, some of whom had dementia, Toba et al. (2002) created an objective index to assess vitality in the context of dementia. This scale was completed by raters who assessed the individual's ability to perform basic ADLs such as ambulation, communication, eating, and toileting. In their study, Toba et al. (2002) note the importance of vitality in predicting important outcomes including mortality. In the everyday cognitive literature, efforts continue to develop multidimensional measures that assess what older adults may be able to do in their day-to-day lives and that predict meaningful outcomes (see Marsiske & Margrett, 2006 for discussion). Two examples developed by Willis and her colleagues are particularly germane to the current discussion of cognitive vitality. The Everyday Problems Test (EPT; Willis & Marsiske, 1993) was designed to assess performance among individuals experiencing normative age-related cognitive changes. The test consists of actual stimuli from everyday life that mirror instrumental ADLs in several domains (e.g., transportation, medication). The Everyday Problems Test for Cognitively Challenged Elderly (EPCCE; Willis, 1993) is an analogous test designed to assess the application of everyday cognitive skills of cognitively impaired individuals. The two tests provide examples of measures that attempt to assess older adults' potential for real-world functioning in normative and nonnormative perspectives, are sensitive to issues of ecological validity, and are easily administered.

Additional theoretical and psychometric work is needed to develop the concept of cognitive vitality more fully. The assessment approaches described herein highlight several important points for future research. First is consideration of the theoretical and practical implications of applying the concept of cognitive vitality to individuals without and with cognitive impairment. Theoretically, how do behaviors indicative of cognitive vitality differ from instrumental activities of daily living (IADL) performance by individuals without dementia and ADL performance by individuals with cognitive impairment and dementia? Reliance on IADL- and ADL-type assessments are likely not the most effective methods for capturing the richness of the concept of cognitive vitality. Theoretically, it is valuable to examine how subjective perceptions factor into assessment of cognitive vitality. How do performance- and behavior-based ratings relate to measures of meta-awareness? Finally, the results of previous studies indicate important correlates and possible contributors to cognitive vitality, such as age, gender, educational attainment, occupational status, physical conditions, and mental health (particularly depression).

CONCLUSIONS

Decrement is too often the focus in cognitive aging. Contrary to the stereotypic impression that cognitive and physical frailty is the norm in extreme old age and that dementia is inevitable, many of the oldest old function quite well. Successful cognitive aging, as indicated by cognitive vitality, is a concept that adds to our understanding of the full spectrum of cognitive health in later life. The literature suggests several resources that promote cognitive health and vitality among older adults, including social relationships, personality, mental and physical health, and nutrition. Future work must dispel myths about cognitive aging, improve assessment techniques related to cognition and functioning, and promote techniques to enhance cognitive health and ultimately vitality.

REFERENCES

Allaire, J. C., & Marsiske, M. (2002). Well- and ill-defined measures of everyday cognition: Relationship to older adults' intellectual ability and functional status. *Psychology and Aging, 17*, 101–115.

Allaire, J. C., & Marsiske, M. (2005). Intraindividual variability may not always indicate vulnerability in elders' cognitive performance. *Psychology and Aging, 20*, 390–401.

Anstey, K. J., Dear, K., Christensen, H., & Jorm, A. (2005). Biomarkers, health, lifestyle, and demographic variables as correlates of reaction time performance in early, middle, and late adulthood. *The Quarterly Journal of Experimental Psychology Section A, 58*, 5–21.

Bäckman, L., Small, B. J., & Wahlin, A. (2001). Aging and memory: Cognitive and biological perspectives. In J. E. Birren & K. W. Schaie (Eds.), *Handbook of the psychology of aging* (pp. 349–377). San Diego: Academic Press.

Baker, T. J., & Bischel, J. (2006). Personality predictors of intelligence: Differences between young and cognitively healthy older adults. *Personality and Individual Differences, 41*, 861–871.

Ballenger, J. F. (2006). *Self, senility, and Alzheimer's disease in modern America.* Baltimore, MD: Johns Hopkins University Press.

Beeri, M. S., Schmeidler, J., Sano, M., Wang, J., Lally, R., Grossman, H., et al. (2006). Age, gender, and education norms on the CERAD neuropsychological battery in the oldest old. *Neurology, 67*, 1006–1010.

Belleville, S., Bherer, L., Lepage, E., Chertkow, H., & Gauthier, S. (2008). Task switching capacities in persons with Alzheimer's disease and mild cognitive impairment. *Neuropsychologia, 46*, 2225–2233.

Bennett, D. A., Schneider, J. A., Arvanitakis, Z., Kelly, J. F., Aggarwal, N. T., Shah, R. C., et al. (2006). Neuropathology of older persons without cognitive impairment from two community-based studies. *Neurology, 66*, 1837–1844.

Bennett, D. A., Schneider, J. A., Tang, Y., Arnold, S. E., & Wilson, R. S. (2006). The effect of social networks on the relation between Alzheimer's disease pathology and level of cognitive function in old people: A longitudinal cohort study. *Lancet Neurology, 5*, 406–412.

Berg, S. (1996). Aging, behavior and terminal decline. J. E. Birren & K. W. Schaie (Eds.), *Handbook of the psychology of aging* (pp. 323–337). San Diego: Academic Press.

Bosma, H., Van Boxtel, M. P. J., Ponds, R. W. H. M., Jelicic, M., Houx, P., Metsemakers, J., et al. (2002). Engaged lifestyle and cognitive function in middle and old-aged, non-demented persons: A reciprocal association? *Zeitschrift für Gerontologie und Geriatrie, 35*, 575–581.

Burke, W. J., Miller J. P., Rubin, E. H., Morris, J. C., Coben, L. A., Duchek, J., et al. (1988). Reliability of the Washington University Clinical Dementia Rating. *Archives of Neurology, 45*, 31–32.

Butler, R., Forette, F., & Greengrass, S. (2004). Maintaining cognitive health in an ageing society. *Journal of the Royal Society for the Promotion of Health, 124*(3), 119–121.

Campbell, J. J., III, & Coffey, C. E. (2001). Neuropsychiatric significance of subcortical hyperintensity. *The Journal of Neuropsychiatry and Clinical Neurosciences, 13*, 261–288.

Collie, A., & Maruff, P. (2000). The neuropsychology of preclinical Alzheimer's disease and mild cognitive impairment. *Neuroscience and Biobehavioral Reviews, 24*, 365–374.

Cutler, S. J., & Hodgson, L. G. (1996). Anticipatory dementia: A link between memory appraisals and concerns about developing Alzheimer's disease. *Gerontologist, 36*, 657–664.

Deci, E. K., & Ryan, R. M. (2008). Hedonia, eudaimonia, and well-being: An introduction. *Journal of Happiness Studies, 9*, 1–11.

de Frias, C. M., Annerbrink, K., Westberg, L., Eriksson, E., Adolfsson, R., & Nilsson, L. G. (2005). Catechol O-methyltransferase Val158Met polymorphism is associated with cognitive performance in nondemented adults. *Journal of Cognitive Neuroscience, 17*, 1018–1025.

de Frias, C. M., Lövdén, M., Lindenberger, U., & Nilsson, L. G., (2007). Revisiting the dedifferentiation hypothesis with longitudinal multi-cohort data. *Intelligence, 35*, 381–392.

Denburg, N. L., Weller, K. L., Yamada, T. H., Shivapour, D. M., Kaup, A. R., & LaLoggia, A., et al. (2009). Poor decision making among older adults is related to elevated levels of neuroticism. *Annals of Behavioral Medicine, 37*, 164–172.

Duff, K., Pattern, D., Schoenberg, M. R., Mold, J., Scott, J. G., & Adams, R. L. (2003). Age- and education-corrected independent normative data for the RBANS in a community dwelling elderly sample. *Clinical Neuropsychologist, 17*, 351–366.

Eriksson, P. S., Perfilieva, E., Bjork-Eriksson, T., Alborn, A.-M., Nordborg, C., Peterson, D. A., et al. (1998). Neurogenesis in the adult human hippocampus. *Nature Medicine, 4*, 1313–1317.

Evert, J., Lawler, E., Bogan, H., & Perls, T. (2003). Morbidity profiles of centenarians: Survivors, delayers, and escapers. *Journal of Gerontology: Medical Sciences, 58A*, 232–237.

Fillit, H. M., Butler, R. N., O'Connell, A. W., Albert, M. S., Birren, J. E., Cotman, C. W., et al. (2002). Achieving and maintaining cognitive vitality with aging. *Mayo Clinic Proceedings, 77*, 681–696.

Folstein, M. F., Folstein, S. E., & McHugh, P. R. (1975). "Mini-Mental State": A practical method for grading the cognitive state of patients for the clinician. *Journal of Psychiatric Research, 12*, 189–198.

Fratiglioni, L., Paillard-Borg, S., & Winblad, B. (2004). An active and socially integrated lifestyle in late life might protect against dementia. *Lancet Neurology, 3*, 343–353.

Galvin, J. E., Powlishta, K. K., Wilkins, K., McKeel, D. W. J., Xiong, C., Grant, E., et al. (2005). Predictors of preclinical Alzheimer disease and dementia: A clinicopathologic study. *Archives of Neurology, 62*, 758–765.

Gillette-Guyonnet, S., Abellan Van Kan, G., Andrieu, S., Barberger-Gateau, P., Berr, C., Bonnefoy, M., et al. (2007). IANA task force on nutrition and cognitive decline with aging. *Journal of Nutrition, Health, and Aging, 11*, 132–153.

Gondo, Y., Hirose, N., Arai, Y., Inagaki, H., Masui, Y., Yamamura, K., et al. (2006). Functional status of centenarians in Tokyo, Japan: Developing better phenotypes of exceptional longevity. *Journal of Gerontology: Biological Sciences and Medical Sciences, 61*, 305–310.

Gorelick, P. (2005). William M. Feinberg Lecture: Cognitive vitality and the role of stroke and cardiovascular disease risk factors. *Stroke, 36*, 875–879.

Gruber-Baldini, A. L., Schaie, K. W., & Willis, S. L. (1995). Similarity in married couples: A longitudinal study of mental abilities and flexibility-rigidity. *Journal of Personality and Social Psychology: Personality Processes and Individual Differences, 69*, 191–203.

Gunning-Dixon, F. M., & Raz, N. (2000). The cognitive correlates of white matter abnormalities in normal aging: A quantitative review. *Neuropsychology, 14*, 224–232.

Hagberg, B., Alfredson, B., Poon, L.W., & Homma, A. (2001). Cognitive functioning in centenarians: A coordinated analysis of results from three countries. *Journal of Gerontology: Psychological Science, 56*, 141–151.

Hendrie, H., Albert, M., Butters, M., Gao, S., Knopman, D., Launer, L., et al. (2006). The NIH Cognitive and Emotional Health Project: Report of the Critical Evaluation Study Committee. *Alzheimer's and Dementia, 2*, 12–32.

Hilborn, J. V., Strauss, E., Hultsch, D. F., & Hunter, M. A. (2009). Intraindividual variability across cognitive domains: Investigation of dispersion levels and performance profiles in older adults. *Journal of Clinical and Experimental Neuropsychology, 31*, 412–424.

Hodgson, L. G., & Cutler, S. J. (2003). Looking for signs of Alzheimer's disease. *International Journal of Aging and Human Development, 56*, 323–343.

Hodgson, L. G., & Cutler, S. J. (2004). Help seeking for personal concerns about developing Alzheimer's disease. *Journal of Applied Gerontology, 23*, 385–410.

Houx, P. J., Vreeling, F. W., & Jolles, J. (1991). Rigorous health screening reduces age effect on memory scanning task. *Brain and Cognition, 15*, 246–260.

Hultsch, D. F., MacDonald, S. W. S., Hunter, M. A., Levy-Bencheton, J., & Strauss, E. (2000). Intraindividual variability in cognitive performance in older adults: Comparison of adults with mild dementia, adults with arthritis, and healthy adults. *Neuropsychology, 14*, 588–598.

Kahn, R. L. (2002). On "Successful aging and well-being: Self-rated compared with Rowe and Kahn." *Gerontologist, 42*, 725–726.

Katzman, R., Brown, T., Fuld, P., Peck, A., Schechter, R., & Schimmel, H. (1983). Validation of a short orientation memory concentration test of cognitive impairment. *American Journal of Psychiatry, 140*, 734–739.

Kovacich, J., Garrett, R., & Forti, E. (2006). New learning programs in cognitive vitality, Alzheimer's disease, and related dementias. *Gerontology and Geriatrics Education, 26*(4), 47–61.

Kramer, A. N., Mailand, C., Lukas, R. G., Syljuasen, C. J., Wilkinson, E. A., Nigg, J., et al. (2004). Centrosome-associated Chk1 prevents premature activation of cyclin-B-Cdk1 kinase. *Nature Cell Biology, 6*, 884–891.

Kramer, A., & Willis, S. (2002). Enhancing the cognitive vitality of older adults. *Current Directions in Psychological Science, 11*, 172–177.

Lindenberger, U., & Baltes, P. B. (1997). Intellectual functioning in old and very old age: Cross-sectional results from the Berlin Aging Study. *Psychology of Aging, 12*, 410–432.

Malaguarnera, M., Cammalleri, L., Gargante, M. P., Vacante, M., Colonna, V., Motta, M. (2007). L-carnitine treatment reduces severity of physical and mental fatigue and increases cognitive functions in centenarians: A randomized and controlled clinical trial. *American Journal of Clinical Nutrition, 86*, 1738–1744.

Margrett, J. A., Allaire, J. A., Johnson, T. L., Daugherty, K., & Weatherbee, S. (2010). Everyday problem solving. In J. Cavanaugh & C. Cavanaugh (Eds.), *Aging in America: Psychological aspects of aging* (pp. 79–101). Westport, CT: Praeger.

Markesbery, W. R., Schmitt, F. A., Kryscio, R. J., Davis, D. G., Smith, C. D., & Wekstein, D. R. (2006). Neuropathologic substrate of mild cognitive impairment. *Archives of Neurology, 63*, 38–46.

Marsiske, M., & Margrett, J. A. (2006). Everyday problem solving and decision making. In J. E. Birren & K. W. Schaie (Eds.), *Handbook of the psychology of aging* (6th ed., pp. 315–342). Burlington, MA: Elsevier Academic Press.

Martin, P., da Rosa, G., Siegler, I. C., Davey, A., Macdonald, M., & Poon, L. W. (2006). Personality and longevity: Findings from the Georgia Centenarian Study. *Age, 28*, 343–352.

Martin, P., Kliegel, M., Rott, C., Poon, L. W., & Johnson, M. A. (2008). Age differences and changes of coping behavior in three age groups: Findings from the Georgia Centenarian Study. *International Aging and Human Development, 66*, 97–114.

Martin, P., MacDonald, M., Margrett, J. A., & Poon, L. W. (2010). Resilience among the oldest-old. In P. S. Fry & C. L. M. Keyes (Eds.), *Frontiers of resilient aging.* Cambridge: Cambridge University Press, 213–238.

Martin, P., Poon, L. W., Clayton, G. M., Lee, H. S., Fulks, J. S., & Johnson, M. A. (1992). Personality, life events, and coping in the oldest old. *International Journal of Aging and Human Development, 34*(1), 19–30.

Martin, P., Rott, C., Poon, L. W., Courtenay, B., & Lehr, U. (2001). A molecular view of coping behavior in older adults. *Journal of Aging and Health, 13*, 72–91.

Masten, A. S. (2001). Ordinary magic: Resilience processes in development. *American Psychologist, 56*, 227–238.

Mitchell, M. B., Miller, L. S., Woodard, J. L., Davey, A., & Poon, L. W. (in press). Predicting observed functional status in centenarians. *The Gerontologist.*

Morris, J. C., Storandt, M., Miller, J. P., McKeel, D. W., Price, J. L., Rubin, E. H. et al. (2001). Mild cognitive impairment represents early-stage Alzheimer disease. *Archives of Neurology, 58*, 397–405.

Morse, C. K. (1993). Does variability increase with age?: An archival study of cognitive measures. *Psychology and Aging, 8*, 156–164.

Nelson, E. A., & Dannefer, D. (1992). Aged heterogeneity – Fact or fiction?: The Fate of diversity in gerontological research. *Gerontologist, 32*, 17–23.

O'Brien, J. T. (2006). Vascular cognitive impairment. *American Journal of Geriatric Psychiatry, 14*, 724–733.

O'Brien, J. T., Erkinjuntti, T., Reisberg, B., Roman, G., Sawada, T., Pantoni, L. et al. (2003). Vascular cognitive impairment. *Lancet Neurology, 2*, 89–98.

Ory, M., Hoffman, M., Hawkins, M., Sanner, B., & Mockenhaupt, R. (2003). Challenging aging stereotypes: Strategies for creating a more active society. *American Journal of Preventive Medicine, 25*, 164–171.

Park, D. C., Gutchess, A. H., Meade, M. L., & Stine-Morrow, E. A. L. (2007). Improving cognitive functioning in older adults: Nontraditional approaches. *Journal of Gerontology, 62B*, 48–52.

Petersen, R. C., Doody, R., Kurz, A., Mohs, R. C., Morris, J. C., Rabins, P. V., et al. (2001). Current concepts in mild cognitive impairment. *Archives of Neurology, 58*, 1985–1992.

Petersen, R. C., & Morris, J. C. (2005). Mild cognitive impairment as a clinical entity and treatment target. *Archives of Neurology, 62*, 1160–1163.

Petersen, R. C., Parisi, J. E., Dickson, D. W., Johnson, K. A., Knopman, D. S., Boeve, B. F., et al. (2006). Neuropathologic features of amnestic mild cognitive impairment. *Archives of Neurology 63*, 665–672.

Plassman, B. L., Langa, K. M., Fisher, G. G., Heeringa, S. G., Weir, D. R., Ofstedal, M. B., et al. (2007). Prevalence of dementia in the United States: The aging, demographics, and memory study. *Neuroepidemiology, 29*, 125–132.

Poon, L. W., & Harrington, C. A. (2006). Commonalities in aging- and fitness-related impact on cognition. In L. W. Poon, W. Chodzko-Zajko, & P. D. Tomporowski (Eds.), *Active living, cognitive functioning, and aging* (Vol. 1, pp. 33–50). Champaign, IL: Human Kinetics.

Poon, L. W., Woodard, J. L., Miller, L. S., Davey, A., Arnold, J., & Martin, P., et al. (2010). Population-based study of dementia prevalence and behavioral staging among the oldest old. Manuscript in preparation.

Randolph, C., Tierney, M. C., Mohr, E., & Chase, T. N. (1998). The Repeatable Battery for the Assessment of Neuropsychological Status (RBANS): Preliminary clinical validity. *Journal of Clinical and Experimental Neuropsychology, 20*, 310–319.

Raz, N. (2005). The aging brain observed in vivo: Differential changes and their modifiers. In R. Cabeza, L. Nyberg, & D. Park (Eds.), *Cognitive neuroscience of aging: Linking cognitive and cerebral aging* (pp. 19–57). New York: Oxford University Press.

Raz, N., & Rodrigue, K. M. (2006). Differential aging of the brain: Patterns, cognitive correlates and modifiers. *Neuroscience and Biobehavioral Reviews, 30*, 730–748.

Raz, N., Rodrigue, K. M., & Acker, J. D. (2003). Hypertension and the brain: Vulnerability of the prefrontal regions and executive functions. *Behavioral Neuroscience, 117*, 1169–1180.

Roberts, R. O., Geda, Y. E., Knopman, D. S., Teresa, J. H., Christianson, B. S., Pankratz, V. S., et al. (2008). Association of duration and severity of diabetes mellitus with mild cognitive impairment. *Archives of Neurology, 65*, 1066–1073.

Rowe, J. W., & Kahn, R. L. (1998). *Successful aging.* New York: Pantheon Books.

Salthouse, T. (2009). When does age-related decline begin? *Neurobiology of Aging, 30*, 507–514.

Schaie, K. W. (1989). Individual differences in rate of cognitive change in adulthood. In V. L. Bengston & K. W. Schaie (Eds.), *The course of later life: Research and reflections* (pp. 65–85). New York: Springer.

Schaie, K. W. (2005). What can we learn from longitudinal studies of adult development? *Research in Human Development, 2*, 133–158.

Schmitt, F. A., Davis, D. G., Wekstein, D. R., Smith, C. D., Ashford, J. W., & Markesbery, W. R. (2000). "Preclinical" AD revisited: Neuropathology of cognitively normal older adults. *Neurology, 55*, 370–376.

Sheline, Y. I., Barch, D. M., Garcia, K., Gersing, K., Pieper, C., Welsh-Bohmer, K., et al. (2006). Cognitive function in late life depression: Relationships to depression severity, cerebrovascular risk factors and processing speed. *Biological Psychiatry, 60*, 58–65.

Sirevaag, A. M., Black, J. E., Shafron, D., & Greenough, W. T. (1988). Direct evidence that complex experience increases capillary branching and surface area in visual cortex of young rats. *Developmental Brain Research, 471*, 299–304.

Starr, J. M., McGurn, B., Whiteman, M., Pattie, A., Whalley, L. J., & Deary, I. J. (2004). Life long changes in cognitive ability are associated with prescribed medications in old age. *International Journal of Geriatric Psychiatry, 19*, 327–332.

Stine-Morrow, E. A. L. (2007). The Dumbledore hypothesis of cognitive aging. *Association for Psychological Science, 16*, 295–299.

Storandt, M., Grant, E. A., Miller, J. P., & Morris, J. C. (2002). Rates of progression in mild cognitive impairment and early Alzheimer's disease. *Neurology, 59*, 1034–1041.

Studenski, S., Carlson, M. C, Fillit, H., Greenough, W. T., Kramer, A. F., & Rebok, G. W. (2006). From bedside to bench: Does mental and physical activity promote cognitive vitality in late life? *Science of Aging Knowledge Environment, 6*, 21.

Thornton, W. J. L., & Dumke, H. A. (2005). Age differences in everyday problem-solving and decision-making effectiveness: A meta-analytic review. *Psychology and Aging, 20*, 85–99.

Toba, K., Nakai, R., Akishita, M., Iijima, S., Nishinaga, M., Mizoguchi, T., et al. (2002). Vitality index as a useful tool to assess elderly with dementia. *Geriatrics and Gerontology International, 2*, 23–29.

Tomporowski, P. D. (2006). Physical activity, cognition, and aging: A review of reviews. In L. W. Poon, W. Chodzko-Zajko, & P. D. Tomporowski (Eds.), *Active living, cognitive functioning, and aging* (Vol. 1, pp. 15–32). Champaign, IL: Human Kinetics.

Wade, D. T., & Collin, C. (1988). The Barthel ADL Index: A reliability study. *International Disability Studies, 10*, 61–63.

Walter-Ginzburg, A., Shmotkin, D., Blumstein, T., & Shorek, A. (2005). A gender-based dynamic multidimensional longitudinal analysis of resilience and mortality in the old-old in Israel: The Cross-sectional and Longitudinal Aging Study (CALAS). *Social Science and Medicine, 60*, 1705–1715.

Walter-Ginzburg, A., Shmotkin, Eyal, N., & Guralnik, J. M. (2008). Can cognitive vitality reduce incident disability? Evidence from the Cross-Sectional and Longitudinal Aging Study (CALAS) of old-old Israelis. Unpublished manuscript.

Willcox, B. J., Willcox, D. C., He, Q., Curb, J. D., & Suzuki, M. (2006). Siblings of Okinawan centenarians share lifelong mortality advantages. *Journal of Gerontology: Biological Sciences, 61*, 345–354.

Willis, S. L. (1991). Cognition and everyday competence. In K. W. Schaie & M. P. Lawton (Eds.), *Annual review of gerontology and geriatrics* (Vol. 11, pp. 80–109). New York: Springer.

Willis, S. L. (1993). *Test manual for the Everyday Problems Test for Cognitively Challenged Elderly.* University Park: Pennsylvania State University.

Willis, S. L. (1996). Everyday cognitive competence in elderly persons: Conceptual issues and empirical findings. *Gerontologist, 36*, 595–601.

Willis, S. L., & Marsiske, M. (1993). *Manual for the Everyday Problems Test.* University Park: Pennsylvania State University.

Wilson, R. S., Beckett, L. A., Bienias, J. L., Evans, D. A., & Bennett, D. A. (2003). Terminal decline in cognitive function. *Neurology, 60*, 1782–1787.

Wilson, R., Schneider, J., Arnold, S., Bienias, J., & Bennett, D. (2007). Conscientiousness and the incidence of Alzheimer disease and mild cognitive impairment. *Archives of General Psychiatry, 6*, 1204–1212.

Wilson, R., Schneider, J., Boyle, P., Arnold, S., Tang, Y., & Bennett, D. (2007). Chronic distress and incidence of mild cognitive impairment. *American Academy of Neurology, 68*, 2085–2092.

World Health Organization. (1948). Preamble to the Constitution of the World Health Organization as adopted by the International Health Conference, New York, 19–22 June, 1946. In *Official Records of the World Health Organization.* Retrieved from http://www.who.int/about/definition/en/print.html.

Yevchak, A., Loeb, S., & Fick, D. (2008). Promoting cognitive health and vitality: A review of clinical implications. *Geriatric Nursing, 29*, 302–310.

Ylikoski, R., Ylikoski, A., Keskivaara, P., Tilvis, R., Sulkava, R., & Erkinjuntti, T. (1999). Heterogeneity of cognitive profiles in aging: Successful aging, normal aging, and individuals at risk for cognitive decline. *European Journal of Neurology, 6*, 645–652.

12

Social Relationships and Well-Being in Very Late Life

HOWARD LITWIN

ABSTRACT

This chapter examines social networks and social exchange in relation to morale and survival among older Jewish Israelis. Using empirical data, the presentation shows that embeddedness in robust social networks and provision of help both decrease as age and disability increase. However, persons who retain robust networks and those who give help have better morale and greater likelihood of 7-year survival. The data underscore the great diversity that prevails among the oldest old.

INTRODUCTION

Study of the association between social relationships and well-being in very old age is an important undertaking. Social relationships are believed to affect well-being and the quality of late life. However, various aspects of social relationships can be considered measures of well-being in their own right, a means through which one may enhance his or her quality of life, or both. It is necessary, therefore, to better understand the ways in which these two domains – social relationships and well-being – are associated and to elucidate the nature of their relationship among the oldest old.

This chapter examines the association of social relationships and well-being in very late life, looking particularly at data that describe the life situations of older Israeli adults. Two interrelated aspects of social relationships are considered in this regard. First is the notion of social network, or the degree to which one is embedded in a structure of social ties. The second aspect is social exchange, that is, the extent to which one is a provider or recipient of funds, goods, or services. Both of these aspects of social relationships constitute measures of well-being. We know, for example, that it is beneficial to be embedded in a supportive social network (Bisschop et al., 2003; Bosworth & Schaie, 1997; Bowling & Browne, 1991; Tesch-Romer, Motel-Klingebiel, & von Kondratowitz, 2002). There is also documentation that it is rewarding to be engaged in mutually enhancing social exchange (Brown, Nesse, Vinokur, & Smith, 2003; Litwin, 2004a).

However, social relationships also constitute a means by which to attain well-being in late life. That is, such relationships can provide the resources and/or the mechanisms by which to attain a range of outcomes that reflect quality of life in very old age. Accordingly, this chapter also examines the association between social relationships and two important well-being outcomes among the very old. It looks specifically in this regard at mental health (Antonucci, Fuhrer, & Dartigues, 1997; Fiori, Antonucci, & Cortina, 2006; Litwin, 2004a) and at survival (Cerhan & Wallace, 1997; Guilley et al., 2005; Rasulo, Christensen, & Tomassini, 2005).

Before beginning the current inquiry, it is necessary to clarify the term *very old age* as employed in this analysis. Late life is frequently defined by chronological age. Accordingly, this discussion adopts the customary distinction among young olds, old-olds, and oldest olds. In the present analysis, the respective age levels considered for these groupings are 60–69, 70–79, and 80 and older. However, the nature of very old age also varies with one's functional capabilities. In general, the greater the degree of physical impairment one experiences, the older one feels (Kleinspehn-Ammerlahn, Kotter-Grühn, & Smith, 2008). Consequently, physical disability is taken into account as an essential factor in this inquiry as well.

The analysis presented in this chapter is based on data from two main sources. The first is the survey of Israelis aged 60 and older that was executed in 1997 by the Israeli Central Bureau of Statistics (CBS). This database was linked, in 2004, to records from the Israeli National Death Registry, thus enabling consideration of factors possibly contributing to mortality and survival. The second source is the Survey of Health, Aging, and Retirement in Europe (SHARE), which studied persons aged 50 and older (Boersch-Supan, Hank, & Juerges, 2005). The first wave of the Israeli sample of SHARE was carried out in 2005–2006. Both surveys included self-report and proxy reports, but the social relationship questions were addressed only to the nonproxy respondents, given their subjective nature. Persons residing in long-term-care institutions were not included in either survey sample.

The current analysis is limited to the population of veteran Jewish Israelis, who comprise the majority segment of the older cohort in Israel (about 80% of all persons aged 60 and older). The term *veteran Jewish Israelis* refers to Jewish persons who were either born in the area that now constitutes the state of Israel or who immigrated to it before 1990. The two other major population groupings in Israeli society are Arab Israelis, that is, Arab citizens of the state of Israel, and new immigrants, primarily from the former Soviet Union, who arrived in massive numbers in the 1990s. Both population groups have distinctive relationship characteristics requiring separate attention (Litwin, 2006a, 2006b); as such, they are not addressed in the constraints of the current chapter.

SOCIAL NETWORKS

The construct of social networks most often refers to the matrix of social ties in which individuals are embedded (Berkman & Syme, 1979; Mitchell, 1969). The study of social ties, or social network analysis, usually focuses on the structural and interactional characteristics of social relationships. The former refer to the architecture of the social network and examine such components as its size and composition; the latter reflect the dynamics that occur in networks, such as frequency of contact with others and the duration of the relationships. An important additional analytic construct has been recently developed that takes into account both the structural and the interactional aspects of one's interpersonal milieu: the notion of network type (Wenger, 1991). Analysis of Israeli data has identified five types of networks among older people using such criteria as marital status, proximate children, frequency of contact with various ties, and attendance at religious and social organizations (Litwin, 2001). These same five network types have also emerged, for the most part, in analysis of data from older persons in the United States (Fiori et al., 2006).

The five network constellations derived in the Israeli typology have been termed *diverse*, *friend focused*, *neighbor focused*, *family focused*, and *restricted* (Litwin, 2007a). Their respective characteristics are summarized in Table 12.1 (Litwin, 2001). As can be seen, the diverse network is the most socially endowed grouping. It has varied sources of support that usually include a living spouse, one or two proximate children, and frequent contact with friends and neighbors. Members of the diverse network are frequently economically advantaged. The friend-focused network is similar to the diverse network in most categories, including family members. Its main distinctive feature is that its members report having frequent contact with friends but almost no contact with neighbors. Moreover, respondents in this network type tend to be a bit younger than those in the other networks. In contrast, the neighbor-focused network shows a reverse pattern. That is, its members have frequent contact with neighbors but almost no contact with persons

TABLE 12.1. *Network type by delineating characteristics and frequencies*

Network type	Delineating characteristic							Frequency (%)
	Married	Proximate children	Contact with children[a]	Contact with friends[a]	Contact with neighbors[a]	Synagogue attendance[b]	Social club attendance[c]	
Diverse	.55	1.1	3.7	4.1	4.4	2.7	1.6	30.2
Friends	.59	1.0	3.7	3.6	0.2	2.5	1.5	23.7
Neighbors	.46	1.2	3.8	0.5	4.4	2.5	1.2	17.1
Family	.59	4.9	4.4	0.8	1.3	3.4	1.3	9.2
Restricted	.44	1.1	3.4	0.1	0.1	2.3	1.4	19.9

[a]Measured on a scale of 0–5: 0 = no contact, 1 = less than monthly, 2 = once or twice a month, 3 = weekly, 4 = once or twice a week, and 5 = daily.
[b]Measured on a scale of 1–5: 1 = does not go at all, 2 = goes only for family celebrations, 3 = goes only on holidays, 4 = goes on Sabbath and holidays, and 5 = goes daily or almost daily.
[c]Measured on a scale of 1–5: 1 = does not go at all, 2 = goes once or twice a month, 3 = goes weekly, 4 = goes once or twice a week, and 5 = goes daily.
Source: "Social network type and morale in old age" by H. Litwin, 2001, *The Gerontologist*, 41, 516–524. Reprinted with permission.

TABLE 12.2. *Network type by age ($n = 2{,}079$) and disability ($n = 2{,}065$) among veteran Jewish Israelis aged 60 and older*

	Network type						
	Diverse %	Friend %	Neighbor %	Family %	Restricted %	%	X^2
Age							
60–69, $n = 809$	30.2	27.4	16.4	12.0	14.0	100.0	
70–79, $n = 835$	33.3	23.6	16.9	8.5	17.7	100.0	
80+, $n = 435$	24.1	17.0	18.6	5.3	34.9	100.0	102.17***
Disability							
Low, $n = 755$	40.0	28.9	15.1	5.2	10.9	100.0	
Medium, $n = 711$	29.0	25.5	16.2	10.0	19.4	100.0	
High, $n = 599$	19.5	14.9	20.7	13.5	31.4	100.0	179.93***

***$p < .001$.

whom they consider friends. Respondents in the neighbor-focused network are also more frequently widowed. The family-focused network is unique in that its members maintain ties mostly with other family members. They also tend to have several children in close geographic proximity, about five on average. People embedded in family-focused networks also tend to frequent a place of worship more than their counterparts in other network types. Finally, people embedded in the restricted network are the least endowed in terms of social contacts. They have virtually no friends or neighbors with whom they are in contact and are the most often widowed relative to those in other network types.

Examination of the associations among age, disability, and network type provides unique insights into the dynamics of social relationships in very late life. Based on data from the CBS survey, Table 12.2 reveals that three robust networks decrease in relative frequency as age increases – the diverse, friend-focused, and family-focused types. The neighbor-focused network maintains its frequency independent of age. The restricted network, in contrast, shows an increase in frequency with age, especially among the oldest old.

Table 12.2 also shows the association between disability and network type. Disability, in this case, was measured on a Hebrew version of the scale of physical capacity that was originally employed in the Yale Health and Aging Project (Cornoni-Huntley et al., 1985). Respondents were asked the extent of difficulty they had in performing such physical tasks as raising their arms above their shoulders and pushing a sofa. The summary scale scores were divided into three levels of difficulty in this analysis; the higher the score, the greater was the disability. Table 12.2 shows an inverse association between disability level and belonging to diverse and friend-focused networks. In contrast, a positive association is evident with the other network types, particularly among those in restricted and family-focused networks.

A separate cross-tabulation of disability level and network type, exclusively in the 80-and-older age group, was also performed, and the same trends were found (not shown). As evident in Table 12.2, about one third of persons aged 80 and older and about one third of persons with high disability were located in a restricted social network. However, the additional cross-tabulation shows that, among the oldest old, almost half of those with a high degree of disability were also embedded in the restricted network constellation. In contrast, more than 40% of the oldest old with low disability maintained diverse social network types, the most gregarious grouping. This suggests that the effect of disability may be more pronounced than that of age.

Network type has been studied in relation to mental health. Findings confirm that persons located in diverse and friend-focused networks report better morale, as measured by an adapted Hebrew version of the General Health Questionnaire (GHQ-12), than do persons in restricted networks (Litwin, 2001). This was the case even after controlling for age and disability. Similar findings have been reported in relation to survival (Litwin & Shiovitz-Ezra, 2006). That is, after controlling for disability and major illness, persons who were embedded in diverse and friend-focused networks and were aged 70 and older at baseline had lower 7-year all-cause mortality risk than did persons in restricted networks. Moreover, the network-survival association remains significant when examined exclusively among respondents aged 80 and older. Thus, it seems that social network type is a critical factor in the well-being of the very old.

SOCIAL EXCHANGE

Another important aspect of social relationships is the exchange of funds, goods, and services (Cox & Rank, 1992; Henretta, Hill, Li, Soldo, & Wolf, 1997; Iecovich & Lankri, 2002; Silverstein, Parrott, & Bengtson, 1995). Of particular consequence in late life is the extent and direction of transfer, as reflected in the exchange of practical support (time) and/or financial support (money) (Kohli & Künemund, 2003; Litwin, 2004b; McGarry & Schoeni, 1995; Silverstein, Conroy, Wang, Giarrusso, & Bengtson, 2002). It can be maintained that the tangible exchange of time or money might be a more meaningful measure of social ties in that variables measuring social network structure reflect potential support only.

The SHARE-Israel project, the Israeli component of the Survey of Health, Ageing, and Retirement in Europe, provides a unique opportunity to examine the nature and direction of social exchange in very late life. The questionnaire asked respondents whether they gave or received practical or financial help to or from others outside the household in the 12 months before the interview. The data showed that some 71% of veteran Jewish Israeli respondents aged 50 and older were engaged in at least one form of exchange. Almost two thirds of the same population gave assistance (time or money), and slightly less than a quarter received assistance. Moreover, age was not associated with the extent of involvement in exchange. Age was related, however, to the direction of the transfers. A negative age gradient appeared in relation to the giving of any assistance (e.g., 75% of persons aged 50–59 gave help, but only 48% of persons aged 80 and older did so). Correspondingly, a positive age gradient was observed in relation to the receipt of any help (17% of those aged 50–59 received help, compared with 54% of those aged 80 and older).

To understand the associations of age, disability, and social exchange, binary logistic regressions were executed for each of the four types of transfer: giving and receiving money and giving and receiving practical help (time). In each procedure the binary transfer outcome (yes/no) was regressed on age and disability, as well as on gender and income as control variables. Disability was measured in this case as the total number of difficulties (0–6) in performing instrumental activities of daily living (IADL), that is, functional disability. The odds ratios presented in Table 12.3 show that neither age nor level of disability was associated with the receipt of financial assistance. Low income was the only correlate of such receipt. A partial age association emerged in relation to giving money. That is, persons aged 60–79 were less likely to give money than those aged 50–59, but this same association was not significant among those 80 years and older. (The table shows a comparable risk ratio in this latter case, but it is not significant because of the smaller number of respondents aged 80 and older.) As for disability, a negative association was evident: the greater the disability, the lower was the probability of giving money. Turning to time transfers, the table shows a clear positive association between age and disability, on the one hand, and receipt of practical help, on the other hand. Conversely, a negative association is evident between both age and disability and the transfer of time. These findings suggest that persons aged 80 and older are more frequently recipients of social exchange than they are providers.

The literature suggests that balanced exchange contributes to better mental health (Litwin, 2004a) and that provision of assistance may protect

TABLE 12.3. *The likelihood of engaging in intergenerational exchange (odds ratios): Binary Logistic Regressions of time and money exchange*

	Exchange of money		Exchange of time	
Variables	Receiving ($n = 1,884$)	Giving ($n = 1,874$)	Receiving ($n = 1,966$)	Giving ($n = 1,966$)
Age Group				
50–59	–	–	–	–
60–69	0.81	0.70**	1.60*	1.01
70–79	0.63	0.75*	2.66***	0.52***
80+	1.35	0.74	5.46***	0.28***
Gender				
Men	–	–	–	–
Women	1.02	0.93	1.50**	1.40**
Income				
Bottom 40%	2.35**	0.75*	0.74	1.42*
Mid 20%	–	–	–	–
Top 40%	1.48	2.32***	0.53***	1.77***
IADL disability				
None	–	–	–	–
One	0.92	0.67*	3.16***	0.70*
Two or more	0.92	0.27***	8.30***	0.17***
Nagelkerke R^2	0.03	0.14	0.29	0.15

*$p < .01$. **$p < .01$. ***$p < .001$.

against mortality risk (Brown et al., 2003). If so, from the point of view of social exchange, the oldest old are at the greatest jeopardy insofar as they tend to receive more than they give. To address that point, a mental health outcome measure was regressed on age, disability, and social exchange, controlling for gender and income. Here, too, the figures stem from the SHARE-Israel database. The outcome measure was the number of symptoms on the Euro-D depression scale, which includes such characteristics as sadness, guilt, suicidal feelings, and sleeplessness (Castro-Costa et al., 2007). The scale score ranged from 0 to 12; the higher the score, the greater was the number of depressive symptoms. Social exchange was measured on two dichotomous variables: giving help of any kind and receiving help of any kind (0–1). Disability was measured once again as functional disability (IADL). The results in Table 12.4 show that functional disability was the strongest predictor of depressive symptoms. As for social exchange, receipt of assistance showed a moderate, positive association with the number of depressive symptoms, and provision of assistance showed a somewhat

TABLE 12.4. *Variables associated with the number of depressive symptoms on the Euro-D depression scale: OLS linear regression ($n = 1{,}817$)*

Variables[a]		Beta
Age group		
60–69		.03
70–79		.06**
80+		–.05*
Gender		
Women		.10***
Income		
Bottom 40%		.09**
Top 40%		–.04
IADL disability		.36***
Gave help		–.15***
Received help		.07**
Adjusted R^2	.24	
F	65.04***	

[a] Reference categories: Age: 50–59; gender: men; income: mid-20%; gave help: no; received help: no.

$^{*}p < .01$. $^{**}p < .01$. $^{***}p < .001$.

stronger, negative association. That is, after controlling for other factors, giving help was associated with better mental health, and receiving help correlated with a poorer mental state. The table also shows that after taking disability and social exchange into account, those age 70–79 had somewhat greater depressive symptoms than did those age 50–59, but those 80 years old and older did not. In fact, a modest, negative association suggests that the oldest old actually have better mental health when the effects of all the other variables are taken into account.

The association between social exchange and mortality risk was addressed in a recent study that used the CBS survey data and the death records mentioned earlier (Litwin, 2007b). The analysis found that, even when taking a range of baseline variables into account (e.g., gender, marital status, social network characteristics, physical activity, morbidity), respondents who reported an unbalanced exchange of instrumental support at baseline (i.e., received more than they gave) had a slightly higher risk of mortality 7 years later. However, the exchange variables in the analysis were less robust in their predictions than were social network indicators, principally ties with friends and attendance at a synagogue. It seems, therefore, that both aspects of social relationships addressed in the current inquiry – social network and social exchange – are related to survival in late life.

DISCUSSION

The findings from this analysis suggest that a significant minority of very old Jewish Israelis is embedded in restricted social networks and that a similar minority tends to be net receivers of social exchange. The same trends are evident among those with high degrees of disability. When both age and disability are taken into account, moreover, the trends become even more pronounced. The findings also show that restricted social networks and higher degrees of disability are negatively associated with well-being in very old age.

At first glance, the findings support the phenomenon of network reduction among the oldest old. Such diminution of the social network may occur as a result of residential relocation, the death of peers (particularly friends), and decreased physical mobility. Although new social ties sometimes replace those that were lost, there is some question as to the intensity and efficacy of newly acquired relationships. This empirical observation is supported by socioemotional selectivity theory, which suggests that older people do benefit from meaningful social relationships (most usually those of longer duration) but also tend to disassociate from ties that are less likely to provide optimal return (Carstensen, 1992; Carstensen, Fung, & Charles, 2003). Thus, a relationship selection process is believed to occur in very late life. However, age per se may be less a trigger of socioemotional selectivity than is one's awareness of limitations on future time (Fung, Carstensen, & Lang, 2001; Fung, Carstensen, & Lutz, 1999). This latter clarification may explain why the degree of disability plays an important role in predicting relationship outcomes in older age.

At the same time, it must be pointed out that the current inquiry also demonstrates that a substantial number of Jewish Israelis aged 80 and older were embedded in gregarious network constellations and that almost half of them provided assistance of some kind. The literature suggests that persons in robust networks and those who provide help report better states of well-being (Bisschop et al., 2003; Brown et al., 2003; Fiori et al., 2006; Giles, Glonek, Luszcz, & Andrews, 2005). In fact, the present analysis shows that, after controlling for disability and exchange, respondents aged 80 and older actually reported fewer depressive symptoms than those in the control group, aged 50–59. The findings in the present inquiry thus add empirical support to the great diversity that prevails among the oldest old (Grundy & Bowling, 1999). As shown, a major proportion of this age group experiences decline in its social relationships and, correspondingly, a reduction in its well-being. However, another significant proportion in the same age group continues to maintain diverse social ties and to actively engage in exchange, thus accruing the associated benefits of each.

The results also suggest that the passage from a socially engaged status to a more restricted one may be sparked by a decline in functional status. That is, an increase in disability may put the oldest old at significantly increased risk of relative social isolation and of limited involvement in social exchange. It cannot be ruled out, however, that this association may also work in the opposite direction. That is, a reduction in social ties and social exchange, for a range of reasons, might possibly lead to functional decline. Additional research is warranted to address this phenomenon.

In conclusion, this chapter considered the nature and scope of social relationships among older people and their associations with well-being in late life. It examined the trends that emerged among the variables in the population of older Jewish Israelis, by using contemporary databases. The results of the inquiry indicate that the nature and scope of social relationships among this particular cohort apparently vary to a large degree, indicating, first of all, that the oldest old is a group characterized by great diversity. The inquiry also emphasizes that part of the observed difference seems to be due to differences in disability. That is, age per se does not predict diminishing social networks and lesser well-being; rather, the combination of older age and increased disability does.

The findings from this analysis suggest that it is strongly desirable to delay as long as possible the onset of disability among the oldest old and to reduce the effect of functional decline on the social networks of persons already subject to some degree of incapacitation. The demonstrated positive association between social relationships and well-being in very late life underscores the need to promote and to preserve functional autonomy among the oldest old. Accordingly, social policy and professional practice should both be recruited to address this important aim. The unprecedented aging of the population requires giving increased attention to the eldest segment of society and to the means that can promote its well-being.

REFERENCES

Antonucci, T. C., Fuhrer, R., & Dartigues, J. F. (1997). Social relations and depressive symptomatology in a sample of community-dwelling French older adults. *Psychology and Aging, 12*, 189–195.

Berkman, L. F., & Syme, S. L. (1979). Social networks, host resistance, and mortality: A 9-year follow-up study of Alameda County residents. *American Journal of Epidemiology, 109*, 186–204.

Bisschop, M. I., Kriegsman, D. M. W., van Tilburg, T. G., Penninx, B., van Eijk, J. T. M., & Deeg, D. J. H. (2003). The influence of differing social ties on decline in physical functioning among older people with and without chronic diseases: The Longitudinal Aging Study Amsterdam. *Aging Clinical and Experimental Research, 15*, 164–173.

Boersch-Supan, A., Hank, K., & Juerges, H. (2005). A new comprehensive and international view on ageing: Introducing the Survey of Health, Ageing and Retirement in Europe. *European Journal of Ageing, 2*, 245–253.

Bosworth, H. B., & Schaie, K. W. (1997). The relationship of social environment, social networks, and health outcomes in the Seattle Longitudinal Study: Two analytical approaches. *Journals of Gerontology: Psychological Sciences, 52*, P197–P205.

Bowling, A., & Browne, P. D. (1991). Social networks, health, and emotional well-being among the oldest in London. *Journals of Gerontology, 46*, S20–S32.

Brown, S. L., Nesse, R. M., Vinokur, A. D., & Smith, D. M. (2003). Providing social support may be more beneficial than receiving it: Results from a prospective study of mortality. *Psychological Science, 14*, 320–327.

Carstensen, L. L. (1992). Social and emotional patterns in adulthood: Support for socioemotional selectivity theory. *Psychology and Aging, 7*, 331–338.

Carstensen, L. L., Fung, H. H., & Charles, S. T. (2003). Socioemotional selectivity theory and the regulation of emotion in the second half of life. *Motivation and Emotion, 27*, 103–123.

Castro-Costa, E., Dewey, M., Stewart, M. D., Banerjee, S., Huppert, F., Mendonca-Lima, C., et al. (2007). Prevalence of depressive symptoms and syndromes in later life in ten European countries: The SHARE study. *British Journal of Psychiatry, 191*, 393–401.

Cerhan, J. R., & Wallace, R. B. (1997). Change in social ties and subsequent mortality in rural elders. *Epidemiology, 8*, 475–481.

Cornoni-Huntley, J. C., Roley, D. F., White, L. R., Suzman, R., Berkman, L. F., Evans, D. A., et al. (1985). Epidemiology of disability in the oldest old: Methodological issues and preliminary findings. *Milbank Memorial Fund Quarterly/Health and Society, 63*, 350–376.

Cox, D., & Rank, M. R. (1992). Inter-vivos transfers and intergenerational exchange. *Review of Economics and Statistics, 74*, 305–314.

Fiori, K. L., Antonucci, T. C., & Cortina, K. S. (2006). Social network typologies and mental health among older adults. *Journals of Gerontology: Psychological Sciences, 61*, P25–P32.

Fung, H. H., Carstensen, L. L., & Lang, F. R. (2001). Age-related patterns in social networks among European Americans and African Americans: Implications for socioemotional selectivity across the life span. *International Journal of Aging and Human Development, 52*, 185–206.

Fung, H. H., Carstensen, L. L., & Lutz, A. M. (1999). Influence of time on social preferences: Implications for life-span development. *Psychology and Aging, 14*, 595–604.

Giles, L. C., Glonek, G. F. V., Luszcz, M. A., & Andrews, G. R. (2005). Effect of social networks on 10 year survival in very old Australians: The Australian Longitudinal Study of Aging. *Journal of Epidemiology and Community Health, 59*, 574–579.

Grundy, E., & Bowling, A. (1999). Enhancing the quality of extended life years: Identification of the oldest old with a very good and very poor quality of life. *Aging and Mental Health, 3*, 199–212.

Guilley, E., Pin, S., Spini, D., d'Epinay, C. L., Herrmann, F., & Michel, J. P. (2005). Association between social relationships and survival of Swiss octogenarians: A five-year prospective, population-based study. *Aging Clinical and Experimental Research, 17*, 419–425.

Henretta, J. C., Hill, M. S., Li, W., Soldo, B. J., & Wolf, D. A. (1997). Selection of children to provide care: The effect of earlier parental transfers. *Journals of Gerontology: Social Sciences, 52*, S110–S119.

Iecovich, E., & Lankri, M. (2002). Attitudes of elderly persons towards receiving financial support from adult children. *Journal of Aging Studies, 16*, 121–133.

Kleinspehn-Ammerlahn, A., Kotter-Grühn, D., & Smith, J. (2008). Self-perceptions of aging: Do subjective age and satisfaction with aging change during old age? *Journals of Gerontology: Psychological Sciences, 63B*, P377–P385.

Kohli, M., & Künemund, H. (2003). Intergenerational transfers in the family: What motives for giving? In V. L. Bengtson & A. Lowenstein (Eds.), *Global aging and challenges to families*. Hawthorne, NY: Aldine de Gruyter.

Litwin, H. (2001). Social network type and morale in old age. *Gerontologist, 41*, 516–524.

Litwin, H. (2004a). Intergenerational exchange and mental health in later-life: The case of older Jewish Israelis. *Aging and Mental Health, 8*, 196–200.

Litwin, H. (2004b). Intergenerational exchange patterns and their correlates in an aging Israeli cohort. *Research on Aging, 26*, 202–223.

Litwin, H. (2006a). The path to well-being among elderly Arab-Israelis. *Journal of Cross-Cultural Gerontology, 21*, 25–40.

Litwin, H. (2006b). Social networks and self-rated health: A cross-cultural examination among older Israelis. *Journal of Aging and Health, 18*, 335–358.

Litwin, H. (2007a). The interpersonal milieu of older people. In S. Carmel, C. Morse, & F. Torres Gil (Eds.), *Lessons on aging from three nations* (Vol. 1, pp. 169–184). Amityville, NY: Baywood.

Litwin, H. (2007b). What really matters in the social network-mortality association? A multivariate examination among older Jewish-Israelis. *European Journal of Ageing, 4*, 71–82.

Litwin, H., & Shiovitz-Ezra, S. (2006). Network type and mortality risk in later-life. *Gerontologist, 46*, 735–743.

McGarry, K., & Schoeni, R. F. (1995). Transfer behaviour in the health and retirement study: Measurement and the redistribution of resources within the family. *Journal of Human Resources, 30*, S184–S226.

Mitchell, J. C. (1969). The concept and use of social networks. In J. C. Mitchell (Ed.), *Social networks in urban situations*. London: Manchester University Press.

Rasulo, D., Christensen, K., & Tomassini, C. (2005). The influence of social relations on mortality in later life: A study on elderly Danish twins. *Gerontologist, 45*, 601–608.

Silverstein, M., Conroy, S. J., Wang, H. T., Giarrusso, R., & Bengtson, V. L. (2002). Reciprocity in parent-child relations over the adult life course. *Journals of Gerontology: Social Sciences, 57*, S3–S13.

Silverstein, M., Parrott, T. M., & Bengtson, V. L. (1995). Factors that predispose middle-aged sons and daughters to provide social support to older parents. *Journal of Marriage and the Family*, *57*, 465–475.

Tesch-Romer, C., Motel-Klingebiel, A., & von Kondratowitz, H. J. (2002). The relevance of the family network for the quality of life of elderly people: Comparing societies and cultures. *Zeitschrift für Gerontologie und Geriatrie*, *35*, 335–342.

Wenger, G. C. (1991). A network typology: From theory to practice. *Journal of Aging Studies*, *5*, 147–162.

13

Spirituality and Religiosity Connections to Mental and Physical Health among the Oldest Old

ALEX J. BISHOP

ABSTRACT

Gerontological examination of spiritual and religious connections in extreme old age has been limited. The purpose of this paper was to expose the connection between religious coping and mental and physical health among centenarians at time 1 and time 2. This involved an examination and identification of longitudinal predictors of religious coping among persons living extremely long lives. It appears that gender, health impairment, and negative affect may represent key predictors of religious coping in extreme old age. Furthermore, religious coping seems to diminish negative affect but increases feelings of stress. This has implications relative to improving theoretical conceptualization and cross-cultural insight into how religious coping contributes to adaptation in very old age. Suggestions for future spirituality and religiosity research with very old populations are highlighted.

INTRODUCTION

Many older adults seek the sacred. Investigators have acknowledged that religious and spiritual behaviors serve as personal resources that improve adaptation and protection against poor physical and mental functioning (Krause, 2006; Pargament, 1997). Although robust physical and mental health status are desirable characteristics in very old age (Quinn, Johnson, Poon, & Martin, 1999; Samuelsson et al., 1997), most exceptionally old persons experience multiple health ailments that threaten individual well-being (Jang, Poon, & Martin, 2004). Physical and mental health challenges in very late life have a reported association with greater religious or spiritual coping practices (e.g., church or synagogue attendance, prayer, beliefs; Krause, 2006; Walter-Ginzburg, Shmotkin, Blumstein, & Shorek, 2005).

Furthermore, religious and spiritual behaviors have been reported to influence longitudinal improvements in physical (e.g., physical impairment and disability) and mental health (e.g., negative mood states) among old-old populations (Benjamins, 2004; Braam, Deeg, Poppelaars, Beekman, & van Tilburg, 2007; Wink, Dillion, & Larsen, 2005). However, knowledge of religious coping behaviors among centenarians has been relatively absent from the gerontological literature. Empirical consideration of religiosity and spirituality among old-old adults representing Jewish, Islamic, Buddhist, and other world-faith orientations has remained limited. Many investigators have continued to rely on oldest-old samples originating from Western religious traditions (Braam, Bramsen, van Tilburg, Van der Ploeg, & Deeg, 2006; Fischer, Nygren, Lundman, & Norberg, 2007; Spini, Pin, & d'Epinay, 2001). This has implications for the improvement of cross-cultural theoretical insights into religious coping and adaptation among persons living extremely long lives.

CONCEPTUALIZING RELIGION AND SPIRITUALITY

Spirituality and religiosity tend to be complex and overlapping constructs (Moberg, 2008). Investigators must often confront the dilemma of how to best conceptualize and measure spiritual and religious phenomena (Moberg, 2002). As discussed in Chapter 17, there are several religious and spiritual measurement scales with potential use in aging research. Historically, religion has been conceptualized as an individual and institutional construct (Hill & Pargament, 2008). In particular, William James (1902) characterized religion as a psychological experience guided by the inherited rituals and traditions of institutional religion. According to Hill and Pargament (2008), the meaning of religion and spirituality has taken on newer and more distinct conceptualizations in research. For instance, religion has come to be defined as a system of ideas or ideological beliefs and commitments, whereas spirituality has been commonly used in reference to the experiential and subjective identification of religious experience (Hill & Pargament, 2008). However, investigators studying physical and mental health must consider several threats that may be introduced by the conceptual division of religion and spirituality (Hill et al., 2000; Hill & Pargament, 2008).

First, the conceptual division of religion and spirituality into individual and institutional domains creates polarization (Hill et al., 2000; Hill & Pargament, 2008). Most organized religions in the world are oriented toward guiding and ordering individual behavior (Hill et al., 2000). Thus, spiritual experiences evolve from a social or institutional context. Second, the evolving duality of religious and spiritual definitions can be easily mistranslated into a simplistic definition in which religion is conceptualized as bad and spirituality is defined as good (Pargament, 2002). In effect, this perspective fails to consider the costs and benefits of engaging in religious or spiritual behaviors. Third, it is important to note that most persons representing diverse religious traditions experience spirituality in an organized religious framework or context (Hill & Pargament, 2008). In effect, religion and spirituality are related rather than independent constructs (Hill et al., 2000). Thus, it may be difficult for persons to distinguish between the two phenomena in the event of coping with physical and mental health problems.

RELIGION, COPING, AND ADAPTATION

Martin et al. (Chapter 7) acknowledged that events in very late life represent some of the "most stressful challenges any individual could experience." Some of those experiences may be traumatic and elicit long-term anxiety. As noted by Hyer and Yeager (Chapter 8), trauma exposure produces an "immediate biological reaction" resulting in psychophysiological responses that continue across time on all exposed individuals. Lazarus and Folkman (1984) theorized that personal stressors (e.g., personal loss, health impairments, emotional trauma) incite primary appraisal, or a cognitive judgment of anticipated threat or loss that may exhaust individual resources. This contributes to increased engagement in coping behaviors. Lazarus and Folkman (1984) referred to this process as secondary appraisal. In secondary appraisal, individuals make an assessment of personal resources for dealing with difficult situations or experiences. Tornstam (2005) hypothesized that old-old adults typically maintain a propensity toward the transcendent. Evidence suggests that those who turn to religious or spiritual behaviors in difficult times also engage in problem-focused behaviors directed at changing a stressful or negative situation (Spilka, Hood, Hunsberger, & Gorsuch, 2003). Furthermore, religious coping behaviors (e.g., prayer, church attendance, seeking religious-based support) may reduce undesirable problems or emotions to the point of enhancing well-being (Folkman & Lazarus, 1988). In devising a theory of religious coping, Pargament (1997) acknowledged that religious coping ultimately results in a "sense of significance" (p. 92) in which persons come to terms with the difficulties of life. Martin et al. (Chapter 7) discussed the finding that cumulative negative life events promote negative affect, whereas positive experiences reduce negative feelings in very late life. Religious experiences are believed to have a restorative influence on diminished physical and mental health abilities (Krause, 2005,

2006, 2008; Pargament, 1997). Thus, religiosity may be a source of positive change despite the trials and tribulations of old-old age.

RELIGIOUS COPING AND THE OLDEST OLD

The Georgia Centenarian Study (Poon et al., 1992) has been one of the only studies in the United States that has provided evidence of a religious and spiritual connection to physical and mental health in extreme old age (Martin, Bishop, Poon, & Johnson, 2006; Martin, Rott, Poon, Courtenay, & Lehr, 2001). Two primary findings have been reported: (a) religiosity is associated with physical health among old-old adults, and (b) religiosity has been acknowledged as a longitudinal predictor of fatigue in late and very late life. Investigators from the Georgia Centenarian Study (Martin et al., 2001) acknowledged that religious coping might yield useful information regarding adaptation among the oldest old.

Older adults appraise stressors (e.g., health problems, feelings of anxiety) as threatening whenever psychosocial resources are scarce (Hobfoll, 1989; Lazarus & Folkman, 1984). When old and very old adults fail to derive basic (e.g., food, shelter), conditional (e.g., education), or personal (e.g., happiness) resources to respond to adversity, they tend to shift their priorities to energies, or spiritually meaningful resources and activities (Hobfoll, 1989; Krause, 2008: Tornstam, 2005). Tornstam (2005) theorized that such behavior reflects developmental movement away from personal desires and toward identification with gerotranscendent concerns in exceptional old age. In advanced old age, persons demonstrate a greater preference for deriving meaning from the complexities and problems of everyday life (Krause, 2008). Religious and spiritual behaviors are acknowledged to enhance the derivation of meaning, which in turn contributes to improvements in physical and mental well-being (Krause, 2008). We propose that religiosity and spirituality represent energy resources that aid adaptation and allow persons in advanced old age to confront stressors (e.g., physical and functional limitations, anxiety) in everyday life.

Although religious and spiritual resources have been documented as beneficial coping resources, it should be noted that most studies on religious coping tend to focus on religious and spiritual predictors of physical and mental health (Hill & Pargament, 2008). Instead, Hill and Pargament (2008) challenged investigators to identify predictors of religion and spirituality. It is feasible to argue that certain life experiences, stressors, or negative situations influence engagement in religious coping more than other variables. Therefore, we attempted to assess how physical and mental health predict religious coping over time, as well as how religious coping influences change relative to physical and mental health outcomes.

METHOD

Sample participants for the study originated from the Georgia Centenarian Study (Poon et al., 1992). Participants included 137 centenarians and 68 longitudinal survivors from a 20-month follow-up. Only community-dwelling and cognitively intact participants were used during initial test, but every participant was contacted again for the follow-up measure. Cognitively intact participants included those with a score of 21 or higher on the Mini-Mental State Examination (Folstein, Folstein, & McHugh, 1975) or a score of 1 or 2 on the Global Deterioration Scale (Reisberg, Ferris, de Leon, & Crook, 1982). Our objective was to explore longitudinal predictors of change in religious coping. Hierarchical multiple regression analyses were used to evaluate health and mental health as predictors of fatigue after controlling for demographic covariates of religious coping at Time 1.

MEASURES

Religious Coping

Religious coping was measured using the Coping Responses Inventory (Moos, Cronkite, Billings, & Finney, 1985). Items reflecting use of prayer, religious beliefs, and church attendance were selected. Participants were asked to indicate whether they used each behavior in response to health problems. Responses were coded as 1 = no; 2 = yes, once or twice; 3 = yes, sometimes; and 4 = yes, fairly often. Scores were summarized for the three items to represent low and high religious coping behavior.

Health

Health was assessed using measures from Older Americans Resources and Services instrument (OARS; Fillenbaum, 1988). Participants were asked to indicate how much current health impairments and illnesses (e.g., arthritis, heart trouble, diabetes) interfered with activities. Participants were asked to respond 1 = not at all, 2 = a little, and 3 = a great deal. Scores were summarized to reflect low and high physical impairment. In addition, instrumental activities of daily living (IADLs) and physical activities of daily living (PADLs) were assessed with the self-care capacity scale of the OARS

(Fillenbaum, 1988). The IADLs were evaluated using seven items (e.g., "Can you prepare your own meals?"), and PADLs were evaluated using six items (e.g., "Can you walk?"). Participants were asked to indicate whether they were 0 = completely unable to perform the activity, 1 = performed that activity with some help, or 2 = performed the activity without help. Summary scores were calculated and used to reflect low and high IADL and PADL performance.

Mental Health

Several measures were used to assess mental health. Fatigue and stress were assessed using items from the Eight State Questionnaire (Institute for Personality and Ability Testing, 1975). Scores were calculated into a summary score to represent high and low feelings of fatigue and stress. Anxiety was assessed by using the second-order factor of the 16PF Personality Factor Inventory (Cattell, Eber, & Tatsuka, 1957). Negative affect was assessed using the Bradburn Affect Scale (see Chapter 17; Bradburn, 1969). This is a scale that measures positive and negative affect. For purposes of this study, only negative subscale items were used. Participants were asked to think how they felt in the last month (e.g., bored, depressed, unhappy) and to respond 1 = not at all, 2 = once, 3 = sometimes, or 4 = often. A summary score of negative affect was used to reflect high and low negative emotion.

Covariates

Age, gender, ethnicity, and education were used as demographic covariates. In addition, participants were asked to report the following: (a) current age; (b) whether they were male of female; (c) whether they were Caucasian, African American, Asian, Hispanic, American Indian, or other; and (d) whether they completed 0–4 years of school, 5–8 years of school, attended some high school, finished high school, attended business or trade school, completed 1–3 years of college, finished college, or attended graduated school.

RESULTS

We assessed health and mental health variables as longitudinal predictors of religious coping. Health impairment ($\beta = .28$, $p < .05$) and negative affect ($\beta = .29$, $p < .05$) emerged as key longitudinal predictors of religious coping (Table 13.1). This suggests that greater health impairment and poor

TABLE 13.1. *Summary of hierarchical regression analyses for longitudinal predictor variables of religious coping at Time 2*

	Model 1			Model 2			Model 3		
Variable	*B*	*SE*	β	*B*	*SE*	β	*B*	*SE*	β
Coping at Time 1	.67	.12	.58**	.57	.13	.51**	.59	.12	.53**
Gender				1.16	.60	.22	1.13	.54	.21*
Ethnicity				−1.15	.63	.22	−1.08	.57	−.21
Education				.04	.13	.04	.04	.11	.04
Age				.18	.17	.12	.16	.15	.11
Physical impairment							.15	.06	.28*
IADLs							.14	.10	.19
PADLs							−.22	.15	−.21
Fatigue							.22	.17	.13
Stress							.01	.13	.01
Anxiety							.06	.17	.04
Negative affect							.20	.07	.29*
$F\Delta$						1.90	3.06		
R^2	.34	.43	.63						
Adjusted R^2	.32	.37	.52						

$^{*}p < .05$. $^{**}p < .01$.

mood influence greater religious coping behaviors. Gender also had a significant association with religious coping at Time 2 ($\beta = .21$, $p < .05$). Thus, women engaged in greater religious coping behaviors than men. To assess the direction of effect for religious coping and health and mental health characteristics, we used religious coping at Time 1 as a predictor of health and mental health characteristics at Time 2 after controlling for stabilities of individual characteristics and demographic confounders (Table 13.2). Religious coping at Time 1 had a significant association with stress at Time 2 ($\beta = .32$, $p < .05$) and with negative affect ($\beta = -.46$, $p < .01$). In effect, greater religious coping appears to increase feelings of stress but enhance emotional feelings across time.

SUMMARY

The primary goal of this investigation was to explore longitudinal predictors of religious coping among centenarians. It appears that gender, greater health impairment, and negative affect are key longitudinal predictors of religious coping behaviors among persons living extremely long lives. Martin et al. (Chapter 7) proposed that survivorship in exceptional old age

TABLE 13.2. *Religious coping at Time 1 predicting change in health and mental health at Time 2*

Criterion	*B*	*SE*	*β*	*t*
Physical impairment	.21	.24	.12	.90
IADLs	.34	.19	.19	1.81
PADLs	.31	.21	.18	1.42
Fatigue	−.15	.09	−.24	−1.64
Stress	.29	.13	.32	2.20*
Anxiety	.05	.10	.07	.46
Negative affect	−.74	.20	−.46	−3.69**

Note: Table data presented are regression coefficients after controlling for stabilities, gender, ethnicity, education, and age.
$^{*}p < .01$. $^{**}p < .05$.

increases the likelihood of stressful events and emotional encounters, which in turn negatively affects physical and mental well-being. We also considered how religious coping might reflect changes in health and mental health characteristics. It appears that religious coping offers a positive benefit of enhanced mood state, but religious coping also increases feelings of stress among centenarians. Based on the results, three key conclusions can be made regarding future directions for cross-cultural research involving religiosity and spirituality behaviors centenarians.

First, an effort should be made to increase understanding of the salience of gender in religious coping. Walter-Ginzburg et al. (2005) indicated that old-old Israeli women have greater physical and functional health problems, yet greater synagogue attendance appears to be one of several key variables that reduce mortality risk for both men and women. However, evidence has been reported that old-old Israeli men express greater transcendent qualities than their younger counterparts. Moen (2001) has advocated for an understanding of a gendered life course. This proposition stems from past research indicating that women in the United States often face multiple jeopardies (e.g., limited work roles, economic strain, poor health) that place them at cumulative disadvantage relative to health and mental health outcomes (Moen, 2001). Future research should determine whether religious and spiritual behaviors across different cultures protect against gender-associated disadvantages in health and mental health in extreme old age.

Second, high levels of coping might have been associated with adverse experiences or problems not covered by the covariates used in the present study. Martin et al. (Chapter 7) provided evidence that many centenarians have endured a lifetime of unique (e.g., automobile accident, water accident, shooting, natural disaster) and historical (e.g., Great Depression) events. According to Hyer and Yeager (Chapter 8), survival of traumatic experiences alters how older adults perceive threatening situations, which in turn influences the adoption of avoidant coping strategies to sustain mental well-being. Investigators should be attentive to understanding how distal and proximal physical and mental health experiences shape resiliency through the use of religious coping behaviors among the oldest old. There is growing evidence that salient experiences earlier in life (e.g., poor health, war, family violence) influence physical and mental health outcomes in late adulthood (Krause, Shaw, & Cairney, 2004; Solomon & Ginzberg, 1998). However, little is known about how these distal and proximal events shape engagement in religious or spiritual coping behaviors among extremely old persons living in different cultural contexts. There is a need for greater cross-cultural research aimed to derive theoretical and developmental models of health and mental health that account for religious coping (see Chapter 15).

Third, it appears that greater use of religious coping behaviors in extreme old age increases feelings of stress over time. This finding warrants further investigation relative to the existence of positive and negative religious coping on mental health outcomes in extreme old age. Perhaps a need to do well in the eyes of a higher being incites religious coping behaviors, which influence feelings of stress. Krause (2005, 2007) has advocated for improved understanding of God-mediated control. According to this perspective, older adults work collaboratively with God to control current experiences in their lives. Krause (2008) theorized that older persons who develop a sense that God is helping solve their everyday problems also adopt a new sense of meaning and appreciation in life. Although a stronger sense of God-mediated control is associated with positive mental health outcomes (Krause, 2005), declining levels of health in advanced old age may initiate the expression of religious and spiritual doubt, which in turn increases age-associated feelings of distress (Schieman, Van Gundy, & Taylor, 2001). Therefore, two central questions must be answered: (a) In what manner do religious coping behaviors increase feelings of stress, enhance positive emotions, or create feelings of doubt among centenarians? (b) Do increases or decreases in stress and negative emotions associated with religious coping hinder or promote adaptation to health problems in extreme later life? These questions have implications relative to clarifying mechanisms by which religious coping increases or decreases stressors and negative emotional feelings among individuals who have lived extremely long lives.

It is important to note that data presented in this chapter were based on a relatively homogenous sample of exceptionally old adults who primarily represented a Baptist religious orientation common to the Southern United States. Relative to the sample in this study, we know now that gender, physical impairment, stress, and emotionality are key influences of religious coping. Therefore, caution is advised in generalizing results across old-old populations representing other world religious traditions or different types of spiritual orientations. However, gerontological literature detailing religiosity and spirituality differences and comparisons among the oldest old in non-Western religious traditions (e.g., Judaism, Buddhism, Hinduism) has also been deficient. Investigators studying old-old adults representing Jewish and Muslim faiths have primarily focused on self-rated associations among religiousness (e.g., synagogue attendance), meaning (e.g., transcendence), mortality, and life satisfaction (Iecovich, 2001; Litwin, 2007; Thomas, 2001), whereas researchers considering old-old members of Far Eastern religious traditions have concentrated more on the associations among religious participation, mortality risk, and perceived well-being (Brown & Tierney, 2009; Zhang, 2008). Although the foci of such studies share similarities, use of independent and homogenous samples has presented limitations relative to cross-cultural comparison. As a result, generalization across multiple and divergent non-Western and Western religious traditions and spiritual perspectives in old-old age remains elusive.

Although data reduction is essential for statistical analyses and hypothesis testing, cultural equivalency is difficult to achieve when only one measurement standard or coding scheme is used (see Chapter 15). Moberg (2002) commented that more inclusive measures of religious and spiritual constructs have the potential to enhance sample diversity and to expand current knowledge on religious or spiritual behaviors. Furthermore, there is an evident need for greater interconnection between gerontological theory and theological perspectives in the assessment and interpretation of religious and spiritual connections (Moberg, 2002). It can be argued that such integration may serve to improve how findings on religious and spiritual connections in very late life may be interpreted and extended across divergent cultures.

Preliminary results and suggestions for future directions stemming from the aforementioned data analysis are intended to encourage other investigators to expanded cross-cultural research efforts in aging. In particular, special emphasis should be placed on the links among religion, spirituality, and well-being of the oldest old. Such research efforts promise to provide a more diverse and comprehensive framework for identifying universal markers of religious and spiritual behaviors that contribute to optimal physical health and positive mental health status.

ACKNOWLEDGMENT

This research was supported by National Institutes of Health Grant No. RO1–43435-10 and 1 PO1 AG17553–01A1.

REFERENCES

Benjamins, M. R. (2004). Religion and functional health among the elderly: Is there a relationship and is it constant? *Journal of Aging and Health, 16*, 355–374.

Braam, A. W., Bramsen, I., van Tilburg, T. G., Van der Ploeg, H. M., & Deeg, D. J. H. (2006). Cosmic transcendence and framework of meaning in life: Patterns among older adults in the Netherlands. *Journals of Gerontology: Psychological Sciences and Social Sciences, 61B*, S121–S128.

Braam, A. W., Deeg, D. J. H., Poppelaars, J. L., Beekman, A. T. F., & van Tilburg, W. (2007). Prayer and depressive symptoms in a period of secularization: Patterns among older adults in the Netherlands. *American Journal of Geriatric Psychiatry, 15*, 273–281.

Bradburn, N. M. (1969). *The structure of psychological well-being.* Oxford, UK: Aldine.

Brown, P. H., & Tierney, B. (2009). Religion and subjective well-being among the elderly in China. *Journal of Socio-Economics, 38*, 310–319.

Cattell, R. B., Eber, H. W., & Tatsuka, M. M. (1957). *The handbook for the 16 Personality Factors Questionnaire.* Champaign, IL: Institute for Personality and Ability Testing.

Fillenbaum, G. G. (1988). *Multidimensional functional assessment of older adults: The Duke Older Americans Resources and Services Procedures.* Hillsdale, NJ: Erlbaum.

Fischer, R. S., Nygren, B., Lundman, B., & Norberg, A. (2007). Living amidst consolation in the presence of God perceptions of consolation among the oldest old: The Umea 85+ study. *Journal of Religion, Spirituality, and Aging, 19*, 3–20.

Folkman, S., & Lazarus, R. S. (1988). Coping as a mediator of emotion. *Journal of Personality and Social Psychology, 54*, 466–475.

Folstein, M. F., Folstein, S. E., & McHugh, R. R. (1975). Mini-Mental State: A practical method for grading the cognitive state of patients for the clinician. *Journal of Psychiatric Research, 12*, 189–198.

Hill, P. C., & Pargament, K. I. (2003). Advances in the conceptualization and measurement of religion and spirituality: Implications for physical and mental health research. *American Psychologist, 58*, 64–74.

Hill, P. C., & Pargament, K. I. (2008). Advances in the conceptualization and measurement of religion and spirituality: Implications of physical and mental health research. *Psychology of Religion and Spirituality, 8*, 3–17.

Hill, P. C., Pargament, K. I., Hood, R. W., Jr., McCullough, M. E., Swyers, J. P., Larson, D. B., et al. (2000). Conceptualizing religion and spirituality: Points of commonality, points of departure. *Journal for the Theory of Social Behaviour, 30*, 51–57.

Hobfoll, S. E. (1989). Conservation of resources: A new attempt at conceptualizing stress. *American Psychologist, 44*, 513–524.

Iecovich, E. (2001). Religiousness and subjective well-being among Jewish female residents of old age homes in Israel. *Journal of Religious Gerontology, 13*, 31–46.

Institute for Personality and Ability Testing. (1975). *Manual for the Eight State Questionnaire (8SQ)*. Champaign, IL: Author.

James, W. (1902). *The varieties of religious experience.* New York: Random House.

Jang, Y., Poon, L. W., & Martin, P. (2004). Individual differences in the effect of disease and disability on depressive symptoms: The role of age and subjective health. *International Journal of Aging and Human Development, 59*, 125–137.

Krause, N. (2005). God-mediated control and psychological well-being in late life. *Research on Aging, 27*, 136–164.

Krause, N. (2006). Religion and health in late life. In J. E. Birren & K. W. Schaie (Eds.), *Handbook of the psychology of aging* (6th ed., pp. 499–518). Amsterdam: Academic Press.

Krause, N. (2007). Social involvement in religious institutions and God-mediated control beliefs: A longitudinal investigation. *Journal for the Scientific Study of Religion, 46*, 519–537.

Krause, N. (2008). Deriving a sense of meaning in late life: An overlooked forum for the development of interdisciplinary theory. In V. L. Bengston, D. Gans, N. M. Putney, & M. Silverstein (Eds.), *Handbook of theories of aging* (2nd ed., pp. 101–116). New York: Springer.

Krause, N., Shaw, B. A., & Cairney, J. (2004). A descriptive epidemiology of lifetime trauma and the physical health status of older adults, *Psychology and Aging, 19*, 637–648.

Lazarus, R. S., & Folkman, S. (1984). *Stress, appraisal, and coping.* New York: Springer.

Litwin, H. (2007). What really matters in the social network-mortality association? A multivariate examination among older Jewish-Israelis. *European Journal of Ageing, 4*, 71–82.

Martin, P., Bishop, A., Poon, L., & Johnson, M. A. (2006). Influence of personality and health behaviors on fatigue in late and very late life. *Journals of Gerontology: Psychological Sciences and Social Sciences, 61B*, P161–P166.

Martin, P., Rott, C., Poon, L. W., Courtenay, B., & Lehr, U. (2001). A molecular view of coping behavior in older adults. *Journal of Aging and Health, 13*, 72–91.

Moberg, D. O. (2002). Assessing and measuring spirituality: Confronting dilemmas of universal and particular evaluative criteria. *Journal of Adult Development, 9*, 47–60.

Moberg, D. O. (2008). Spirituality and aging: Research implications. *Journal of Religion, Spirituality, and Aging, 20*, 95–134.

Moen, P. (2001). The gendered life course. In R. H. Binstock & L. K. George (Eds.), *Handbook of aging and the social sciences* (5th ed., pp. 179–196). Boston: Academic Press.

Moos, R. H., Cronkite, R. C., Billings, A. G., & Finney, J. W. (1985). *Health and daily living manual.* San Francisco: Stanford University Medical Centers.

Pargament, K. I. (1997). *The psychology of religion and coping: Theory, research, practice.* New York: Guilford Press.

Pargament, K. I. (2002). The bitter and the sweet: An evaluation of the costs and benefits of religiousness. *Psychological Inquiry, 13*, 168–181.

Poon, L. W., Clayton, G. M., Martin, P., Johnson, M. A., Courtenay, B. C., Sweaney, A. L., et al. (1992). The Georgia Centenarian Study. *International Journal of Aging and Human Development, 34*, 1–17.

Quinn, M. E., Johnson, M. A., Poon, L. W., & Martin, P. (1999). Psychosocial correlates of subjective health in sexagenarians, octogenarians, and centenarians. *Issues in Mental Health Nursing, 20*, 1151–1171.

Reisberg, B., Ferris, S. H., de Leon, M. J., & Crook, T. (1982). The Global Deterioration Scale for assessment of primary degenerative dementia. *American Journal of Psychiatry, 139*, 1136–1139.

Samuelsson, S. M., Alfredson, B. B., Hagberg, B., Samuelsson, G., Nordbeck, B., Brun, A., et al. (1997). The Swedish Centenarian Study: A multidisciplinary study of five consecutive cohorts at the age of 100. *International Journal of Aging and Human Development, 45*, 223–253.

Schieman, S., Van Gundy, K., & Taylor, J. (2001). Status, role, and resource explanations for age patterns in psychological distress. *Journal of Health and Social Behavior, 42*, 80–96.

Solomon, Z., & Ginzburg, K. (1998). War trauma and the aged: An Israeli perspective. In J. Lomranz (Ed.), *Handbook of aging and mental health: An integrative approach* (pp. 135–152). New York: Plenum Press.

Spilka, B., Hood, R. W., Jr., Hunsberger, B., & Gorsuch, R. (2003). *The psychology of religion* (3rd ed.). New York: Guilford Press.

Spini, D., Pin, S., & d'Epinay, C. J. L. (2001). Religiousness and survival in the Swiss Interdisciplinary Longitudinal Study on the oldest old. *Zeitschrift für Gerontopsychologie und-psychiatrie, 14*, 181–186.

Thomas, L. E. (2001). The job hypothesis: Gerotranscendence and life satisfaction among elderly Turkish Muslims. In S. H. McFadden & R. C. Atchley (Eds.), *Aging and the meaning of time: A multidisciplinary exploration* (pp. 207–227). New York: Springer.

Tornstam, L. (2005): *Gerotranscendence: A developmental theory of positive aging.* New York: Springer.

Walter-Ginzburg, A., Shmotkin, D., Blumstein, T., & Shorek, A. (2005). A gender-based dynamic multidimensional longitudinal analysis of resilience and mortality in the old-old in Israel: The Cross-Sectional and Longitudinal Study. *Social Science and Medicine, 60*, 1705–1715.

Wink, P., Dillion, M., & Larsen, B. (2005). Religion as moderator of the depression-health connection: Findings from a longitudinal study. *Research on Aging, 27*, 197–220.

Zhang, W. (2008). Religious participation and mortality risk among oldest old in China. *Journals of Gerontology: Psychological and Social Sciences, 63B*, S293–S297.

14

The Impact of Leisure Activity and Innovation on the Well-Being of the Very Old

GALIT NIMROD

ABSTRACT

This chapter discusses the role of leisure in the well-being in the old and the oldest old and, in particular, the potential benefit of innovative activity. Using a case study approach, this chapter demonstrates that innovation (i.e., adding a brand new activity into one's life) is possible even under extreme health constraints, and that its benefits may be quite diverse. Innovation seems to offer relief and distraction from physical and emotional losses, and creates an opportunity for a more meaningful daily life. It is consequently suggested that innovation at a very old age may contribute to an enhanced sense of well-being.

WHAT IS LEISURE?

Defining leisure may seem an easy task, but scholars often refer to different phenomena while using the same terminology. The most common concepts associated with leisure are: time, activity, and experience (Katz et al., 2000; Kelly, 1996). When defining leisure as time, writers refer to it as residual, or leftover, time. This time is what is left after completing all duties (e.g., work and home chores) and necessary activities (e.g., eating and sleeping). This time is distinctive by being relatively free from obligations and by a high level of choice.

Defining leisure as an activity, however, refers to what people do in their free time. Most leisure studies examine participation in leisure activities, the frequency and duration of participation, and activity companions. Such investigations provide descriptive pictures of forms and content of leisure (e.g., physical, social, creative), and enable trend analysis over time, as well as cultural and subgroup comparison. The departure point of this approach is that leisure, to some extent, is active and purposive. Such a definition may overlook activities that appear to be passive or useless (e.g., daydreaming).

Defining leisure as an experience is an attempt to capture the subjective and deeper meanings of leisure. This approach defines leisure as a state of mind or mental condition, usually associated with pleasure. The focus is not the time or the activity but the participant's experience, yet it is often difficult to separate the experience from its form (i.e., the activity) or from other mental states not attributable to the activity.

In an attempt to combine these different concepts, Kelly (1996) defined leisure as the "quality of activity defined by relative freedom and intrinsic satisfaction" (p. 22). This definition concentrates on the experience but in the context of an activity that occurs in time and place. Similarly, Kleiber (1999) defined leisure as a "combination of free time and the expectation of preferred experience" (p. 3). He recognized the context of leisure as time that is perceived as free and suggested that leisure experiences occur in intrinsically rather than extrinsically motivated activities.

LEISURE IN LATER LIFE

Leisure in later life has three unique characteristics, the first of which is being a challenge. The challenge starts with retirement. Although some retirees seek part-time or even full-time jobs, most devote their additional free time to leisure interests (Harvard Center for Health Communication, 2004; Robinson and Godbey, 1997). This transition may require some level of adjustment. After lifelong involvement in work, newly retired persons need to create a lifestyle that will be at least as satisfying as their prior lifestyle. Some welcome the opportunity to explore a wide range of activities and to do things they have wanted to do for years, but others are troubled by the emptiness created when work ceases. Successful adaptation to the substantial extra free time is a major challenge of retirement, and many do not face it well. According to an Israeli study (Nimrod & Adoni, 2006), for more than half of the recent retirees surveyed, leisure is a challenge for which they are inadequately prepared. As a result, they gravitate toward familiar and simple activities like watching television or visiting shopping malls, and they report significantly lower life satisfaction than retirees who have broader and more diverse leisure repertoire.

Even when people adapt well to retirement, the challenge continues, as there is a continuous increase in the number and level of constraints to leisure. Four types of constraints influence older adults' leisure (Nimrod, 2003): (a) cultural-environmental constraints, such as the need to behave according to certain age-related norms, social isolation, and lack of companions as a result of friends and relatives' increasing limitations and mortality; (b) health-related constraints, including physiological (e.g., disabilities, chronic illness, less energy) and psychophysiological (e.g., concentration or memory problems); (c) psychological constraints, such as lower motivation, low self-esteem, and fears; and (d) technical constraints, such as lower income, availability of activities, mobility, and lack of time. Research on constraints has provided contradictory findings regarding the strength and dominance of different constraints. Yet it has been consistently demonstrated that the number and impact of leisure constraints increase as people age (McGuire, 1985; McGuire & Norman, 2005).

The second characteristic of older adults' leisure is that it becomes a main source of meaning in life. During adulthood, people have three main sources for meaning in life: their careers, their families, and their leisure activities. When people retire from work and their children leave home and start their own families, the first two sources lose some of their significance; thus, the significance of leisure increases. It can become the major domain in which people find meaning. This does not mean that individuals cease finding meaning in their family relationships. As described in Chapter 12, contact with family members is central in older adults' lives, but its nature usually changes from responsibility to mutual and freely chosen activity; leisure thus becomes the main framework for maintaining family relations as well. In addition, leisure can become a work replacement, especially when a person is involved in hobbies or amateur and volunteer activities that can be described as "serious" leisure. This category of leisure activities (suggested by Stebbins, 2006) is characterized by considerable commitment and perseverance, and usually involves belonging to a group of associates and identifying with it. Serious leisure may involve some inconveniences (e.g., long and exhausting rehearsals when belonging to a theater group), yet it may also lead to many durable psychological benefits such as self-esteem and sense of belonging.

The last characteristic of leisure in later life is that it plays a key role in older adults' well-being. The role of leisure activity in later life has been examined in numerous studies. Although its effect on older adults' well-being appears to vary somewhat in different contexts and among different subgroups, most evidence shows a strong positive association between activity involvement and subjective well-being in old age (e.g., Fernandez-Ballesteros, Zamarron, & Ruiz, 2001; Hall & Havens, 2002; Kelly, 1987; McKenna, Broome, & Liddle, 2007; Nimrod, 2007a, 2007b; Riddick & Stewart, 1994; Searle, Mahon, Iso-Ahola, Sadrolias, & Van Dyck, 1995, 1998;

Shmanske, 1997). In addition, leisure seems to be a central factor explaining successful coping with later-life transitions and negative life events (Duggleby, Bateman, & Singer, 2002). Maintaining relationships with family and friends, spirituality, and staying physically and mentally active and involved were found to be effective mechanisms for coping with retirement (Nimrod, 2007a, 2007b; Nimrod, Janke, & Kleiber, 2008), spousal loss (e.g., Janke, Nimrod, & Kleiber, 2008a, 2008b, 2008c; Utz, Carr, Nesse, & Wortman, 2002), and adapting to a major health decline (e.g., Duke, Leventhal, Brownlee, & Leventhal, 2002; Silverstein & Parker, 2002).

LEISURE IN THE LIFE OF THE OLDEST OLD

The described unique characteristics of leisure in later life are valid for all older adults, including the oldest old. In fact, research on older adults' leisure usually focuses on populations that have passed a certain age without limiting the upper end. Therefore, most existing knowledge about the leisure of the oldest old comes from inclusive research. But exclusive studies focusing on the oldest old also exist.

When comparing the oldest old with younger elders, leisure seems to pose an even greater challenge. Having more physiological, cognitive, and psychological limitations; reduced social networks; and other technical constraints (e.g., losing one's driver's license as a result of low vision, thus constraining mobility), the oldest old need greater persistence to stay involved with favored activities. Similar to the younger old, this involvement is a main source of meaning and plays a key role in their well-being (Keith, 1980; Kochniuk, 2004; McKee, 2002; Nilsson, Bernspång, Fisher, Gustafson, & Löfgren, 2007; Silverstein & Parker, 2002), but this does not always apply to all activities and subgroups. For example, in a study of Swedish adults aged 85 and older, Nilsson (2006) found that participants were most likely to be interested in, motivated by, take part in, and perceive well-being from social activities, cultural activities, and media. Participants were least likely to be interested in, motivated by, take part in, and perceive well-being from equipment sports and ball games. Studies in the United States (Barer, 1994; Keith, 1980) have found significant gender differences. Men seemed to benefit most from active, instrumental, and solitary leisure pursuits (e.g., hobbies, household maintenance, outdoor activities). Women showed more life satisfaction when involved in social activities and informal interactions.

Facing more constraints to leisure, the oldest old are commonly forced to quit activities they love. It is possible that their way of resolving the dissonance between what they would like to do and what they can do is to decrease the significance of leisure. According to Frazier (2002), possible "selves" represent individuals' ideas of what they might become, what they would like to become, and what they fear becoming. He compared possible selves of three cohorts of older adults and found that the domains of leisure, good health, and abilities and education were most frequently reported as the most important hoped-for components of possible selves. However, leisure was more salient for the youngest group, whereas the salience of health emerged among individuals in their eighth and ninth decade of life. Prager (1997) found that hedonistic activities were significantly less important to the oldest old than to middle-aged or young-old groups. The preservation of human values and ideals, in contrast, increased in importance among older age groups. Similarly, when investigating life domains in older adults' self-definition, Freund (1999) found that the majority of participants considered hobbies and interests, social participation, and daily living routine as self-defining domains. However, among the oldest old, life review, personal assessment, and health also played important roles. This indicates that, as people age, they are not exclusively activity oriented but also self-reflecting and preoccupied with their private lives. These findings are consistent with several theories of adult development, which emphasize internal growth in later life, such as Vaillant's model (2002) and gerotranscendence theory (Tornstam, 1997, 1999); these suggest that, in very old age, successful aging is associated with a shift in perspective to a less materialistic and more philosophic point of view.

Such findings may be the results of cohort effects, but they also suggest that leisure is less a goal and more a means as people age. Among their reasons for choosing specific activities, very old adults mention various instrumental motives such as maintaining and improving fitness, keeping healthy, exercising the mind, testing the memory, and keeping up with language proficiency (Geiger & Miko, 1995; Hoppes, Hally, & Sewell, 2000; Kolt, 2002). Moreover, some leisure activities, such as exercising or social activities, are perceived as preserving one's youth (Dionigi, 2006; Fournier & Fine, 1990; Yarnal, 2006).

Leisure seems to have a unique role in oldest-old lives. This role may be described as a resource for resilience. The aging process poses cumulative risk factors to the oldest old; leisure provides cumulative protective factors that help them cope with, and resist, those risks. In fact, numerous studies have demonstrated that involvement in various leisure activities contributes to oldest persons' health. Leisure protects against cognitive decline and dementia (Ghisletta, 2006; Leung & Lam, 2007; Scarmeas, Levy, Tang, Manly, & Stern, 2001), functional impairment (Benjamins, 2004;

Graham, 2006), incompetence (Baltes, 1993), and frailty (Levers, Estabrooks, & Ross-Kerr, 2006). It also reduces mortality risk (Glass, 1999; Landi, 2004; Lennartsson, 2001). This protective effect is reflected in the profile of individuals who survive and thrive independently at age 85 and beyond, which has been portrayed by several scholars (McNellis, 2004; Vaillant, 2002; Ward-Baker, 2006). These individuals were described as highly vital human beings, committed to maintaining social ties, caring about an active body and mind, continuing to be energized by new ideas and learning, still viewing life as full of possibilities, and setting and attaining short-term goals.

CONTINUITY AND CHANGE IN LEISURE WITH AGING

The leisure activities of older people have been well researched since the early 1960s, with types of activities, benefits, constraints, and family and social contexts receiving the most attention (Nimrod, 2003). In addition, studies have provided strong evidence of older adults' tendency for continuity. Although older adults have considerable discretionary time in retirement and few parental or other caregiving responsibilities (at least initially), they tend not to participate in activities different from those they enjoyed before retirement (Janke, Davey, & Kleiber, 2006; Long, 1987; Nimrod, 2007a); rather, either they continue participating in the same activities (Iso-Ahola, Jackson, & Dunn, 1994; Levinson, 1986; Parker, 1982; Parnes et al., 1985), or take up activities in which they had been interested or proficient in the past (Atchley, 1993; Kelly, 1987). At most, the consensus holds, they increase their participation in the same activities (Janke et al., 2006; Robinson & Godbey, 1997; Rosenkoetter, Garris, & Engdahl, 2001; Verbrugge, Gruber-Baldini, & Fozard, 1996), and as they age, are less inclined to be interested in acquiring new knowledge or developing new skills (Ballard, 2003).

The major evidence for change in activity in later life was associated with reduction of the levels of activity or simple substitution to less challenging alternatives (Armstrong & Morgan, 1998; Bennett, 1998; Janke et al., 2006; Strain, Grabusic, Searle, & Dunn, 2002). There is a decline in participation in leisure activities with age (Iso-Ahola et al., 1994; Katz et al., 2000; Klumb, 1999; Lefrancois, Leclerc, & Poulin, 1998; Van Der Meer, 2008). In addition, there is a transition from physical activities to those demanding less physical effort and a corresponding shift from outdoor to indoor activities (Gordon, 1980; Gordon, Gaitz, & Scott, 1976; Rapoport & Rapoport, 1975; Vail & Berman-Ashcenazi, 1976). The outcome, as it comes into practice in the lives of the oldest old, is substantial time in discretionary activities done alone and at home, with television viewing being most prevalent (Horgas,

Wilms, & Baltes, 1998; Robinson & Godbey, 1997). Many of these oldest old, especially those with personal resources and a wide range of opportunities in their spatial environments, still have broad activity patterns (Van Der Meer, 2008) and maintain a high level of leisure satisfaction due to continued participation in more limited but still valued activities (Griffin & McKenna, 1998).

In offering an explanation for older adults' inclination toward constancy, Atchley (1989, 1993, 1999) proposed the continuity theory, which posits that continuity is a primary adaptive strategy for dealing with the changes associated with normal aging. It argues that individuals aspire to maintain stability in familiar roles that they had formerly engaged in, even though their advancing age could raise obstacles reducing the availability of those roles. Individuals tend to maintain the psychological and social patterns adopted during their life course (e.g., attitudes, opinions, personality, preferences, behavior) by developing stable activity patterns that help them preserve continuity. Continuity may also serve as a coping strategy when facing negative events in later life (see Kleiber, Hutchinson, & Williams, 2002). Familiar leisure activities that are personally expressive and that provide continuity with significant past relationships have great importance in restoring meaning and direction after negative life events. Such activities are also likely to restore feelings of competence, control, and freedom (Hutchinson, Loy, Kleiber, & Dattilo, 2003), qualities considered to moderate the impact of stress on one's well-being (Coleman & Iso-Ahola, 1993).

INNOVATION THEORY

Unlike continuity, innovation at an advanced age is a relatively unexplored phenomenon. A major reason for neglecting this issue is that most evidence indicates that the tendency for innovation is rather rare. Another reason is that the major evidence for change in activity in later life, as noted earlier, is its association with reduction of the levels of activity (rather than in the kind of activity).

According to previous studies, adding new activities in old age is not a common phenomenon – it occurs more often among women – and usually takes place in the domains of exercise, indoor activities, and hobbies (Iso-Ahola et al., 1994). Among men, there may be new activity in the domestic domain, which in many cases had been dominated for years by their wives (Long, 1987; Parnes et al., 1985; Strain et al., 2002). With regard to the benefits of starting a new activity, it has been argued that those who do develop new activities experience enjoyment and happiness (Thompson, 1992), higher life satisfaction (Nimrod, 2007a), and improvement in self-perception (Parry & Shaw, 1999). These arguments are supported by many studies conducted in recent years on the psychological benefits older adults gain from learning computer skills and using the Internet (for a review, see Nimrod, 2009).

A recent study (Nimrod & Kleiber, 2007) focused primarily on the issue of innovation in later life. This exploratory study, utilizing a qualitative approach with a sample of adult learners, led to the proposal of innovation theory. According to innovation theory, (a) the motivation for innovation is most often intrinsic, though it may result from various triggers; (b) in some cases, innovation represents an opportunity for renewal, stimulation, and growth that is continuous in some respects with earlier interests and capacities (self-preservation innovation), but in others, it represents an opportunity for reinvention of self (self-reinvention innovation); (c) there is a consistency in individuals regarding the type of innovation to which they are attracted; and (d) innovation has a positive impact on older persons' well-being.

The last proposition, namely the suggested association between innovation and well-being, was further researched using quantitative data. A study focusing on recently retired individuals (Nimrod, 2008) demonstrated that the occurrence of innovation among recently retired Israelis was not as rare as previous studies suggest. Fifty percent of the sample reported adding at least one new type of leisure activity to their daily lives after retiring from work. In addition, the study indicates that the innovators exhibited a significantly higher level of life satisfaction, thus providing preliminary support for innovation theory.

According to innovation theory, innovation is simply adding a new activity to one's leisure repertoire. Innovative activity is not necessarily creative activity. Creative activity (whether artistic or not) is a process whereby the individual seeks an original solution to a problem or challenge at hand (Mariske & Willis, 1998). Creative and innovative activities share some features: both involve openness, risk taking, flexibility, and adaptability. But where creativity is about seeking new solutions, innovative activity is about seeking new experiences; creativity is about different paths to the same goal, whereas innovation may lead to defining new goals.

Literature on creativity and aging (e.g., Cohen et al., 2006; Fisher & Specht, 1999) shows that creativity contributes to older adults' well-being and suggests that it promotes better management of everyday life and may be viewed as a coping mechanism for changing circumstances. Nimrod and Kleiber (2007) suggest considering innovation as a growth mechanism, thus enabling one to broaden and deepen one's sense of meaning in life and leading to greater well-being and satisfaction with life.

INNOVATION AMONG OLDER AND CONSTRAINED ADULTS

Following a study of innovation among older adults with chronic health conditions (Nimrod & Hutchinson, 2010), it was suggested that (a) similar to innovation among healthy older adults, innovation among older adults with chronic health conditions may result from internal, external, or instrumental triggers; (b) changes in health may serve as precursors for innovation, having either direct or indirect influence; (c) innovation during a time of declining health may involve various inconveniencies, but many find ways to adjust; and (d) although innovation among healthy older adults may be either self-preservation innovation or self-reinvention innovation (as suggested earlier by Nimrod & Kleiber, 2007), the main role of innovation among older adults with chronic health conditions is preserving a sense of continuity (i.e., self-preservation innovation).

On the basis of data from Nimrod and Hutchinson's study (2010), this chapter argues that innovation is both possible and beneficial among the oldest old. To support this premise, stories of two participants in this study are presented. The stories are vastly different from each other. They represent two extremes of innovation: one somewhat mild and minimal, another more significant and powerful. However, both exemplify the potential contribution of innovation in leisure to the well-being of the oldest old.

Jacob and the Garden Club

Jacob is a 78-year-old retired policeman. He has been married for 53 years, and he has three children and four grandchildren. Six years ago he suffered a severe stroke resulting in partial paralysis of the left side of his body. His leg and arm are "still not cooperating" with him and his throat is paralyzed, which causes him problems with speaking, eating, and drinking. Before the stroke, Jacob lived in a single-family dwelling and was an enthusiastic gardener; after the stroke, he couldn't garden any more. However, after moving into a condominium, he became an active member of the residents' garden club. The club includes 15 residents; they are in charge of planning, planting, purchasing flowers, watering, and so on. They also run a recycling project of the complex's bottles and cans, using the proceeds to purchase flowers.

When Jacob was asked what he liked about participating in the club he tapped with two fingers on his forehead and said: "I do it purposely because I'm trying to keep my brain occupied, try to keep it exercised," but it seems that there were other benefits as well. The club facilitated social relationships in the condominium, thus providing a sense of contribution and significance, as well as enjoyment of the outcome:

> I do get some satisfaction of seeing it. . . . We have a meeting to decide what we're going to get, we see each other almost every day, passing by the hallway. . . . I was there when they were planting everything and people, we call it deadhead, they pick off the dead blooms . . . but I don't do that, I just enjoy seeing it. . . . There's one bench right there in front. On fine days, if it's not too hot, I just sit there and admire the beauty.

Using the terms of innovation theory, the garden club, though a new activity, preserved a sense of Jacob's internal continuity (from his prestroke home gardening) and thus could be regarded as self-preservation innovation. To an extent, it replaced gardening and preserved the previous self-image of a person whose mind was always occupied and who devoted his life to public service.

Beth and the Quaker Church

Beth is an 82-year-old widow. She has two children living far away from her and one grandson. She has many chronic health conditions, including chronic lung diseases, fibromyalgia, back problems, bleeding bowels, swollen legs, high blood pressure, migraines, hiatal hernia, heart murmur, low potassium and low salt, and glaucoma, as well as two hearing aids. In addition, she had a series of strokes that damaged her short-term memory and upset her balance, so that she cannot walk without a walker.

Because of her health condition, she had to quit many favored leisure activities, including walking, exercising at a health club, using the computer, playing bridge, and participating in guided philosophical discussions. Nevertheless, she decided to join the Quaker church and became a keen member. The trigger for adding this activity was external: a friend, who was a member, suggested that Beth try it. However, Beth had an internal motivation to become more spiritual. Her inspiration was another friend who had already died but was her role model:

> I know if I were more spiritual she would come over to me, I know that. She was definitely psychic and I couldn't praise her enough. . . . [S]he said the best thing that you can do for [a grandchild who had drug problems]

> is to send him positive love . . . so that's what I did and that's what I do. . . . [T]he biggest thing about her was her spirituality. . . . [She] could have written all the materials from the Quakers, everything that's there, that's what she would talk about.

Attending church was never a significant part of Beth's life. She grew up as a Lutheran; when she married, she turned to the United Church of Christ, but she reported that she and her husband were always "very lazy" about attending church. In contrast, she said that now she "wouldn't miss the Quaker meeting." When asked about the things that she liked in the Quaker services, she mentioned several: she liked the way the services were held in silence and how "if you had something you wanted to share, you just said it." She liked the discussions, which probably provided some replacement for her lost philosophical discussions; and she also very much enjoyed the fact that her social network had expanded. However, it seemed that the most significant thing she experienced since joining the church was being accepted and loved just as she was.

Beth had unfinished business with education, because she did not complete an academic degree; and she loved to get dressed and put on jewelry and makeup. The church members did not seem to care about either "weakness":

> I'm so lucky, I've got really good friends and the Quakers are unbelievable, they're so caring. They're so kind. I don't think there's anybody there without two or three [academic] degrees, but you'd never, ever know it. Sometimes I feel a little out of my depth. When I left grade 12 in [my hometown] I had a scholarship to [college] so I went there for a year [but I had to work] at all kinds of different things to make money. . . . These people, they're unbelievable[;] you can talk about anything to them. They're so kind and so helpful and so modest. . . . I'm the only one who wears lots of jewelry and make-up because simplicity is in the documents, but they all have nice homes and things like that but they don't bring that up. They don't dress up, they're clean and they look fine, but I'm the only one who dresses up. Yeah, I said I should take some of this jewelry off, and they say no, no, no, we love to see it on you, so I wear it.

In terms of innovation theory, Beth reinvented herself not only as a Quaker and as a more spiritual person but also as someone equal and worthy of being loved.

SUMMARY

If we use the common division of older adults into young old, middle old (or old old), and oldest old, both Jacob and Beth would be included in the middle group (i.e., 75–84 years old). However, it has been established that people in their 90s or older are often healthier and more robust than those 20 years younger (Perls, 1995; Philp, 2004). Therefore, there is no reason to differentiate between the middle old and the oldest old when discussing the potential benefits of innovation for older adults. Furthermore, the health challenges that these individuals were facing demonstrate that innovation can still occur, even when there are significant constraints.

Is innovation possible among older adults? Yes. Innovation is not necessarily a grandiose step such as learning to fly an airplane or joining a group of mountain climbers. It can be reflected in rather minor changes, such as joining a garden club or a spiritual group. A more significant question is, Is adding a new activity adaptive and beneficial? Does it hold a potential contribution to old people's well-being?

Innovation theory (Nimrod & Hutchinson, 2010; Nimrod & Kleiber, 2007) suggests that innovation's impact is not direct; its key role is in creating opportunities for broadening and deepening one's sense of meaning in life. The two previous examples demonstrate that the benefits of each new activity can be quite different. For Jacob, it was a sense of competence and contribution; enjoyment of the outcome; and pride, occupation, and affiliation. The new activity helped him preserve old interests and roles, and it provided a sense of inner continuity. For Beth, the benefits were increased spirituality, intellectual stimulation, and social affiliation. However, the new activity also helped her reinvent herself and feel good about her spirituality and self-worth. To an extent, it provided a sense of renewal and new self-perception.

Although for Jacob it was his physical condition that led to innovation, for Beth health was not a precursor. In both cases, however, innovation offered relief and distraction from physical and emotional losses the respondents had experienced and created opportunities for a more meaningful daily life. It is suggested, then, that similar innovative behavior among the oldest old can contribute to an enhanced sense of well-being.

Although the oldest old tend to report a reduced significance of leisure (Frazier, 2002; Freund, 1999; Prager, 1997), leisure is still an important component in their lives. It contributes to well-being (Keith, 1980; Kochniuk, 2004; McKee, 2002; Nilsson, Bernspång, Fisher, Gustafson, & Löfgren, 2007; Silverstein & Parker, 2002), and seems to have a unique role as a resource for resilience. Adding new activities to their leisure repertoire may replace activities abandoned as a result of various constraints. Moreover, innovation – creating significantly new experiences through new activities – may enhance the well-being of the oldest old by preserving their sense of self and by allowing for self-discovery and growth even at very advanced age. Innovation reinforces their view of themselves as individuals who are aging well in spite of limiting conditions and enhances a sense of freedom, control, and self-worth.

REFERENCES

Armstrong, G. K., & Morgan, K. (1998). Stability and change in levels of habitual physical activity in later life. *Age and Ageing, 27*(Suppl. 3), 17–23.

Atchley, R. (1989). The continuity theory of normal aging. *The Gerontologist, 29*, 183–190.

Atchley, R. (1993). Continuity theory and the evolution of activity in later adulthood. In J. R. Kelly (Ed.), *Activity and aging: Staying involved in later life* (pp. 5–16). Thousand Oaks, CA: Sage.

Atchley, R. (1999). *Continuity and adaptation in aging.* Baltimore: Johns Hopkins University Press.

Ballard, S. M. (2003). Family life education needs of midlife and older adults. *Family Relations, 52*, 129–136.

Baltes, M. M. (1993). Everyday competence in old and very old age: An interdisciplinary perspective. *Ageing and Society, 13*, 657–680.

Barer, B. M. (1994). Men and women aging differently. *International Journal of Aging and Human Development, 38*, 29–40.

Benjamins, M. R. (2004). Religion and functional health among the elderly: Is there a relationship and is it constant? *Journal of Aging and Health, 16*, 355–374.

Bennett, K. M. (1998). Gender and longitudinal changes in physical activities in later life. *Age and Ageing, 27*(Suppl. 3), 24–28.

Cohen, G. D., Perlstein, S., Chapline, J., Kelly, J., Firth, K. M., & Simmens, S. (2006). The impact of professionally conducted cultural programs on the physical health, mental health, and social functioning of older adults. *The Gerontologist, 46*, 726–734.

Coleman, D., & Iso-Ahola, S. E. (1993). Leisure and health: The role of social support and self-determination. *Journal of Leisure Research, 25*, 111–128.

Dionigi, R. (2006). Competitive sport as leisure in later life: Negotiations, discourse, and aging. *Leisure Sciences, 28*, 181–196.

Duggleby, W., Bateman, J., & Singer, S. (2002). The aging experience of well elderly women: Initial results. *Nursing and Health Sciences, 4*(3), 10.

Duke, J., Leventhal, H., Brownlee, S., & Leventhal E. A. (2002). Giving up and replacing activities in response to illness. *Journals of Gerontology Series B: Psychological Sciences and Social Sciences, 57*, 367–376.

Fernandez-Ballesteros, R., Zamarron, M., & Ruiz, M. (2001). The contribution of socio-demographic and psychosocial factors to life satisfaction. *Ageing and Society, 21*, 25–43.

Fisher, B. J., & Specht, D. K. (1999). Successful aging and creativity in later life. *Journal of Aging Studies, 13*, 457–473.

Fournier, S. M., & Fine, G. A. (1990). Jumping grannies: Exercise as a buffer against becoming "old." *Play and Culture, 3*, 337–342.

Frazier, L. D. (2002). Psychosocial influences on possible selves: A comparison of three cohorts of older adults. *International Journal of Behavioral Development, 26*, 308–317.

Freund, A. M. (1999). Content and function of the self-definition in old age and very old age. *Journals of Gerontology: Series B: Psychological Sciences and Social Sciences, 54B*, 55–67.

Geiger, C. W., & Miko, P. S. (1995). Meaning of recreation/leisure activities to elderly nursing home residents: A qualitative study. *Therapeutic Recreation Journal, 29*, 131–138.

Ghisletta, P. (2006). Does activity engagement protect against cognitive decline in old age? Methodological and analytical considerations. *Journals of Gerontology: Series B: Psychological Sciences and Social Sciences, 61B*, 253–261.

Glass, T. A. (1999). Population based study of social and productive activities as predictors of survival among elderly Americans. *British Medical Journal, 319*(7208), 478–491.

Gordon, C. (1980). Development of evaluated role identities. *Annual Review of Sociology, 6*, 405–433.

Gordon, C., Gaitz, C., & Scott, J. (1976). Leisure and lives: Personal expressivity across the life span. In R. Binstock & E. Shanas (Eds.), *Handbook of aging and the social sciences* (pp. 310–341). New York: Van Nostrand Reinhold.

Graham, S. A. (2006). *Effects of a home-based physical activity program implemented by a trained caregiver on the physical function of community-dwelling older adults.* Unpublished dissertation, University of Texas at Austin.

Griffin, J., & McKenna, K. (1998). Influences on leisure and life satisfaction of elderly people. *Physical and Occupational Therapy in Geriatrics, 15*, 1–16.

Hall, M., & Havens, B. (2002). *Aging in Manitoba: Selected findings.* Retrieved September 12, 2002, from http://www.umanitoba.ca/faculties/medicine/community_health_sciences/AIM.html.

Harvard Center for Health Communication. (2004). *Reinventing aging: Baby boomers and civic engagement.* Cambridge, MA: Harvard School of Public Health-Metlife Foundation.

Hoppes, S., Hally, C., & Sewell, L. (2000). An interest inventory of games for older adults. *Physical & Occupational Therapy in Geriatrics, 18*(2), 71–83.

Horgas, A. L., Wilms, H. U., & Baltes, M. M. (1998). Daily life in very old age: Everyday activities as expression of successful living. *The Gerontologist, 38*, 556–568.

Hutchinson, S. L., Loy, D., Kleiber, D. A., & Dattilo, J. (2003). Leisure as a coping resource: Variations in coping with traumatic injury and illness. *Leisure Sciences, 25*, 143–161.

Iso-Ahola, S. E., Jackson, E., & Dunn, E. (1994). Starting, ceasing and replacing leisure activities over the life-span. *Journal of Leisure Research, 26*, 227–249.

Janke, M., Davey, A., & Kleiber, D. (2006). Modeling change in older adults' leisure activities. *Leisure Sciences, 28*, 285–303.

Janke, M. C., Nimrod, G., & Kleiber, D. A. (2008a). Leisure activity and depressive symptoms of widowed and married women in later life. *Journal of Leisure Research, 40*, 250–266.

Janke, M. C., Nimrod, G., & Kleiber, D. A. (2008b). Leisure patterns and health among recently widowed adults. *Activities, Adaptation, and Aging, 32*, 19–39.

Janke, M. C., Nimrod, G., & Kleiber, D. A. (2008c). Reduction in leisure activity and well-being during the transition to widowhood. *Women and Aging, 20*, 83–98.

Katz, E., Hass, H., Weitz, S., Adoni, H., Gurevitch, M., Schiff, M., et al. (2000). *Tarbut hapnai belsrael: Tmurot bedfusei hapeilut hatarbutit 1970–1990* [Leisure patterns in Israel: Changes in cultural activity 1970–1990]. Tel Aviv: Open University.

Keith, P. M. (1980). Life changes, leisure activities, and well-being among very old men and women. *Activities, Adaptation and Aging, 1*, 67–75.

Kelly, J. R. (1987). *Peoria winter, styles and resources in later life.* Lexington, MA: Lexington Books.

Kelly, J. R. (1996). *Leisure* (3rd ed.). Boston: Allyn and Bacon.

Kleiber, D. (1999). *Leisure experience and human development.* New York: Basic Books.

Kleiber, D. A., Hutchinson, S. L., & Williams, R. (2002). Leisure as a resource in transcending negative life events: Self-protection, self-restoration and personal transformation. *Leisure Sciences, 24*, 219–235.

Klumb, P. L. (1999). Time use of old and very old Berliners: productive and consumptive activities as functions of resources. *Journals of Gerontology: Series B: Psychological Sciences and Social Sciences, 54B*, 271–278.

Kochniuk, L. (2004). *We never buy green bananas: Oldest old. Phenomenological study.* Unpublished dissertation, University of Idaho.

Kolt, G. S. (2002). Exercise participation motives in older Asian Indians. *Psychological Studies, 47*, 139–147.

Landi, F. (2004). Physical activity and mortality in frail, community-living elderly patients. *Journals of Gerontology: Series A: Biological Sciences and Medical Sciences, 59A*, 833–837.

Lefrancois, R., Leclerc, G., & Poulin, N. (1998). Predictors of activity involvement among older adults. *Activity, Adaptation and Aging, 22*, 15–29.

Lennartsson, C. (2001). Does engagement with life enhance survival of elderly people in Sweden? The role of social and leisure activities. *Journals of Gerontology: Series B: Psychological Sciences and Social Sciences, 56B*, 335–342.

Leung, G. T. Y., & Lam, L. C. W. (2007). Leisure activities and cognitive impairment in late life – A selective literature review of longitudinal cohort studies. *Hong Kong Journal of Psychiatry, 17*, 91–100.

Levers, M.-J, Estabrooks, C. A., & Ross-Kerr, J. (2006). Factors contributing to frailty: Literature review. *Journal of Advanced Nursing, 56*, 282–291.

Levinson, S. (1986). *Bhirat peiluiot pnai beprisha – Glisha oh pitzui shel isuk vepeiluiot pnai lifnei haprisha legimlaot?* [Leisure choices in retirement – Overflow or compensation from pre-retirement activities?]. Unpublished master's thesis, Bar-Ilan University, Ramat Gan, Israel.

Long, J. (1987). Continuity as a basis for change: Leisure and male retirement. *Leisure Studies, 6*, 55–70.

Mariske, M., & Willis, S. L. (1998). Practical creativity in older adults' everyday problem solving: Life span perspectives. In C. E. Adams-Price (Ed.), *Creativity and successful aging: Theoretical and empirical approaches* (pp. 73–113). New York: Springer.

McGuire, F. (1985). Constraints in later life. In M. G. Wade (Ed.), *Constraints on leisure* (pp. 335–353). Springfield, IL: Thomas.

McGuire, F., & Norman, W. (2005). The role of constraints in successful aging: Enabling or inhibiting? In E. Jackson (Ed.), *Constraints to leisure* (pp. 89–101). State College, PA: Venture Press.

McKee, K. J. (2002). Methods for assessing quality of life and well-being in frail older people. *Psychology and Health, 17*, 737–751.

McKenna, K., Broome, K., & Liddle, J. (2007). What older people do: Time use and exploring the link between role participation and life satisfaction in people aged 65 years and over. *Australian Occupational Therapy Journal, 54*, 273–284.

McNellis, C. K. (2004). *Lived experiences of the independent oldest old in community-based programs: Heideggerian hermeneutical analysis (Martin Heidegger)*. Unpublished dissertation, University of Chicago.

Nilsson, I. (2006). Focus on leisure repertoire in the oldest old: The Umea 85+ Study. *Journal of Applied Gerontology, 25*, 391–405.

Nilsson, I., Bernspång, B., Fisher, A. G., Gustafson, Y., & Löfgren, B. (2007). Occupational engagement and life satisfaction in the oldest old: The Umeå 85+ study. *Occupation, Participation and Health, 27*, 131–139.

Nimrod, G. (2003). Leisure after retirement: Research review and mapping. *Gerontology, 30*, 29–46. [In Hebrew].

Nimrod, G. (2007a). Expanding, reducing, concentrating and diffusing: Post retirement leisure behavior and life satisfaction. *Leisure Sciences, 1*, 91–111.

Nimrod, G. (2007b). Retirees' leisure: Activities, benefits, and their contribution to life satisfaction. *Leisure Studies, 26*, 65–80.

Nimrod, G. (2008). In support of innovation theory: innovation in activity patterns and life satisfaction among recently retired individuals. *Ageing and Society, 28*, 831–846.

Nimrod, G. (2009). The Internet as a resource in older adults' leisure. *International Journal of Disability and Human Development, 8*, 207–214.

Nimrod, G., & Adoni, H. (2006). Leisure styles and life satisfaction among recent retirees in Israel. *Ageing and Society, 26*, 607–630.

Nimrod, G., & Hutchinson, S. (2010). Innovation among older adults with chronic health conditions. *Journal of Leisure Research, 41*, 1–23.

Nimrod, G., Janke, M., & Kleiber, D. A. (2008). Retirement, activity, and subjective well-being in Israel and the United States. *World Leisure Journal, 50*, 18–32.

Nimrod, G., & Kleiber, D. A. (2007). Reconsidering change and continuity in later life: Toward an innovation theory of successful aging. *International Journal of Aging and Human Development, 65*, 1–22.

Parker, S. (1982). *Work and retirement*. London: George Allen and Unwin.

Parnes, H. S., Crowley, J. E., Haurin R. J., Less, L. J., Morgan, W. R., Mott, F. L., et al. (1985). *Retirement among American men*. Lexington, MA: Lexington Books.

Parry, D. C., & Shaw, S. M. (1999). The role of leisure in women's experiences of menopause and mid-life. *Leisure Sciences, 21*, 205–218.

Perls, T. T. (1995). The oldest old. *Scientific American, 272*, 70–75.
Philp, I. (2004). *Better health in old age.* Retrieved online on October 18, 2007, from England's Department of Health (DH) Web site: http://www.dh.gov.uk/en/Publicationsandstatistics/Publications/PublicationsPolicyAndGuidance/DH_4092957.
Prager, E. (1997). Sources of personal meaning in life for a sample of younger and older urban Australian women. *Journal of Women and Aging, 9*, 47–65.
Rapoport, R., & Rapoport, R. N. (1975). *Leisure and the family life cycle.* London: Routledge and Kegan Paul.
Riddick, C. C., & Stewart, D. G. (1994). An examination of the life satisfaction and importance of leisure in the lives of older female retirees: A comparison of blacks to whites. *Journal of Leisure Research, 26*, 75–87.
Robinson, J. P., & Godbey, G. (1997). *Time for life: The surprising way Americans use their time.* State College: Pennsylvania State University Press.
Rosenkoetter, M. M., Garris, J. M., & Engdahl, R. A. (2001). Postretirement use of time: Implications for pre-retirement planning and postretirement management. *Activities, Adaptation and Aging, 25*, 1–18.
Scarmeas, N., Levy, G., Tang, M. X, Manly, J., & Stern, Y. (2001). Influence of leisure activity on the incidence of Alzheimer's disease. *Neurology, 57*(12), 2236–2242.
Searle, M. S., Mahon, M. J., Iso-Ahola, S. E., Sadrolias, H. A., & Van Dyck, J. (1995). Enhancing a sense of independence and psychological well-being among the elderly: A field experiment. *Journal of Leisure Research, 27*, 107–124.
Searle, M. S., Mahon, M. J., Iso-Ahola, S. E., Sadrolias, H. A., & Van Dyck, J. (1998). Examining the long term effects of leisure education on a sense of independence and psychological well-being among the elderly. *Journal of Leisure Research, 30*, 331–340.
Shmanske, S. (1997). Life-cycle happiness in a discounted utility model. *Kyklos, 50*, 383–407.
Silverstein, M., & Parker, M. G. (2002). Leisure activities and quality of life among the oldest old in Sweden. *Research on Aging, 24*, 528–547.
Stebbins, R. A. (2006). Serious leisure. In C. Rojek, T. Veal, & S. Shaw (Eds.), *A handbook of leisure studies* (pp. 448–456). New York: Palgrave Macmillan.
Strain, L. A., Grabusic, C. C., Searle, M. S., & Dunn, N. J. (2002). Continuing and ceasing leisure activities in later life: A longitudinal study. *The Gerontologist, 42*, 217–223.
Thompson P. (1992). "I don't feel old": Subjective ageing and the search for meaning in later life. *Ageing and Society, 12*, 23–47.
Tornstam L. (1997). Gerotranscendence: The contemplative dimension of aging. *Journal of Aging Studies, 11*, 143–154.
Tornstam L. (1999). Gerotranscendence and the functions of reminiscence. *Journal of Aging and Identity, 4*, 155–166.
Utz, R. L., Carr, D., Nesse, R., & Wortman, C. B. (2002). The effect of widowhood on older adults' social participation: An evaluation of activity, disengagement, and continuity theories. *The Gerontologist, 42*, 522–533.
Vail, H., & Berman-Ashcenazi, A. (1976). *Leisure use of the 70+ years old.* Jerusalem: Brookdale Institute. [In Hebrew].
Vaillant, G. (2002) *Aging well.* Boston: Little, Brown.

Van Der Meer, M. J. (2008). Sociospatial diversity in the leisure activities of older people in the Netherlands. *Journal of Aging Studies*, 22, 1–12.

Verbrugge, L. M., Gruber-Baldini, A. N., & Fozard, J. L. (1996). Age differences and age changes in activities: Baltimore longitudinal study of aging. *Journals of Gerontology Series B: Psychological Sciences and Social Sciences*, *51B*, 30–41.

Ward-Baker, P. D. (2006). *Remarkable oldest old: New vision of aging.* Unpublished dissertation, Union Institute and University, Cincinnati, OH.

Yarnal, C. M. (2006). The Red Hat Society: Exploring the role of play, liminality, and *communitas* in older women's lives. *Journal of Women and Aging*, *18*, 51–73.

PART IV

SIGNPOSTING PARADISE: MEASUREMENT OF WELL-BEING

15

Culture and Meaning: Strategies for Understanding the Well-Being of the Oldest Old

CHRISTINE L. FRY AND CHARLOTTE IKELS

ABSTRACT

Well-being has been a central variable in understanding the experiences of older people including the oldest old. For subjective well-being cultural understandings and meaning are central. A long standing question has been how to measure well-being within one culture and across cultures. Two major strategies have evolved. The first uses psychometric measures and multivariate analysis to explore different components of well-being. The second is more open-ended using ethnographic and qualitative strategies to elicit dimensions of well-being from the experiences of older people in the contexts in which they live. The promises and difficulties of each methodology are reviewed. The appropriateness of each strategy for diverse contexts and populations of the oldest old are considered.

INTRODUCTION

A prominent and persistent effort of gerontology is directed toward understanding the well-being of older people. The quality of life in a community can be assessed directly through indicators of life expectancy, levels of education, quality of housing, and income. How well-being is experienced and evaluated calls for more subjective measurement. For more than a half a century, researchers have devised scales and alternative strategies for measuring what may well be a gerontological holy grail. As early as the late 1970s, however, researchers expressed concern about the appropriate use of the then-available scales and even about whether gerontologists should want to measure well-being (Nydegger, 1977)

One of the major goals of measuring subjective well-being is to acquire data that will permit the researcher or policy maker to assess the quality of life of a population or individual. To achieve this goal, the researcher must settle on a measurement strategy that is both valid and reliable. As Bishop and Martin (Chapter 17) demonstrate in their review of the literature on the measurement of subjective well-being, gerontologists for decades have employed a host of scales that attempt to assess general well-being and/or domain-specific well-being. The vast majority of the scales have been developed for use with populations in the developed nations of North America and Europe. Their applicability to populations in developed nations outside of these areas, such as Japan, or in developing nations, such as Botswana, is highly questionable (Draper, 2007; Torres, 1999). Cultural issues involving the salience of emotional states, communicative style, familiarity with the interview format, and the local hierarchy of values (what is considered necessary or desirable for the "good life") may render the data collected through scales invalid or uninterpretable. If the researcher also has the goal of making comparisons across culturally distinctive groups, the problems of validity and interpretability are magnified.

Well-being turns out to be a variable that is fairly clear conceptually (see Chapters 5, 7, and 17) but that is very difficult to operationalize. Nevertheless, there are many hypotheses suggesting variables that have impacts on well-being (see Chapter 7). The intent of this chapter is to look at the reasons well-being is so difficult to measure. First, we look at cultural knowledge and the ways well-being is defined and how individuals use their understandings to evaluate subjective experiences. Second, we examine the major strategies used to measure well-being. These are the familiar psychometric indices and the less familiar ethnographic strategies. Third, we consider the measurement and use of well-being for older adults, especially for the oldest old.

CULTURE AND THE MEASUREMENT OF WELL-BEING

Measuring subjective well-being is easy, but interpreting the measure is difficult. For example, we could simply ask, "How's it going?" We would get our answer, but we may not know what it means or how to analyze it across individuals or contexts because at its core well-being is individual and shaped by experience in a cultural context. Likewise from another perspective, that of the investigator, well-being is equally culturally shaped (see Chapter 8, which highlights the impact of trauma on self-concepts). The way researchers conceptualize well-being as a variable is a product of the history of the field of measurement theory. The questions we ask, the eliciting frames we design, and the scales we construct are all derived from shared assumptions made on the part of the researcher or the research tradition. As investigators, we must be aware of how our research culture shapes us and use that knowledge to construct culturally sensitive instruments, aware of distortions in communication with our respondents, and cognizant of potential pitfalls in the interpretation of our results.

Well-being as it has been conceived in gerontology is a variable anchored in an individual. It is a psychological variable in that a researcher obtains an understanding of how a person feels about his or her life in a specified temporal framework. Most researchers explore linkages of that feeling with issues in the life context of that person, especially health, material security, and social concerns. The most usual way to elicit this information is to interview respondents. Two main strategies have been used. The first involves the construction of psychometric scales, which consist of forced-choice items, to arrive at a summary score indicative of well-being. The second strategy also involves interviews but often includes longer-term observations of the person in context. In the interview format, questions are open ended to elicit the perspective of the person being interviewed. This second approach is an ethnographic strategy.

The discussion that follows is based on the authors' experience in a major cross-cultural project (Project AGE) designed to examine the linkages between community contexts and pathways to well-being in old age (Keith et al., 1994). Project AGE selected seven communities around the globe.[1] Christine L. Fry and Jennie Keith codirected the project. (For the specific research sites and their respective principal investigators, see Table 15.1.) With a multiple-site project with individual investigators distributed around the globe, the codirectors theoretically and methodologically integrated the research design around a number of linked hypotheses. Before beginning the actual fieldwork, the team members agreed to employ multiple similar methodologies that were suitably adapted to meet local conditions (see Table 15.2. for an outline of methods employed). The multiplicity of methods meant that team members would be able to obtain multiple pathways to understand the local meaning of subjective well-being. These methods included (among others) discussions with key informants and formal interviews with a random sample of adults (usually individuals ranging in age from the late teens to the late 80s or early 90s) but with oversampling of the older population. In the interview, the major sources of data derived from a card sort referred to as the age game and from a set of

[1] Project AGE was supported by Grant No. AG03110 through the National Institute on Aging.

TABLE 15.1. *Project AGE: Research communities*

Geographic location	Community	Principle investigator
Africa Kalahari Desert Botswana	Jo/hoansi (!Kung) Small communities located near permanent water source consisting of families who subsist primarily by foraging combined with gardening and working for the Herero	Patricia Draper – University of Nebraska, Lincoln
	Herero Small communities of cattle stations consisting primarily of lineage members under the leadership of an influential male. Subsistence is the herding of cattle and smaller animals combined with gardening.	Henry C. Harpending – University of Utah
Europe Ireland	Clifden, County Galway A small community in western Ireland based on tourism, lobster fishing, raising of sheep, and state services.	Anthony P. Glascock – Drexel University
	Blessington, County Wicklow A small town in eastern Ireland within commuting distance to Dublin.	Jennette Dickerson-Putman – Indiana University, Indianapolis
North America United States	Momence, Illinois A Midwestern small town with a mixed economy of light industry, agriculture, retail, and service.	Christine L. Fry – Loyola University of Chicago
	Swarthmore, Pennsylvania A suburban college town near Philadelphia.	Jennie Keith – Swarthmore College
Asia	Hong Kong Four neighborhoods in Kowloon. Hong Kong is an urban and industrial port of trade in the global economy.	Charlotte Ikels – Case Western Reserve University

TABLE 15.2. *Project AGE: Methods*

Instruments	Research activities	
Participant observation	Participant observation involves taking up long-term residence in a community to get to know the people and the way of life of the community. This involves participating in public events, observing public spaces, and getting to know the cast of characters and their views of community life and issues, as well as the local knowledge.	
Key informant interviewing	Informants share their knowledge of specific issues in the community. Individuals are selected for their different perspectives on community life. Key informants are instrumental in the design of formal research instruments.	
Life histories	A sample of older adults is invited to share an overview of their lives from childhood to the present. This involves a semistructured interview to organize the history in meaningful units (e.g., chapters, timeline). Interviews are taped and follow-ups are made for corrections and elaborations.	
Structured interviews	Formal interviews with a probability sample of adults and an over sample of older adults are conducted in each community. Topics covered in the interview included personal background information, family and kinship, community involvement, health and functionality, and well-being. A component of the interview is the age game, a card-sort technique to elicit data on the life course and questions to obtain information on such issues as age transitions and evaluations of different life stages.	
Instruments to obtain data on well-being	Respondents' own well-being	Respondents are asked to rate their own present well-being using the Cantril ladder or a culturally meaningful metaphor involving ranking. Reasons for present placement and the high and low ends of the ladder are obtained. Also, the past and expected future rankings are asked for, along with reasons for the respective rankings.
	Well-being of older person known to respondent	As a part of the age game for the older groups defined by the respondent, they are asked to select two older people known to them in those groups. One is to be perceived as experiencing a good old age and the other as having difficulties. Reasons for a good and difficult old age are asked for, along with information on age and gender.
	Well-being across the life course in different age groups	In the age-game interview, respondents are asked for each age group differentiated to indicate the good things about being in that life stage and the hard things about that life stage. Because of its abstractness, these data are normative.

questions associated with a scale adapted from the Cantril (1965) ladder. In addition, in the course of carrying out the research, each fieldworker spent a year in his or her respective field site observing and participating in the daily round of life; thus, their interpretations of the data are grounded in a rich understanding of the local context. Given the nature of the research question, the key methodological issue was how to operationalize well-being in such a way that we would be able to interpret the resulting data and at the same time resolve issues of reliability, validity, and comparability. In the end, comparability in meaning proved challenging in the coding of data for cross-site interpretation. Our initial research design called for both psychometric and ethnographic measurement.

PSYCHOMETRIC STRATEGIES OF MEASUREMENT

Within gerontology, the most familiar way of measuring well-being is through the use of scales. Scales are congruent with a long tradition of psychological testing. By the middle of the 20th century, scales such as the Neugarten Life Satisfaction Scale (see Chapter 17; Neugarten, Havighurst, & Tobin, 1961), the Philadelphia Geriatric Center Morale Scale (Lawton, 1975), and the Affect Balance Scale (Bradburn, 1969) had been developed and rapidly became popular research instruments. They were fairly straightforward to administer; could be used in a variety of settings; and could be used for different purposes, from assessment of subjective well-being to evaluating the effectiveness of interventions such as relocation to specialized housing. Since that time, these scales have evolved into a second generation scales of subjective well-being and to more restrictive domain-specific instruments (see Chapter 17). Comparative research across nations has resulted in psychometric scales to empirically explore cultural diversity in the nature of well-being (Basabe et al. (2002); Biswas-Diener, Diener, & Tamir (2004); Diener & Suh (2000); Diener, & Tov, (2007); Oishi, Diener, Lucas, & Suh (1999)).

Why have these scales persisted and proliferated for more than 50 years in gerontological research? The reason is because they are powerful instruments. They do what scales should do. First, the design of scales is theory driven. Scales are usually constructed by a panel of experts to operationalize the concept of subjective well-being. Scales are tested for reliability and validity. Also, because a scale consists of multiple items, it is possible to insert questions that are a check on internal consistency. This further increases confidence in validity. In addition, because the responses used to score the scale are mathematically constructed, the resulting level constitutes a near-interval-level measurement. We can be fairly confident that individuals scoring a 30 are very similar to one another in their level of well-being. With such scales, it is possible to analyze and interpret results with sophisticated multivariate statistical packages.

In the case of Project AGE, the American site researchers were amenable to adapting such a scale, but team members who were responsible for other sites that differed not only in languages but also in culture raised concerns. These concerns centered on validity and assumptions made in test taking:

1. *Validity*: Because our instruments are products of the investigators' research culture and are designed to measure well-being that is the product of a different culture, we must ask the question of which culture we are measuring. Is it the observer's or the observed's? Obviously, we want to design instruments appropriate for the individuals answering the questions. Transfer of a well-being scale to another culture and population is far more complicated than translating the items into another language. The respondents may be able to respond to the questions, but they will be using their local cultural knowledge about well-being. If cultural sensitivity is ignored, we run the risk of obtaining results that are an artifact of the instrument. A prime example comes from race and IQ research in the early 20th century. World War I soldiers participated in psychological testing as part of their induction into the army. A pattern emerged that Southern Blacks did not perform as well as their White counterparts. How do we interpret this? Are Blacks less intelligent, or are they using different cultural knowledge to answer the questions?
2. *Culture and the culture of testing*: Any interview in standardizing the eliciting procedure takes on the format of a formal examination – even with qualitative questions. Test taking is an acquired skill that requires learning and practice to master. In communities with universal education, children rapidly learn this skill to survive formal educational institutions. Once they graduate, however, they have little use for test-taking abilities and soon lose them. Some 70 or 80 years later, a standardized test may be a puzzle indeed. Without formal education, respondents find standardized tests frustrating. In Project AGE, we saw this reaction with older respondents who made comments about test taking. In Africa, especially our Ju/hoansi respondents were quick to point to redundancies in our instruments. As a result, our researchers became more aware of the cultural assumptions in instrument construction.

In the end, we did not use a psychometric measurement strategy. All team members agreed that it would possible to adapt an existing scale and make it reliable and valid for each site. It was clear that the African sites and Hong Kong would be the riskiest in terms of successful adaptation. Our conclusion was that the adaptation of such an instrument was not the most efficient use of project resources, especially when we had an alternative measurement strategy that was designed to be culturally sensitive.

ETHNOGRAPHIC STRATEGIES OF MEASUREMENT

As psychometric well-being scales were being developed in the 1960s, another line of research designed to explore quality-of-life issues and life satisfaction cross-nationally emerged (Campbell, Converse, & Rodgers, 1976) Best known is the work of Cantril (1965), who conducted an 11-nation study using a direct, open-ended strategy of measurement. Because of the comparative nature of his study, he made few assumptions about the cultural content of life satisfaction. His eliciting frame involved a metaphor entailing a linear rank (a ladder) and a number of direct and open questions about meaning. Although not culturally neutral, the simplicity of the instrument lends itself to adaptation and cross-cultural comparisons. The Cantril ladder is also congruent with a line of anthropological research that emerged in the 1950s and 1960s. Ethnoscience, or ethnosemantics, is a long-standing research strategy to investigate the knowledge of native peoples about the world they live in (e.g., classifications of plants and animals). With cross-fertilization from psychology and anthropological linguistics, a paradigm that became known as cognitive anthropology was formalized, with distinctive measurement strategies (see D'Andrade, 1995). Although the Cantril ladder is not an anthropologically developed instrument, it has strong parallels with cognitive anthropological measurement theory in that it seeks (a) to bring forth native understandings and meaning (emic as opposed to the observer's point of view, or etic) and (b) to ask informants to use their knowledge and make judgments about specific issues. A number of eliciting frames and analytic strategies have expanded our ethnographic tool kit (de Munck & Sobo, 1998). For instance, in gerontological research, triad testing has been used to examine the pleasures and work of old age in a hill-tribe people of Thailand (Harman, 1998).[2] Freelisting has been used to document diversity in cultural domains (including emotions) in the United

[2] Triad testing involves asking informants to examine three objects, words, or concepts and to use their judgment to indicate which two of the three are the most similar. The two items most similar are scored the same and the third item is scored as different. The results

States and Mexico (Schrauf & Sanchez, 2008).[3] Likewise, Project AGE used a card sort to explore the meaning of age and the life course in our seven research communities. Because the Cantril ladder is a qualitative, open-ended instrument, adaptable to different cultural circumstances, Project AGE incorporated it as the central strategy to ethnographically document and describe the meanings of well-being.

WELL-BEING, EVALUATION, AND MEANING

The Cantril self-anchoring ladder was used by the project team to elicit evaluations and explanations of present, past, and future life. Essentially, the bottom of the ladder represents the worst things could possibly be, and the top represents the best. The respondent is asked where he or she would be on the ladder and why. Basically, the instrument measures life satisfaction rather than morale, and for that reason, it is considered a stabler indicator of well-being. Its simplicity made it seem ideal for Project AGE, though the researchers decided to reduce the ladder from ten rungs to six. Yet this instrument required further adaptation in at least two of the sites. In Hong Kong in the pretest, some informants just could not seem to see the rungs of the ladder and fixated instead on the spaces between the rungs. In the final interview schedule the ladder was replaced by a flight of six stairs. This change did not eliminate all problems, however, as more than a few people thought they were being asked how many stairs they could climb.[4] For many Ju/hoansi, a ladder (and likewise a flight of stairs) was not a sufficiently familiar item to be useful for elicitation. The researcher instead held out five fingers. Once the informant had rated his or her present life, he or she was also asked to rate life five years ago and five years hence (with explanations for both ratings). Thus, as shown here, the researcher had a

across a number of informants are entered into appropriate statistical software, such as factor analysis, cluster analysis, consensus analysis, or multidimensional scaling.

[3] Freelisting is a procedure whereby informants are asked to list as many different kinds of items in a specific domain, such as emotions. Variation across informants is compared using such analytic software as consensus analysis for a specific cultural context and can be used to compare different cultural contexts.

[4] When Ikels later used the flight-of-stairs diagram in her research on older Chinese in China, she found that a common misunderstanding was that the informant was being asked which floor they would like to live on. Three was the favorite answer, as it was high enough to avoid the dust and dirt of the street but low enough to be reachable at a time when most buildings of eight or fewer stories did not have elevators. Ikels was conducting the research while housing reform was under way and hundreds of thousands of people were being relocated to newer dwellings.

wide variety of data from which to evaluate the meaningfulness of any given respondent's answers.

Although the Cantril ladder enabled the team members to collect valid and culturally meaningful data on life satisfaction, when we approached our analytic procedures, we faced a number of challenges. In this context, we discuss the two that are most pertinent to the measurement of well-being. The first is the reduction of textual data to consistent and comparable codes across our research sites. The second is the issue of level of life satisfaction and numeric ranking and the meaning of numbers.

Data Reduction Strategies

Whether within a single population or across populations, data reduction is essential to perform statistical analyses or to test hypotheses. Yet reduction can also lead to distortion when very different cultures are subjected to the same coding scheme. This dilemma was encountered on numerous occasions by the Project AGE researchers. An early version of the codebook developed for the first phase sites (Momence, Illinois; Swarthmore, Pennsylvania; and Hong Kong) was organized around 15 dimensions with subdimensions and sub-subdimensions. Unfortunately, when we approached the questions of intercoder reliability and cross-site comparability, it became all too clear that the coding protocol was too complicated. When the data from Ireland and Botswana became available, the coding protocols were reevaluated, which resulted in the elimination of all but the four dimensions of health, wealth, sociality, and personal attributes and/or matters. Evaluating the narrative portions of the interviews proved arduous and hazardous. Are coders at different universities coding the same level of unit, or are some going phrase by phrase or sentence by sentence and assigning multiple codes while others assimilate the whole answer and assign a single code? If two people in two different sites say what appears to be the same thing – "I seldom see anyone" – do they mean the same thing objectively or subjectively? In the process of coding, an abstraction from the text of an answer to a specific question is being made by assigning themes to the textual data. Judgments are being made about the meaning in that text. To resolve the issue of reliability and comparability, all text data are organized in electronic database files with fields for codes. The team members checked one another's coding and questioned either appropriate codes or number of codes used. In an additional step, one researcher read the entire data set to check for coding consistency. Queries were returned to the original coders for response (revision or justification). Constant interaction and checking was essential to be sure that everyone was reducing and coding in comparable ways. Also, the electronic management of textual data enabled a much more sensitive interpretation of tables, because data could be readily retrieved to see what individual Herero or Hong Kong respondents were saying about health or material security when texts were coded with that theme.

Scales and the Meaning of Numbers

Given the difficulties inherent in working with open-ended narrative data, researchers understandably find working with straightforward numbers – "I'd give myself a five" – a relief. Numbers, after all, practically code themselves, but unfortunately they do not necessarily mean what they seem to say. For example, there is a strong emphasis in Chinese philosophy on the mean, or the middle way, which can be understood at the popular level as encouraging moderation in all things. If given an odd number of stairs in their diagram for the Cantril ladder, Hong Kong informants would have put themselves smack in the middle of the scale unless they were doing exceptionally well or poorly. Even when told that they could not choose 3.5 – that they had to place themselves on the third or fourth step – a substantial number of Hong Kong informants successfully resisted the researcher. Respondents in other sites avoided giving themselves a six because it seemed immodest or because they still had goals to achieve so they hadn't reached the top yet, even though in both situations they felt their lives were terrific. In Clifden, Ireland, stoicism was highly valued, so informants gave themselves high ratings despite the fact that they were clearly experiencing great hardships (and referred to them elsewhere in the interview). A discourse of "poor me" depressed self-rating for both the Ju/hoansi and the Herero. Among the Ju/hoansi low ratings were a way to elicit support from the interviewer and/or onlookers, whereas among the Herero, low ratings were a way to discourage or fend off people seeking favors or a handout. Without access to data beyond the immediate responses to the well-being scale, researchers could easily be led astray by the numbers.

The researchers' resolution of the problem was to proceed with caution. It would be nonsensical to rank order the sites in terms of their absolute well-being scores, but the scores can be used to look for internal variation within each of the sites and for patterned variation across the sites. For example, do older people in one site on average rate themselves higher or lower than other age groups? Do well-being scores vary directly with health in all sites? Do the same factors elevate older people's scores across the sites?

For example, most people's definitions of the material aspects of the good life are set early in life. When economies expand and living standards rise, older people find themselves living a much richer old age than their parents in terms of diet, health care, and consumer amenities. Yet younger people are more likely to take those features for granted and material wealth will be less likely to elevate well-being.

An additional problem with numbers on the Cantril ladder relates to analytic protocols. When a respondent points to a rung of the ladder, the stair step, or a finger, they are being asked to place themselves between the extremes of the best and worst possible life. A problem with self-anchoring is that it does not result in a true interval scale. There is no way we can be confident that all individuals who placed themselves at a 5 are nearly of the same level of life satisfaction or if those who placed themselves at a 6 or a 4 are all that different from a 5. We have discussed problems of meaning already. We do, however, have ranking, but at best it is an ordinal rank. This limits the statistical analytic procedures we can use.

CULTURAL UNDERSTANDING AND MEASURING WELL-BEING

Diversity in cultures creates barriers to understanding. This becomes particularly evident when differences are vast. However, even when culture appears to be shared, distortions occur that affect the data collection process. In contrast, distortions and differences do not deter us from understanding the underlying phenomena. In the following sections, we first examine cultural distortions in individuals' presentation of their own well-being. Second, for the domain of well-being, we outline equivalencies across cultures through which we can better comprehend diversity.

CULTURAL DISTORTIONS

Response bias is a long-standing issue in social research, including in the well-being of older people. It is widely recognized that there is a tendency of older people to say they are satisfied with conditions judged by observers to be definitely unsatisfactory (see Chapter 8 on the impact of trauma). Interpretations range from "older people like it like that" to the sweet-lemon rationalization or the basic mechanism of denial, which automatically comes into play to defend a person from anxiety and feelings of inadequacy. Because well-being is culturally constructed and evaluated, distortion is more complicated than denial.

Well-being is far more than a rating of an internal state and a cultural evaluation of a current circumstance. Well-being enters into social interaction in a variety of ways. Well-being is in many respects the socioemotional dimension of interaction. All social animals (including nonhumans) use their limbic systems to access clues as to the state of another. Are they relaxed, contented, upbeat? Or are they agitated, depressed, and possibly prone to violence? If the state is positive, interaction can proceed with little concern. If the state is negative, then supportive behavior may be called for or interaction avoided if dangerous. Affective states are an important lubricant to social life. From a U.S. perspective, individuals who present a positive sociality are more likely to be popular and to attract sustained interactions. "Toxic" individuals with negative sociality are dealt with, but with more truncated interaction and sometimes avoidance. When asked to rate well-being or to discuss life satisfaction, an individual uses his or her cultural knowledge of what it is to be a "good" person. We also know that a good deal of stage management goes on before and during social interaction. Image management involves knowledge and values about social interaction. When we ask about well-being or life satisfaction, we are asking a person to present him- or herself to the researcher.

We become aware of distortions when there is an incongruity between observable conditions and what the informant tells us of his or her circumstance. For instance, conditions are problematic, but well-being is rated overly high and the opposite. Data collectors are aware of these disconnects. But unfortunately, the notes in the margin are usually not coded and the information not retrieved. In reducing data to codes and numbers, they are reified into tables that are the object of interpretation. To illustrate the incongruities and distortions, we present portions of four life histories from Project AGE and offer interpretations of how the informants present themselves.

"Life is wretched, but I am fine"

The pattern "life is wretched, but I am fine" is the most familiar distortion pattern and the one researchers are most familiar with. In Momence, Illinois, we encountered a man who had rated his well-being quite high, but who had major health problems. In presenting himself, Eldon, at the time 78 years old, described himself as follows:

> I am a hot headed Frenchman. That is the kind of guy I am. I am not much good now, I can tell you that. My health isn't much good. You

> don't want to know what the matter with me is. I have emphysema and I have cancer, but it isn't active. I have colitis. It gives me hell sometimes. I have arthritis and I get disability in both legs. I have had hard labor. That is all I can remember – just hard work.

Indeed, his work involved stoop labor, many accidents, and long periods of ill health culminating in two industrial accidents a month apart that forced him into retirement. Yet in spite of health issues and hard, low-paying jobs, Eldon does see factors that promote his well-being:

> The most important things about my life are that I have raised three kids. They are the most important things in my life. I have eight grandchildren and two great-grandchildren. They are the most important things of my life. Without a family, if you die tomorrow, you would have nothing to leave behind. I also own my own home.

In fact, for many working-class older men in Momence, it was seeing children raised to adulthood and paying the mortgage that gave them a sense of completion and well-being – not health and prosperity. Eldon is using his cultural knowledge in outlining his life satisfaction. Health as a source for well-being became negative, but he still reports good well-being. He simply moved on and focused on other sources of well-being. Consequently, he presented himself as an interesting character who had lived long and accomplished things. Eldon is not an unfortunate being because he has health problems.

"Life is fine, but I am miserable"

Presentation of self as negative when all signs of well-being indicate positive circumstances is not the response bias that is especially common for American and European populations. Here we turn to two older Herero men in the Kalahari Desert of Botswana. The first is an "owner of his village," age 77 at the time of his interview:

> I am not very well off; I am behind everyone else in the region. I am doing poorly. Other villages have many cattle and lots of food while my village is hungry. I have no garden because there is never any rain around here. But this year I cried like a baby – there were good rains and if I had planted a garden I would be eating well. [His ethnographer noted that he is one of the most prosperous men in the area.]

Another 77-year-old Herero man also sees his life as troublesome. His ethnographer asked how his life was going on the day of the interview:

> It is quite bad. I am in very bad shape and life is not good today. All my friends and people have died and there is no one left. When one is old and ill, there is no good life to be had.

His ethnographer responded, "I see a neat well-built village, a pretty and healthy wife who takes good care of things, many children of good heart, many cattle, good water." To which the man replied:

> Yes, that is true, the recent rains have made things better for my people, and this makes me glad, but I myself am living badly and am in very bad shape.

Both of these men are well off, but because of their responsibilities for others in their respective villages, they are complaining about a drought that threatens food supply and well-being and their ability to attract and retain village members. Why were they complaining?

Complaints are social strategies to accomplish desired ends. The end may be as simple as making needs known. In contrast, in face-to-face communities and lifelong social arenas, complaints rival negative gossip as a social control mechanism. Rosenberg (2009) noted that complaint discourse among the Ju/hoansi is a way to try to control the behavior of others through embarrassment. Ethnographically, the interviews collected by Project AGE researchers are notable, with complaints directed toward individuals present during the interview (interpreters, relatives). Most common are statements about lazy children (people in their 50s) and how young people no longer respect their elders by becoming Europeanized. The Herero elders are anchoring their complaint about how poorly they are doing in the drought, but they also are making a social statement about their needs and importance. They are also trying to avoid requests for a handout by painting a negative picture of their material situation. In addition, they are making a statement about how terrible the world could be if everyone behaved badly (i.e., became Europeanized).

"Life is wretched and I am miserable"

When something is wrong and the individual lets us know, we see it as understandable and consequently do not see the response as a distortion. A 70-year-old Ju/hoansi man, in presenting the story of his life, told of hunting and working for the Herero herding cattle. He also described anger and violence that periodically would erupt and injuries that would result. Of great importance were his strength and his sexuality, with several marriages and many affairs. He concluded that for the present things are pretty bad:

> But today I am old and helpless. I am like a child newly born. I am not like a child that can take its mother's breasts and nurse. I am like a baby for which the mother takes her breast and puts it in the baby's mouth. I have no way to help myself. I look to others for help. Blankets, clothing food can come from people like you. I can't even go to the well anymore. Some days I am just thirsty because there is no water and no one has brought me water. My wife is having leg trouble and she's not able to do much. When I see you Europeans I am glad because you kind of people can help me.

His ethnographer asked, "You say that you are now glad to have this fine wife. Have you finished with chasing women?"

> No[.] I was through with that once I married her. At first I chased Herero women and Zhun/wa woman and really ran. But once with my present wife I put all that behind me. Today I am a castrated beast. Today you can hitch me up to the plough like an ox. When the European doctors fixed my hernia they took my testicles.

His ethnographer responded, "Nonsense! They don't take testicles when they do hernia operations. You must be teasing":

> I am not teasing. No you don't understand. I still have testicles. But when you sleep with a woman her buttocks are pushing against your abdomen. Since then I am afraid to sleep with my wife because I am afraid I will tear open the old incision. I can't ride a donkey, I can't ride a horse. Don't pick up anything heavy, don't walk around a lot. If you pick up anything heavy your guts will come back out like before. They said when winter comes and it is cold, the operation will be mostly healed. But in fact I don't feel like it is better.
>
> Think about an old bull, aged almost dead. His testicles hang down and are shriveled up. He puts his nose up the backside of a cow and sniffs. Haven't you seen this? He just puts his nose at her backside and doesn't do anything else.

The ethnographer asked, "Are you like this?" To which the informant and all listening break into laughter. Was he lamenting the loss of his strength and sexuality and really feeling miserable? The hyperbole involved in his statement suggests that, by putting himself in such a bad light, he was making a joke. But the joke also reminds his audience of how bad his life (and theirs) could really become.

"Life is fine and I am fine"

A 77-year-old Herero man, in discussing his life, told of the death of his father and the confidence of his father in him as he died:

> When my father died, I was playing in the bush. People called me and brought me to my father. He held my wrist as he lay there with his head in my mother's lap. He said to my mother[,] "My child is of the Omukuenambura matrilineage." My father told my mother, "You are my wife, take care of this child of mine and do not give him away. Ask food from our relatives but do not send this child out to other villages." He was still holding my wrist. "As I look at this child, I see that he will be able to do anything. Let him build his own house and his own village and live there." Then his hand fell from my arm, my mother was crying. I shivered, my heart raced, I wondered why people were crying. My father was dead. He died on a Friday, December 10, and he was buried the following Saturday between the calf corral and the cattle corral in our village.

From that point, he talked about how he achieved adult status through marriages, establishing a village and attracting relatives and managing his herd of cattle. By way of conclusion:

> These were my works that I have told you. When my father died, I had only four cows. I did many things. I became very rich; my father gave me a good *oruzo.*

In the cases of positive well-being and positive presentation of self, there is little reason to question distortions. In the preceding examples and many more, ethnographic knowledge helps in the interpretation of evaluation of life satisfaction and what informants are trying to accomplish as they present themselves and their evaluation.

CULTURAL EQUIVALENCIES

Despite the enormous differences found in lifestyle, values, language, and social organization around the world and among the sites in Project AGE, well-being or satisfaction with one's life is nevertheless anchored in a limited set of major domains (and subdomains). This finding has been demonstrated in Britain (Bowling & Gabriel 2007; Bowling et al., 2003) and in

Thailand (Grey, Rukumnuaykit, Kittisuksathit, & Thongthai, 2008) as well as in Cantril (1965) and Project AGE. Based on ethnographic eliciting of the meaning of well-being in Project AGE (Fry et al., 1997), the domains are as follows:

1. *Health and body status:* Every society has a body of knowledge about the way the human body works and how it must function to accomplish the everyday tasks of living.
2. *Material security:* Collective knowledge offers protection from environmental insults. Generally, this domain includes such things as subsistence, work, shelter, and wealth. The first two domains are undoubtedly the major domains affecting well-being.
3. *Social issues:* Human cultures are noted for interdependency among individuals, which shape expectations about the nature of relationships.
4. *Ideas about personhood:* Culture, in addition to providing a design for living, also supplies a blueprint of what it means to be a good citizen and human being. This includes a wide spectrum of ideas about coping styles, personal strengths, and personal qualities.

Although the domains have been isolated on the basis of qualitative work, they are by no means absent from the psychometric scales and the majority of work on subjective well-being and life satisfaction (see Chapter 9) As domains, they are found across cultures. It is within domains that we find differences. For instance, when we examine what the Ju/hoansi and Herero tell us about their life satisfaction, it is difficult to separate material security from health and body states. Nearly all Ju/hoansi informants discuss hunger (rumbling stomachs) and poor health. These are obviously linked when one procures or produces food directly from the environment. In contrast, our U.S. informants saw material issues such as financial security, as money enables purchases of food and services from markets. Health is quite separate, as health providers constitute another market. Social issues reveal underlying differences. Herero children contribute to material security in that they work for their parents. Many Herero informants indicated that the ability to command children was a reason for their life satisfaction. In the United States, parents saw the maturation of their children and the empty nest as a combined benefit of reduced responsibility and the joy of seeing them find their ways in the world. Equivalencies such as the four domains of well-being enable us to see the reasons for differences in meaning within diverse local cultures or communities.

CONCLUSION

Although well-being of older adults is well charted, very little is known about the well-being of the oldest old, with the exception of the chapters in this volume and a handful of other studies. As the predictable sources of well-being and satisfaction with one's current life become more restricted, what qualities of life are activated and possibly invented to move on and continue living comfortably? Certainly, among the oldest old, bodies become increasingly frail and senses compromised. Resources accumulated earlier in life become more restricted (see Chapters 9 and 18). Social worlds shrink, and environments become more circumscribed (see Chapter 12). In a study of individuals older than 85 in San Francisco, Johnson and Barer (1997) used a combination of psychometric and ethnographic methods. The participants in the study were followed for 6 years with five points of measurement. When administered the Bradburn Affect Balance Scale, the individuals talked around the forced-choice format to explain their responses and how they avoided negative issues. The respondents redefined their ideas of self, detached themselves from aggravating issues, and lived almost exclusively in the present. Ethnographically, we need to explore the worlds of the oldest old to further understand continuities in the sources of satisfaction as well as emergent resources in extreme old age. Because well-being is culturally mediated and self-generated, we will not find one answer. Heterogeneity and diversity are to be expected when investigating the worlds of people who have lived to become the oldest old.

REFERENCES

Basabe, N., Paez, D., Valencia, J., Gonzalez, J. L., Rime, B., & Diener, E. (2002). Cultural dimensions, socioeconomic development, climate, and emotional hedonic level. *Cognition and Emotion, 16*, 103–125.

Biswas-Diener, R., Diener, E., & Tamir, M. (2004). The psychology of subjective well-being. *Daedalus, 133*, 18–25.

Bowling, A., & Gabriel, Z. (2007). Lay theories of quality of life in older age. *Aging and Society, 27*, 827–848.

Bowling, A., Gabriel, Z., Dykes, J., Marriott-Dowdling, L., Evans, L., Fliessig, A., et al. (2003). Let's ask them: a national survey of definitions of quality of life and its enhancement among people aged 65 and over. *International Journal of Aging and Human Development, 56*, 269–306.

Bradburn, N. M. (1969). *The structure of psychological wellbeing.* Chicago: Aldine.

Campbell, A., Converse, P. E., & Rodgers, W. L. (1976). *The quality of American life: Perceptions, evaluations and satisfactions.* New York: Russell Sage Foundation.

Cantril, H. (1965). *The pattern of human concerns.* New Brunswick, NJ: Rutgers University Press.

D'Andrade, R. (1995). *The development of cognitive anthropology*. Cambridge: Cambridge University Press.

De Munck, V. C., & Sobo, E. J. (Eds.). (1998). *Using methods in the field: A practical introduction and casebook*. Walnut Creek, CA: Altamira Press.

Diener, E., & Suh, E. M. (Eds.). (2000). *Culture and subjective well-being*. Cambridge: Massachusetts Institute of Technology Press.

Diener, E., & Tov, W. (2007). Culture and subjective well-being. In S. Kitayama & D. Cohen (Eds.), *Handbook of cultural psychology* (pp. 691–713). New York: Guilford Press.

Draper, P. (2007). Conducting cross-cultural research in teams and the search for the "culture proof" variable. *Menopause*, *14*, 680–687.

Fry, C. L., Dickerson-Putman, J., Draper, P., Ikels, C., Keith, J., Glascock, P., & Harpending, H. C. (1997). Culture and the meaning of a good old age. In J. Sokolovsky (Ed.), *The cultural context of aging: Worldwide perspectives* (pp. 99–124). Westport, CT: Bergin and Garvey.

Grey, R. S., Rukumnuaykit, P., Kittisuksathit, S., & Thongthai, V. (2008). Inner happiness among Thai elderly. *Journal of Cross-Cultural Gerontology*, *23*, 211–224.

Harman, R. C. (1998). Triad questionnaires: Old age in Karen and Maya cultures. In V. C. De Munck & E. J. Sobo (Eds.), *Using methods in the field: A practical introduction and casebook* (pp. 121–138). Walnut Creek, CA: Altamira Press.

Johnson, C. L., & Barer, B. M. (1997). *Life beyond 85 years: The aura of survivorship*. New York: Springer.

Keith, J., Fry, C. L., Glascock, A. P., Ikels, C., Dickerson-Putman, J., Harpending, H. C. et al. (1994). *The aging experience: Diversity and commonality across cultures*. Thousand Oaks, CA: Sage.

Lawton, M. P. (1975). The Philadelphia Geriatric Center Morale Scale: A revision. *Journal of Gerontology*, *30*, 85–89.

Neugarten, B. L., Havighurst, R. J., & Tobin, S. S. (1961). The measurement of life satisfaction. *Journal of Gerontology*, *16*, 134–143.

Nydegger, C. N. (Ed.). (1977). *Measuring morale: A guide to effective assessment*. Washington, DC: Gerontological Society.

Oishi, S., Diener, E., Lucas, R. E., & Suh, E. (1999). Cross-cultural variations in predictors of life satisfaction: Perspectives from needs and values. *Personality and Social Psychology Bulletin*, *25*, 980–990.

Rosenberg, H. G. (2009). Complaint discourse: Aging and caregiving among the Ju/hoansi of Botswana. In J. Sokolovsky (Ed.), *The cultural context of aging: Worldwide perspectives* (pp. 30–52). Westport, CT: Praeger.

Schrauf, R. W., & Sanchez, J. (2008). Using freelisting to identify, assess, and characterize age differences in shared cultural dimensions. *Journal of Gerontology Social Sciences*, *63B*, S385–S392.

Torres, S. (1999). A culturally relevant theoretical framework for the study of successful aging. *Aging and Society*, *19*, 33–51.

16

The Will to Live as an Indicator of Well-Being and Predictor of Survival in Old Age

SARA CARMEL

ABSTRACT

The will to live (WTL) is presented in this chapter as an important indicator of general well-being due to its diagnostic and prognostic value. Conceptually, the WTL is defined as the psychological expression of a natural instinct of human beings – the striving for life, which is comprised of rational and irrational components, and can be self-assessed. The WTL can be measured by a single item or by four- and five-item scales. All three tools showed good psychometric characteristics and generated similar results in four large-scale studies of elderly Israelis, two of which used a longitudinal design. The WTL was also a powerful predictor of long-term survival among old women.

Conceptually, considering that the WTL not only expresses a state of general well-being, but also one's commitment to life and the desire to continue living, it is a unique and valuable indicator of well-being. Empirical findings lend support to its special features. Practically, the tools for evaluating the WTL are parsimonious, easy to use, and well accepted by older people. All of these lead us to recommend using the WTL for diagnostic and prognostic purposes.

INTRODUCTION

The will to live (WTL) is perceived as the psychological expression of the basic, natural, and built-in instinct of every living creature – the striving for life. This existential concept has been addressed in philosophy, poetry, and prose, but until recently it has not attracted much attention in the behavioral sciences. Although some scholars have used related terms such as *morale* and *disengagement*, to the best of our knowledge, until the 1990s, only one study focused directly on the will to live (Ellison, 1969). The purpose of this chapter is to present the concept of WTL, to suggest measures for evaluating it, and to provide a summary of the current knowledge regarding this construct.

What Is the WTL?

The natural instinct to continue living can be viewed in three ways: as a vital need, as a drive, and as the ultimate aspiration of living creatures. Among human beings, the WTL is the psychological expression of this natural instinct. As such, it is a psychobiological phenomenon combining irrational and rational components (Carmel, 2001). The irrational component is "a fundamental manifestation of instinct that takes precedence over any thought," whereas the other component is an outcome of a thinking process (Beadle et al., 2004, p. 34). These components were described by Selye (1976) on the physiological level as a spontaneous, generalized reaction of the organism when confronted by a threat to life. On the cognitive level, a person who testifies to having a strong WTL actually expresses a sense of well-being and his or her commitment to life, as well as a desire to continue living (Carmel, 2001). It has been further suggested that people are aware of the strength of the irrational component in their WTL and include it in the cognitive assessment of their will to live. Thus, the intensity of WTL can be self-assessed, on the basis of a combination of one's self-evaluation of the strength of the irrational component and one's perception of the quality and meaningfulness of life – the rational component.

As humans are social creatures, the rational component of WTL is shaped and influenced by a person's social environments (including cultural and religious values and beliefs) and unique life experiences. The existential needs of societies throughout history led most of them to strengthen their members' natural drive to preserve their lives by internalizing the importance and sacredness of life, to the degree that losing the will to live is perceived as a pathological symptom demanding treatment. There are, however, exceptions in which the WTL is significantly weakened and people become either indifferent or wish to end their lives. This can happen as a result of personal causes or social indoctrination. For example, people may lose interest in life because of physical and/or mental suffering combined with a lack of hope for improvement, as occurs in severe and terminal health conditions or in chronic or temporary mental pathologies, including diseases, anxieties, and depression. In other cases, cultural and religious beliefs and ideologies influence people to disregard and overcome their natural instincts and purposely end their lives. This kind of outcome can be seen in mass suicides conducted by certain cults or in the current phenomenon of suicide bombers.

Irrational and Rational Components of the WTL: Empirical Support

The WTL is thus shaped and influenced by nature as well as by physical and sociocultural factors. As such, it is expected to vary among people, given the variability in both dimensions. Support for this perception of the WTL can be found in some empirical findings. In a multivariate analysis, the WTL was found to be an important predictor of elderly persons' wishes for the use of life-sustaining treatments in severe and terminal health conditions. For the same hypothetical severe-illness conditions, people with a stronger will to live were more likely to prefer receiving life-sustaining treatments than people with a weaker will to live (Carmel & Mutran, 1997). These findings are indicative of the natural and often irrationally strong instinct to continue living under any condition, an instinct that people are aware of and able to assess.

The hypothesis that the WTL is a product of people's cognitive rational evaluations of the quality and meaningfulness of life, as based on their set of values, religious or other existential beliefs, and unique life experiences, was supported by comparative analyses of different social groups. For example, in an Israeli national sample of people aged 70 and older, the WTL of elderly new immigrants from the former Soviet Union was significantly weaker than that of their Israeli counterparts (3.83, $SD = 0.98$ vs. 4.09, $SD = 0.99$, $t = -3.98$, $p = 0.001$). The new immigrants also scored lower than their counterparts on activities of daily living (ADL), self-rated health, number and severity of chronic diseases, social support, self-esteem, and satisfaction with life (Carmel & Lazar, 1998). Similarly, in the same study, women scored significantly lower than men on WTL, as well as on ADL, self-rated health, self-esteem, and satisfaction with life (Carmel & Bernstein, 2003). These findings indicate that the WTL is weaker in groups that evaluate their quality of life as less satisfying. Results of longitudinal studies also show that the WTL weakens with aging (Studies 1 and 3 in Table 16.1). Moreover, the WTL is explained by multiple variables and is differently shaped in different social groups, as exemplified in results of a multivariate analysis conducted on the same data. Women's WTL was mainly explained by psychological indicators of well-being, including self-esteem, satisfaction with life, and fear of death, whereas in men it was explained by living with a partner and physical indicators of health, including age, somatic symptoms, and

TABLE 16.1. *Psychometric characteristics of the will to live in four studies of Israeli elderly people*

Factor analysis	Median	Mean (SD)	Cronbach's alpha	Scale	Type of scale	Research design	Studies
	4.00 4.00	4.15 (0.99) (in 1994) 3.96* (1.05) (in 1996)		0–5	Single item	Longitudinal, 1994, 1995, 1996 (3 stages)	1. Random sample of 1,138 elderly aged 70+[a]
1 factor (PCA)	3.75	3.50 (1.01)	0.85	0–5	4-item scale	Cross-sectional, 2006	2. National random sample of 1,255 elderly aged 65+[b]
1 factor (PCA)	3.75 3.75	3.75 (0.80) 3.69* (0.76)	0.89 (in 2005) 0.85 (in 2006)	0–5	5-item scale	Longitudinal, 2005, 2006 (2 stages)	3. Sample of convenience of 262 elderly aged 75+[c]
1 factor (PCA)	3.80	3.81 (0.69)	0.82	0–5	5-item scale	Cross-sectional, 2007	4. Random sample of 861 drivers aged 70+[d]

Note: PCA = principal component analysis.
[a]Carmel (2001). [b]Carmel, Iecovich, & Sherf (2007), unpublished results. [c]Carmel & Tovel (2008), unpublished results. [d]Carmel (2008), unpublished results.
*$p < .05$.

number of chronic diseases. However, in both genders, it was explained by multiple indicators of quality of life (Carmel, 2001).

Associations between the WTL and various indicators of quality of life and perceived well-being were also reported in a study of retired steelworkers, which showed that a weak WTL was associated with poor health, loss of function, and social isolation (Ellison, 1969). In studies of patients with advanced cancer, significant correlations were found between the WTL and physical symptoms, anxiety, and a sense of well-being (Beadle et al., 2004; Chochinov, Tataryn, Clinch, & Dugeon, 1999). The relative importance of each of these factors in explaining patients' WTL varied according to different stages of the terminal disease. This indicates that the WTL is not just an expression of depression or explained by only one variable but rather a generalized phenomenon, explained by various physical and psychological factors, the importance of which in influencing the WTL varies with the physical changes that occur in the different stages of a severe disease and their psychosocial implications. Furthermore, in a more recent study conducted on patients with end-stage cancer, Chochinov et al. (2005) showed that existential variables, such as a sense of hopelessness, feelings of becoming a burden to others, and being subject to violation of dignity, were the most important factors in explaining the WTL.

These conclusions were further supported by the unpublished results of data from three recent studies conducted on different samples of elderly persons aged 65 and older, 70 and older, and 75 and older (Carmel, 2008; Carmel, Iecovich, & Sherf, 2007; Carmel & Tovel, 2008). In two of these studies, the association between the WTL and depression (measured by GDS-15 – Sheikh & Yesavage, 1986; Zalsman, Aizenberg, & Sigler, 1998) was assessed. The results in both studies (−0.45 and −0.56 Pearson correlation coefficients) indicated that, although a strong and statistically significant linear correlation exists between both measures, they do not measure the same phenomenon. In addition, significant, high-to-moderate Pearson correlation coefficients were found in all three studies between the WTL and indicators of well-being such as satisfaction with life (from .41 to .53), happiness (from .40 to .58), self-rated health (from .32 to .43), and ADL (from −.25 to −.47). All these findings systematically support the perception of the WTL as a concept encompassing both a basic instinctual drive to continue living and a calculated outcome of one's subjective evaluation of the quality, meaningfulness, and worthiness of life.

Self-Awareness of the WTL

The young and the healthy take the WTL for granted. It is not an issue occupying their thoughts. However, it becomes a matter actively contemplated when people face their approaching death and/or when life turns into a burden too heavy to bear. When experiencing terminal disease and/or a significant decline in physical or mental functioning, as well as other significant difficulties, such as overload of demands in the context of diminishing resources and feelings of helplessness, people start questioning whether life is worth living and become aware of their WTL. Frankl (1972) addressed the importance of the WTL when trying to understand survival under the harsh conditions of the Nazi concentration camps. He argued that prisoners who found some meaning and purpose in their lives had higher chances of survival than others because of their psychological commitment to continue living.

Regarding old age, both Butler (1963), in his description of the life-review process, and Erickson (1968), in presenting the eighth stage of his developmental theory, argue that elderly people's increased awareness of their approaching death initiates new psychological processes. We further suggest that the closeness of death and such psychological processes enhance old people's self-awareness and understanding of their will to live. Taking this into consideration, and the fact that, for many elderly persons, life becomes more and more difficult to live because of accumulated losses in all areas of life, we hypothesized that the motivation to struggle for life weakens with age and that older persons become increasingly aware of this. Our findings in the cross-sectional and longitudinal studies (Table 16.1) repeatedly support this hypothesis by showing that the WTL weakens with age. Recent publications about the high and increasing rates of suicide among older Americans, especially men, also indicate that more and more older persons commit suicide with no sign of mental illness such as major depression (Brody, *New York Times*, 2007), probably because they find life not worth living (Conwell, Duberstein, & Caine, 2002).

MEASURING THE WTL

A Single-Item Measure

In a previous study, the WTL was measured by the single item, "If you could describe your will to live, on a scale of 0 to 5, would you say that it is: 5 = very strong, 4 = strong, 3 = intermediate, 2 = weak, 1 = very weak, 0 = no will to live," and validated in a sample of 1,138 elderly Israelis. Analyses using this tool showed statistically significant, positive associations between the WTL and a number of indicators of well-being (Carmel, 1995, 2001; Carmel, Baron-Epel, & Shemi, 2007; Carmel & Mutran, 1997). For example, Pearson correlation coefficients were .34 with self-esteem, .23 with control over life, .34 with life satisfaction, .15 with mood, .23 with self-rated health, .24 with ADL, .16 with economic status, and –.10 with year of immigration (Carmel, 1995). The statistically significant explanatory variables of the WTL, in order of importance, were self-esteem, life satisfaction, having a partner, age, mood, and warm social relations (Carmel, 1995). In a multivariate analysis, the WTL was found to be an important explanatory factor of preferences for the prolongation of life in hypothetical severe illness conditions when controlled for age, gender, religiosity, health and functioning, social support, fear of death, and fear of dying (Carmel & Mutran, 1997). Furthermore, it was a powerful predictor of long-term survival, especially among women, when controlled for age, ADL, self-rated health, self-esteem, and working outside the home or volunteering (Carmel et al., 2007).

Four- and Five-Item Tools

Since 2006, a four-item scale and a five-item scale have been developed and used in three new studies of elderly Israelis (Table 16.1). Similar to the single-item measure, both scales comprise direct questions regarding the strength of the will to live, unlike the seven-item scale developed by Ellison (1969). Psychometric characteristics of the scales were found to be similarly good in all three studies: both scales were found to load on one factor, and the internal reliability was relatively high, with Cronbach's alpha values ranging from .82 to .89.

Preliminary analyses of the recent three studies showed similar outcomes to those found when only one item was used. In cross-sectional and longitudinal studies, statistically significant negative correlations were found between age and the WTL, thus indicating that the WTL weakens with age. Women consistently ranked their WTL lower than men, and in a longitudinal analysis conducted on the same persons with a 1-year interval, the WTL significantly declined over time for both genders. Cultural differences were also expressed in differences in the WTL found between religious and nonreligious groups, and among groups of different ethnic origins. Religious persons ranked their WTL significantly higher than did nonreligious, and Israeli-born and veteran immigrants reported a stronger will to live than did new immigrants from the former Soviet Union.

SUMMARY AND CONCLUSION

Previous studies (using a single-item scale) have shown that the will to live has diagnostic and prognostic value. Its value as a diagnostic tool of general well-being was shown by its statistically strong positive correlations with often-used indicators of well-being, such as self-esteem, happiness, satisfaction with life, self-rated health, and physical functioning. The WTL is, however, a unique indicator of well-being; in addition to being an expression of a general sense of well-being, it also conveys one's commitment to life and desire to continue living, as demonstrated in its power to predict preferences for the prolongation of life in hypothetical terminal illness conditions. The prognostic value of the WTL was presented by its power in predicting survival among elderly women for a period of 7.5 years while controlling for other good predictors of survival, such as age, self-rated health, and physical and social status (Carmel et al., 2007). Replications conducted in three recent studies on different samples of elderly persons (using four- and five-item scales) support previous findings about the WTL being an indicator of older persons' well-being.

The special features of the construct of the WTL; the accumulated repeated empirical findings; and the simple, easy-to-use tools for evaluating it – which are well accepted by elderly persons – lead us to suggest viewing the will to live as an important indicator of elderly persons' well-being. Furthermore, we recommend using the WTL as a tool for diagnostic and prognostic purposes, as well as for evaluating psychosocial interventions.

REFERENCES

Beadle, G. F., Yates, P. M., Najman, J. M., Clavarino, A., Thomson, D., Williams, G., et al. (2004). Illusions in advanced cancer: The effect of belief systems and attitudes on quality of life. *Psychological Oncology*, *13*, 26–36.

Brody, J. E. (2007). *A common casualty of old age: The will to live.* The New York Times (Nov. 2007). http://query.nytimes.com/gst/fullpage.html.

Butler, R. N. (1963). The life review: An interpretation of reminiscence in the aged. *Psychiatry*, *26*, 65–76.

Carmel, S. (1995). *Concerns, attitudes and wishes about the use of life-sustaining treatments among elderly persons in Israel.* Comprehensive Science Report, U.S.A. – Israel Binational Science Foundation (BSF), Jerusalem, Israel.

Carmel, S. (2001). The will to live: Gender differences among elderly persons. *Social Science and Medicine*, *52*, 949–958.

Carmel., S. (2008). *Driving-related adaptation patterns among elderly drivers in Israel: Description, antecedents and well-being outcomes.* Final Science Report, Ran Naor Foundation for the Advancement of Road Safety Research, Ramat Hasharon, Israel.

Carmel, S., Baron-Epel, O., & Shemi, G. (2007). The will to live and survival at old age: Gender differences. *Social Science and Medicine, 65*, 518–523.

Carmel, S., & Bernstein, J. (2003). Gender differences in physical health and psychosocial well-being among four age groups of elderly people in Israel. *International Journal of Aging and Human Development, 56*, 113–131.

Carmel, S., Iecovich, E., & Sherf, M. (2007). *Reality and desires in respect to provision of health care services to various groups of elderly persons by age, sick fund, geographical region, ethnicity, and socioeconomic status.* Final Science Report, Israel National Institute for Health Policy and Health Services Research, Tel Hashomer, Israel.

Carmel, S., & Lazar, A. (1998). Health and well-being among elderly persons: The role of social class and immigration status. *Ethnicity and Health, 3*, 31–43.

Carmel, S., & Mutran, E. (1997). Wishes regarding the use of life-sustaining treatments among elderly persons in Israel: An explanatory model. *Social Science and Medicine, 45*, 1715–1727.

Carmel, S., & Tovel, H. (2008). Determinants of successful aging. Unpublished results.

Chochinov, H. M., Hack, T., Hassard, T., Kristjanson, L. J., McClement, S., & Harlos, M. (2005). Understanding the will to live in patients nearing death. *Psychosomatics, 46*, 7–10.

Chochinov, H. M., Tataryn, D., Clinch, J. J., & Dugeon, D. (1999). Will to live in the terminally ill. *Lancet, 354*, 816–819.

Conwell, Y., Duberstein, P. R., & Caine, E. D. (2002). Risk factors for suicide in later life. *Biological Psychiatry, 52*, 193–204.

Ellison, D. L. (1969). Alienation and the will to live. *Journal of Gerontology, 24*, 361–367.

Erikson, E. (1968). *Identity: Youth and crisis.* Canada: North and Company.

Frankl, V. E. (1972). *Man's search for meaning.* New York: Washington Square Press.

Selye, H. (1976). *The stress of life.* New York: McGraw Hill.

Sheikh, J. I., & Yesavage, J. A. (1986). Geriatric Depression Scale (GDS): Recent evidence and development of a shorter version. In Brink, T.L.(ed.), *Clinical gerontology: A guide to assessment and intervention* (pp. 165–173). New York: Haworth Press.

Zalsman, G., Aizenberg, D., & Sigler, M. (1998). Geriatric Depression Scale Short Form: Validity and reliability of the Hebrew version. *Clinical Gerontologist, 18*, 3b–9b.

17

The Measurement of Life Satisfaction and Happiness in Old-Old Age

ALEX J. BISHOP AND PETER MARTIN

ABSTRACT

Happiness and satisfaction with life has emerged as a renewed topic of interest among gerontological investigators. However, the conceptualization of life satisfaction and happiness in advanced later life can present challenges relative to selection of proper measurement instrumentation. This chapter addresses the conceptualization and measurement of life satisfaction and happiness in very old age in three key ways. First, the conceptualization of subjective well-being is addressed in reference to the oldest old. Second, psychometric properties pertaining to past and current use of classical (e.g., Life Satisfaction Index-A), second-generation (e.g., Satisfaction with Life Scale), and domain-specific (e.g., Retirement Satisfaction Index) measures of subjective well-being within old and very old populations is addressed. Third, future directions for the advancement of measurement of subjective well-being in old-old populations are highlighted.

INTRODUCTION

In Chapter 3, Shmotkin referred to subjective well-being as a "dynamic and flexible agent of adaptation" in old-old age. Gerontologists have a long history of developing quantitative instruments to assess feelings of satisfaction and the pursuit of happiness in later life (Ferraro & Schafer, 2008). Yet reliable and valid psychometric tools to evaluate subjective well-being among exceptionally old adults can be difficult to find. As Fry and Ikels highlighted in Chapter 15, the well-being construct is conceptually sound but often too complex to operationalize. This is a possible explanation for why quantitative assessments of subjective well-being have yielded mixed results. Some investigators have reported a decline in life satisfaction after age 65, with substantial losses occurring in old-old age (Mroczek & Spiro, 2005), whereas others have acknowledged that happiness remains moderately stable across time (Diener, Suh, Lucas, & Scollon, 2006; Diener, Suh, Lucas, & Smith, 1999; Lucas, 2008). In effect, subjective well-being represents a paradox in aging.

Ambiguous evidence supports what Cohen-Mansfield described as the shifting baseline of well-being in Chapter 4. This is commonly referred to as the stability-despite-loss phenomenon in gerontological literature (Mroczek & Kolarz, 1998). In other words, most old-old adults express great contentment and appreciation with life despite being challenged by biopsychosocial limitations (e.g., poor health, cognitive impairment, diminished social opportunity; Yang, 2008). Variation of decline in exceptional longevity may be so great that commonly used standardized quantitative measurements of well-being may become relatively ineffective (Poon et al., 2007). Thus, gerontologists investigating subjective well-being must remain cautious but strategic in the selection of developmentally appropriate instrumentation.

Fry and Ikels covered cultural aspects in the measurement of well-being in Chapter 15, as well as the relative contribution of qualitative assessment in well-being research. As a companion piece, the purpose of this chapter is to summarize quantitative measures of subjective well-being. We first address the conceptualization of subjective well-being. Then, we examine classical or first-generation measures, identify contemporary or second-generation instruments, and address domain-specific scales. Finally, we discuss future directions for subjective well-being measurement of the oldest old.

CONCEPTUALIZING SUBJECTIVE WELL-BEING

Subjective well-being has been defined as a cognitive orientation of life based on positive and negative emotions, domain satisfactions, and global judgments of life satisfaction and happiness (Diener, Suh, Lucas, & Smith, 1999; Eid & Larsen, 2008). Cognitive-affective processes are salient components of perceived quality of life in exceptional old age. For instance, many old-old adults appraise distal life achievements and current ambitions relative to basic resources (e.g., food, shelter, economic security; Jopp & Rott, 2006; Yang, 2008). Negative circumstances (e.g., poor health status) can compromise resources above and beyond pleasant memories and positive happenings (Larsen & Prizmic, 2008). Yet late adulthood is often reported to be one of the happiness developmental periods of life (Mehlsen, Platz, & Fromholt, 2003). Aberg, et al. (2005) acknowledged that old-old individuals frequently engage in the cognitive review and recall of past pleasantries in life. Such behavior is believed to bolster emotional satisfaction and contentment with present life conditions (Aberg et al., 2005). This is one plausible explanation that persons aged 70 and older tend to report greater happiness and positive well-being than younger age groups (Berg, Hassing, McClearn, & Johansson, 2006). In effect, adaptive behaviors appear to regulate the ebb and flow of emotions, which evolve into judgments of life satisfaction during extreme old age.

Some investigators have also highlighted the relevance of time in shaping perceptions of well-being (Hoyt & Creech, 1983; Pavot, Diener, & Suh, 1998). Temporality is a definitive characteristic of subjective well-being involving a comparative assessment of past, present, and anticipated future events (Pavot et al., 1998). Exceptionally old persons often perceive their time as limited (Lang & Carstensen, 2002). Some may have found fulfillment many years ago but feel that there is nothing left to accomplish in very late life. In turn, an expression of discontentment with life may persist. Other persons may have experienced numerous hardships, failures, traumas, or losses earlier in life, yet remain presently happy with life in extreme old age. Therefore, the age and developmental period during which persons encounter life events as well as the meaning and value assigned to such experiences can alter feelings of happiness (Diener et al., 2006; Krause, 2007a, 2009. Thus, it is not enough to assess whether old-old adults are happy or unhappy. Rather, it is essential that quantitative evaluations of life satisfaction also account for the occurrence of distal and proximal experiences which compromise or improve feelings of happiness (Diener et al., 2006). In other words, life satisfaction is a cumulative and developmental process.

Relative to advanced old age, subjective well-being may be indicative of gerotranscendence. Joan Erikson (1997) equated gerotranscendence as the ninth stage of psychosocial development. During this developmental period, exceptionally old persons may experience significant physical and mental decline followed by a significant loss in autonomy, increased dependence on others, and increased feelings of despair. However, Tornstam (2005) theorized that persons in exceptional old age typically remain emotionally connected to humanity, retain an affinity for the past, seek redefinition of self in space and time, prefer solitary or meditative moments, and lack concern for material possessions. This suggests that evaluation of subjective well-being requires sophisticated measurement instrumentation to capture transcendent dimensions of living an exceptionally long life. There has been a progression of attempts made by investigators to enhance quantitative assessment of life satisfaction and happiness in late and very late life. Such efforts can be classified into three main categories, including early or first-generation measures, contemporary or second-generation assessments, and domain-specific evaluations.

FIRST-GENERATION MEASURES

No other measures have had greater impact on the quantitative assessment of subjective well-being in late adulthood than the Life Satisfaction Index-A (Neugarten et al., 1961), the Affect Balance Scale (Bradburn, 1969), and the Philadelphia Geriatric Morale Scale (Ferraro & Schaefer, 2008; Lawton, 1975). These classical scales were devised as multidimensional assessments of subjective well-being. In the process, these first-generation measures have emerged as the most widely used quantitative instruments cited in aging research (Ferraro & Schafer, 2008). As Fry and Ikels emphasized in Chapter 15, several of these measures have persisted in gerontological research for more than 50 years because they represent some of the most "powerful instruments" and "do what scales do ." In essence, they remain the standard by which most contemporary psychometric measures of subjective well-being must achieve.

Life Satisfaction Index-A

The Life Satisfaction Index-A (LSI-A) (Neugarten, Havighurst, & Tobin, 1961) is often recognized as the gold standard in the measurement of life satisfaction among older adults (Ferraro & Schaefer, 2008; Pavot & Diener 2008). The LSI-A is a 21-item scale used to measure five factors: (a) zest (e.g., degree of engagement in activities with other people), (b) resolution (e.g., extent to which persons take responsibility for their own lives), (c) congruence (e.g., the degree to which desired life goals are accomplished), (d) self-concept (e.g., concept of self physically, psychologically, and socially), and (e) mood tone (e.g., feelings of happiness). Respondents are asked to rate their level of agreement on a three-point Likert scale (–1 = disagree, 0 = uncertain, and 1 = agree). Neugarten et al. (1961) reported interitem correlations ranging from .57 to .84. Original reliability of the LSI-A was also reported to be strong at .78 (Neugarten et al., 1961).

In more recent studies, the LSI-A has evinced strong test-retest reliability in culturally diverse samples. For example, Chou and Chi (1999) investigated determinants of life satisfaction among 544 Hong Kong Chinese elders and reported test-retest reliability to be .81 at baseline and .84 during a 3-year

TABLE 17.1. *Summary of original psychometric properties of subjective well-being measures*

Measure	Item response			Reliability		
	Scale	Scoring	Rating	Interitem	Alpha	Test-retest
First generation						
LSI-A (Neugarten et al., 1961)	21 items	3 point	–1 = disagree; 1 = agree 1 = agree	r = .57 to .84	.78	–
BABS (Bradburn, 1969)	10 items	Dichotomous	0 = no; 1 = yes	r = −.43 to .30	.76	–
Positive affect	5 item			r = .23 to .74.	.83	.86 to .96
Negative affect	5 items			r = .40 to .71	.81	.90 to .97
PGMS-R (Lawton, 1975)	17 items	Dichotomous	0 = no; 1 = yes	–	–	–
Agitation	6 items			–	.85	–
Attitude	5 items	–	–		.81	
Lonely-dissatisfaction	6 items			–	.85	–
Second generation						
SWLS (Diener et al., 1985)[a]	5 items	7 point	1 = strongly disagree; 7 = strongly agree	r = .61 to .81	–	.82 to .87
SHS (Lyubomirsky & Lepper, 1999)[b]	4 items	7 point	1 = not at all; 7 = a great deal		.86	.55 to .90
PANAS (Watson et al., 1988)	20 items	5 point	1 = very slightly 5 = extremely	r = −.12 to −.23	–	–
Positive Affect	10 items			–	.86 to .90	.47 to .68
Negative Affect	10 items			–	.84 to .87	.39 to .71

Ryff PWB Scales (Ryff, 1989a)	120 items	6 point	1 = strongly disagree;	–	–	–
			6 = strongly agree	–	–	–
Self-acceptance	20 items			–	.93	.85
Positive relations	20 items			–	.91	.83
Autonomy	20 items			–	.86	.88
Environmental mastery	20 items			–	.90	.81
Purpose in life	20 items			–	.90	.82
Personal growth	20 items			–	.87	.81
Domain-specific						
Retirement						
RDI (Smith et al., 1969)	63 items	Dichotomous	0 = no; 1 = yes	r = .19 to .43	–	–
RSI (Floyd et al., 1992)	51 items	4 point	1 = unimportant;	r = .45 to .71	.81	.56 to .77
			4 = important			–
		6 point	1 = very ungratifying;			–
			6 = very gratifying			–
WCI (Karasek & Theorell, 1990)	8 items	5 point	1 = strongly agree;	r = .37 to .62	.64 to .85	–
			5 = strongly disagree			
Housing						
HOOP (Heywood et al., 2002)	1 item	5 point	1 = definitely not;	–	–	
			5 = yes, definitely			
Family						
PAI (Bengston & Black, 1973)	10 items	6 point	1 = not well;	r = .41 to .73		.92
			6 = extremely well			
FII (Bengston & Lovejoy, 1973)	12 items	8 point	1 = almost never;	–	.58 to .89	.81
			8 = almost every day			

(continued)

TABLE 17.1 *(continued)*

Measure	Item response			Reliability		
	Scale	Scoring	Rating	Interitem	Alpha	Test-retest
Religiosity & Spirituality						
CSQ-Revised (Silverman et al., 1983)	72 items	5 point	1 = not at all; 5 = completely	–	.79 to .94	–
SWBS (Paloutzian & Ellison, 1982)[c]	20 items	6 point	1 = strongly disagree; $r = .32$ 6 = strongly agree	–		.82 to .99
RWB	10 items	–	–			.88 to .99
EWB	10 items	–	–			.73 to .98
GTG (Krause, 2006)	4 items	4 point	1 = strongly disagree; 4 = strongly agree	–	.96	– –
Meaning in Life						–
GQ-6 (McCullough et al., 2002)	6 items	7 point	1 = strongly disagree; 7 = strongly agree	–	.76 to .84 –	– –
GQ-6-Adapted (Krause, 2007b)	3 items	4 point	1 = disagree strongly; 4 = agree strongly	–	.86	
VOL (Lawton et al., 2001)	19-items	5 point	1 = disagree very strongly; 5 = agree very strongly	–	–	–
Positive VOL	13 items			$r = .37$ to .73	.94	–
Negative VOL	6 items			$r = .38$ to .55	.83	–

[a]Interitem correlations of SWLS reflect original test of scale with older adult sample. [b]Depicted reliability indices of SHS refer to original test with sample of older adult residents from retirement community. [c]Interitem correlation for full SWBS reflects association of all items representing RWB and EWB subscales.

follow-up. Furthermore, Chipperfield and Havens (2001) reported Cronbach's alpha of the LSI-A to be .77 at initial testing and .74 during a 7-year follow-up of 2,180 old and very old adults of diverse cultural decent in Manitoba, Canada (Chipperfield & Havens, 2001). In effect, the LSI-A appears to be a reliable quantitative assessment of life satisfaction in diverse cultural settings.

Investigators should be aware that the LSI-A has undergone extensive methodological critique and factor reconstruction. For example, Adams (1969) examined the reliability and multidimensionality of the LSI-A and reported inconclusive evidence of a five-factor structure. In particular, Adams (1969) was unable to identify any factor that corresponded to the self-concept dimension but did provide support for the dimensions of zest, congruence, and mood tone. In effect, Adams (1969) recommended a shorter 13-item version of the LSI-A designated as the LSI-Z. Investigating a sample of octogenarians, Lyyra, Törmäkangas, Read, Rantanen, and Berg (2006) reconfirmed Adams's (1969) critique and concluded that the zest, congruence, and mood tone dimensions of the LSI-A should be used to evaluate the life satisfaction of old-old persons.

Similar to Adams (1969), Hoyt and Creech (1983) failed to support the five-factor structure of life satisfaction originally proposed by Neugarten et al. (1961). Using a nationally representative sample, Hoyt and Creech (1983) reported evidence of an alternative temporal factor structure reflecting satisfaction with the past, present, and future. Hoyt and Creech (1983) concluded that the LSI-A appeared to capture developmental components of life satisfaction.

Relative to developmental factors, Liang (1984) noted that congruence (e.g., past satisfaction with life) and mood tone (e.g., current happiness) dimensions of the LSI-A were distinct developmental components of life satisfaction. Liang (1984, 1985) structurally integrated these two factors with positive and negative affect dimensions of the Bradburn Affect Balance Scale (Bradburn, 1969) and established an acceptable measurement model of fit using structural equation modeling. Stock, Okun, and Benin (1986) reported success in replicating similar findings in the integration of congruence and mood tone items of the LSI-A with the positive and negative affective dimensions of the Bradburn Affect Balance Scale.

We recommend investigators use LSI-A items representing the mood tone (three items) and congruence (four items) dimensions. This equates to a brief seven-item scale that can be easily administered as a developmental assessment of life satisfaction with old-old respondents. In two previous studies, we used the seven-item LSI-A form and reported alpha reliabilities of .78 across a sample including 60-, 80-, and 100-year-olds, as well as .53 in an sample consisting of only 100-year-olds (Bishop, Martin, MacDonald, & Poon, 2010; Bishop, Martin, & Poon, 2006). It appears that the seven-item short form of the LSI-A is a rather reliable measure across participant samples that include young-old, old, and old-old adults. However, this does not seem to be the case for exceptionally old samples. Further testing of these items required determining whether the structure of life satisfaction was developmentally different among the oldest old.

Bradburn Affect Balance Scale

The Bradburn Affect Balance Scale (BABS; Bradburn, 1969) is a 10-item scale originally designed to assess positive and negative affect. Respondents are typically asked to think how they have felt (e.g., excited, on top of things, depressed or very unhappy) during the previous few weeks. The initial BABS instructed respondents to answer using a dichotomous scale (0 = no, not at all; 1 = yes, often). However, there is evidence to support use of a four-point Likert scale (1 = not at all; 4 = often) across old and very old adults (Martin, Kliegel, Rott, Poon, & Johnson, 2008).

Bradburn (1969) hypothesized that positive and negative affect are distinct and reliable dimensions of subjective well-being. Relative to internal consistency, Bradburn (1969) reported a Cronbach's alpha of .76 for the full Affect Balance Scale. Interitem correlations across items of the full scale ranged from $r = -.43$ to $r = .30$ (Bradburn, 1969). Bradburn (1969) also provided initial reliability of the positive and negative affect subscales. First, the positive affect subscale was acknowledged to have a Cronbach's alpha of .83, with a test-retest reliability ranging from .86 to .96. Interitem correlations among positive affect items ranged from $r = .23$ to $r = .74$. Second, the negative affect subscale was reported to have an alpha reliability of .81, with test-retest reliability ranging from .90 to .97. Interitem correlations among negative affect items ranged from $r = .40$ to $r = .97$. Thus, original reliability testing of the BABS indicated a reliable measure with two distinct constructs.

Bradburn (1969) also validated that positive and negative affect were unique dimensions across gender and a single-item indicator of happiness. For instance, small gamma associations were reported between summary scores, ranging from .04 to .15 for men and −.10 to .04 for women. In addition, positive affect had a reported correlation of .34 (gamma) at Time 1 and .38 (gamma) at Time 2, with a single-item indicator of happiness (e.g., feeling very happy, pretty happy, not happy), whereas values for negative affect were reported at −.33 and −.38 respectively (Bradburn, 1969). Bradburn (1969) concluded that the positive and negative affect subscales are separate dimensions indicative of psychological well-being across gender and measures of happiness.

Stacey and Gatz (1991) tested the longitudinal integrity of the BABS and reported internal consistency to range from .60 to .73. The correlation between positive and negative affect was also low ($r = .06$; Stacey & Gatz, 1991). Stacy and Gatz (1991) acknowledged that positive and negative affect showed good convergent validity with the Center for Epidemiological Studies of Depression Scale (CES-D; Radloff, 1977) and with the Brief Symptoms Inventory (BSI; Derogatis & Melisaratos, 1983). Finally, 14-year stability coefficients for negative affect were determined to be more stable across all old and very old age groups than coefficients for positive affect (Stacy & Gatz, 1991).

Key findings of measurement equivalence using the BABS have also been reported (Maitland, Dixon, Hultsch, & Hertzog, 2001). Maitland et al. (2001) reported that longitudinal comparisons showed a lack of measurement equivalence pertaining to the pleased items (e.g., pleased about having accomplished something), as well as the upset items (e.g., vaguely uneasy or upset) among old-old adults. In addition, Maitland et al. (2001) acknowledged that factor correlations displayed only moderate stability across 3 years, thus indicating significant individual change in affect. Maitland et al. (2001) concluded that investigators should not be deterred from using all 10 items of the BABS. However, use of cumulative or summary scores may be problematic in studies that involve very old adults (Maitland et al., 2001). Nonetheless, the BABS is a brief scale easily administered within a short period of time. This may be advantageous for investigators wishing to garner pilot or cross-sectional data on old-old adults.

Philadelphia Geriatric Morale Scale – Revised

The Philadelphia Geriatric Morale Scale – Revised (PGMS-R; Lawton, 1975) is a 17-item scale used to evaluate three components of psychological well-being: agitation, attitude toward aging, and feelings of loneliness and dissatisfaction. The PGMS-R was also established as an alternative measure to the LSI-A. Lawton (1975) specifically designed the PGMS to be a comprehensible and user-friendly measure for very old adults. In particular, all items are scaled on a dichotomous (i.e., yes or no) response format. Original

Cronbach's alpha for the PGMS included .84 for the agitation items, .81 for the attitude toward aging items, and .85 for the lonely-dissatisfaction items (Lawton, 1975). Lawton (1975) also reported that the PGMS items correlate well with indicators of physical health, engagement in activities, social relations, and functional ability.

More recent reports on the psychometric characteristics of the PGMS-R have confirmed original findings. For instance, Adkins, Martin, and Poon (1996) reported Cronbach's alpha of the full PGMS-R scale at .83 across a sample of sexagenarians, octogenarians, and centenarians. Martin et al. (1996) also computed a separate test of reliability for centenarians. This yielded an internal consistency of .81 across PGMS-R items. Furthermore, Martin, Grünendahl, and Martin (2001) reported Cronbach's alphas for the three separate subscales: agitation, attitude toward own aging, and lonely and dissatisfaction in a cross-sectional investigation in Germany. In particular, they reported alpha reliabilities of .70, .65, and .70, respectively. Finally, Anstey, Burns, von Sanden, and Luszcz (2008) acknowledged test-retest reliabilities of the PGMS-R to range from .81 and .82 at each wave of an 8-year population-based study that included a subsample of adults 85 years of age and older. Thus, the PGMS-R appears to maintain strong reliability within cross-sectional and longitudinal examinations involving exceptionally old adults.

Furthermore, the PGMS-R subscales have demonstrated a wide range of significant interitem correlations relative to satisfaction with activities ($r = .17$ to $r = .31$), quality of social contacts ($r = .16$ to $r = .30$), and stressors linked to health ($r = -.20$ to $r = -.36$), finances ($r = -.18$ to $r = -.26$), and the environment ($r = -.10$ to $r = -.12$; Martin et al., 2001). The PGMS-R items have also maintained associations with social network characteristics in late and very late life (Fiori, Smith, & Antonucci, 2007). In particular, Fiori et al. (2007) reported significant interitem correlations between the PGMS-R items and social network size ($r = .10$), frequency of contact with family ($r = .09$), number of social activities ($r = .17$), instrumental support ($r = -.20$), emotional support ($r = -.16$), and satisfaction with family and friends ($r = .23$). In effect, the PGMS-R appears to be a flexible measure offering nice utility with key indicators of well-being in late life.

However, investigators should be aware that Liang and Bollen (1983) restructured the PGMS into a 15-item inventory based on empirical evidence that the PGMS-R can be used as a multidimensional or unidimensional measure. Furthermore, Liang, Lawrence, and Bollen (1986) reviewed the factor structure of the 15-item scale and verified it to be invariant across age and gender in older adult samples (Liang, Lawrence, & Bollen, 1986). Use of the 15-item version has increased in recent years. This is especially true in cases where the scale was adapted as a brief instrument to assess oldest-old adults (Anstey et al., 2008; Fiori et al., 2007; Wong, Woo, & Ho, 2005; Wong, Woo, Hui, & Ho, 2004). Initial evidence suggests that the PGMS-R consists of a two-factor structure that may work better with old-old sample populations (Wong et al., 2004). However, further testing is needed.

SECOND-GENERATION MEASURES

Classical measures of subjective well-being have been criticized for excluding global judgment of life satisfaction (Diener, Emmons, Larsen, & Griffin, 1985). This has resulted in second-generation measurement tools designed to capture global cognitive-affective or subjective judgments of life. Three instruments have had relative success as measures of subjective well-being among old and very old adults.

Satisfaction with Life Scale

The Satisfaction with Life Scale (SWLS; Diener, Emmons, et al., 1985) was designed to be a brief multi-item and global evaluation of life satisfaction. This measure is a five-item scale consisting of three factors: positive affect, negative affect, and satisfaction. Each item is rated on a seven-point scale (1 = strongly disagree; 7 = strongly agree). The SWLS has been confirmed to measure a single construct: life satisfaction (Pavot & Diener, 1993; Shevlin & Bunting, 1994). The SWLS was initially administered to young adult samples and to an older adult sample. Relative to the young adult samples, the SWLS evinced strong reliability, with a 2-month test retest coefficient of .82 and coefficient alpha of .87 (Diener, Emmons, et al., 1985). Internal consistency across items ranged from $r = .61$ to $r = .84$ (Diener, Emmons, et al., 1985). In addition, the SWLS was reported to demonstrate sound validity, as indicated by intercorrelations across other measures of well-being, including Cantril's (1965) self-anchoring ladder ($r = .57$ to $r = .58$), Bradburn's (1969) Positive Affect Balance Subscale ($r = .50$ to $r = .51$), and Bradburn's (1969) Negative Affect Balance Subscale ($r = -32$ to $r = -37$) (Diener, Emmons, et al., 1985). Furthermore, Diener, Emmons, et al. (1985) reported the SWLS to be strongly correlated with personality measures including self-esteem ($r = .54$), symptom checklist ($r = -.41$), neuroticism ($r = -.48$), emotionality ($r = -.25$), activity ($r = .08$), sociability ($r = .20$), and impulsivity ($r = -.03$).

Original psychometric testing of the SWLS with the older adult sample was not as extensive and consisted of a relatively small convenience sample ($N = 53$) of older persons with an average age of 75 (Diener, Emmons, et al., 1985). Nonetheless, item-total correlations between the five SWLS items ranged from $r = .61$ to $r = .81$ (Diener, Emmons, et al., 1985). Thus, the SWLS demonstrated good internal consistency across items when used with older adults.

Since its initial psychometric development, the SWLS has been tested for factorial invariance across multiple age groups (Pons, Atienza, Balaguer, & García-Merita, 2000). Although dimensionality of the SWLS appeared to remain the same across young and old age groups, Pons et al. (2000) indicated that the SWLS exhibited age sensitivity relative to the item reflecting whether the conditions of life were excellent. In particular, older respondents tended to vary significantly on this item when compared with persons of younger age.

Relative to old-old adults, the SWLS has demonstrated good utility. For instance, Shmotkin, Berkovich, and Cohen (2006) used the SWLS in a study of old and very old Israelis, many of whom were survivors of the Holocaust. In this study, the SWLS had a reported alpha reliability of .66. Shmotkin et al. (2006) acknowledged that a lower than expected scale reliability may have been due to an oral interview format rather than a standard self-administered survey. It is plausible that internal consistency of the SWLS may be hindered because of methodological procedures. However, investigators conducting other culturally based studies with old and very old adults residing in the Netherlands (Steverink & Lindenberg, 2006) and in Germany (Westerhof & Barrett, 2005) have reported internal consistency of the SWLS to be strong at $\alpha = .85$ and $\alpha = .86$, respectively. Further investigation and comparison across cultures is needed to confirm Shmotkin et al.'s (2006) methodological hypothesis.

Although the SWLS has been used to assess life satisfaction of oldest-old adults, the SWLS has primarily served as a measure of life satisfaction in young adulthood and middle adulthood (Vassar, Ridge, & Hill, 2008). Most important, many investigators who have used the SWLS with older adults have failed to report psychometric properties such as reliability and validity (Vassar et al., 2008). Therefore, it is difficult to make a confident final determination of scale utility in exceptionally old populations. Nonetheless, the SWLS is an effective brief measure of life satisfaction that can be easily administered using an oral interview or self-report format with high functioning or frail older persons. As a result, investigators are encouraged to integrate this brief measure into future research involving old-old adults.

Subjective Happiness Scale

An alternative measure to the Diener, Emmons, et al. (1985) Satisfaction with Life Scale is the Subjective Happiness Scale (SHS; Lyubomirsky & Lepper, 1999). This measure was constructed as a global subjective assessment of happiness. The scale consists of four items using seven-point Likert-scale formats. One item used to evaluate unhappiness is reverse coded. A single composite score of subjective happiness is then computed by averaging responses across the four items (Lyubomirsky & Lepper, 1999).

The SHS was validated using 14 different studies across multiple samples representing varying ages and cultures (Lyubomirsky & Lepper, 1999). Test-retest reliability across studies of the SHS ranged from .79 to .94. Relative to construct validity across studies, Lyubomirsky and Lepper (1999) reported that the SHS correlated highly with other happiness scales such as the Bradburn Affect Balance Scale ($\alpha = .52$ to $\alpha = .64$) and the Satisfaction with Life Scale ($\alpha = .61$ to $\alpha = .72$). Furthermore, correlations between the SHS and other theoretically and empirically related happiness and well-being constructs (e.g., self-esteem, optimism, emotionality, extraversion, neuroticism, depression) did not exceed $r = .70$. Lyubomirsky and Lepper (1999) concluded that the SHS maintains strong reliability across time and is unique to other happiness measures.

It is important to note that Lyubomirsky and Lepper (1999) originally tested the SHS using a large retirement community sample of 622 older adults. Cronbach's alpha of the SHS relative to this population was reported to be .86. However, investigators have not extensively used the SHS to assess happiness in old or very old populations. Lee and Im (2007) conducted one of the few aging studies in which SHS served as the primary happiness measure. This investigation involved a cross-sectional sample of 140 Korean elderly, age 60–88. Lee and Im (2007) adapted the four items to the Korean language and reported a Cronbach's alpha coefficient of .76. In effect, the SHS seems to demonstrate strong reliability when used in older adult populations. Further testing and use of the SHS in research involving exceptionally old adults is recommended. The SHS contains a very brief protocol of items to assess happiness. Investigators may find this advantageous when conducting research with frail old-old adults who may experience high levels of mental fatigue during interview or self-report processes.

The Positive and Negative Affect Schedule

The Positive and Negative Affect Schedule (PANAS; Watson, Clark, & Tellegen, 1988) was constructed as a brief evaluation of high-arousal emotions that elicit positive and negative affect. The scale consists of 10 positive adjectives (e.g., *alert, excited*) and 10 negative adjectives (e.g., *upset, jittery*). Respondents are usually asked to rate the degree to which each adjective describes how they felt on a five-point Likert scale (1 = very slightly or not at all; 5 = extremely). Watson et al. (1988) originally administered, tested, and compared this scale across six different time-oriented ratings of emotionality, including at the moment, during the day, over the past few days, during the past few weeks, over the past year, and in general. Interitem reliabilities among positive affect ratings ranged from .86 (e.g., year) to .90 (e.g., general), whereas internal consistency among negative affective items ranged from .84 (e.g., year) to .87 (e.g., general, past few weeks, today). Thus, the PANAS demonstrated high internal consistency across different time orientations. In addition, Watson et al. (1988) reported test-retest reliabilities of time-oriented ratings of positive affective adjectives to range from .47 (e.g., today) to .68 (e.g., general). Test-retest reliability for time-oriented negative affective adjectives ranged from .39 (e.g., today) to .60 (e.g., year). Finally, interitem correlations between positive and negative affective adjectives ranged from $r = -.15$ to $r = -.23$, thus indicating two distinct constructs (Watson et al., 1988).

The PANAS has been widely adopted to assess emotionality of old-old adults residing in Germany. For example, Isaacowitz and Smith (2003) used the PANAS to examine positive and negative affect in a large sample ($N =$ 516) of German residents aged 70–100+ years of age ($M = 85$ years) from the Berlin Aging Study (BASE). Cronbach's alphas were reported to be relatively high for the 10 positive affect items ($\alpha = .78$) and the 10 negative affect items ($\alpha = .81$). Isaacowitz and Smith (2003) acknowledged that the PANAS subscales were associated with personality and intellectual functioning in the oldest old. In particular, extraversion was reported to have a positive association with positive affect ($\beta = .39$, $p < .01$), whereas neuroticism ($\beta = .65$, $p < .01$) and general intelligence ($\beta = .39$, $p < .01$) were predictive of negative affect (Isaacowitz & Smith, 2003). Thus, personality and general intelligence variables appear to be useful in predicting positive and negative affect items of the PANAS.

The PANAS has also demonstrated good convergent validity in studies involving oldest-old adults. In particular, Kunzmann, Little, and Smith (2000) reported that a single-item indictor of life satisfaction was positively associated with positive affect ($r = .35$, $p < .01$) but negatively related to negative affect ($r = -.33$, $p < .01$). Similarly, Steverink and Lindenberg (2006) indicated evidence of convergent validity between the PANAS subscales and the Satisfaction with Life Scale (SWLS; Diener, Emmons, et al., 1985). Life satisfaction scores on SWLS were positively associated with positive affect items of the PANAS ($r = .32, p < .01$) and negatively associated with negative affective items ($r = -.39, p < .01$). In effect, PANAS works well with measures of life satisfaction. Therefore, investigators studying life satisfaction in very old age should seriously consider using the PANAS scale. The measure appears to be psychometrically sound and is easily administered in old-old populations.

Ryff Scales of Psychological Well-Being

The Ryff Scales of Psychological Well-Being (Ryff, 1989a, 1989b; Ryff & Keyes, 1995) were constructed to provide a theoretically derived set of six distinct self-report instruments to assess dimensions of psychological well-being: self-acceptance, positive relationships with others, autonomy, purpose in life, personal growth, and environmental mastery. Respondents are typically asked to provide a ratings on a six-point scale (1 = strongly disagree; 6 = strongly agree). Ryff (1989) originally computed item-to-scale correlations to create six separate 20-item scales (Ryff, 1989a). Original internal consistency or alpha coefficients for the 20-item scales were reported as self-acceptance, .93; positive relations with others, .91; autonomy, .86; environmental mastery, .90; purpose in life, .90; and personal growth, .87 (Ryff, 1989a). Test-retest reliability coefficients of the original 20-item scales over a 6-week period were reported as self-acceptance, .85; positive relations with others, .83; autonomy, .88; environmental mastery, .81; purpose in life, .82; and personal growth, .81 (Ryff, 1989a). Furthermore, construct validity with other theoretically derived scales of well-being was considered. Ryff (1989a) reported the range of intercorrelations of the six dimensions with other measures: Bradburn Affect Balance Scale (Bradburn, 1969), .25 to .62; Life Satisfaction Index-A (Neugarten et al., 1961), .26 to .73, and the Zung Depression Scale (Zung, 1965), −.33 to −.60.

The six psychological well-being scales were further operationalized into six 14-item scales (Ryff, Lee, Essex, & Schmutte, 1994). Similar to previous analyses (Ryff, 1989a, 1989b), items were selected on the basis of item-to-scale coefficients (Ryff et al., 1994). Correlations between the original 20-item scales and the 14-item scales ranged from .97 to .98 (Ryff et al., 1994). Internal consistency of the reduced item scales ranged from .82 to .90 (Ryff et al., 1994). Furthermore, test-retest reliability of the 14-item scales over a 6-week period ranged from .81 to .88 (Ryff et al., 1994). Ryff et al. (1994) also noted that the 14-item scales correlated positively with established measures of positive well-being (e.g., life satisfaction, affect balance, and self-esteem) and negatively with measures of depression and external control. In addition, intercorrelations between the six 14-item scales were reported to range between .32 and .76 (see Ryff et al., 1994).

Ryff and Keyes (1995) retested the factor structure of the six psychological well-being constructs across the original 20-item scales, the 14-item shortened versions, and 3-item indices. All scales demonstrated psychometric properties appropriate for aging research (see Ryff & Keyes, 1995). Confirmatory factor analysis was also used to examine latent constructs. Reported interitem correlations among the latent constructs ranged from .24 to .85 (Ryff & Keyes, 1995). Correlations of the six latent dimensions were then examined to establish convergent validity. Ryff and Keyes (1995) reported correlations between the six dimensions and single-item measures of happiness (e.g., how much time during the past month participants felt happy) and life satisfaction (e.g., how things were going in life), as well as depression, using an eight-item version of the CES-D (Radloff, 1977). Correlations ranged from .31 to .54 and from .21 to .64, respectively, on the single-item measures of happiness and satisfaction, whereas correlations between the six scales and the CES-D ranged from −.22 to −.70 (Ryff & Keyes, 1995).

Administration of the Ryff Scales of Psychological Well-Being primarily originated with the 1995 National Survey of Midlife Development in the United States (MIDUS; Greenfield & Marks, 2004, 2007; Keyes, Shmotkin, & Ryff, 2002). This study has concentrated on the well-being of young and middle-aged persons, with sample participants ranging from age 25 to 74. The extent to which alpha reliability, predictive or convergent validity, or factor structure among a sample of old-old adults would yield consistent or comparable findings remains unknown. Certain subscales do appear to work well with old and very old adults. For example, Bishop (2006) used the 14-item personal growth subscale from Ryff's Psychological Well-Being Scales with old and very old men and women residing in Benedictine Order religious monasteries. Cronbach's alpha for the personal growth scale in this study was reported at .80 (Bishop, 2006). Although the personal growth subscale demonstrated strong reliability, further integration and testing of the Ryff Scales of Psychological Well-Being in secular and nonsecular (e.g., individualistic vs. collectivistic) old-old populations is warranted.

Implementation of the 20-item or 14-item versions of all six scales in research with old-old adults may create a risk of mental fatigue. Researchers are advised to be selective as to which of the six subscales to use. Relative to large sample surveys involving special older populations, the three-item index of the Ryff Scales of Psychological Well-Being may work best (Greenfield & Marks, 2007). However, application of the Ryff scales in exceptionally old populations needs to be expanded for improved understanding of psychometric properties and user feasibility.

DOMAIN-SPECIFIC MEASURES

As second-generation measures continue to be used in advancing the science of subjective well-being research, it remains important that aging researchers consider the cultural-domain (see Chapter 15). Domain experiences elicit a retrospective or immediate judgment of satisfaction with life, which further influences an adult's memory of an event, affective emotions, or interpersonal relationships (Kahneman & Krueger, 2006). For example, happiness may be judged as the difference between what persons were able to achieve through work (e.g., income, wealth) versus what they aspire to attain in retirement (e.g., health, economic security; Diener & Biswas-Diener, 2008). The net effect of this judgment on subjective well-being is greatest when individuals are able to remain engaged in work, to invest in close family ties, or to pursue personally meaningful activities (e.g., attending church or other social functions; Kahneman & Krueger, 2006). Therefore, domain measures of work and retirement satisfaction, housing satisfaction, family solidarity, satisfaction with church, purpose, and meaning are relevant to the well-being of old-old adults.

RETIREMENT SATISFACTION

Retirement Descriptive Index

The Retirement Descriptive Index (RDI; Smith, Kendall, & Hulin, 1969) is a classical measure originally designed to evaluate affective responses to retirement. The RDI consists of 63 items representing four dimensions of retirement satisfaction: activities and work (e.g., sense of accomplishment), finances (e.g., satisfactory), health (e.g., never felt better), and interpersonal relations (e.g., stimulating). Respondents are asked to indicate whether each item reflects their current retirement situation using dichotomous ratings (0 = no; 1 = yes). Smith et al. (1969) reported interitem correlations across dimensions to range from .19 to .43 in a sample of men. Smith and colleagues (1969) also recognized that older retirees maintain low satisfaction scores on the RDI. However, Smith et al. (1969) failed to provide detailed psychometric information of internal consistency relative to original construction of the RDI.

Dorfman, Kohout, and Heckert (1985) used the RDI to assess retirement satisfaction among rural older adults and reported a Cronbach's alpha of.85. Dorfman et al. (1985) also reported that the RDI evinces high subscale reliabilities relative to activities ($\alpha = .78$), finances ($\alpha = .74$), health ($\alpha = .74$), and interpersonal relations ($\alpha = .77$). Furthermore, Dorfman et al. (1985) confirmed that personal characteristics, including perceived health ($r = .37$), functional health ($r = .19$), and monetary spending ($r = -.24$), maintain strong predictive associations with overall RDI scores.

In an alternative use of the RDI, MacEwen, Barling, Kelloway, and Higginbottom (1995) adapted only two subscales – financial satisfaction and satisfaction with activities – in a study of middle-age adults. MacEwen et al. (1995) transformed these subscales into dichotomous items to assess expected satisfaction in retirement. Internal consistency of the financial and activity subscales was reported to be $\alpha = .78$ and $\alpha = .79$, respectively. MacEwen et al. (1995) also summed three additional items of the RDI (i.e., expected change in marital relationship, mood, self-esteem following retirement) to assess overall well-being in retirement but reported a lower than expected Cronbach's alpha of .62. Low reliability of this three-item global index most likely reflected the use of few items. However, the MacEwen et al. (1995) application of the RDI suggests that the RDI offers flexibility when using brief subscales or easily administered item ratings. However, use of the RDI has remained limited, and knowledge regarding psychometric properties or factorial structure relative to old-old populations is unclear. Thus, an opportunity exists to retest the measurement properties and factorial structure in a contemporary sample of old-old adults.

Retirement Satisfaction Index

A more widely accepted measure of retirement satisfaction in aging research is the Retirement Satisfaction Index (RSI, Floyd et al., 1992). Floyd et al. (1992) derived the RSI based on life-span development theory and life-span transition theory. The RSI includes a 51-item questionnaire consisting of six dimensions: preretirement work functioning (e.g., retrospective report of work-related activities and job involvement), adjustment and change (e.g., perception of stress associated with event of retirement), reasons for retirement (e.g., voluntary and involuntary control over retirement), satisfaction with life in retirement (e.g., satisfaction and dissatisfaction with retirement), sources of enjoyment (e.g., access to economic and social provisions), and leisure and physical activities (e.g., continuity of skills, hobbies, and behaviors). The RSI also involves use of separate four-point (1 = unimportant; 4 = important) and six-point (1 = very ungratifying; 6 = very gratifying) Likert-type ratings across various items.

Floyd et al. (1992) conducted a series of factor analyses on three sections of questions to achieve three factor-analytically-derived subscales. Tested subscale items included questions measuring reasons for retirement (15 items), satisfaction with life in retirement (11 items), and sources of enjoyment (15 items). Remaining items reflecting other subscales were treated as single-item scores. Cronbach's alpha across the three factor-analytically-derived subscales was reported at .81 (Floyd et al., 1992). Test-retest reliability over a 14-day interval ranged from $r = .56$ to $r = .77$ for multiple items representing the three factor-analytic subscales and $r = .45$ to $r = .71$ for single-item ratings (Floyd et al., 1992). Furthermore, Floyd et al. (1992) reported concurrent validity of the overall mean satisfaction score, the three subscale scores, and the global rating of retirement satisfaction for the Satisfaction with Life Scale (SWLS; Diener, Emmons, et al., 1985) and the Marital Satisfaction Questionnaire for Older Persons (MSQOP; Haynes et al., 1992). Correlations for the SWLS ranged from $r = .30$ to $r = 48$, whereas correlations associated with the MSQOP ranged from $r = .32$ to $r = .56$. Thus, specificity of RSI factor scores was supported.

There is evidence that RSI is a culturally competent measure. In particular, the RSI has demonstrated strong utility across older adult samples from European Union countries (Fouquereau, Fernandez, Fonseca, Paul, & Uotinen, 2005; Fouquerequ, Fernandez, & Mullet, 1999; Stephen, Fouquereau, & Hernandez, 2008). Fouquereau et al. (1999) retested the factor structure of RSI using a French sample and confirmed support of the factors derived from Floyd et al. (1992) reflecting reasons for retirement, satisfaction with life in retirement, and sources of enjoyment. Furthermore, Fouquereau et al. (2005) reported the RSI to be a successful measure of global retirement satisfaction across six countries, including Belgium, Finland, France, Portugal, Spain, and the United Kingdom.

In effect, the RSI represents a useful measure for cross-cultural comparison. Although it may potentially be a time-intensive instrument to administer with old-old samples, researchers may still want to consider using one or all three of the factor-analytically-derived subscales (e.g., reasons for retirement, satisfaction with life in retirement, and sources of enjoyment). Use of the three subscales will reduce the number of self-report items without compromising scale integrity (Floyd et al., 1992).

Work-Control Index

Although labor participation has continued to decline among old-old persons, there has been continued growth in the number of old and very old adults who may continue to work part-time or volunteer in various jobs (Choi, 2003). Jopp and Rott (2006) reported evidence that past acquisition of skill and abilities through formal job training continues to influence feelings of optimism and happiness into exceptional old age. Thus, it may be valuable to assess how old-old adults reconstruct their work lives to deriving a mastery over well-being. Work-control items from the Job Content Questionnaire (JCQ; Karasek & Theorell, 1990; Karasek et al., 1998) represent a measurement index that has proved useful for evaluating perceived control and satisfaction in work. In particular, work-control items of the JCQ were designed to assess the degree to which individuals felt content with the way work matches their education, skills, training, and desired autonomy. Sample items include "My job allows me to use my skills and abilities" and "My job matches what I like to do." All items are rated on a five-point Likert scale (1 = strongly disagree; 5 = strongly agree). Items representing the work-control index of the JCQ have demonstrated good psychometric reliability in aging research. Cronbach's alpha has been reported to range from .59 to .86 among male study participants representing workers in the United States, Canada, the Netherlands, and Japan. For female workers from those same countries, the work-control index of the JCQ has a reported alpha reliability ranging from .64 to .85. Furthermore, Karasek et al. (1998) reported interitem correlations across work-control index items to range from $r = .37$ to .62 among male and female workers from different countries. Thus, work-control items from the JCQ evince high reliability and strong interitem correlations across culturally diverse and gender specific samples.

Wickrama, Surjadi, Lorenz, and Elder (2008) adopted an eight-item work-control index from the JCQ to investigate work-control trajectories among middle-aged and older men across three measurement waves. Coefficient alphas for each measurement wave were reported at .83, .84, and .81, respectively. Thus, the JCQ appears to be a strongly reliable measure across time. We recommend that investigators further test and incorporate the eight-item work control index in studies involving old-old adults who may continue to work or engage in volunteer service. This index provides a brief and easy way to evaluate work-related happiness and well-being in advanced old age. Furthermore, it has the potential to offer a contemporary assessment of how old-old adults may reframe perceived productivity relative to feeling satisfied with life.

HOUSING SATISFACTION

Most old-old adults continue to age in place after retirement. In effect, housing often becomes a reflection of individual satisfaction in very old age (Oswald, Schilling, et al., 2006; Oswald, Wald, et al., 2007). Housing satisfaction can be conceptualized as a complex outcome of health-related well-being and a objective and subjective indicator of satisfaction with the environment, but a readily available psychometric or standardized assessment tool does not exist (Pinquart & Burmedi, 2004). Instead, contemporary measurement of housing satisfaction has been limited to a single-time indicator adapted from the Housing Options for Older People (HOOP) questionnaire (Heywood, Oldman, & Means, 2002). In particular, respondents are asked the following question: "Are you happy with the condition of your home?" Responses are typically scored on a five-point Likert scale (1 = definitely not; 5 = yes, definitely). Oswald, Wald, et al. (2007) reported patterns in which housing satisfaction was related to autonomy among old-old adults residing in Sweden ($r = .47$) and Germany ($r = .66$). In an earlier investigation, Oswald, Schiller, et al. (2006) reported that housing satisfaction maintained a mean of 4.62 with a standard deviation of 1.46 across a sample of $N = 1223$ older adults, age 80–89, from Sweden, Britain, and Germany. Furthermore, Oswald, Schiller, et al. (2006) examined the factor structure of perceived housing domains. Housing satisfaction maintained a factor loading of .96. Oswald, Schiller, et al. (2006) concluded that housing satisfaction is one of four key domains of perceived housing among older adults residing in various cultural settings. Other domains included meaning of home, usability, and housing control beliefs. Despite these findings, researchers should expand on this current work. In particular, a more sophisticated psychometric assessment of housing satisfaction is needed to compare with the more often used single-item indicator.

FAMILY SOLIDARITY

Positive Affective Index

The Family Solidarity Inventories (Bengston & Lovejoy, 1973) were originally developed as separate measurement indices to assess two primary dimensions of intergenerational relations: affection (e.g., degree of positive sentiment toward family members) and association (e.g., degree to which family members engage in the interaction, sharing, or exchange or activities) (see Mangen, Bengston, & Landry, 1988). Both measurement indices were also created for the purposes of assessing family cohesion across two or three living generations (Mangen & Peterson, 1982; Mangen et al., 1988).

To assess positive affective family solidarity, Bengston and Lovejoy (1973) established the Positive Affective Index (PAI). This is a 10-item scale designed to assess feelings of positive sentiment or affect among family members as perceived and reported by family members. The PAI is used to evaluate five dimensions: (a) understanding, (b) fairness (c) trust, (d) respect, and (e) affection. Additional single-item questions include quality of communication among family members, sense of closeness, and getting along. All items are rated on a six-point Likert scale (1 = not well; 6 = extremely well). Scores are generally summarized across items to provide an index of positive affect. Original dimensionality was assessed using a sample of 100 older adult parent–adult child dyads (Mangen & Peterson, 1982). Moderate to high homogeneity was reported across items. In particular, interitem correlations ranged from .41 to .73. Factor analyses of items also resulted in uniform loadings (.60 to .80). Finally, Bengston and Black (1973) reported a strong Cronbach's alpha of .92.

Construct validity of PAI items has been assessed for indicators reflecting interaction frequency among the two generations. All index items were reported to load highly on the same factor relative to different types of interaction among family members (.50 to .85) (Mangen & Peterson, 1982). In addition, construct validity was tested by separating the two generations. High factor loadings were determined relative to the oldest (G1: .60 to .84) and the younger generation (G2: .56 to .78) (Mangen & Peterson, 1982).

The PAI has demonstrated good utility in more recent intergenerational investigations. For instance, Long and Martin (2000) considered relationship closeness among oldest-old adults and their children. They reported a Cronbach's alpha of .92 across old-old parents and .96 among older adult children. In addition, Goodman and Silverstein (2002) investigated a sample of grandmothers raising grandchildren. The coefficient alpha for positive affectual solidarity in that study ranged from .83 for the grandmother-grandchild relationship to .93 and .95 for other relationships. Internal consistency has also been reported to be strong in other studies that considered level of affection between adult children and older adult mothers (.93) and fathers (.91) (Silverstein, Conroy, Wong, Giarrusso, & Bengston, 2002).

Furthermore, some investigators have demonstrated success in using a three-item index of the PAI. For instance, Silverstein, Cong, and Li (2006) used an adapted three-item version of the PAI with a sample of older adults residing in rural China. Silverstein et al. (2006) reported a reliability coefficient of .82 for this adapted form. Thus, the PAI appears to work well across young, old, and very old family members and is easily adaptable as a brief measurement index in other cultures.

Family Interaction Index

Bengston and Lovejoy (1973) also framed a family interaction index (FII) to compliment the PAI (see Mangen et al., 1988). This instrument consists of a 12-item checklist designed to measure the type and frequency of informal (e.g., recreation outside the home activities representing informal) and ceremonial (e.g., family gatherings) family activities. Activities were categorized around five dimensions: (a) interactions outside the home, (b) visitation and conversation, (c) family get-togethers, (d) written or spoken communication, and (e) exchange of gifts or assistance. Respondents are typically asked to indicate how often they engage in various activities with an identified family member using an eight-point Likert scale (1 = almost never; 8 = almost every day). One additional item is used to assess proximity or the distance the respondent lives from the target individual. This item is used as a reflective indicator to determine which activities may be more or less salient for the older family member (Mangen & Peterson, 1982). Original Cronbach's alpha for ceremonial and informal family activity subscales was reported to be .58 and .89, respectively, whereas test-retest reliability of the full index over a 4-week period was reported at .81 (Bengston & Black, 1973). Despite good internal consistency, investigators should remain aware that the types of activities used in the FII may carry divergent levels of meaning and importance across various families living in various cultural contexts (Mangen & Peterson, 1982). In other words, the FII may have limited measurement utility in diverse family systems.

Other investigators have noted that the FII demonstrates strong reliability across old and very old adults. For instance, Long and Martin (2000) reported an internal consistency of $\alpha = .71$ among old-old parents and $\alpha = .73$ among their adult children. Furthermore, Silverstein et al. (2002) reported scale reliability to range from .88 to .90 for time spent in activities with older adult fathers and mothers, respectively. Finally, interitem correlations between items of the PAI and items from the FII have been reported to range from .29 to as low as .01 (Silverstein et al., 2002). According to Silverstein et al. (2002), this indicates that affectual and associative forms of solidarity are unique ways in which older adult parents invest in relationships with their adult children. Thus, researchers are advised to treat and measure items reflecting affectual solidarity and family interaction independently.

RELIGIOSITY AND SPIRITUALITY

Beyond the family context, religiosity represents a central domain of health, happiness, and well-being (Koenig, 1998; Koenig, McCullough, & Larson, 2001. The oldest old often represent the "forgotten" aged in religious faith communities (Dickerson & Watkins, 2003). Most religiosity scales have been designed to measure organized religious activities and rituals, including church attendance or frequency of engagement in religious activities (Hill & Wood, 1999). Although old-old members want to attend church or synagogue as well as engage in religious activities, many are limited by physical frailty (e.g., poor vision and hearing, mobility problems) or resource deficits (e.g., transportation, pastoral senior programs and services) that restrict participation. Some old-old members of religious congregations may become disenfranchised with organized religion to the point of feeling dissatisfied with clergy, lay members, or other church-affiliated programs or outreach services (Dickerson & Watkins, 2003). In effect, many may desire to turn away from formal religious institutions and engage in more solitary existential pursuits (e.g., private or contemplative prayer, forming a relationship with God or the Divine) to find meaning and fulfillment in what lies beyond themselves. Thus, alternative religiosity and spirituality measures that more directly focus on happiness or satisfaction are needed.

Congregational Satisfaction Questionnaire

The Congregation Satisfaction Questionnaire (CSQ; Silverman, Pargament, Johnson, Echemendia, & Snyder, 1983) is a psychometric measure designed to assess member satisfaction with church or synagogue. The CSQ was originally normed using a sample of 353 members across 13 congregations from Roman Catholic and Protestant churches ranging from 100 to 6,200 members. In addition, the scale was designed to be applicable in investigations involving members of Jewish synagogues. Silverman et al. (1983) reported a mean sample age of 44 years among participants, indicating an average length of membership of 18 years.

The original CSQ consisted of eight subscales. For each dimension, respondents were asked to rate how accurately words or short phrases described their congregation. Respondents were asked to rate items on a three-point Likert scale (0 = no, 1 = yes, and 3 = uncertain). Silverman et al. (1983) reported an alpha reliability ranging from .67 to .90, with a test-retest reliability range of .62 to .82. Convergent validity was established between the measured subscales and reported to range from $r = .32$ to $r = .43$. Each of the scales also maintained significant correlations with at least one or more demographic or religiosity indicators (i.e., age, education, frequency and number of religious activities, frequency of attendance, number of close members, frequency of prayer, and importance of religion). Furthermore, all subscales maintained small but significant correlations with life satisfaction, ranging from $r = .13$ to $r = .24$. According to Silverman et al. (1983), this finding demonstrated evidence of the interrelatedness between the religious domain and life satisfaction.

It is important to note that the original CSQ was revised. Several revisions were made to the original scale, including the omission of one subscale, the introduction of several new and additional items across subscales, and a change in the response option from a three-point to five-point Likert scale (1 = not at all; 5 = completely; Brant, Jewell, & Rye, 1999). The revised CSQ resulted in a 70-item scale that asks respondents to rate 10 positively and negatively worded phrases across seven dimensions. The revised CSQ has demonstrated improved reliability across the seven newly established subscales: religious services ($\alpha = .85$), members ($\alpha = .85$), special programs and services ($\alpha = .79$), child education ($\alpha = .85$), adult education ($\alpha = .88$), leaders ($\alpha = .82$), and facilities ($\alpha = .94$; Brant et al., 1999). On the basis of this information, it appears that the CSQ is a reliable and valid measure of congregation satisfaction. Although there is no reported evidence that the CSQ has been widely or exclusively tested using older adult populations, the CSQ has strong face validity as a potentially useful evaluation of religious satisfaction in old-old age. In particular, researchers who conduct applied gerontological research might find the CSQ a worthwhile quantitative assessment to determine religious needs of old-old adults who maintain or desire an active religious life. However, investigators are advised to adopt the revised CSQ for greater reliability in outcomes.

Spiritual Well-Being Scale

The Spiritual Well-Being Scale (SWBS; Ellison, 1983; Paloutzian & Ellison, 1982, 1991) was developed as a 20-item global psychological measure of self-reported spiritual well-being. Paloutzian and Ellison (1982) designed the SWBS to capture two key dimensions: (a) religious well-being (RWB), or the vertical dimension of perceived well-being of one's spiritual life as reflected by a relationship with God, and (b) existential well-being (EWB), or the horizontal dimension of perceived well-being of one's spiritual life as indicated in sense of purpose, life satisfaction, and positive or negative experiences. Each subscale contains 10 items rated on a six-point Likert scale (1 = strongly agree; 6 = strongly disagree). All RWB items contain the word *God* (e.g., "I don't find much satisfaction in private prayer with God"), whereas EWB items are more global and include no specific religious language (e.g., "I feel very fulfilled and satisfied with life"). Paloutzian and Ellison (1982) originally tested the SWBS using a sample of 206 college students. They reported a moderate correlation between RWB and EWB ($r = .32$) during the initial construction of the scale. Furthermore, Paloutzian and Ellison (1982) reported test-retest reliability over 1, 4, 6, and 10 weeks to range from .88 to .99 for RWB, .73 to .98 for EWB, and .82 to .99 for the full SWBS. Thus, it is evident that the SWBS evinces high internal consistency and reliability. For additional information regarding reliability norms across various empirical studies, researchers should refer to the manual for the SWBS (Paloutzian & Ellison, 1991) or work by Bufford, Paloutzian, and Ellison (1991).

Paloutzian and Ellison (1982) also conducted a factor analysis of scale items. They concluded that factors correspond to two subscales. In particular, RWB items clustered strongly together on one factor, whereas EWB items were more indicative of two subfactors reflecting life direction and satisfaction. Subsequent research has posed a more complex factor structure (Ledbetter, Smith, Fischer, & Vosler-Hunter, 1991). This is a result of ceiling effects, which tend to occur more in sample populations of evangelical religious orientations. Therefore, investigators need to be aware that the factorial structure of the SWBS may make interpretation of scores ambiguous across divergent religious orientations.

Relative to original findings on predictive validity, Ellison (1983) reported that the SWBS tends to share an association with measures used to evaluate mental and family well-being. For instance, the SWBS has been reported to be predictive of loneliness ($r = .37$ to $r = .55$), purpose in life ($r = .52$), self-esteem ($r = .16$ to $r = .44$), parent-child relationship quality ($r = .19$ to $r = .38$), and family closeness ($r = .26$ to $r = .34$). Thus, the SWBS tends to be an appropriate measure in research that focuses on mental health functioning as well as family relations.

Nonetheless, the SWBS is noted as one of the most widely adopted spirituality scales in clinical research (Boivin, Kirby, Underwood, & Silva, 1999). Although the SWBS has not been exclusively used to investigate spiritual well-being in old-old age, there is evidence to support its use in clinical aging research. This appears to be most true relative to health and caregiving outcomes. First, investigators have used the SWBS to assess spiritual well-being among middle-aged and older adults living with chronic illness (e.g., breast or prostate cancer) and disability (e.g., amputation, postpolio, spinal cord injury; Riley et al., 1998). Reported alpha reliabilities of .87 for RWB, .78 for EWB, and .89 for the full SWBS indicate the measure maintains strong reliability in clinical applications where sample participants may have chronic or age-associated physical or functional health problems (Riley et al., 1998).

In addition, the SWBS has been reported as a reliable measure among family members caring for terminally ill relatives (Kirschling & Pittman, 1989). Cronbach's alpha pertaining to EWB, RWB, and the full SWBS scale in this investigation were reported to be high at .95, .94, and .84, respectively. Furthermore, Kirschling and Pittman (1989) provided evidence that confirmed the predictive validity of the SWBS and mental health indicators. In particular, they reported a significant negative association between EWB and negative affect ($r = -.38$). Similarly, reliability of the full SWBS has also been reported as strong across a sample of Alzheimer's caregivers ($\alpha = .91$; Spurlock, 2005). Among this sample, the full SWBS was reported to be predictive of caregiver burden ($r = -.49$). In effect, clinical gerontologists and other aging researchers should consider adopting the SWBS to evaluate spiritual well-being among physically frail or terminally ill old-old adults and among their respective family care providers.

Gratitude toward God

Consideration of one's relationship with God is an additional and alternative way to evaluate contentment and satisfaction with life. Krause (2006) devised a brief four-item measure indicative of gratitude toward God. Krause (2006) specifically selected and modified indicators originating from an existing empirical research and measurement of gratitude in daily life (Emmons, McCullough, & Tsang, 2003). These indicators were used to form a construct reflective of one's appreciation for their relationship with God. Measurement items included (a) "I am grateful to God for all He has done for me," (b) "If I were to make a list of all the things God has done for me, it would be a very long list," (c) "As I look back on my life, I feel I have been richly blessed by God," and (d) "I am grateful to God for all He has done for my family members and close friends." Krause (2006) used a restricted sample of older practicing Christians ($M = 77.6$ years, $SD = 6.0$ years) to evaluate the brief composite scale. Respondents were asked to rate their level of agreement using a four-point Likert scale (1 = strongly disagree; 4 = strongly agree). Krause (2006) reported internal consistency reliability of this brief composite scale to be $\alpha = .96$.

It is important to note that Krause and Ellison (2009) also derived a modified three-item version to assess gratitude with God. This composite index included all original items from Krause's (2006) implementation with exception of one item. In particular, the family-oriented item was omitted to create a more specific measure of gratitude toward God. Relative to psychometric properties, Krause and Ellison (2009) tested a measurement model in which the three-item index was used to create a measurable latent variable construct. Reported factor loadings across the three items were .87, .88, and .88, respectively, for feeling grateful to God, making a list of all things God had done, and feeling blessed. Thus, the modified three-item version appears to be useful in forming a latent construct reflecting gratitude toward God.

Although this short composite measure of gratitude toward God has not been widely used among old-old populations, it does provide a brief and alternative assessment that can be used to capture satisfaction derived from a religious or spiritual relationship with God. However, Krause (2006) highlighted a key shortcoming of the measure. In particular, the composite scale may not be comprehensive enough to be suitable for use among persons representing non-Western monotheistic religious traditions (e.g., Jews, Muslims).

MEANING IN LIFE

There has been a contemporary movement in gerontology toward the development of psychometric measurement tools that transcend religious and spiritual domains (Krause, 2009). Relative to the theory of gerotranscendence, Tornstam (2005) proposed that persons living exceptionally long lives experience a shift in perspective from a materialistic and pragmatic view of the world to a more transcendent and cosmic pursuit of meaning in old-old age. Krause (2009) posited meaning in life as a theoretical and measurable construct closely linked to subjective well-being. It represents a key source of satisfaction and happiness and is often expressed through feelings of gratitude in old-old age. When old-old adults are provided an ability to achieve individual values, sense of purpose, personal goals, and reconciliation with the past, they feel more grateful and fulfilled for the positive and negative happenings of life (Krause, 2004, 2009). As highlighted in chapters by Shmotkin (Chapter 3), Martin, daRosa, and Poon (Chapter 7), and Hyer and Yeager (Chapter 8), life experiences tend to be crucial in the derivation of subjective well-being in old-old age.

The Gratitude Questionnaire – Six-Item Form (GQ-6)

The Gratitude Questionnaire – Six-Item Form (GQ-6; McCullough, Emmons, and Tsang, 2002) is a six-item self-report questionnaire designed to evaluate the experience of gratitude in everyday life. Respondents are typically asked to rate the six items using a seven-point Likert scale (1 = strongly disagree; 7 = strongly agree). Sample items include "I have so much in life to be thankful for" and "As I get older I find myself able to appreciate the people, events, and situations that have been part of my life history."

The GQ-6 was originally tested and developed across samples of undergraduate college students and community-dwelling adults. McCullough et al. (2002) used EQS and conducted confirmatory factor analyses that yielded a one-factor measurement model. This model was reported to have acceptable goodness-of-fit indices relative to the comparative fit index (.90 to .95), and standardized root mean residuals (.05 to .10). In addition, Cronbach's alpha estimates have been reported to range from .76 to .84 (Emmon, McCullough, & Tsang, 2003; McCullough et al., 2002). Thus, the GQ-6 evinces strong reliability across a unidimensional construct.

McCullough et al. (2002) also tested the construct validity of the GQ-6. Correlations between the GQ-6 and positive affective traits (e.g., positive emotionality, life satisfaction, vitality, optimism, hope) were reported to be positive and ranged from .30 to .50, whereas correlations with measures of negative affectivity, depression, and anxiety were negative and were reported to be less than or equal to .40. In other words, high scorers on the GQ-6 report more frequent positive emotions and lower levels of negative affect (Emmons et al., 2003). Furthermore, McCullough et al. (2002) noted that measures of the big-five personality traits accounted for an estimated 20 to 30% of variance across GQ-6 scores. In effect, the GQ-6 typically maintains significant associations with other measures designed to assess positive and negative emotionality as well as personality.

Although the GQ-6 appears to have good face validity, the original six-item version has had little to no application in aging research to date. This perhaps is because the GQ-6 is a relatively new measure. However,

Krause (2007b) reported using an adapted three-item version taken from the McCullough et al. (2002) scale in a large sample study of older adults originating from the Centers for Medicare and Medicaid Services beneficiary list. The adapted GQ-6 items included (a) "I have much in life to be thankful for," (b) "If I could list everything that I feel grateful for it would be a very long list," and (c)"I stop and count my blessings nearly every day." The three items were rated on a four-point Likert scale (1 = disagree strongly; 4 = agree strongly). Reliability of the three-item measure was not reported. Instead, Krause (2007b) tested a structural equation measurement model and reported that factor loadings of the three measurement items ranged from .90 to .70. This suggests that Krause's (2007b) three-item adaption of the GQ-6 can be used as a key indicator of the gratitude construct. Krause (2007b) also acknowledged that the three-item measure of gratitude maintained a significant, negative association with depressive symptoms ($r = -.135$). Thus, Krause (2006) was able to provide supportive evidence that items of GQ-6 maintain a negative association with negative affect or emotionality.

A priority for future well-being research involving old-old adults should be the implementation of the GQ-6 or the version reflective of Krause's (2007b) three-item adaptation. It is virtually unknown whether feeling appreciation or gratitude makes old-old adults feel happier or more satisfied in life. The GQ-6 offers a brief protocol that gerontological investigators can easily implement with old-old adults residing in various contexts (e.g., community dwelling, assisted living, long-term care). Further testing and cross-comparison of the GQ-6 with classical and contemporary life satisfaction and happiness measures in aging research is warranted.

Valuation of Life Scale

The Valuation of Life Scale (VOLS; Lawton et al., 2001) was derived to assess global constructs reflecting the cognitive-affective embrace of life. The VOLS consists of 19 items designed to capture sense of purpose in life (e.g., espousal of meaning and goals in life), persistence (e.g., personal conviction toward worthwhile efforts to solve problems), futurity (e.g., optimistic outlook toward life), self-efficacy (e.g., judgment of future competence), and hope (e.g., positive expectation of current and future occurrences). Respondents are asked to rate their level of agreement on a five-point scale (1 = disagree very strongly; 5 = agree very strongly). Lawton et al. (2001) psychometrically tested the scale using old and very old adults and reported evidence of a two-factor structure. The first factor consisted of 13 items and reflected positive valuation of life (e.g., "Life has meaning for me"). The second factor included the remaining six items and reflected negative valuation of life (e.g., "I'm just putting in time for the rest of my life"). Internal consistency of positive VOL was reported at .94, whereas a Cronbach's alpha of .83 for negative VOL was acknowledged (Lawton et al., 2001). Interitem correlations for positive VOL were also reported to range from .37 to .73, whereas interitem correlations reflecting negative VOL ranged from .38 to .55.

With the exception of Ryff's Autonomy Scale, Lawton et al. (2001) reported that the VOLS displayed significant concurrent validity with remaining subscales of Ryff's Psychological Well-Being Scale ($r = .44$ to $r = .62$), measures of hardiness ($r = .23$ to $r = .40$), and assessments of individual mastery ($r = .35$ to $r = .52$). In addition, Lawton et al. (2001) acknowledged significant but weak correlations between the VOLS and measures of health (e.g., health conditions, activities of daily living), whereas correlations to measures of depression were moderate. Lawton et al. (2001) concluded that the VOLS may lack full independence from indicators of health and depressive symptomatology and therefore demonstrate marginal discriminant validity. Yet the VOLS has been reported to independently explain desired years of life above and beyond indices of health or depression (Lawton et al., 2001).

Evidence has suggested that negative dimension items of the VOLS are not well understood among old-old persons with lower levels of education (Lawton et al., 2001). Therefore, recent use of the VOLS with old-old samples has primarily been concentrated on implementation of the 13-item subscale of positive VOL (Jopp, Rott, & Oswald, 2008; Rott, Jopp, d'Heureuse, & Becker, 2006). This subscale has demonstrated satisfactory psychometric properties relative to investigations on old-old adults. For example, Lawton et al. (2001) reported that the positive VOLS subscale demonstrated high internal consistency ($\alpha = .83$) in a diverse community-dwelling sample of White and African American older adults over the age of 70. Similarly, Jopp et al. (2008) reported a Cronbach's alpha of .90 among old-old adults age 85 and older. Jopp et al. (2008) also indicated that demographic indicators including age ($\beta = -.22$) and marriage ($\beta = -.51$) were strongly predictive of the VOLS in the oldest old. However, health indicators (e.g., vision, Instrumental Activities of Daily Living) tended to explain a greater proportion of the variance in VOLS subscale for young-old adults than for old-old individuals (33% vs. 39%, respectively).

Investigators should continue to incorporate the 13-item positive VOLS subscale in research with old-old populations. The fact that this scale provides a brief assessment indicative of how very old persons positively embrace the meaning of life is advantageous toward advancing theoretical understanding of spirituality in very old age. Yet convergent and discriminant validity of VOLS relative to established religious and spiritual measures used with old-old adults remains unclear. Further psychometric evaluation is warranted.

FUTURE DIRECTIONS

The future of subjective well-being measurement applied to oldest-old populations may emphasize three important areas of study: (a) multiple group comparisons, (b) cross-cultural validation, and (c) cross-fertilization of existing measures. Sophisticated statistical software packages including but not limited to LISREL, Mplus, and AMOS have made it more convenient to critique the factorial integrity, reliability, and validity of quantitative instrumentation across age groups, cultural contexts, and other measurements. Many first-generation measures of subjective well-being tended to be derived using older adult samples who exclusively resided in the United States, whereas many second-generation and domain-specific measures of well-being were originally developed using young-adult and middle-aged samples but have been successfully tested in various cultural settings. In particular, second-generation and domain-specific measures, such as the Satisfaction with Life Scale (Diener, Emmons, et al., 1985), the Positive-Negative Affect Schedule (Watson et al., 1988), and the Retirement Satisfaction Index (Floyd et al., 1992) appear to work well in diverse cultural settings.

Nonetheless, there has been limited consideration of whether past measures of well-being are age or culturally invariant relative to contemporary scales. As Fry and Ikels alluded in Chapter 15, there needs to be greater appreciation and awareness of the cultural forces in the science of subjective well-being research. Investigators should be aware that some classical measures may have factorial structures that may be developmentally appropriate for use with exceptionally old populations and culturally sensitive for application across older diverse or special populations. Furthermore, classical measurement tools that appear outdated may actually withstand the test of time and remain effective evaluations of happiness or life satisfaction across a wide array of old-old populations.

In addition, the Satisfaction with Life Scale (Diener, Emmons, et al., 1985) appears to capture culturally relevant components of life satisfaction across diverse global context (Diener, Suh, Lucas, & Smith, 1999; Eid & Larsen, 2008). However, it remains unclear whether classical instrumentation, second-generation measures, or domain-specific measurement tools capture theoretically derived subjective well-being constructs (e.g., cognitive-affective) across multiple groups of old-old adults representing more than one cultural context. We believe that there is a need for greater testing, comparison, and cross-cultural validation of established instrumentation across multiple old-old groups (e.g., U.S. vs. international, community-dwelling vs. care facility, religious nonsecular vs. nonreligious secular). Multiple-group comparisons will help advance conceptual and theoretical modeling of subjective well-being in extreme old age.

There is a vast array of well-being measures from which investigators can select. Past and present investigators have acknowledged a need to cross-fertilize existing subjective well-being measures to derive more sophisticated theoretical conceptualizations of life satisfaction and happiness in old and very old age (Krause, 2003, 2004; Liang, 1984, 1985). Cross-fertilization involves the integration or blending of similar factors (e.g., cognitive-affective, happiness) across different multidimensional measures of subjective well-being. This was best demonstrated by Liang (1984), who used the LSI-A (Neugarten et al., 1961) and Bradburn Affect Scale (Bradburn, 1969) and established a new factorial structure of subjective well-being in old age. In particular, results from Liang's (1984, 1985) work conceptually redefined how to measure life satisfaction among older populations. As the field of gerontology continues to advance theories of aging and well-being, there will be an increasing need to restructure and adapt measurement instruments for the development and application of interdisciplinary and cross-cultural research (Krause, 2009). We believe that the cross-fertilization of measurement will help prevent the reinvention of previously established instrumentation and contribute to the identification of unique and common facets or subjective well-being indicators that universally represent the phenomenon in very late life.

This chapter aimed to inform investigators of several key classical, second-generation, and domain-specific measures of subjective well-being in late and very late life. Many of the presented measures have had limited use in domestic or cross-cultural research studies on the oldest old. Furthermore, there has been limited cross-cultural comparison involving subjective well-being measurement of old-old adults. One promising area for improvement would be the combination of quantitative assessments with ethnographic approaches (see the discussion of Cantril's self-anchoring ladder in Chapter 15) or clinical treatment therapies (see discussion of treatment review and Hyer and Sohnle model in Chapter 8). After all, not all psychometric instruments were originally devised as universal measures suitable for use among people representing divergent orientations, contexts, and cultures. Religious and spiritual measurements discussed earlier in this chapter are a clear example of this reality.

Cross-disciplinary integration of quantitative and ethnographic methods of assessment or clinical interventions could have two profound outcomes. First, it would improve clarity of understanding relative to how complex and dynamic biopsychosocial processes and systems contribute to the ebb and flow of happiness and life satisfaction in old-old age (see the discussion regarding baseline theory in Chapter 4). Second, it would foster greater interdisciplinary and transdisciplinary efforts to develop more sophisticated and practical measurement instruments or techniques applicable to a broader sector of old-old adults. We believe that greater integrative methods of measurement, assessment, and application will further necessitate a demand for innovative modes of psychometric inquiry. Such advances will serve to better inform scientific understanding of the richness and diversity of happiness and satisfaction in exceptional old age. Consequently, we hope that this chapter will encourage gerontologists worldwide to consider adopting psychometric measures into a repertoire of examination. We believe this will foster cutting-edge research and quantitative analyses of subjective well-being in exceptional old age.

REFERENCES

Aberg, C. A., Sidenvall, B., Hepworth, M., O'Reilly, K., & Lithell, H. (2005). On loss of activity and independence, adaptation improves life satisfaction in old age – a qualitative study of patients' perceptions. *Quality of Life Research, 14*, 1111–1125.

Adams, D. (1969). Analysis of a life satisfaction index. *Journal of Gerontology, 24*, 470–474.

Adkins, G., Martin, P., & Poon, L. W. (1996). Personality traits and states as predictors of subjective well-being in centenarians, octogenarians, and sexagenarians. *Psychology and Aging, 11*, 408–416.

Andrews, F. M., & Whitney, S. B. (1976). Social indicators of well-being: America's perception of life quality. New York: Plenum Press.

Anstey, K. J., Burns, R., von Sanden, C., & Luszcz, M. A. (2008). Psychological well-being is an independent predictor of falling in an 8-year follow-up of older adults. *Journals of Gerontology, 63B*, P249–P257.

Bengtson, V. L., & Black, K. D. (1973). Inter-generation relations and continuities in socialization. In P. Baltes & K. W. Schaie (Eds.), *Life-span developmental psychology: Personality and socialization* (pp. 207–234). New York: Academic Press.

Bengston, V. L., & Lovejoy, M. C. (1973). Values, personality, and social structure: An intergenerational analyses. *American Behavioral Scientist, 16*, 880–912.

Berg, A. I., Hassing, L. B., McClearn, G. E., & Johansson, B. (2006). What matters most for life satisfaction in the oldest-old? *Aging and Mental Health, 10*, 257–267.

Bishop, A. J. (2006). Age and gender differences in adaptation and subjective well-being of older adults residing in monastic religious communities. *Pastoral Psychology, 55*, 131–144.

Bishop, A. J., Martin, P., MacDonald, M., & Poon, L. (2010). Predicting happiness among centenarians. *Gerontology, 56*, 88–92.

Bishop, A. J., Martin, P., & Poon, L. (2006). Happiness and congruence in late adulthood: A structural model of life satisfaction. *Aging and Mental Health, 10*, 445–453.

Boivin, M. J., Kirby, A. L., Underwood, L. K., & Silva, H. (1999). Spiritual Well-Being Scale. In P.C. Hill and R. W. Hood, Jr. (Eds.), *Measures of religiosity* (pp. 382–385). Birmingham, AL: Religious Education Press.

Bradburn, N. M. (1969). *The structure of psychological well-being.* Chicago: Aldine.

Brant, C. R., Jewell, T. A., & Rye, M. S. (1999). *Congregational Satisfaction Questionnaire.* In P. C. Hill & R. W. Wood (Eds.), Measures of religiosity (pp. 484–487). Birmingham, AL; Religious Education Press.

Bufford, R. K., Paloutzian, R. F., & Ellison, C. W. (1991). Norms for the Spiritual Well-Being Scale. *Journal of Psychology and Theology, 19*, 56–70.

Cantril, H. (1965). *The pattern of human concerns.* New Brunswick, NJ: Rutgers University Press.

Chipperfield, J. G., & Havens, B. (2001). Gender differences in the relationship between marital status transitions and life satisfaction in later life. *Journal of Gerontology, 56B*, P176–P186.

Choi, L. H. (2003). Factors affecting volunteerism among older adults. *Journal of Applied Gerontology, 22*, 179–196.

Chou, K. L., & Chi, I. (1999). Determinants of life satisfaction in Hong Kong Chinese elderly: A longitudinal study. *Aging and Mental Health, 3*, 328–335.

Clayton, R. R. (1971). 5-D or 1? *Journal for the Scientific Study of Religion, 10*, 37–40.

Clayton, R. R., & Gladden, J. W. (1974). The five dimensions of religiosity: Toward demythologizing a sacred artifact. *Journal for the Scientific Study of Religion, 13*, 135–144.

Davis, J., & Smith, T. W. (1998). In *General social survey cumulative file.* Ann Arbor: University of Michigan, Inter-University Consortium for Political and Social Research.

Derogatis, L. R., & Melisaratos, N. (1983). The Brief Symptom Inventory: An introductory report. *Psychological Medicine, 13*, 595–605.

Dickerson, B., & Watkins, D. R. (2003). The Caleb Effect: The oldest-old in church and society. *Journal of Religious Gerontology, 15*, 201–213.

Diener, E., & Biswas-Diener, R. (2008). *Happiness: Unlocking the mysteries of psychological wealth.* Malden, MA: Blackwell Publishing.

Diener, E., Emmons, R. A., Larsen, R. J., & Griffin, S. (1985). The Satisfaction with Life Scale. *Journal of Personality Assessment, 49*, 71–75.

Diener, E., Lucas, R. E., & Scollon, C. N. (2006). Beyond the hedonic treadmill: Revising the adaptation theory of well-being. *American Psychologist, 61*, 305–314.

Diener, E., Suh, E. M., Lucas, R. E., & Smith, H. L. (1999). Subjective well-being: Three decades of progress. *Psychological Bulletin, 125*, 276–302.

Dorfman, L. T. (1989). Retirement preparation and retirement satisfaction in the rural elderly. *Journal of Applied Gerontology, 8*, 432–450.

Dorfman, L. T. (1995). Health conditions and perceived quality of life in retirement. *Health and Social Work, 20*, 192–199.

Dorfman, L. T., Kohout, F. J., & Heckert, D. A. (1985). Retirement satisfaction in the rural elderly. *Research on Aging, 7*, 577–599.

Eid, M., & Larsen, R. J. (Eds.). (2008). *The science of subjective well-being.* New York: Guilford Press.

Ellison, C. W. (1983). Spiritual well-being: Conceptualization and measurement. *Journal of Psychology and Theology, 11*, 330–339.

Emmons, R. A., McCullough, M. E., & Tsang, J. A. (2003). The assessment of gratitude. In S. L. Lopez & C. R. Snyder (Eds.), *Positive psychological assessment: A handbook of models and measures* (pp. 327–341). Washington, DC: American Psychological Association.

Erikson, J. M. (1997). Gerotranscendence. In E. H. Erikson (Ed.), *The life cycle completed* (pp. 123–129). New York: Norton.

Faulkner, J. E., & DeJong, G. (1966). Religiosity in 5-D: An empirical analysis. *Social Forces, 45*, 246–254.

Ferraro, K. F., & Schafer, M. H. (2008). Gerontology's greatest hits. *Journals of Gerontology: Psychological and Social Sciences, 63*, S3–6.

Fiori, K. L., Smith, J., & Antonucci, T. C. (2007). Social network types among older adults: A multidimensional approach. *Journals of Gerontology, 62*, P322–P330.

Floyd, F. J., Haynes, S. N., Doll, E. R., Winemiller, D., Lemsky, C., Burgy, T. M., et al. (1992). Assessing retirement satisfaction and perceptions of retirement experiences. *Psychology and Aging, 7*, 609–621.

Fouquereau, E., Fernandez, A., Fonseca, A. M., Paul, M. C., & Uotinen, V. (2005). Perceptions of and satisfaction with retirement: A comparison of six European union countries. *Psychology and Aging, 20*, 524–528.

Fouquereau, E., Fernandez, A., & Mullet, E. (1999). The Retirement Satisfaction Inventory: Factor structure in a French sample. *European Journal of Psychological Assessment, 15*, 49–56.

Goodman, C., & Silverstein, M. (2002). Grandmothers raising grandchildren: Family structure and well-being in culturally diverse families. *Gerontologist, 42*, 676–689.

Greenfield, E. A. & Marks, N. F. (2004). Formal volunteering as a protective factor for older adults' psychological well-being. *Journals of Gerontology, 59B*, S258–S264.

Greenfield, E. A., & Marks, N. F. (2007). Continuous participation in voluntary groups as a protective factor for the psychological well-being of adults who develop functional limitations: Evidence from a national survey of families and households. *Journals of Gerontology, 62B*, S60–S68.

Hall, D. E., Meador, K. G., & Koenig, H. G. (2008). Measuring religiousness in health research: Review and critique. *Journal of Religion and Health, 47*, 134–163.

Haynes, S. N., Floyd, F. J., Lemsky, C., Rogersdoll, E., Winemiller, D., Heilman, N., et al. (1992). The Marital Satisfaction Questionnaire for older persons. *Psychological Assessment, 4*, 473–482.

Heywood, F., Oldman, C., & Means, R. (2002). *Housing and home in later life.* Buckingham, England: Oxford University Press.

Hill, P. C., & Wood, R. W., Jr. (Eds.). (1999). *Measures of religiosity.* Birmingham, AL: Religious Education Press.

Hoyt, D. R., & Creech, J. C. (1983). The Life Satisfaction Index: A methodological and theoretical critique. *Journal of Gerontology, 38*, 111–116.

Isaacowitz, D. M., & Smith, J. (2003). Positive and negative affect in very old age. *Journal of Gerontology, 58B*, P143–P152.

Jopp, D., & Rott, C. (2006). Adaptation in very old age: Exploring the role of resources, beliefs, and attitudes for centenarians' happiness. *Psychology and Aging, 21*, 266–280.

Jopp, D., Rott, C., & Oswald, F. (2008). Valuation of life in old and very old age: The role of sociodemographic, social, and health resources for positive adaptation. *Gerontologist, 48*, 646–658.

Kahneman, D., & Krueger, A. B. (2006). Developments in the measurement of subjective well being. *Journal of Economic Perspectives, 20*, 3–24.

Kalkstein, S., & Tower, B. R. (2008). The Daily Spiritual Experiences Scale and well-being: Demographic comparisons and scale validation with older Jewish adults and a diverse Internet sample [Electronic version]. *Journal of Religion and Health.* Retrieved March 20, 2009 from http://www.springerlink.com/content/n328jm68v8pqojv1/fulltext.pdf.

Karasek, R. Brisson, C., Kawakami, N., Houtman, I., Bongers, P., & Amick, B. (1998). The Job Content Questionnaire (JCQ): An instrument for internationally comparative assessments of psychosocial job characteristics. *Journal of Occupational Health Psychology, 3*, 322–355.

Karasek, R., & Theorell, T. (1990). *Healthy work: Stress, productivity, and the reconstruction of work life.* New York: Basic Books.

Keyes, C., Shmotkin, D., & Ryff, C. D. (2002). Optimizing well-being: The empirical encounter of two traditions. *Journal of Social Psychology and Personality, 82*, 1007–1022.

Kirschling, J. M., & Pittman, J. F. (1989). Measurement of spiritual well-being: A hospice caregiver example. *Hospice Journal, 5*, 1–11.

Koenig, H. G. (Ed.). (1998). *Handbook of religion and mental health.* San Diego: Academic Press.

Koenig, H. G., McCullough, M. E., & Larson, D. B. (2001). *Handbook of religion and health.* New York: Oxford University Press.

Krause, N. (2003). Religious meaning and subjective well-being in late life. *Journal of Gerontology, 58B*, S160–S170.

Krause, N. (2004). Common facets of religion, unique facets of religion, and life satisfaction among older African-Americans. *Journal of Gerontology, 59B*, S109–S117.

Krause, N. (2006). Gratitude toward God, stress,and health in later life. *Research on Aging, 28*, 163–183.

Krause, N. (2007a). Evaluating the stress-buffering function of meaning in life among older people. *Journal of Aging and Health, 19*, 792–812.

Krause, N. (2007b). Self-expression and depressive symptoms in late life. *Research on Aging, 29*, 187–206.

Krause, N. (2009). Deriving a sense of meaning in late life: An overlooked forum for development of interdisciplinary theory. In V. L. Bengston, D.. Gans, N. M. Putney, & M. Silverstein (Eds.), *Handbook of theories of aging* (2nd ed., pp. 101–116). New York: Springer.

Krause, N., & Ellison, C. G. (2009). Social environment of the church and feelings of gratitude toward God. *Psychology of Religion and Spirituality, 1*, 191–205.

Kunzmann, U., Little, T. D., & Smith, J. (2000). Is age-related stability of subjective well-being a paradox? Cross-sectional and longitudinal evidence from the Berlin Aging Study. *Psychology and Aging, 15*, 511–526.

Lang, F. R., & Carstensen, L. L. (2002). Time counts: Future time perspective, goals and social relationships. *Psychology and Aging, 17*, 125–139.

Larsen, R. J., & Prizmic, Z. (2008). Regulation of emotional well-being. In M. Eid & R. J. Larsen (Eds.), *The science of subjective well-being* (pp. 258–289). New York: Guilford Press.

Lawton, M. P. (1975). The Philadelphia Geriatric Morale Scale: A revision. *Journal of Gerontology, 30*, 85–89.

Lawton, M. P., Moss, M., Hoffman, C., Kleban, M. H., Ruckdeschel, K., & Winter, L. (2001). Valuation of life: A concept and scale. *Journal of Aging and Health, 13*, 3–31.

Ledbetter, M. F., Smith, L. A., Fischer, J. D., Vosler-Hunter, W. L., et al. (1991). An evaluation of the construct validity of the Spiritual Well-Being Scale: A confirmatory factor analytic approach. *Journal of Psychology and Theology, 19*, 94–102.

Lee, J. Y., & Im, G. S. (2007). Self-enhancing bias in personality, subjective happiness, and perception of life-events: A replication in a Korean aged sample. *Aging and Mental Health, 11*, 57–60.

Liang, J. (1984). Dimensions of the Life Satisfaction Index A: A structural formation. *Journal of Gerontology, 39*, 613–622.

Liang, J. (1985). A structural integration of the Affect Balance Scale and the Life Satisfaction Index A. *Journal of Gerontology, 40*, 552–561.

Liang, J., & Bollen, K. A. (1983). The structure of the Philadelphia Geriatric Center Morale Scale: A reinterpretation. *Journal of Gerontology, 38*, 181–189.

Liang, J., Lawrence, R. H., & Bollen, K. A. (1986). Age differences in the structure of the Philadelphia Geriatric Morale Scale. *Psychology and Aging, 1*, 27–33.

Long, V., & Martin, P. (2000). Personality, relationship closeness, and loneliness of oldest old adults and their children. *Journal of Gerontology, 55*, P311–P319.

Lucas, R. E. (2008). Personality and subjective well-being. In M. Eid & R. J. Larsen (Eds.), *The science of subjective well-being* (pp. 171–194). New York: Guilford Press.

Lyubomirsky, S., & Lepper, H. S. (1999). A measure of subjective happiness: Preliminary reliability and construct validation. *Social Indicators Research, 46*, 137–155.

Lyya, T. M., Törmäkangas, T. M., Read, S., Rantanen, T., & Berg, S. (2006). Satisfaction with present life predicts survival in octogenarians. *Journals of Gerontology, 61B*, P319–P326.

MacEwen, K. E., Barling, J., Kelloway, E. K., & Higginbottom, S. F. (1995). Predicting retirement anxiety: The roles of parental socialization and personal planning. *Journal of Social Psychology, 135*, 203–213.

Maitland, S. B., Dixon, R. A., Hultsch, D. F., & Hertzog, C. (2001). Well-being as a moving target: Measurement equivalence of the Bradburn Affect Balance Scale. *Journals of Gerontology, 56B*, P69–P77.

Mangen, D., Bengston, V. L., & Landry, P. H., Jr. (Eds.). (1988). *The measurement of intergenerational relations.* Beverly Hills, CA: Sage.

Mangen, D. J., & Peterson, W. A. (Eds.). (1982). *Research instruments in social gerontology: Vol. 2, Social roles and social participation.* Minneapolis: University of Minnesota Press.

Martin, M., Grünendahl, M., & Martin, P. (2001). Age differences in stress, social resources, and well-being in middle and older age. *Journal of Gerontology, 56B,* P214–P222.

Martin, P., Kliegel, M., Rott, C., Poon, L. W., & Johnson, M. A. (2008). Age differences and changes in coping behavior in three age groups: Findings from the Georgia Centenarian Study. *International Journal of Aging and Human Development, 66,* 97–114.

McCullough, M. E., Emmons, R. A., & Tsang, J. A. (2002). The grateful disposition: A conceptual and empirical topography. *Journal of Personality and Social Psychology, 82,* 112–127.

Mehlsen, M., Platz, J., & Fromholt, P. (2003). Life satisfaction across the life course: Evaluations of the most and least satisfying decades of life. *International Journal of Aging and Human Development, 57,* 217–236.

Mroczek, D. K., & Kolarz, C. M. (1998). The effect of age on positive and negative affect: A developmental perspective on happiness. *Journal of Personality and Social Psychology, 75,* 1333–1349.

Mroczek, D. K., & Spiro, A., III. (2005). Change in life satisfaction during adulthood: Findings from the Veterans Affairs Normative Aging Study. *Journal of Personality and Social Psychology, 88,* 189–202.

Neugarten, B. L., Havighurst, R. J., & Tobin, S. S. (1961). The measurement of life satisfaction. *Journal of Gerontology, 16,* 134–143.

Oswald, F., Schilling, O., Wahl, H. W., Fänge, A., Sixsmith, J., & Iwarsson, S. (2006). Homeward bound: Introducing a four-domain model of perceived housing in very old age. *Journal of Environmental Psychology, 26,* 187–201.

Oswald, F., Wahl, H. W., Schilling, O., Nygren, C., Fänge, A., Sixsmith, A., et al. (2007). Relationships between housing and healthy aging in very old age. *Gerontologist, 47,* 96–107.

Paloutzian, R. F., & Ellison, C. W. (1982). Loneliness, spiritual well-being, and quality of life. In L. A. Peplau & D. Perlman (Eds.), *Loneliness: A sourcebook of current theory, research, and therapy* (pp. 224–237). New York: Wiley Interscience.

Paloutzian, R. F., & Ellison, C. W. (1991). *Manual for the Spiritual Well-Being Scale.* Nyack, NY: Life Advance.

Pavot, W., & Diener, E. (1993). Review of the Satisfaction with Life Scale. *Psychological Assessment, 52,* 164–172.

Pavot, W., & Diener, E. (2008). The Satisfaction with Life Scale and the emerging construct of life satisfaction. *The Journal of Positive Psychology, 3,* 137–152.

Pavot, W., Diener, E., & Suh, E. (1998). The temporal satisfaction with life scale. *Journal of Personality Assessment, 70,* 340–354.

Pinquart, M., & Burmedi, D. (2004). Correlates of residential satisfaction in adulthood and old age: A meta-analysis. In H. W. Wahl, R. J. Scheidt, & P. G. Windley (Eds.), *Annual review of gerontology and geriatrics* (Vol. 23, pp. 195–222). New York: Springer.

Pons, D., Atienza, F. L., Balaguer, I., & García-Merita, M. L. (2000). Satisfaction with life scale: Analysis of factorial invariance for adolescents and elderly persons. *Perceptual and Motor Skills, 91*, 62–68.

Poon, L. W., Clayton, G. M., Martin, P., Johnson, M. A., Coutenay, B. C., Sweaney, A. L., et al. (1992). The Georgia Centenarian Study. *International Journal of Aging and Human Development, 34*, 1–17.

Poon, L. W., Jazwinski, M., Green, R. C., Woodard, J. L., Martin, P., Rodgers, W. L., et al. (2007). Methodological considerations in studying centenarians: Lessons learned from the Georgian Centenarian Studies. In L. W. Poon, T. T. Perls, & K. W. Schaie (Eds.), *Annual review of gerontology and geriatrics. Vol. 27: Biopsychosocial approaches to longevity* (pp. 231–264). New York: Springer.

Radloff, L. S. (1977). The CES-D scale: A self report depression scale for research in the general population. *Applied Psychological Measurement, 1*, 385–401.

Riley, B. B., Perna, R., Tate, D. G., Forchheimer, M., Anderson, C., & Luera, G. (1998). Types of spiritual well-being among persons with chronic illness: Their relations to various forms of quality of life. *Archives of Physical Medicine and Rehabilitation, 79*, 258–264.

Roff, L. L., Klemmack, D. L., Simon, C., Cho, G. W., Parker, M. W., Koenig, H. G., et al. (2006). Functional limitations and religious service attendance among African-American and white older adults. *Health and Social Work, 31*, 246–255.

Rott, C., Jopp, D., d'Heureuse, V., & Becker, G. (2006). Predictors of well-being in very old age. In H. W. Wahl, H.. Brenner, H. Moleenkopf, D. Rothenbacher, & C. Rott (Eds.), *The many faces of health, competence, and well-being in old age: Integrating epidemiological, psychological, and social perspectives* (pp. 119–129). New York: Springer.

Ryff, C. D. (1989a). Happiness is everything or is it? Explorations on the meaning of psychological well-being. *Journal of Personality and Social Psychology, 57*, 1069–1081.

Ryff, C. D. (1989b). In the eye of the beholder: Views of psychological well-being among middle aged and older adults. *Psychology and Aging, 2*, 195–210.

Ryff, C. D., & Keyes, C. L. M. (1995). The structure of psychological well-being revisited. *Journal of Personality and Social Psychology, 4*, 719–727.

Ryff, C. D., Lee, Y. H., Essex, M. J., & Schmutte, P. S. (1994). My children and me: Midlife evaluations of grown children and of self. *Psychology and Aging, 9*, 195–205.

Schilling, O. K. (2005). Cohort- and age-related decline in elder's life satisfaction: Is there really a paradox? *European Journal of Ageing, 2*, 254–263.

Shevlin, M. E., & Bunting, B. P. (1994). Confirmatory factor analysis of the satisfaction with life scale. *Perceptual and Motor Skills, 79*, 1316–1318.

Shmotkin, D., Berkovich, M., & Cohen, K. (2006). Combining happiness and suffering in a retrospective view of anchor periods in life: A differential approach to subjective well being. *Social Indicators Research, 77*, 139–169.

Silverman, W. H., Pargament, K. I., Johnson, S. M., Echemendia, R. J., & Snyder, S. (1983). Measuring member satisfaction with the church. *Journal of Applied Psychology, 68*, 664–677.

Silverstein, M., Cong, Z., & Li, S. (2006). Intergenerational transfers and living arrangements of older people in rural China: Consequences for psychological well-being. *Journal of Gerontology*, *61B*, S256–S266.

Silverstein, M., Conroy, S. J., Wang, H., Giarrusso, R., & Bengston, V. L. (2002). Reciprocity in parent-child relations over the adult life course. *Journal of Gerontology*, *57*, S3–S13.

Smith, P. M., Kendall, L. M., & Hulin, C. L. (1969). *The measurement of satisfaction in work and retirement.* Skokie, IL: Rand McNally.

Spurlock, W. R. (2005). Spiritual well-being and caregiver burden in Alzheimer's caregivers. *Geriatric Nursing*, *26*, 154–161.

Stacey, C. A., & Gatz, M. (1991). Cross-sectional age differences and longitudinal change on the Bradburn Affect Balance Scale. *Journals of Gerontology*, *46*, P76–P78.

Stephen, Y., Fouquereau, E., & Fernandez, A. (2008). Body satisfaction and retirement satisfaction: The meditational role of subjective health. *Aging and Mental Health*, *12*, 374–381.

Steverink, N., & Lindenberg, S. (2006). Which social needs are important for subjective well being? What happens to them with aging? *Psychology and Aging*, *21*, 281–290.

Stock, W. A., Okun, M. A., & Benin, M. (1986). Structure of subjective well-being among the elderly. *Psychology and Aging*, *1*, 91–102.

Tornstam, L. (2005). *Gerotranscendence: A developmental theory of positive aging.* New York: Springer.

Vassar, M., Ridge, J. W., & Hill, A. D. (2008). Inducing score reliability from previous reports: An examination of life satisfaction studies. *Social Indicators Research*, *87*, 27–45.

Watson, D., Clark, L. A., & Tellegen, A. (1988). Development and validation of brief measures of positive and negative affect: The PANAS scales. *Journal of Personality and Social Psychology*, *54*, 1063–1070.

Westerhof, G. J., & Barrett, A. E. (2005). Age identity and subjective well-being: A comparison of the United States and Germany. *Journal of Gerontology*, *60B*, S129–S136.

Wickrama, K. A. S., Surjadi, F. F., Lorenz, F. O., & Elder, G. H., Jr. (2008). The influence of work control trajectories on men's mental and physical health during the middle years: Mediational role of personal control. *Journal of Gerontology*, *63B*, S135–S145.

Wong, E., Woo, J., & Ho, E. H. (2005). Depression is the predominant factor contributing to morale as measured by the Philadelphia Geriatric Morale Scale in elderly Chinese aged 70 years and over. *International Journal of Geriatric Psychiatry*, *20*, 1052–1059.

Wong, E., Woo, J., Hui, E., & Ho, S. C. (2004). Examination of the Philadelphia Geriatric Morale Scale as a subjective quality-of-life measure in the elderly Hong Kong Chinese. *Gerontologist*, *44*, 408–417.

Yang, Y. (2008). Social inequalities in happiness in the United States, 1972 to 2004: An age period-cohort analysis. *American Sociological Review*, *73*, 204–226.

Zung, W. W. (1965). A self-rating depression scale. *Archives of General Psychiatry*, *12*, 63–70.

18

Late-Life Psychotherapy: Challenges and Opportunities to Enhance Well-Being in the Oldest Old

LEE HYER, CATHERINE A. YEAGER, AND CIERA V. SCOTT

ABSTRACT

This chapter discusses problems with psychosocial treatments for the oldest old. We attempt to straddle the tenets of the Developmental Adaptation and Changes of Adaptation models as well as the offerings in other chapters. We highlight how the distal and proximate variables noted in the previous chapters are necessary but not sufficient for the eventual understanding of treatment outcomes in the oldest old. To date, the psychosocial adjustment and treatment of the oldest old have been largely ignored, having been given short shrift as a result of the medical model. The present chapter considers the biopsychosocial model as it applies to this developmental stage – issues, problems, strengths, and future directions. Given inherent biological limits, we specify the role of a life lived, one's life history, and how this might influence current stress and well-being. Finally, we discuss treatment models for other age groups and their applicability to empirically supported principles for oldest-old adults.

INTRODUCTION

In our chapter on posttraumatic stress disorder (PTSD), we argued that the trauma response is fundamentally a diathesis-stress response. The role of aging as a largely moderating influence in the expression of psychological trauma was construed as somewhat distinct, especially for the oldest old. Trauma itself is multidimensional and mixes with age, a variable that owns both positive and negative features as it relates to health and well-being. In that chapter, treatment required a focus on the "person" of the victim of trauma. Memories can be modified or transformed in the context of factors related to aging: mourning for losses, giving meaning to experiences, reestablishing self-coherence and self-continuity, and encouraging reliance on social supports. As with most psychotherapies, empirically supported interventions that apply to younger groups were borrowed and applied to the oldest old. In this chapter, we expand on this and address psychotherapy in general for the oldest old. We have several battles to wage when considering the extreme old age and psychotherapy, especially in regard to stressors carried into late life or experienced in late life.

First, there is the battle of ineluctable decline. Aging is seen as a stochastic process that occurs after reproductive maturation. It unfolds from the diminishing energy available to maintain molecular fidelity (Hayflick, 1988). Just one fact captures the panoply of problems and maladies for the oldest old: most lethal illnesses increase exponentially with age in late life, so that even a cure for any one disease has only a slight effect on healthy life expectancy (Smits et al., 2008). In fact, the recent emphasis on the construct of health span reflects the issue that increased longevity simply amplifies ill health encountered in the oldest old. At 85 years of age, the prevalence of disability jumps to greater than 50%, the percentage in long-term care (LTC) is slightly less than 20%, and the percentage still married is 24% (Hyer & Intieri, 2006). Psychiatrically, prevalence rates of degenerative diseases among the oldest old is concerning (approximately 50%) and even worse for those with memory complaints at extreme old age (approximately 66%) (Blazer, 2003). Perhaps there are certain ages when antiaging maneuvers ("windows of sensitivity") can result in beneficial long-term effects, but this remains to be seen (Perls, 2004).

Consistent predictors of debility among the oldest old are advanced age, gender (being male), physical disability, and poor self-rated health (Ben-Ezra & Shmotkin, 2006). Additionally, the negative side of such psychosocial predictors as social networks, volunteering activity, emotional support, and solitary leisure activities (see Shmotkin, Chapter 3) conspire to reduce well-being. In this book, too, MacDonald (Chapter 9) noted that time orientation (present vs. future), risk aversion, and preference for passive versus active participation in leisure activities affect older adults' resource consumption and, therefore, well-being. In highlighting Johnson and Barer's (1997) work, MacDonald also emphasized that very old adults are critically dependent on having someone who is able to manage ostensibly small changes that nonetheless have powerful and lasting impacts on quality of life (QoL) (e.g., a residential change). He added that even small cultural and environmental differences in the quality and redundancy of interpersonal relationships likely have very big effects on the comparative well-being of the oldest old. In the context of very late life's intensifying needs and depleted personal resources, cultural differences in the degree of social isolation may even contribute to mortality.

Shmotkin (Chapter 3) provided the challenges of the oldest old as a paradigm for the essential tensions of resilience and vulnerability. He identified several relevant theories: the common-cause theory (Fried & Guralnik, 1997), in which a decline of biological capability is posited to overshadow all other adaptive functions; Baltes's (1997) theory of incomplete architecture of human ontology, which asserts that human development is not programmed to function optimally in the fourth age because the compensatory role of knowledge and skill-based resources become less able to overcome biological dysfunction; the gerodynamics theory (Birren & Schroots, 1996), which argues that old systems cannot readily stabilize equilibrium conditions, thus requiring downward adaptation. It would seem, then, that the psychological status of the oldest old has little choice but to give way to necessary biological determinants at this age.

Second, there is the issue of psychotherapy at advanced age. Simply put, data for the oldest old regarding psychotherapy is burdened by the tentacles of senescence, especially health and cognition, and encapsulated largely in models of care represented in LTC settings involving the environment, major unmet needs, speculative stress, and fancied ideas of well-being at advanced age (e.g., see Cohen-Mansfield, Chapter 4). Data on outcomes are virtually nonexistent and what does exist is case based. This is due in part to the nature of the oldest old, whose health teeters on impending frailty (Beekman et al., 2002); in part, because actually knowing the entrails of generativity or wisdom is more mysterious than otherwise; in part, because our technology is too youth focused and/or too primitive to isolate extreme old age constructs without our own filters. Adding insult to injury, our filters, too, are wanting.

Third, we lack good constructs for the oldest old. Previous chapters in this book have wrestled nobly with this issue (and we address some here) but have largely offered no definitive findings for this group. Their writings remain in the hypothetical construct ranges of science. Depression in extreme old age, as one example, is distinct as it has more medical comorbidities, more middle and terminal insomnia, less positive affect, and less negative ideation (Hussain et al., 2005). Posttraumatic stress disorder is woefully understudied for the oldest old. What can be exported from younger groups is that PTSD exists, is susceptible to late-life slights as much as those fought earlier in life, and seems to become reinvigorated when there is a degenerative process (see Hyer & Sohnle, 2001).

In fact, the central models of this book (the Georgia Models; Martin, Poon, & Johnson, Chapter 5), models carefully considered, explain less than half the variance of adjustment. The developmental adaptation model integrates distal influences, resources, behavioral skills, and developmental outcomes. Individual, social, and economic resources; proximal life events; and behavioral coping skills act as mediators and do contribute to the adaptational processes associated with positive developmental outcomes. Exogenous variables (life events and past personal achievements) also point to the influence of distal experiences and events. Outcomes (functional capacity and subjective health, cognitive status, mental health, economic cost and burden, psychological well-being, and longevity) reflect fundamental quality-of-life characteristics. It is less a fact that we are trying to explain the whole elephant by pointing out different parts, and more a fact that we have imperfect proxies for what QoL or well-being really is at late life and our models of individual change are too loose.

There are other battles. In this chapter, we address the care of the oldest old from a theoretical perspective and then from a psychotherapy viewpoint. We highlight how the current science of psychology is wanting in this regard. We then provide 10 issues that emphasize concerns about the oldest old from a practical and psychotherapy context. We also borrow from other chapters for assistance in making these arguments. We end with some thoughts about possible solutions for this group.

CRITICAL MODEL OF CARE FOR OLDEST OLD

Macrolevel

We start with a challenge: How can the oldest old possibly adapt and thrive in a sea of frailty? As a species, we are in a state of permanent incompleteness as we seek personal growth and change across the life span (Baltes & Freund, 2003). There are several worthy models that address person-centered issues of the oldest old. In the not so distant past, Lawton's environmental press theory (Lawton & Nahemow, 1973) highlighted the importance of the environment in aging – when the demands of the environment cannot be met (environmental press), the individual's level of competence (person capacity) falters. In other words, if environmental demands and individual competence are not in sync, functional maladaptation will result. Lawton also held that the well-being of older adults depended on their ability to adapt to life, and that this could be accomplished by modifying the social and environmental context (Lawton, 1996). In so doing, the older individual attempts to control not only the sources of affect but also his or her response to affect.

Perhaps the best adaptive explanation of extreme old age is encapsulated in the Selection, Optimization, and Compensation (SOC) model of Baltes and Baltes (1980, 1990). This model posits that the ways in which an individual in decline selects, optimizes, and compensates for debility is critical for good quality of life. This model represents a holistic approach to aging: successful aging is reflective of doing the best with what one has. This model allows for problems, disease, and loss while emphasizing coping and a positive view of the inevitable. The three strategies of SOC promote adaptive responding to everyday demands and functional decline in later life, and they are associated with optimal functioning. However, they require resources. The more resources available to the aging individual, the better he or she can engage in SOC. Given the emergence of frailty and debility in extreme old age, the challenge then becomes how to apply SOC strategies. In effect, the elder must minimize the impact of age-related changes while maximizing potential gains from his or her environment.

The SOC model is really one of adaptive development, a framework for understanding the processes of developmental regulation over the life span. Baltes, Wahl, and Reichert (1991) view successful aging as adaptive functioning irrespective of environmental context. Selection in everyday life is defined as actively or passively reducing the number of activities, goals, or domains to focus on those areas that are most important in one's life. This is a loss-based selection. It is perhaps a matter of the "best" selection if the person selects emotionally meaningful experiences (Carstensen, Isaacowitz, & Charles, 1999). With age, adults tend to adjust for a more satisfying emotional contact. Socioemotional selectivity theory (SST)(Carstensen & Turk-Charles, 1994), a variant of SOC, posits that older adults prioritize the goal of emotional regulation. Consequently, they prune their social ties to eliminate unsatisfying relationships and to retain satisfying ones. Perceptions of a limited future, for example, were found to be associated with prioritizing generative and emotionally meaningful goals (Lang & Carstensen, 2002). Selection, then, involves a convergence of environmental demands, individual motivations, skills, and biological capacities.

Optimization is defined as enhancing the means to refine one's resources in a selected domain. It refers to adaptive processes or strategies in which indirect aging losses have occurred and there is an actual amelioration or maximization of means in spite of loss. Investing more time and effort in specific tasks or activities that provide meaning and less in others that are not as salient is an example of optimization. Optimization thus ensures the possibility of maintaining high levels of functioning in extreme old age in some selected domains through practice and acquisition of new knowledge and technology.

Compensation entails the use of new and alternative means to reach a goal or to maintain a desired state once a loss has occurred. Compensation demands a substitute by acquiring new strategies or reactivating older ones. People may alter or expand routines once a functional loss has resulted. Again, this occurs best when there are resources available. Compensation becomes important when life tasks require a capacity beyond that of one's current skills.

The SOC model embraces the potential of lowered performance in which behavioral dependency can be adaptive. In essence, the effective coordination of the three processes (SOC) ensures successful aging. The transition to extreme old age is accompanied by an increased awareness of what one cannot do in the context of what one can do. This transition influences the type of goals selected in late life. Because the central task of late life is adjusting to decline, one's possibilities can adjust accordingly. One's choices are probably most often a function of health, identity and personal characteristics, and attachments (social relationships and positive contacts). This can be positive.

In this book, Cohen-Mansfield (Chapter 4) presents a new conceptualization of well-being in old age. She describes the shifting baseline theory, which has significant implications for the way in which well-being can be assessed. This theory of adaptation across the life span argues four tenets: (a) multiple levels of well-being exist at any given time; (b) well-being is affected by both a trait and a state component; (c) people tend to return to their baseline level of well-being after change in their baseline level of functioning; and (d) there are specific exceptions to returning to baseline, such as cases in which a new baseline emerges that involves physical pain. The shifting baseline theory focuses attention on the notion that well-being is based on day-to-day experiences and thus captures how well-being could be enhanced in extreme old age despite substantial decline and devastating loss.

Microlevel

Emotion and memory are notable markers of late-life adjustment because they have been studied and because they provide information. Emotion is generally understood to refer to the biologically based multichannel response (physiological responses, subjective experience, and expressive behavior) to environmental stimuli. Research typically finds that the emotion system maintains itself into old age, with the capacity to experience and express both positive and negative emotions intact. J. Smith and Baltes (1993), for example, showed that, compared to young-old individuals, the very old experienced some decline in frequency of positive mood states but no change in negative affect. Mroczek and Kolarz (1998) identified linear relationships between age and positive and negative affect: younger participants reported the highest level of negative affect, whereas older participants reported the lowest level. Utilizing an experience sampling design, Carstensen, Pasupathi, Mayr, and Nesselroade (2000) found no age differences for the frequency of positive emotional experiences, whereas the relationship between age and negative affect was described as curvilinear.

As noted above, a well-formulated perspective on emotion regulation in adulthood is SST (Carstensen, 1993; Carstensen, Gross, & Fung, 1998; Carstensen, Isaacowitz, & Charles, 1999; Fredrickson & Carstensen, 1990). Socioemotional selectivity theory emerged as an explanation for the extremely well replicated finding of age-related declines in social interaction (Carstensen, 1992; Lang & Carstensen, 1994). Carstensen has suggested that older adults regulate emotions by acknowledging the social nature of emotional experience. Arguing that decline reflects an active selection process, SST proposes that, over time, the individual increasingly chooses to invest limited personal and psychological resources in close emotional relationships that maximize opportunities for the experience of positive affect and/or the avoidance of negative affect. In other words, older adults manage emotional experiences by selectively managing the social context. Choosing to spend time with a small number of intimate friends and engaging in activities known to be pleasant is an incredibly effective strategy for maximizing positive outcomes. Presumably the elder maintains this investment in close ties, conserves energy, and maximizes positive affect and/or minimize negative affect. This is a fertile area for study.

Where memory is concerned, there is more confusion: old (trauma) memories can be for the better or the worse. On the one hand, the autobiographical memory of older people is positively biased, which means that positive memories are more durable than negative memories, probably because of improved affect regulation, optimization, savoring the positive, and minimizing the negative (see Shmotkin, Chapter 3). On the other hand, negative outcomes (e.g., negative memories, bad events, poor health) may have more lasting effects on people's functioning and well-being than good outcomes. In an effort to explain this, Shmotkin (2005) has depicted subjective well-being (SWB or happiness) as a force for creating a positive psychological state in the face of life adversity. Its complement, the hostile world scenario (HWS), refers to the perception of impending actual or potential threats to one's life. The HWS is the embodiment of trauma. Then, SWB and the HWS are believed to regulate each other by various mechanisms to promote and maintain pleasantness and a sense of accomplishment. This can be done in many ways, as, for example, by adaptation (habituation to adverse experiences), counteracting (antidotes for dismantling HWS-induced negative emotions), or coactivation (mutual support of SWB and HWS). Finally, meaning-in-life is considered a system that functions in parallel to SWB for dealing with life adversity and refers to the ability to reframe negative or traumatic circumstances through reconstructive processes. The interplay between the regulatory function of SWB and the HWS to maintain stasis and meaning is complex and involves the mediators of several psychological mechanisms as well as life situations.

In summary, there is a homeostatic accommodation that unfolds in the oldest-old victim of trauma. Emotion and memory are at the forefront but are far from being understood or predictable. In addressing trauma, the health-care provider glimpses at these variables and attempts to measure and use them. In truth, at present, one wonders whether such themes can be applied as heuristics or possibly as therapeutic interventions for improved meaning in life.

PSYCHOTHERAPY AND VERY OLD AGE

As we turn to psychotherapy and the oldest old, we consider the broad context and the specifics of late life.

Context

We have a poor background from which to assert certainty. More than 50 years of research has led to few absolute truths regarding psychotherapy. From this broad perspective we know that (a) the differential effectiveness of competing therapeutic approaches does not seem to exist; (b) the superiority of psychopharmacological over psychological approaches has yet to be proved; and (c) the utility of psychiatric classification as determining the course of treatment is poor. In fact, our psychiatric nosology is vastly superior to our treatments, and this is because we can make our disorders reasonably reliable. We are also aware that only about 50% of those with a psychiatric diagnosis go to therapy, and of that number, only half are adequately treated. These numbers are considerably lower for older adults and even lower yet for the very old.

Psychology continues to make assertions "rich in bombast but bereft of fact" (p. 407; Hubble, Duncan, & Miller, 1999). There has been a conceptual and practical war in the science and practice of psychotherapy in the past two decades. The fundamental premise of evidence-based therapies is that research alone will suffice to answer most clinical decisions; the fundamental premise of evidence-based practice is that this will not suffice, as real-world practice is too complex. The latter asks, What does research tell us, what does the patient want, and what is available and realistic for the patient? Therapists make dozens of minidecisions for which there will be no empirical research to provide guidance. Certainly, practitioners do not expect that every therapeutic decision will be guided by research data. In the scientific sense, the influence of the independent variable is a temporary fiction that is modified over time by the complexity of the context. It is easily alterable by subsequent mediators and moderators. Chronological age, while often confounded, constitutes an important moderator on the studied variable to influence any main effect on outcome. With trauma, for example, it is hard to imagine an effect on which age does not have such an influence. It is generally accepted that experiencing past trauma or significant loss complicates the current trauma process (Green, 2000). But it also influences current physical health and, collaterally, health-care utilization. Felitti et al. (1998), for example, found that patients who experienced several types of adverse childhood events had increased risk of ischemic heart disease, stroke, cancer, emphysema, diabetes, hepatitis, and fractures. Finally, the interface of psychotherapy and medication (additive, synergistic, or attenuation) on positive outcomes in just about every psychiatric disorder is simply not known.

The conventional wisdom is that there are promising psychological treatments for most common psychiatric conditions. This means that there are therapies that improve upon the passage of time (efficacious) or outperform an alternative active treatment (efficacious and specific). If we as practitioners rely on the randomized clinical trial (RCT) to assess treatment efficacy and effectiveness for the oldest old, the use of randomization, clean subjects, a fair placebo or alternative therapy, blindedness of raters, and multiple perspectives of comparison is required. If the RCT shows significance, we must still do more to establish a measure of certainty by dismantling the intervention to reveal why the difference (e.g., relaxation, extinction, parasympathetic system, attentional processes, different cognitions). And finally, if we do have an efficacious therapy, we must do two more steps:

(a) Is it cost efficient? (Is the effect large enough?) and (b) Does it work differently on different types of patients? We can see the problem for the oldest old.

In this scenario, even if we extrapolate from younger ages, empirically supported treatments (ESTs) are never pure therapies to be used off the shelf for older adults. The oldest old, especially, almost invariably have medical and other neuropsychiatric comorbidities. And just coming to therapy can in itself be self-correcting. Therapy cannot be of a fixed duration; patients often seek out a given therapy or therapist; and first-rate therapy is aimed to improve QoL, not just symptoms. So we cannot always know what is common and therapeutic and specific and therapeutic. The gap between research and clinical practice for the older adult is not a newly created tourist attraction. It is real.

To drive this issue home, the most empirically validated treatment for PTSD involves cognitive behavioral treatment (CBT). About this technique, DeRubeis & Feeley, 1990 noted:

> In order to benefit from CT the patient must engage in, day-to-day, the methods and strategies learned in therapy. In order to do so fruitfully, the patient must already have experienced some changes in relevant thinking and attitudes. He or she must be more hopeful, he or she must have begun to rethink dysfunctional attitudes, and he or she must be able to generate sanguine reactions to events. . . . We might speculate, in contrast, that for pharmacotherapy the psychological state requisite for improvement is the belief that taking the pill is important. (p. 82)

This is hardly modal for the oldest-old individual.

Among the oldest old there appear to be a few truisms. First, nonspecific factors are prepotent in therapy. These assert a substantial influence on outcomes. A perusal of the components of therapy that apply include the therapeutic alliance (.25 ES), empathy (.32 ES), goal consensus and collaborative involvement (<.3 ES), homework compliance (<.3 ES), positive regard (.3 ES), congruence and genuineness (small ES), feedback from patient (small ES), repairing alliance ruptures (small ES), self-disclosure (small ES), relational interpretations (negative ES), stage of change (moderate ES), personality (moderate ES), and expectations and preferences (small ES). Second, there are many moderating and mediating factors that make small differences between therapies but are powerful enough to matter for older adults and certainly for the oldest old (Cuijpers, van Straten, Andersson, & van Oppen, 2008). In the context of PTSD, for example, outcomes following the diagnosis of a chronic health problem are mediated by, in part, behavioral and social pathways, and in part by posttraumatic symptoms (e.g., Friedman & Schnurr, 1995; Kendall-Tackett, 2009).

Third, we do know many of the factors that are central for psychotherapy for the oldest old. The core components of therapy involve a healing setting, an explainable rationale for symptoms and change, a confiding relationship, and a ritual or procedure for change. From the trenches, therapists who work with frail elders rely on behavioral activation, pleasant events, and simple coping or, if it can be managed, on meaning-centered strategies. One involves increasing pleasant activities, monitoring one's emotions, and practicing present-focused living, as well as listening to the narrative of the elder beset with a psychological issue. In general, older adults can successfully change from without in the form of behavior activation (Jacobson, Martell, & Dimidjian, 2001) or from within (meaning making). Krause (2007) has shown that developing a deep sense of meaning in life leads to healthier functioning, longer lives, and improved well-being.

PTSD

In this book, Hyer & Yeager (Chapter 8) identified the Developmental Adaptation and Changes of Adaptation models (see Chapter 1) as providing person, social, and economic variables that encourage or prevent older adults from processing and/or accepting PTSD ownership and carryover. Trauma at late life is both brought on and fostered by many variables, such as new small traumas, kindling effects, and conditioning effects. Those authors identified the distal and proximate elements of the expression of the trauma response in aging: from the scaffolding of the agents that subserve PTSD (genetics, perceptions of control and predictability, direct and vicarious conditioning, and prior trauma and emotional vulnerability) to the core components of PTSD (anxiety and panic), to health and its components (lifestyle habits and morbidity), and eventually to the expression of PTSD. They presented how an individual experiences a trauma, is conditioned by trauma's cues, encodes this as danger, and develops a panic or fight-flight-freeze response. This response yields to a series of avoidant behaviors to ensure that the trauma response will persist. Resulting symptoms are the phenomenology of the person's trauma reaction, which is perpetuated by negative self-related schemas and ruminations.

Characteristically, older adults fail to recognize the link between psychological symptoms and mental illness. They similarly fail to perceive the connection between psychological distress and physical health status, and they often reject out of hand the possibility of ameliorating suffering through a psychological intervention. Efficacious treatment of PTSD seems to rely on two mechanisms: (a) emotional processing of the trauma memory by repeated exposure and (b) alteration of the traumatic event's meaning. There is, of course, more to think about when considering the oldest old. Shmotkin, Shrira, and Palgi's (Chapter 6) study of Holocaust survivors at extreme old age reveals that the impact of trauma generally proves stronger than that of many good experiences. Traumatic memories remain vivid and personally significant, especially among clinical populations. Nevertheless, community-dwelling Holocaust survivors demonstrate a general resilience that may be reflected by, as well as derived from, the positive features in their life narratives. Trauma survivors probably enjoy positive memories, though their negative memories may overshadow the overall positivity bias seen in the general elderly population. Although it seems that happiness can maintain predictive power in comparison with suffering, which suggests that the past can keep life pleasant even after substantial trauma, suffering did maintain its predictive power among the Holocaust survivors, especially among clinical populations. Whether these findings apply to the general population of very old adults is unknown.

The will to live (WTL) also is relevant, defined as the psychological expression of a natural instinct of human beings – the striving for life, which can be self-assessed (Chapter 16). Its diagnostic value derives from its being a unique indicator of well-being among elderly persons, which expresses not only a state of general well-being but also one's commitment to life and desire to continue living. Findings from five large-scale studies of elderly Israelis, two of which used a longitudinal design, have shown that WTL significantly weakens with age. In all five studies, women systematically reported a weaker WTL than men, and it is explained by different variables for each gender. These findings indicate that, in elderly persons, gender roles and the aging process, with its related losses, influence people's WTL. Subcultural differences are also expressed in the WTL. Finally, these studies demonstrated that the WTL has been shown to be a product of rational evaluations of the quality and meaningfulness of life, as based on one's set of values, religious or existential beliefs, and unique life experiences.

ISSUES TO CONSIDER IN TREATMENT

For treatment of the oldest old, something different is required. Unfortunately, data on outcome studies for this age group are virtually nonexistent, and what does exist is case based and most often applies to LTC settings.

That said, we discuss 10 issues here that walk a shaky line between concerns of the oldest old and concerns of psychotherapy.

Issue 1: Maximize the Environment

An approach to managing problems associated with frailty and dementia is based on the philosophy of reducing disability through reducing demands of the task or environment. The emphasis is on recapturing lost or abandoned abilities, or on restructuring activities so that they can be successfully accomplished in spite of deficits attributable to dementia. Interventions that could accommodate or compensate for losses in cognitive abilities should have a substantial impact on reducing problematic behaviors in persons with dementia (Camp, 1999; Camp, Cohen-Mansfield, & Capezuti, 2002). For example, researchers in cognition and aging report that normal older adults' most preserved abilities, on which interventions should be based, involve the use of environmental supports and cues found in familiar surroundings, along with the use of aspects of cognition that are relatively spared by aging, such as automatic skills and implicit memory (Hess & Pullen, 1996; A. D. Smith & Earles, 1996).

Lawton and Nahemow's (1973) environmental press theory, described earlier, argues that an imbalance between environmental press and competence result in negative affect and maladaptive behaviors. An important point of this model is that the gap between environmental demands and person capacity can be lessened by adjusting environmental stimulation. In the Disablement Model, interventions in environments that provide appropriate levels of stimulation might prove effective in reducing disability (Verbrugge & Jette, 1994). From this perspective, for persons with frailty or degenerative dementias, a reasonable approach to reducing their level of disability is to lower the demand level of the task environment. Verbrugge and Jette (1994) note: "Disability can be diminished swiftly and markedly if the physical or mental demands of a given task are reduced" (p. 9). This can be accomplished by presenting persons with tasks that do not exceed their capabilities and but provide stimulation and challenge. Similarly, Cohen-Mansfield (2001) and Camp, Cohen-Mansfield, & Capezuti (2002) have written extensively about the need to determine the underlying cause of problematic behaviors associated with dementia. They ascribe such behaviors as generally associated with unmet basic human needs and argue that the most common of these needs is for social and physical stimulation, which are often not available because of a combination of dementia effects and the monotony of the typical nursing home environment.

Litwin (Chapter 12) examined the association of social relationships and well-being in very late life among older Israeli adults. He assessed social networks, the degree to which one is embedded in a social structure, social exchange, and the extent to which one is a provider or recipient of goods and services. Viewing these as measures of well-being, he concluded that the oldest old are more frequently the recipients of social exchange than they are providers. These findings indicate the diversity that prevails among the very old; many in this age group experience decline in social relationships and, correspondingly, a reduction in well-being, and many continue to maintain diverse social ties and to actively engage in exchange, accruing the associated benefits of each.

Clearly, not all of the oldest old are frail or dementing. However, most experience some measure of decline – in health; in social relationships; or, if traumatized, in psychological distress as well. A tenet, therefore, for extreme old age and for the practitioner treating the oldest old is to always be vigilant regarding environmental and social supports in the form of tangible help, environmental accommodation, social support, behavioral activation, and rehabilitation.

Issue 2: Individual Variability in the Treatment of the Oldest Old

To successfully cope with psychological distress, most people stumble into their own combination of lifestyle adaptations, therapeutic techniques, and mental adjustments. However, the oldest old have problems in therapy for reasons explained earlier. Therefore, the most successful therapeutic approaches encourage the person to take action in the face of a disorder that saps his or her resolve. Personalizing treatment is critical because the elderly face a bewildering array of health threats and social constraints that need special attention and because the services available in treatment settings may be confusing to them.

Comprehensive care algorithms may be required to target the modifiable predictors of poor outcomes and organizational barriers to care. The care model should, therefore, (a) target clinical and/or biological predictors of adverse outcomes of the psychiatric condition; (b) enhance the competencies of the oldest old so they can effectively use their resources; (c) provide psychoeducation, accommodate preferences, and maximize treatment engagement; (d) address unmet needs through linkages to appropriate social or case management services; (e) coordinate care among medical, psychiatric, and social services; and (f) provide continuity of care, prevent relapses or recurrences of depression, and preempt medical events and social stressors. The problem of adjusting to life as it presents itself is difficult indeed, with further slights in store for the elder. They not only require assistance in navigating environmental demands but also must engage in an almost perpetual redoing of life tasks and goals. The dance between assimilation and accommodation (Brandstadler, 1999) is endless, often requiring creativity on the part of health-care providers and family, which can be frustrating for all involved.

Issue 3: CBT as Psychotherapy Model for Oldest Old

The utility of the psychosocial treatment, CBT, and its conceptual relatives (problem-solving therapy, behavioral activation, and interpersonal process therapy) in the treatment of depression and PTSD has been established. Cognitive behavioral therapy is also time limited, educative, collaborative and active, goal oriented and problem focused – it emphasizes the present, requires therapeutic alliance, and has structured sessions. In addition, CBT monitors outcomes, builds rapport carefully, targets real goals, and focuses on relapse prevention. Of course, even the construct of relapse is different for the oldest old. Behaviors that are triggers for problems, negative self-schemas, and maladaptive interpersonal styles, as well as stress, continue to be prime suspects in therapy. But the attention paid to these issues is not as aggressive as it is for younger age groups.

Cognitive behavioral therapy utilizes case formulation. This is a deliberative, reiterative, and conjoint effort of identifying the etiological, precipitant, and maintaining problems of the person. It represents the formulation of theory, its transformation into practice, and the ongoing measurement of its impact. Case formulation is integrative and dynamic. It looks for the whole picture. Symptoms are placed in the context of cyclic patterns, both internal and externally driven. The elder becomes a participant-observer, becomes informed about the therapy, and grows into an active collaborator in his or her care. It is in this exercise that the whole of treatment is decided and measured. And it is here that we can tell whether treatment receipt (i.e., is the client getting what is called for?) and treatment enactment (is the patient doing what is requested?) are having the intended effect.

In extreme old age, there are differences and weaknesses that must be accommodated. The therapist's ability to relieve the negative, for example, is less viable than helping the oldest old build a pleasant, meaningful life. The therapist must be very person-centric and holistic to wrestle with meaning-making issues and end-of-life concerns as they affect current adjustment.

This is not typical CBT. Some time ago, Goldfried and Davidson (1976) noted other limits to CBT. It does not focus on appropriate expectations, optimal alliance (nonspecific techniques), or increasing awareness (via feedback); it does not encourage corrective experiences (either in or between sessions); and it does not provide reality testing in an ongoing way. These issues are often central to successful treatment of those at very old ages.

Issue 4: Power of the Therapeutic Alliance and the Therapist

Almost 50 years ago, Jerome Frank (1961) noted that therapy needs to facilitate healing by persuasion. Perhaps more than any feature related to treatment of the oldest old, the therapeutic alliance (TA) is critical. In general, TA correlates with outcome for adults in therapy (Krupnick et al., 1996). This is within range of many other effect sizes in therapy. The TA is even more relevant for the oldest old. In studies done at the University of Medicine and Dentistry of New Jersey (Hyer & Intieri, 2006), we found that older adults preferred the therapeutic relationship over any CBT technique. In LTC facilities, TA was an essential marker for change.

The road to change in therapy is mediated by the person of the therapist. Norcross (2002) holds that research indicates that more effective psychotherapists principally offer a strong relationship in the individualizing of therapy methods for a particular patient and condition. This requires considerable training and experience, the antithesis of the idea that anyone can do psychotherapy. For example, there is much more variance explained by therapist differences than treatment differences. In the National Institute of Mental Health Collaborative Health Study, Elkin et al. (1989) found that competent and liked therapists in the placebo condition had better outcomes than those in the psychotherapy and medicine conditions.

The TA has phases that must be addressed and met: goal agreement (i.e., therapist and patient collaborate on goals), task agreement (i.e., both agree on the steps of action), and bond (i.e., both respect each other). If the elder does not find the therapist helpful or likeable, there will be problems at best and treatment dropout at worst. The successful therapist, above all, is creating a kind of greenhouse, using empowerment and the TA, to help the elder flourish. On the basis of the client's assessment of the alliance, the TA becomes the resource that facilitates, supports, and focuses self-healing. We add here that the critical feature of the TA is how well the therapist matches the client's view of help and support (i.e., the client's theory of change). There is little evidence that matching on cultural or demographic factors assists in the positive association between client and therapist. It is simply the elder's liking of and feeling understood by the therapist.

Issue 5: Maximize the Elder's Positive Traits

Strengths are not always highlighted in therapy. Earlier we discussed the SOC model and how those variables lead to positive in outcomes. A sense of control, for example, has repeatedly been identified as an important factor in successful aging and emotional well-being. By adulthood, and particularly by older adulthood, the perception of control has stabilized (Seeman & Lewis, 1995). As a global personality trait, high internal locus of control has been related to greater life satisfaction, more positive self-concept, better ratings of health status, and greater participation in activities among the elderly (Eizenman, Nesselroade, Featherman, & Rowe, 1997; Rodin, Timko, & Harris, 1985). The few studies that have attempted to examine and enhance perceived personal control in residential care settings have found that greater levels of choice and internal control are associated with better well-being, less reliance on facility services, and greater participation in community activities (Langer & Rodin, 1976; Timko & Moos, 1989).

As individuals age, then, their primary control (e.g., creating modifiable goals that conform to their wishes) may decrease, but their secondary control (e.g., adjusting beliefs and goals in response to nonmodifiable conditions) may be more stable and malleable. Thus, elderly individuals who continue to place great import on primary control may experience poorer adjustment to the aging process than those persons who shift their paradigms and gradually place a greater emphasis on secondary control. When conceptualized in this manner, poor adjustment (e.g., general distress, depression, anxiety) may result from frustration associated with continuing to attempt to exert control on aspects of one's life that are no longer controllable. Individuals may poorly adjust to the changes associated with aging because they repeatedly place a high priority on controlling their environment, when often their ability to control the environment has declined considerably as a function of stage of life. It would be expected that elders who accept that declining control over the environment comes with aging, and who focus on their ability to control their own internal states and their own behaviors, demonstrate a more successful adjustment to aging.

Applying this concept to therapy, the majority of the variance of change in therapy is due to the patient. Bergin and Garfield (1988) noted that, rather than argue over whether therapy "works," we should discuss whether or not the client "works." Client involvement and the highlighting of client strengths are the keys. This refers to the background factors of therapy: cooperation (vs. resistance), openness, psychological mindedness, and collaborative style, as well as such trait components of self-control, efficacy, and mastery. Nimrod (Chapter 14) proposed the innovation theory, which is one way to optimize positivity and promote strengths at very old age. According to innovation theory, innovation is an opportunity for renewal, refreshment, and growth that is a continuation, in some respects, of earlier interests and capacities. As such, innovation has a positive impact on elders' well-being. Innovation and continuity can therefore serve as a coping strategy when facing negative events and restore perceptions of competence, control, and freedom. Bishop, Martin, and Poon (Chapter 13) proposed religiosity as another positive trait. Religiosity has been associated with better physical health among the oldest old and has been acknowledged as a longitudinal predictor of vigor in late and very late life. Bishop et al. also proposed that religiosity and spirituality represent energy resources that aid adaptation in very late life. There are many worthy roads to Rome.

Issue 6: Placebo as Therapy

Although placebo may seem a strange concept to introduce here, the placebo is important in therapy and for the very old individual. It represents a change in the mind-body unit that occurs because of the symbolic significance one attributes to an event or object in the healing environment. Weil (1998) held that the placebo response is a pure example of healing elicited by the mind. He considered this process as an ally for doctors used in the mitigation of disease. The art of medicine was seen as the presentation of treatments to patients to increase their effectiveness. This involved the placebo response (Weil, 1998).

The placebo response occurs when we receive certain types of messages from the environment. The messages work in some fashion to alter the meaning of our state of health. In effect, we sense a new meaning, and the body activates an inner pharmacopeia. It is often in the early stages of an intervention that the placebo is most active: the recipient knows that she or he is reacting better, which reinforces later changes. As psychiatry has lower rates of success than just about any other area of medicine, the placebo component can add measurably to the properties of change. Havel (1985) noted:

> Hope is not the same as optimism. It is not the conviction that something will turn out well, but the certainty that something makes sense, regardless of how it turns out.... It is also this hope, above all, which gives us the strength to live and continually try new things.

Regarding the oldest old, the types of messages capable of activating the placebo are ones that involve an explanation of what the illness means to the patient and family and what is likely to happen and change. A positive change occurs when the patient senses the illness has been explained, that she or he is surrounded by those who care, and that she or he can exercise some control. From this comes meaning; stories about what happened then can be integrated or changed. The placebo (the inner pharmacopeia) is a necessary condition for this to occur. On the one hand, as the elder believes in therapy, its effects are enhanced; on the other hand, as the practitioner believes in his or her treatments, the therapist communicates this confidently, thus maximizing patient hope and expectations.

Issue 7: Enhancing Self-Identify

Older people do best when they are self-organizing, proactive, self-reflecting, and self-regulating, not just reactive to external events (Bandura, 1999). A parsimonious and realistic view of the older individual's actions is that the person is neither driven solely by global traits nor automatically shaped by the environment. Rather, actions are guided by a person(ality) system that mediates the relationship between types of situations and the cognitive, affective, or behavior patterns of the person (Shoda & Mischel, 2000). Thus, there are predictable, characteristic patterns of variation in an individual's behavior across situations and age. Organisms self-organize and do so naturally, consistently, and holistically.

The self-identity of the elder persists. Even people with dementia retain a sense of personal identity, despite the fact that functional losses prevent them from clearly expressing that identity. Usita, Hyman, and Herman (1998) analyzed narrative life stories of six persons with dementia and found that the participants were able to retrieve and share stories, as well as update their sense of selves to include the present. In an exploratory study, Cohen-Mansfield, Golander, and Arnheim (2000) examined a systematic approach for the assessment of self-identity. Four domains of role identity were investigated (professional, family, leisure activities, and personal attributes) through information obtained from the persons themselves, their family members, and their formal caregivers. The familial role was found most likely to be remembered even during advanced stages of progressive dementia, possibly because stronger past roles and connections are more likely to be maintained. The self-identity in persons with dementia may depend on interactions with others that allow the identity to be expressed (Li & Orleans, 2002; Sabat and Harre, 1992; Small, Geldart, Gutman, & Scott,

1998; Vittoria, 1998). Golander and Raz (1996), for example, demonstrated the importance of caregivers' reminding, constructing, and reediting past biographies of their loved ones with dementia.

Along with the creative methods to unearth the identity of the elder noted previously, reminiscence therapy, especially, and encouraging personal narratives and fostering life stories seem particularly effective in promoting and expressing self-identity (Basting, 2003; Usita et al., 1998). Shmotkin, Shrira, and Palgi (Chapter 6) also discussed time as a way to guide life stories of different times, governed largely by the individual's level of functioning and less by the variables of age, marital status, residential patterns, gender, ethnic origin, and education. But the majority of research is still in the early stages of exploring the phenomenon of selfhood in dementia; as such, relevant outcome measures are still in their infancy.

Issue 8: Personality as Guide

Research on personality has made considerable progress in the past 30 years. The overall focus has been on trait consistency across the life span, its phenomenology, and ways to improve measurement. The broad outline of personality across the life span is now better understood (Caspi, Roberts, & Shiner, 2005; Helson, Kwan, John, & Jones, 2002; Jones & Meredith, 1996; McCrae & Costa, 2003; Mroczek & Spiro, 2003; Small, Herzog, Hultsch, & Dixon, 2003; Steunenberg, Twisk, Beekman, Deeg, & Kerkhof, 2005). Perhaps this is due to improved scales based on sound personality models (Millon, 1969, 1983), as well as the actuarial data based on the Five Factor Model (Digman, 1990; McCrae, 2002). In addition, recent progress in the use of statistical methods has provided newer tools to examine longitudinal trajectories of personality traits (Helson et al., 2002; Jones & Meredith, 1996; Mroczek & Spiro, 2003; Small et al., 2003; Steunenberg et al., 2005).

Personality traits are linked to adaptational processes and outcomes. Martin, Bishop, Poon, and Johnson (2006) noted that the cluster of emotional stability, conscientiousness, and extraversion is particularly prevalent in long-lived individuals. Gender differences in centenarians' personality traits suggest that higher levels of conscientiousness and extraversion were found in female centenarians than in controls. Personality traits are salient predictors of behavioral skills and mental and physical health outcomes. Perhaps the strongest predictor linked to poor mental health outcome is neuroticism or anxiety (Costa et al., 1987; Staudinger, Freund, Linden, & Maas, 1999). DeNeve and Cooper (1998) also reported that anxiety (as a trait) predicted lower levels of life satisfaction, happiness, and greater negative affect.

These developments in personality theory have special application for the oldest old. Mroczek and Spiro (2003), for example, followed a sample of 1,600 men from the Normative Aging Study for 12 years and found curvilinear slopes for neuroticism, which declined up to age 80, and an overall linear trajectory for extraversion, indicating no average change. Extraversion declined in men older than 80 years. As with many such studies, there were considerable intraindividual differences. Helson et al. (2002), too, found that dominance and independence peaked in middle age and that measures of social vitality declined with age. Some measures of norm adherence, such as self-control, increased with age. In a recent study, Terracciano, McCrae, and Costa (2006) examined personality traits over a 42-year period. Cumulative mean-level trait changes averaged about .5 standard deviations (SD) across adulthood. Extraversion showed distinct developmental patterns: activity declined from ages 60–90 years, restraint increased, ascendance peaked at 60, and sociability declined slightly. Scales related to neuroticism showed curvilinear declines up to age 70 and increased thereafter. Agreeableness and openness to experience changed little. Masculinity declined linearly.

In summary, personality is important because it encompasses the biopsychosocial patterns of the person and is predictive of adjustment, both psychosocial and medical. At late life, personality continues to influence the nature and severity of symptoms and overall adjustment of treatment-seeking patients. On this template can be mapped the probable behaviors and trajectories of the oldest old. In an effort to inquire about diverse strategies of coping with old-old age, Shmotkin, Shrira, and Palgi (Chapter 6) identified adaptational trajectories from a data set in Israel: the equilibrated, the descending, and the no-future trajectories. The equilibrated trajectory group, which conveyed the meaning of self-preservation, revealed the highest level of functioning on central markers of adaptation. The descending trajectory, although prevalent in extreme old age, was found to be a moderately effective strategy. The no-future trajectory suggested the lowest level of functioning. These findings open stimulating views on the adaptive roles of time-related perceptions of life at very old age.

Issue 9: Expand the Definition of Patient

Many issues that arise with the oldest individuals demand interaction with family and social agencies. Indeed, the family should be considered central to quality care of the elder. Two concerns are relevant here. One is caregiving.

Caregiving, in general, is commonly associated with burden, especially when the caregiver and care receiver are older adults. In fact, in addition to burden, estimates show that 40–70% of caregivers of medically ill older adults experience depression, with approximately one quarter to one half of them meeting criteria for a depressive disorder (Zarit, 2006). The added burden of dementia in the care recipient has been attributed to increased intensity of caregiving in terms of time involved in caregiving over the course of a day and degree of assistance needed for basic and complex activities of daily living (Russo & Vitaliano, 1995). When the care receiver exhibits behavior problems in addition to cognitive deterioration, caregiver distress is even more intense.

Certain caregiver characteristics influence burden as well, such as concomitant health problems (Brodaty, Griffin, & Hadzi-Pavlovic, 1990), being female (Mausbach et al., 2006), having poor coping behaviors (Mausbach et al., 2006), showing high expressed emotion (EE; Vitaliano, Young, Russo, Romano, & Magana-Amato, 1993), and being the care receiver's spouse (Lyons, Zarit, Sayer, & Whitlach, 2002). Caregiver overload, poor life satisfaction, perceived role captivity, and depression also add to burden. When caregiver vulnerabilities interact with care receiver problem behaviors, there is heightened risk for elder abuse. In their study of caregivers, Cooney, Howard, and Lawlor (2006) found that 52% of caregivers admitted to having carried out some form of abuse, including verbal (51%), physical (20%), and neglect (4%). Caregiver high EE was associated with all types of abuse; caregiver poor health was related to verbal abuse, whereas caregiver self-reported good health was associated with physical abuse.

It may be safe to assume that the presence of a caregiver in distress is modal for the oldest old. This person will require help and direction. The TA is as important to working with a caregiver as it is with the client. Development of a TA with the caregiver relies not only on an empathic understanding of the caregiver's unique situation but also on an appreciation of the influence of ethno-cultural beliefs about dementia and the caregiving role (e.g., Cloutterbuck, Mahoney, & 2003). Several models of effective caregiver assistance can apply (see Hepburn, Lewis, Sherman, & Tornatore, 2003), but those that target caregiver stress individually and those that are multimodal and intensive in nature appear to be the most effective (Mittleman, Roth, Haley, & Zarit, 2004; Roth, Mittelman, Clay, Madan, & Haley, 2005; Schulz & Martire, 2004).

The second issue involves the family or an appreciation for the family system. As an individual with dementia gradually loses the capacity for self-care and informed decision making, family members are under increased pressure to become involved in the decision making for that person (Karel & Moye, 2006). Such situations are bound to create conflict and even divisiveness among family members as to whose interests should be considered. Past filial relationships and present changes in family dynamics are potent variables that add substantially to burden. Family conflict and distress may be further heightened when family members are of the so-called sandwich generation – that is, individuals or couples who are between the ages of 45 and 65 and find themselves faced with balancing the needs of their own children with the demands and needs of aging parents (Riley & Bowen, 2005). In effect, when there are indicators of family strife, the therapist will want to consider a family systems component in the treatment to help reduce burden and foster decision making in the best interests of the elder.

Issue 10: Differences That Make a Difference – Cognition and Health

The cognition and health constructs both have been discussed in various ways here. The frameworks proposed by Martin and Martin (2002), Schaie (2005), and Willis (1991) allow us to address several important challenges to cognitive and health research in later life by adopting the life-span approach and the dynamics of continuity and change in the prediction of adaptation across the life span. Margrett et al. (Chapter 11) remind us of the complexity of assessing cognition in later life. In our previous chapter, we outlined several cognitive issues of concern for PTSD and certainly for the oldest old. This also applies to sensory deficits that may explain substantial age-related variation in cognitive performance (Li & Lindenberger, 2002).

The very nature and structure of cognitive abilities appears to change throughout older adulthood. Findings suggest that constituent cognitive abilities become less differentiated and more similar with increasing age (see Chapter 11). Although this phenomenon has not been well addressed in very late life, Margrett et al. (Chapter 11) remind us that a related developmental phenomenon, accelerated decline, which is evident as older adults approach death, has been studied. Research in that area demonstrates terminal decline (evident approximately 3 years before death) and drop (evident within 1 year of death; see Bäckman, Small, & Wahlin, 2001; Berg, 1996). This issue, too, has particular bearing on understanding the course of cognitive and problem-solving ability in very late life.

In addition, the increased heterogeneity observed in older adults' functioning, including group-level differences and the increasing prevalence of dementia in very late life, represents further problems and perhaps strengths.

Specifically, in Chapter 8, we noted that severe or prolonged trauma, or a history of such early exposure, places the aging individual at increased risk for cognitive decline or dementia. Particularly, deficits in binding and retrieval access to recollective information require additional executive functioning strategies to overcome recall deficits. However, older adults do poorly at late life where executive functioning is concerned. This is then compounded by trauma de novo or carried across time. The trauma memory is active, variable, and present during virulent stages. In summary, this is a special area that requires attention, assessment, and altered treatment when the typical older victim seeks help.

Health, of course, influences everything related to psychotherapy. Previously, we noted that across the age board, people who have traumatic events in their life or who are depressed and/or anxious have considerably higher rates of cardiovascular disease, diabetes, gastrointestinal disorders, and cancer. They are also much more likely to have worse lifestyle habits, to be heavy health-care utilizers and show poor compliance with prescriptives, and to have higher mortality rates (Kendall-Tackett, 2009). Exercise, stress reduction, and good health compliance habits are recommended as components of therapy and assert more variance than medications, procedures, and hospital admissions combined (Kendall-Tackett, 2009). It is no longer the case that treatment of the oldest old is just a psychological intervention in an office with soft chairs. The action is clear: mental health problems lead to physical health problems and vice versa. Those with trauma histories, even at late life, can be treated successfully and will adjust their lives even at extreme old age to down-regulate their stress response.

CONCLUSION

Hazan (Chapter 2), among others in this book, used the phrase "the fourth age," representing this time period as a subversive factor that undermines the tenets on which gerontology as a discipline is supported. With such bad press, the rationale for understanding very old age is strained, and concepts such as role, identity, mobility, memory, story, meaning, adaptability, continuity, productivity, and the like, pale in the service.

From the classic positions of psychotherapy, we have noted in so many ways that most change is self-change with loving support. We also have argued that core change involves more than just the usual strong-arm therapy necessities of accountability. The meter sways in the direction of self-validation and support in therapy for the oldest old. Whether this involves severe debilitation and a shifting balance of therapy, with the frail elder treated for well-being and not function (Chapter 4) or whether we are treating a more robust client, the need for stroking for the sake of support and providing tangible help is fundamental first-rate therapy for the oldest old. The focus in therapy, then, for those in the fourth age is remoralization, not remediation or rehabilitation.

In this context, the therapist's belief system trumps other issues in treatment. The wise therapist is not strongly change focused (i.e., solution focused) but, rather, encourages self-healing and fosters competencies, potentiates the past, and is attuned to patient. The therapist also takes on the role of therapy manager. In a sense, the therapist is an authentic chameleon. With the oldest old, too, the therapist may wish to make adjustments to traditional therapeutic techniques, such as being more active or task focused with a only few clearly outlined goals and using a psychoeducational label and collaborative approach. Techniques assist the therapist only as replicable and structured ways for developing and practicing values, attitudes, and behaviors consistent with core ingredients of effective therapy. Techniques then enhance the potency of the common factors; they are a magnifying glass.

Interpersonal process therapy (IPT), often practiced on elders, especially applies here. For CBT to be successful, IPT tenets need to be applied. Binder (1999) noted that the most competent therapist is the one who is flexible and autonomous. Similarly, Lazarus and Davidson (1998) too held that the clinician approaches therapy with a tenuous plan, a changeable framework for ordering the complex data, and, like any other applied scientist, must ultimately pay honor to the individual case that always calls for input/knowledge/skills beyond basic psychological principles.

We are a long way from a knowledge base for the systematic exploration of phenomena associated with therapeutic change that includes throughput and output. Throughput entails the cognitive and attention processes that are subserved by attentional resources, online cognitions, and coping strategies. As we showed, these are problematic for very old adults. Output involves the exploration of phenomena associated with therapeutic change – and activates the metatherapeutic processes associated with characteristics of transformation – acknowledging mastery, mourning the self, and receiving affirmation, plus their respective affective markers (joy, emotional pain, and healing). We find that these processes lead to an awakening of adaptive action tendencies; increased confidence; access to states of well-being; liveliness; and deepened capacity for intimacy, insight, creativity, and empathy. In effect, the patient becomes an active healer.

For the very old, it is time for psychotherapists to put distance between themselves and the classical medical model that focuses on the dichotomies of sickness versus health or disease versus cure. In a similar vein, scientifically validated treatments for the oldest only encourage therapists to create a Procrustean bed for their clients, where the client has to fit into a preconceived notion of disease and a corresponding structured cure is mechanically applied. Most very old individuals who seek help from a therapist are sick medically, but the humanistic issue involves experiencing mental or emotional pain and unearthing the fact that they are functioning below their optimal capacity. In the end, the oldest old are not cured but are helped to achieve improved functioning vis-à-vis the challenges and opportunities currently facing them through more productive and meaningful relationships with significant persons in their lives.

REFERENCES

Bäckman, L., Small, B. J., & Wahlin, A. (2001). Aging and memory: Cognitive and biological perspectives. In J. E. Birren, K. Schaie, & K. Warner (Eds.). *Handbook of the psychology of aging* (5th ed., pp. 3419–3377). San Diego, CA: Academic Press.

Baltes, P. B. (1997). On the incomplete architecture of human ontogeny: Selection, optimization, and compensation as foundation of developmental theory. *American Psychologist*, *52*, 366–380.

Baltes, P. B., & Baltes, M. M. (1980). Plasticity and variability in psychological aging: Methodological and theoretical issues. In G. E. Gurski (Ed.), *Determining the effects of aging on the central nervous system* (pp. 41–66). Berlin: Schering.

Baltes, P. B., & Baltes, M. M. (Eds.). (1990). *Successful aging: Perspectives from the behavioral sciences.* New York: Cambridge University Press.

Baltes, P. B., & Freund, A. M. (2003). The intermarriage of wisdom and selective optimization with compensation (SOC): Two meta-heuristics guiding the conduct of life. In C. L. M. Keyes & J. Haidt (Eds.), *Flourishing: Positive psychology and the life well-lived* (pp. 249–273). Washington, DC: American Psychological Association Books.

Baltes, M. M., Wahl, H. W., & Reichert, M. (1991). Successful aging in long-term care institutions. In K. W. Schaie (Ed.), *Annual Review of Gerontology and Geriatrics* (Vol. 11, pp. 311–337). New York: Springer-Verlag.

Bandura, A. (1999). Moral disengagement in the perpetration of inhumanities. *Personality and Social Psychology Review*, *3*, 193–209.

Basting, A. D. (2003). Looking back on loss: Views of the self in Alzheimer's disease. *Journal of Aging Studies*, *17*, 87–99.

Beekman, A., Geerlings, S., Deeg, D., Smit, J., Schoevers, R., de Beurs, E., et al. (2002). The natural history of late life depression: A 6 year prospective study in the community. *Archives of General Psychiatry*, *59*, 605–611.

Ben-Ezra, M., & Shmotkin, D. (2006). Predictors of mortality in the old-old in Israel: The cross-sectional and longitudinal aging study. *Journal of American Geriatrics Society*, *54*, 906–911.

Berg, S. (1996). Aging, behavior, and terminal decline. In J. E. Birren, K. W. Schaie, R. P. Abeles, M. Gatz, & T. A. Salthouse (Eds.), *Handbook of the psychology of aging* (4th ed., pp. 323–337). San Diego, CA: Academic Press.

Bergin, S. L., & Garfield, A. E. (1988). *Handbook of psychotherapy and behavior change.* New York: Wiley.

Binder, J. L. (1999). Issues in teaching and learning time-limited psychodynamic psychotherapy. *Clinical Psychology Review, 19*, 705–719.

Birren, J. E., & Schroots, J. J. F. (1996). History, concepts and theory in the psychology of aging. In J. E. Birren & K. W. Schaie (Eds.). *Handbook of the psychology of aging,* 3rd ed., (pp. 3–23). San Diego, CA: Academic Press.

Blazer, D. (2003). Depression in late life: Review and commentary. *Journal of Gerontological Science, 58A*, 1693–1699.

Brandtstädter, J. (1999). Sources of resilience in the aging self: Toward integrating perspectives. In T. M. Hess & F. Blanchard-Fields (Eds.), *Social cognition and aging* (pp. 123–141). San Diego, CA: Academic Press.

Brodaty, H., Griffin, D., & Hadzi-Pavlovic, D. (1990). A survey of dementia carers: Doctors' communications, problem behaviours, and institutional care. *Australian and New Zealand Journal of Psychiatry, 24*, 362–370.

Camp, C. J. (1999). *Montessori-based activities for persons with dementia.* Cleveland, OH: Menorah Park Center for Senior Living.

Camp, C. J., Cohen-Mansfield, J., & Capezuti, E. A. (2002). Mental health services in nursing homes: Use of nonpharmacologic interventions among nursing home residents with dementia. *Psychiatric Services, 53*, 1397–1404.

Carstensen, L. L. (1992). Social and emotional patterns in adulthood: Support for socioemotional selectivity theory. *Psychology and Aging, 7*, 331–338.

Carstensen, L. L. (1993). Motivation for social contact across the lifespan: A theory of socioemotional selectivity. In J. Jacobs (Ed.), *Nebraska Symposium on Motivation* (Vol. 39, pp. 209–254). Lincoln: University of Nebraska Press.

Carstensen, L. L., Gross, J. J., & Fung, H. H. (1998). The social context of emotional experience. *Annual Review of Gerontology and Geriatrics, 17*, 325–352.

Carstensen, L. L., Isaacowitz, D. M., & Charles, S. T. (1999). Taking time seriously: A theory of socioemotional selectivity. *American Psychologist, 54*, 165–181.

Carstensen, L. L., Pasupathi, M., Mayr, U., & Nesselroade, J. R. (2000). Emotional experience in everyday life across the adult life span. *Journal of Personality and Social Psychology, 79*, 644–655.

Carstensen, L. L., & Turk-Charles, S. (1994). The salience of emotion across the adult life span. *Psychology and Aging, 9*, 259–264.

Caspi, A., Roberts, B. W., & Shiner, R. (2005). Personality development. *Annual Review of Psychology, 56*, 453–484.

Cloutterbuck, J., & Mahoney, D. F. (2003). African American dementia caregivers: The duality of respect. *Dementia: The International Journal of Social Research and Practice, 2*, 221–243.

Cohen-Mansfield, J. (2001). Managing agitation in elderly patients with dementia. *Geriatric Times, 2*, 22–30.

Cohen-Mansfield, J., Golander, H., & Arnheim, G. (2000). Self-identity in older persons suffering from dementia: Preliminary results. *Social Science and Medicine, 51*, 381–394.

Cooney, C., Howard, R., & Lawlor, B. (2006). Abuse of vulnerable people with dementia by their carers: Can we identify those most at risk? *International Journal of Geriatric Psychiatry, 21*, 564–571.

Costa, P. T., Zonderman, A. B., McCrae, R. R., Cornoni-Huntley, J., Locke, B. Z., & Barbano, H. E. (1987). Longitudinal analyses of psychological well-being in a national sample: Stability of mean levels. *Journal of Gerontology, 42*, 50–55.

Cuijpers, P., van Straten, A., Andersson, G., & van Oppen, P. (2008). Psychotherapy for depression in adults: A meta-analysis of comparative outcome studies. *Journal of Consulting and Clinical Psychology, 76*, 909–922.

DeNeve, K. M., & Cooper, H. (1998). The happy personality: A meta-analysis of 137 personality traits and subjective well-being. *Psychological Bulletin, 133*, 197–229.

DeRubeis, R. J., & Feeley, M. (1990). Determinants of change in cognitive therapy for depression. *Cognitive Therapy and Research, 14*, 469–482.

Digman, J. M. (1990). Personality structure: Emergence of the five-factor model. *Annual Review of Psychology, 41*, 417–440.

Eizenman, D. R., Nesselroade, J. R., Featherman, D. L., & Rowe, J. R. (1997). Intraindividual variability in perceived control in an older sample: The MacArthur successful aging studies. *Psychology and Aging, 12*, 489–502.

Elkin, I., Shea, M., Watkins, J., Imber, S., Sotsky, S., Collins, J., et al. (1989). National Institute of Mental Health Treatment of Depression Collaborative Research Program: General effectiveness of treatments. *Archives of General Psychiatry, 46*, 971–982.

Felitti, V. J., Anda, R. F., Nordenberg, D., Williamson, D. F., Spitz, A. M., Edwards, V., et al. (1998). Relationship of childhood abuse and household dysfunction to many of the leading causes of death in adults: The Adverse Childhood Experiences (ACE) Study. *American Journal of Preventive Medicine, 14*, 245–258.

Frank, J. D. (1961). *Persuasion and healing*. Baltimore, MD.: Johns Hopkins Press.

Frederickson, B. L., & Carstensen, L. L. (1990). Choosing social partners: How old age and anticipated endings make people more selective. *Psychology and Aging, 5*, 335–347.

Fried, L. P., & Guralnik, J. M. (1997). Disability in older adults: Evidence regarding significance, etiology, and risk. *Journal of American Geriatrics Society, 45*, 92–100.

Friedman, M. J., & Schnurr, P. P. (1995). The relationship between trauma, posttraumatic stress disorder, and physical health. In M. J. Friedman, D. S. Charney, & A. Y. Deutch (Eds.), *Neurobiological and clinical consequences of stress: From normal adaptation to posttraumatic stress disorder*. Philadelphia: Lippincott-Raven.

Golander, H., & Raz, A. E. (1996). The mask of dementia: Images of demented residents in a nursing war. *Ageing and Society, 16*, 269–285.

Goldfried, M., & Davidson, G. (1976). *Clinical behavioral therapy*. New York: Holt, Rinehart, and Winston.

Green, B. L. (2000). *Traumatic loss: Conceptual and empirical links between trauma and bereavement*. New York: Routledge.

Havel, V. (1985). *Power of the powerless*. Armonk, NY: Sharpe.

Hayflick, L. (1988). Why do we live so long? *Geriatrics, 43*, 77–87.

Helson, R., Kwan, V. S. Y., John, O. P., & Jones, C. (2002). The growing evidence for personality change in adulthood: Findings from research with personality inventories. *Journal of Research in Personality, 36*, 287–306.

Hepburn, K., Lewis, M., Sherman, C., & Tornatore, J. (2003). The savvy caregiver program: Developing and testing a transportable dementia family caregiver training program. *Gerontologist, 43*, 908–915.

Hess, T. M., & Pullen, S. M. (1996). Memory in context. In F. Blanchard-Fields & T. M. Hess (Eds.), *Perspectives on cognitive change in adulthood and aging* (pp. 387–427). New York: McGraw-Hill.

Hubble, M. A., Duncan, B. L., & Miller, S. D. (1999). *The heart and soul of change: What works in therapy.* Washington, DC: American Psychological Association.

Hussain, M. M., Rush, A. J., Sackeim, H. A., Wisniewski, S. R., McClintock, S. M., Craven, N., et al. (2005). Age-related characteristics of depression: A preliminary STAR*D report. *American Journal of Geriatric Psychiatry, 13*, 852–860.

Hyer, L., & Intieri, R. (2006). *Geropsychological interventions in long-term care.* New York: Springer.

Hyer, L., & Sohnle, S. (2001). *Trauma among older people: Issues and treatment.* Philadelphia: Brunner-Routledge.

Jacobson, N. S., Martell, C. R., & Dimidjian, S. (2001). Behavioral activation treatment for depression: Returning to contextual roots. *Clinical Psychology: Science and Practice, 8*, 255–270.

Johnson, C. L., & Barer, B. M. (1997). *Life beyond 85 years.* New York: Springer.

Jones, C. J., & Meredith, W. (1996). Patterns of personality change across the life span. *Psychology and Aging, 11*, 57–65.

Karel, M. J., & Moye, J. (2006). The ethics of dementia caregiving. In S. M. Lobo-Prabhu, V. A. Molinari, & J. W. Lomax (Eds.), *Supporting the caregiver in dementia: A guide for health care professionals* (pp. 261–284). Baltimore: John Hopkins University Press.

Kendall-Tackett, K. (2009). *Trauma and physical health: Understanding the effects of extreme stress and of psychological harm.* New York: Routledge.

Krause, N. (2007). Longitudinal study of social support and meaning in life. *Psychology and Aging, 22*, 456–469.

Krupnick, J. L., Sotsky, S. M., Elkin, I., Simmens, S., Moyer, J., Watkins, J., et al. (1996). The role of the therapeutic alliance in psychotherapy and pharmacotherapy outcome: Findings in the National Institute of Health treatment of depression collaborative research program. *Journal of Consulting and Clinical Psychology, 64*, 532–539.

Lang, F. R., & Carstensen, L. L. (1994). Close emotional relationships in late life: Further support for proactive aging in the social domain. *Psychology and Aging, 9*, 315–324.

Lang, F. R., & Carstensen, L. L. (2002). Time counts: Future time perspectives, goals, and social relationships. *Psychology and Aging, 17*, 125–139.

Langer, E. J., & Rodin, J. (1976). The effects of choice and enhanced personal responsibility for the aged: A field experiment in an institutional setting. *Journal of Personality and Social Psychology, 34*, 191–198.

Lawton, M. P. (1996). Quality of life and affect in later life. In C. Magai & S. H. McFadden (Eds.), *Handbook of emotion, adult development, and aging* (pp. 327–348). San Diego, CA: Academic Press.

Lawton, M. P., & Nahemow, L. (1973). *Ecology and the aging process.* Washington, DC: American Psychological Association.

Li, K., & Lindenberger, U. (2002). Relations between aging sensory/sensorimotor and cognitive functions. *Neuroscience and Biobehavioral Reviews, 26*, 777–783.
Li, K., & Orleans, M. (2002). Personhood in a world of forgetfulness: An ethnography of the self-process among Alzheimer's patients. *Journal of Aging and Identity, 7*, 227–244.
Lyons, K. S., Zarit, S. H., Sayer, A. G., & Whitlach, C. J. (2002). Caregiving as a dyadic process: Perspectives from caregiver and receiver. *Journals of Gerontology Series B: Psychological Sciences and Social Sciences, 57*, 195–204.
Martin, P., Bishop, A., Poon, L., & Johnson, M. A. (2006). Influence of personality and health behaviors on fatigue in late and very late life. *Journals of Gerontology: Psychological Sciences, 61B*, P161–P166.
Martin, P., & Martin, M. (2002). Proximal and distal influences on development: The model of developmental adaptation. *Developmental Review, 22*, 78–96.
Mausbach, B. T., Aschbacher, K., Patterson, T. L., Ancoli-Israel, S., von Kanel, R., Mills, P. J., et al. (2006). Avoidant coping partially mediates the relationship between patient problem behaviors and depressive symptoms in spousal Alzheimer caregivers. *American Journal of Geriatric Psychiatry, 14*, 299–306.
McCrae, R. R. (2002). *The five-factor model of personality across cultures*. New York: Kluwer Academic.
McCrae, R. R., & Costa, P. T. (2003). *Personality in adulthood: A five-factor theory perspective* (2nd ed.). New York: Guilford Press.
Millon, T. (1969). *Modern psychopathology*. Philadelphia: Saunders.
Millon, T. (1983). *Theories of personality and psychopathology*. New York: Holt, Rinehart, and Winston.
Millon, T., & Davis, R. (1996). *Disorders of personality: DSM-IV and beyond*. New York: Wiley.
Mittleman, M., Roth, D., Haley, W., & Zarit, S. (2004). Effects of a caregiver intervention on negative caregiver appraisals of behavior problems in patients with Alzheimer's disease: Results of a randomized trial. *Journals of Gerontology B: Psychological Sciences and Social Sciences, 59B*, 27–34.
Mroczek, D. K., & Kolarz, C. M. (1998). The effect of age on positive and negative effect: A developmental perspective on happiness. *Journal of Personality and Social Psychology, 75*, 1333–1349.
Mroczek, D. K., & Spiro, A. (2003). Modeling intraindividual change in personality traits: Findings from the normative aging study. *Journals of Gerontology Series B: Psychological Sciences and Social Sciences, 58*, 153–165.
Norcross, J. N. C. (2002). *Psychotherapy relationships that work: Therapist contributions and responsiveness to patients*. New York: Oxford University Press.
Perls, T. T. (2004). Antiaging quackery: Human growth hormone and tricks of the trade, more dangerous than ever. *Journal of Gerontology: Biological Sciences, 59A*, 682–691.
Riley, L. D., & Bowen, C. P. (2005). The sandwich generation: Challenges and coping strategies of multigenerational families. *Family Journal, 13*, 52–58.
Rodin, J., Timko, C., & Harris, S. (1985). The construct of control: Biological and psychosocial correlates. *Annual Review of Gerontology and Geriatrics, 5*, 3–55.
Roth, D. L., Mittleman, M. S., Clay, O. J., Madan, A., & Haley, W. E. (2005). Changes in social supports as mediators of the impact of a psychosocial intervention for

spouse caregivers of persons with Alzheimer's disease. *Psychology and Aging, 20*, 634–644.

Russo, J., & Vitaliano, P. P. (1995). Life events as correlates of burden in spouse caregivers of persons with Alzheimer's disease. *Experimental Aging Research, 21*, 273–294.

Sabat, S. R., & Harre, R. (1992). The construction and deconstruction of self in Alzheimer's disease. *Ageing and Society, 12*, 443–461.

Schaie, K. W. (2005). *Developmental influences on adult intellectual development: The Seattle longitudinal study.* New York: Oxford University Press.

Schulz, R., & Martire, L. M. (2004). Family caregiving of persons with dementia prevalence, health effects, and support strategies. *American Journal of Geriatric Psychiatry, 12*, 240–249.

Seeman, M., & Lewis, S. (1995). Powerlessness, health, and mortality: A longitudinal study of older men and mature women. *Social Science and Medicine, 41*, 517–525.

Shmotkin, D. (2005). Happiness in the face of adversity: Reformulating the dynamic and modular bases of subjective well-being. *Review of General Psychology, 9*, 291–325.

Shoda, Y., & Mischel, W. (2000). Reconciling contextualism with the core assumptions of personality psychology. *European Journal of Personality, 14*, 407–428.

Small, B. J., Hertzog, C., Hultsch, D. F., & Dixon, R. A. (2003). Stability and change in adult personality over 6 years: Findings from the Victoria Longitudinal Study. *Journals of Gerontology: Series B. Psychological Sciences and Social Sciences, 58*, 166–176.

Small, J. A., Geldart, K., Gutman, G., & Scott, M. C. (1998). The discourse of self in dementia. *Ageing and Society, 18*, 291–316.

Smith, A. D., & Earles, J. L. (1996). Memory changes in normal aging. In F. Blanchard-Fields& T. Hess (Eds.), *Cognitive changes in adulthood and aging.* New York: McGraw-Hill.

Smith, J., & Baltes, P. B. (1993). *Differential psychological ageing: Profiles of the old and very old.* New York: Cambridge University Press.

Smits, F., Smits, N., Schoevers, R., Deeg, D., Beekman A., & Cuijpers, A. (2008). An epidemiological approach to depression in old age. *American Journal of Geriatric Psychiatry, 16*, 444–453.

Staudinger, U. M., Freund, A. M., Linden, M., & Maas, I. (1999). Self, personality, and life regulation. Facets of psychological resilience in old age. In P. B. Baltes & K. U. Mayes (Eds.). *The Berlin Aging Study: Aging from 70 to 100* (pp. 302–328). New York: Cambridge University Press.

Steunenberg, B., Twisk, J. W. R., Beekman, A. T. F., Deeg, D. J. H., & Kerkhof, A. J. F. M. (2005). Stability and change in neuroticism in aging. *Journals of Gerontology Series B: Psychological Sciences and Social Sciences, 60*, 27–33.

Terracciano, A., McCrae, R. R., & Costa, P. T. (2006). Personality plasticity after age 30. *Personality and Social Psychology Bulletin, 32*, 999–1009.

Timko, C., & Moos, M. (1989). Choice, control, and adaptation among elderly residents of sheltered care settings. *Journal of Applied Social Psychology, 19*, 636–655.

Usita, P., Hyman, I., & Herman, K. (1998). Narrative intentions: Listening to life stories in Alzheimer's Disease. *Journal of Aging Studies, 12*, 185–197.

Verbrugge, L. M., & Jette, A. M. (1994). The disablement process. *Social Science and Medicine, 38*, 1–14.

Vitaliano, P. P., Young, H. M., Russo, J., Romano, J., & Magana-Amato, A. (1993). Does expressed emotions in spouses predict subsequent problems among care recipients with Alzheimer's disease? *Journals of Gerontology, 48*, 202–209.

Vittoria, A. K. (1998). Preserving selves: Identity and dementia. *Research on Aging, 20*, 91–136.

Weil, A. T. (1998). *The natural mind: A new way of looking at drugs and the higher consciousness.* Boston: Houghton Mifflin.

Willis, S. L. (1991). Cognition and everyday competence. In K. Schaie & M. Lawton (Eds.). *Annual Review of Gerontology and Geriatrics* (11th vol., pp. 80–129). New York: Springer.

Zarit, S. (2006). Assessment of family caregivers: A research perspective. In Family Caregiver Alliance (Ed.), *Caregiver assessment: Voices and views from the field – Report from a National Consensus Development Conference* (Vol. 2, pp. 12–37). San Francisco: Family Caregiver Alliance.

19

An Integrative Summary and Future Directions in the Study of Well-Being

JISKA COHEN-MANSFIELD AND LEONARD W. POON

ABSTRACT

This chapter integrates and summarizes our collective thinking on well-being among the old-old by answering five central questions: 1) What is old-old age?; 2) What is well-being in old-old persons?; 3) What affects well-being in old-old age?; 4) What theory, if any, is appropriate for old-old age?; 5) What interventions, if at all, are needed to enhance well-being in old-old age? It is hoped that our discourse will generate new research and directions toward well-being among old-old at the end stage of life.

INTRODUCTION

We began this volume with a road map to increase our knowledge on well-being among the oldest old. We designed this volume to include different views on well-being, the impact of experiences and trauma accumulated over the lifetime, mediating and moderating influences, and measurement issues.

At the end of this journey of inquiry, we are able to summarize and integrate our effort. As a scientific endeavor, this book both answers questions and raises others. The book aims to answer questions about the essence of well-being in very old age and the predictors of such status. Some findings repeat and are consistent across populations and studies, whereas some of the chapters present diverse and conflicting points of view. To integrate the results of the different chapters and focus the discussion, we concentrate on five questions that traverse the chapters:

1. What is old-old age?
2. What is well-being in old-old persons?
3. What affects well-being in old-old age?

4. What theory, if any, is appropriate for old-old age?
5. What interventions, if at all, are needed to enhance well-being in old-old age?

1. What Is Old-Old Age?

What is the problem with old-old age? It is quite obvious that chronological age is vastly inadequate as an indication for classifying the level of well-being among individuals. About half the chapters of this book focused on research on centenarians, whereas another half focused on old-old persons using other definitions. Yet the main question arising from such a discussion is, What is it about old-old age, be it centenarian or any other definition, that makes this population unique? In other words, is it age per se, as represented by life span on this planet and length of telomeres in the DNA, that affects reactions to the environment or to trauma? Alternative hypotheses are that it is physical frailty and disability, cognitive decline, diminished resources, or a combination of those that affects responses and life experience in old age. On all these factors, the old-old differ from the old. As seen in Chapter 9, centenarians differ from octogenarians in economic and social resources. Yet are the actual mechanisms with which they cope with decline different from each other? Which of these and which combination of these represents the fourth age as described in Chapter 2? Are healthy, cognitively intact centenarians different psychologically from healthy and cognitively intact sixty-year-olds? Are centenarian persons with dementia different from their seventy-year-old counterparts? Most likely, the main difference relates to the dimension of vigor, frailty, weakness, and fatigue. If so, could we better characterize the relative impact of cognitive decline, disability, frailty, and diminished resources on the living experience of the oldest old? Such impact will be evident on the living experience of the person, but it may or may not be seen for well-being. Another concept that is not well explored is distance from death. Is the well-being of individuals in their seventies and hundreds different when they are one year from death? Does the amount and depletion of resources affect these individuals differently based on their chronological age?

How far does middle age extend? As chartered in Chapter 2, the distinction between middle age and the third age is hazy and becoming more blurred. Although there are gradual changes in biological and functional processes, such as vision or drug absorption, throughout the lifetime, as well as some that are accelerated in old age, such as sarcopenia (an involuntary loss of muscle mass; see Chapter 10), it is possible that, from a psychological and sociological point of view, these ages are blending. If so, the work of gerontology and geriatrics may be to attend to the psychological and sociological sequelae of cognitive decline, functional decline, and predeath phenomena rather than to a specific age group.

One illustration of the confusion surrounding the impact of age can be examined through the discussion of socioemotional selectivity theory in Chapter 12. The theory "suggests that older people do benefit from meaningful social relationships... but also tend to disassociate from ties that are less likely to provide optimal return.... Thus, a relationship selection process is believed to occur in very late life. However, age per se may be less a trigger of socioemotional selectivity than is one's awareness of limitations on future time.... This latter clarification may explain why the degree of disability plays an important role in predicting relationship outcomes in older age." These findings highlight central questions: Is the decrease in social network a function of age, of disability, of the realization of limited available time, or of more limited opportunity (Cohen-Mansfield & Parpura-Gill, 2007)? One important inference from this question relates to whether this selection is at will or due to lack of options. An understanding of this has implications to theory (e.g., the former interpretation being closer to disengagement theory and the latter to continuity) and to intervention (e.g., are establishment of new social ties appropriate for this population?).

2. What Is Well-Being in Old-Old Persons?

The conceptualizations of well-being. Our authors presented diverse definitions of well-being. Dwelling on the subjective aspects of well-being, Shmotkin (Chapter 3) presents happiness and subjective well-being as referring to "self-evaluations that people make about their general life condition, basically in positive-negative terms." A similar definition is used in Chapter 17: "Subjective well-being is best defined as a cognitive orientation of life based on positive and negative emotions, domain satisfactions, and global judgments of life satisfaction and happiness." Both definitions stress a cognitive and an evaluative component, a positive-negative dimension, and an emphasis on a general or a global point of view. Alternatively, in Chapter 15, emphasis is placed on psychological aspects of well-being such as emotion, happiness, and satisfaction, and well-being is described as "a psychological variable in that a researcher obtains an understanding of how a person feels about their life in a specified temporal framework." A somewhat different approach is presented in Chapter 4, where multiple levels of well-being are presumed to coexist at any given time and where well-being is conceptualized to involve both trait and state components. Still a different approach is presented in the examination of well-being through the will to live: "defined as the psychological expression of a natural instinct of human beings – the striving for life, which is comprised of rational and irrational components, and can also be self-assessed" (Chapter 16). The inclusion of persons with dementia in the discussion of well-being (Chapter 4) suggests that well-being can also be estimated by an observed state of mind rather than only through self-evaluation. Finally, low levels of well-being are characterized by appetite loss in the old-old. Nonetheless, this symptom may be moderated by environmental conditions as nursing-home residents had a lower risk for appetite loss (Chapter 10).

Social biases in the reporting of well-being. Not only are symptoms of well-being affected by the environment; the very core expressions of well-being and the interpretation of responses to well-being questions are socially determined and affected by social norms about how to view life and what responses are appropriate. When older persons are questioned regarding their well-being, responses may also represent messages intended for the person's social network (Chapter 15). Although social norms and expectations are most evidently affecting diverse well-being reports across societies, these social forces affect individuals' responses in a given society as well. Ethnographic studies address this issue by investigating the content and context of individual responses and pointing out their influences (Chapter 15). In contrast, quantitative studies regard such biases in reports as noise and address problems in measurements by using large samples, using relatively robust assessments, comparing different social and cultural subgroups, and searching for findings that are stronger than the variability introduced by the biases inherent in responses to inquiries regarding well-being. Different chapters in the book illustrate both approaches (Chapter 17). A central question on the measurement of well-being and quality of life is, Whose perspectives, the individual's or the researcher's, are relevant?

Well-being versus quality of life. Well-being is differentiated from quality of life, as quality of life covers more domains and takes account of more indicators, including "life expectancy, levels of education, quality of housing and income" (Chapter 15). A construct similar to quality of life is developmental outcomes, which includes functional capacity and subjective health, cognitive impairment, mental health, economic cost and burden, psychological well-being, and longevity, and reflects fundamental quality-of-life characteristics (Chapter 5). A related distinction is made between hedonic and eudaimonia well-being. Whereas subjective well-being relates to current positive and negative affect, eudaimonia refers to the striving toward realization of one's true potential and toward perfection (Chapter 3). Eudaimonia is also construed as psychological well-being in contrast with subjective hedonic well-being, and it is operationalized to include the constructs of growth and autonomy (Chapters 3 and 9). This distinction raises the question, Is eudaimonia a goal to be achieved or is it a means of reaching subjective well-being? On the one hand, for many older adults, eudaimonia is a necessary condition for reaching subjective well-being. Meaning and a sense of achievement are crucial even in very old age and even in dementia (Cohen-Mansfield et al., 2010; Marx et al., 2005), and therefore are highly significant to the development of leisure roles and activities for the old-old (Chapter 14). For others, such as the severely cognitively impaired, eudaimonia may not be possible or meaningful. Are meaning and self-actualization a necessary criterion for quality of life? Such inquiry is related to the debate over what is successful aging and over whether health and functional status should be construed as criteria for successful aging. Indeed, older persons view themselves as aging successfully despite chronic disease (Montross et al., 2006). Thus, it is important to query, Whose decision is it? Who determines the criteria for quality of life or successful aging? As stated in Chapter 2, "these criteria for quality of life reflect issues and concerns pertinent . . . to midlife, such as continuity, success, and meaning," which may not be pertinent at the end of existence. The issue of what is included under the definition of *quality of life* and who determines this inclusion is a philosophical question with practical implications for society's goals and practices, as it allows us to rate persons as successful or not, as attaining quality of life, and as with or without the potential to attain it.

What do we measure when assessing well-being? As described in Chapter 17, current measures of well-being span a large range of constructs and dimensions. These reflect the dichotomy between the more narrow definitions of subjective well-being and the broader constructs of quality of life, developmental outcomes, eudaimonia, and successful aging. Among the assessments with the narrower and more focused definition, we have examples from Chapter 17, such as the Bradburn Affect Balance Scale, which assesses positive and negative affect. The Positive and Negative Affect Schedule, while eliciting positive and negative affect, assesses emotionality. The Satisfaction with Life Scale evaluates life satisfaction. A somewhat intermediate measure is the Life Satisfaction Index, measuring the dimensions of zest (i.e., degree of engagement in activities with other people), congruence (i.e., the degree to which desired life goals were accomplished), and mood (i.e., feelings of happiness). An example capturing the quality of life end of the spectrum is the Ryff Scales of Psychological Well-Being, which assess the following dimensions of psychological well-being: self-acceptance, positive relationships with others, autonomy, purpose in life, personal growth, and environmental mastery. Other measures focus on specific life conditions, such as retirement, assessed via the Retirement Descriptive Index, and the Retirement Satisfaction Index. Similarly, the Family Interaction Index measures the type and frequency of family activities. Other types of assessment focus on religious and spiritual aspects of well-being, such as the Duke University Religiosity Index, the Valuation of Life Scale, the Daily Spiritual Experiences Scale, and the Attachment to God Scale (see Chapter 17). Finally, another approach to the measurement of well-being is the assessment of the will to live (Chapter 16). Most chapters in this book focused on subjective well-being, and as can be seen in Chapter 9, the use of other constructs, such as growth and autonomy, results in different explanatory models. Although there is confusion as to which measures are most appropriate, a guiding principle in the selection is the research question and the context in which the questions are posed.

3. What Affects Well-Being in Old-Old Age?

Quantitative results: Distal and proximal influences. On the whole, people report adequate levels of well-being well into very old ages, yet there is a wide variability in the ratings of well-being. Empirical findings document some influences on or relationships with well-being, such as those of personality, self-reported health, quality of relationships, and adequacy of economic resources (see Chapter 1). Chapter 5 reports both distal and proximal variables to be related to well-being. Findings concerning distal influences were as follows: (a) having more children was related to diminished loneliness, whereas poor health in childhood was associated with higher loneliness scores; (b) losing a father earlier in life was related to depressive symptoms, a relationship mediated by level of extraversion; and (c) lifetime (cumulative) negative events eroded the personality trait of competence, which was significantly related to positive coping and lower levels of depression. Several findings illustrated the influence of proximal factors. Engaged lifestyle (e.g., volunteering, traveling, giving public speeches) was related to higher cognitive status, though proximal events were only marginally associated with depressive symptoms. Chapter 12 highlights the importance of robust social networks and helping others (related both to social support system and to eudaimonia) to well-being in older persons. Religious coping is another proximal variable associated with improved well-being (Chapter 13).

Qualitative results: Distal and proximal influences. In contrast to the regression methodologies most often used to examine determinants of well-being, an alternative approach is to inquire about the perceptions of older persons themselves about those determinants. When examining the impact of distal and proximal life events as perceived by very old persons, distal events were more likely to be positive and to include normative life transitions, such as marriage, whereas proximal life events tended to involve decline in health and thus be perceived as diminishing well-being (Chapter 7).

The effect of trauma. In examining multiple studies of the distal effects of major past trauma of the Holocaust, Chapter 6 reports of negative effects on well-being in old-old age, yet some studies did not find such effects, which underscores the wide heterogeneity in responses to major distal events. The study of major distal trauma in old-old age is limited by its very nature due to a selection bias, in that researchers are restricted to those who survived for many years beyond such trauma. Those manifesting a more major traumatic response most likely have not survived to this age (Chapter 6). When experiencing trauma in old age, the old-old are neither more nor less prone to its effects; indeed, what may constitute a trauma eliciting posttraumatic symptoms may greatly vary across people (Chapter 8). These findings demonstrate the resiliency of humans in dealing with life-changing trauma, which is frequently underestimated.

The effect of trauma on the cognitively impaired. Another deviation from the common study methodology of contributors to well-being is a focus on persons with dementia, who account for about 30% or more of those age 90 and older (Ebly, Parhad, Hogan, & Fung, 1994; Farrer & Cahan, 2007). In Chapter 6, Shmotkin discusses dementia-molded survival and raises the question of whether cognitive impairment sensitizes traumatic memories or blunts them. Similarly, in Chapter 8, Hyer speaks about severe trauma as a contributor to the risk of dementia, and in turn, dementia may contribute to a rekindling of trauma, to a decreased ability to cope with traumatic stressors, or to the forgetting of trauma.

The knotty meshing of explanatory variables. One of the most difficult issues in explaining well-being in the old-old is the intricate blending of explanatory variables. In most aging samples, income and education are closely tied, both related to health and to mental health, which have cyclical relationships between them. Distal variables often affect proximal variables, which then affect well-being. One such example is presented in

Chapter 9, where distal resources (e.g., education) relate to the proximal variable of income, which allows centenarians to better cope with functional limitations and thus affects subjective mental health. Proximal resources are affected by distal processes, as the impact of income on subjective mental health may reflect not only current income but also life-long constructive attitudes and activities, which were also responsible for the attainment of income. Similarly, in results presented here, is number of children (Chapter 5) a distal or proximal resource? Although the acquisition of this resource is distal, it is probably through social contact with the children and the economic and social resources provided by them, both of which represent proximal resources that result, but are not a necessary outcome, of distal events. At times, the proximal resource is both a resource and an indicator or an outcome of well-being. For example, is volunteering a result or a predictor of mental health? Is experiencing PTSD rather than recovering from trauma affected by the same variables that predispose a person to poor outcomes? Is it possible to disentangle the recursive relationships between affect and PTSD? Although some design and statistical methodologies can partially disentangle those relationships, they most often represent a real-life entanglement, in that cycles of causes and outcomes affect each other. This intricate relationship between causal and outcome variables is clear in quantitative methods, but it is also evident in qualitative ones, as stated in Chapter 15, where in the discussion of life satisfaction among persons from various African tribes, material security was so closely linked with health, that it was difficult to separate these constructs.

The well-being paradox in old-old age. Empirical data present consistent findings of well-being levels in old-old age that are comparable to those of other ages. Yet the mechanism for this is currently addressed only by theoretical explanations. Although research findings concerning predictors of well-being do exist, as outlined herein, the apparent paradox of well-being, despite worsening physical, cognitive, and diminished resources, is not yet explained by empirical findings.

4. What Theory Is Appropriate for Old-Old Age?

The bounty of theories. The dominant theoretical framework in this book is the developmental adaptation model (Chapter 5). This model includes distal experiences and past achievements as important predictors of well-being and adaptation in later life. Although both distal and proximal events have a direct effect on adaptation, the effect of distal variables on adaptation is often mediated by proximal resources. A very different approach is presented in the shifting baseline theory (Chapter 4), which describes well-being as a function of a relatively constant baseline trait and of states representing periods of change and stability in health, function, and other resources. In addition to these two theories, corresponding to specific chapters in the book, other chapters refer to a multitude of other theories, some of which are age specific. Erickson's developmental stages theory is used in Chapter 16. Disengagement theory is referred to in Chapter 2. Continuity and innovation theories are discussed in Chapter 14. Chapter 3 presents a theoretical model of the pursuit of happiness in the face of adversity. According to this model, persons are involved in an active adaptation process in order to face threats in their environment and to maximize well-being. Chapter 3 also refers to other theories such as the common-cause theory and the gerodynamics theory, whereas Chapter 12 discusses socioemotional selectivity theory. Lawton's environmental press theory and the Selection, Optimization, and Compensation (SOC) model of Baltes and Baltes are discussed in Chapter 18. More general cognitive behavioral and social learning theories are mentioned in the discussion of interventions (Chapters 8 and 18).

How do these theories differ from each other, and what is the meaning of having such a diverse range of theories? Some theories describe old age as constituting a new stage in life with different developmental tasks (e.g., Erickson, disengagement theory), whereas others emphasize the continuity with prior life (e.g., continuity theory, innovation theory). Some theories focus on the decreased ability to cope with life tasks in old-old age (e.g., common-cause theory, the theory of incomplete architecture of human ontology, gerodynamics theory), whereas others address the well-being paradox and aim to explain how older persons cope with adversity, frailty, or decline (e.g., the pursuit of happiness in face of adversity, the environmental press theory, SOC, the shifting baseline theory). The latter theories therefore address some form of adaptation. It is our belief that the construct of adaptation is at the heart of the controversies among these theories. It is important to note that, overall, the proliferation of theories probably attests to their limitations in capturing the phenomena under discussion and to insufficient research to discern among them. Despite this general limitation, future work needs to clarify which of these provides a better representation of reality in general or for types of phenomena in particular.

What is adaptation? The centrality of adaptation in many of the theories makes this construct particularly important to comprehend, yet an understanding of basic tenets of this construct is lacking. How does adaptation differ from resilience? Or from coping? In fact, could *adaptation* be the term used for achieving well-being despite an adverse-world scenario (Chapter 3)? In that case, adaptation may signify a pattern of living sustained by ongoing processes, such as the pursuit of well-being in labile life conditions. Schlossberg (1981) described adaptation as the balance of individual resources and deficits (Chapter 5). Which resources and deficits have a direct or indirect effect on balance and adaptation? Is adaptation an active process, as suggested in several chapters (e.g., Chapter 3), or a passive one (Chapter 4)? What affects adaptation? If it is an active process, what cognitive and behavioral activities are necessary and sufficient for adaptation? If it is a passive process, which conditions are more likely to promote it and which will hinder it? Furthermore, to what degree does *adaptation* describe the individual, and to what extent is adaptation a dialectical process in that the social context and environment adapt to the presence and exigencies of the old?

5. What Interventions Are Needed to Enhance Well-Being in Old-Old Age?

Several approaches to intervention to enhance well-being are discussed in this book. Maximizing the benefits of leisure activities (Chapter 14) is one important avenue. Such activities can offer relief and distraction from physical and emotional losses and create an opportunity for a more meaningful daily life, thus creating the potential to enhance both subjective well-being and eudaimonia. As stated in Chapter 14, new activities can replace those activities that are discontinued due to limitations or disabilities. When new activities are innovative and successful, they can go beyond replacement of prior habits in providing a sense of control and a new sense of worth, thus promoting an enhanced sense of growth and well-being.

Cognitive behavior therapy, adapted to the old and sometimes frail individual, can be useful in older adults both in the treatment of posttraumatic stress disorder (Chapter 8) and in other interventions that aim to increase subjective well-being (Chapter 18). Hyer, in Chapter 18, highlights principles that are central to interventions with old-old persons. Some of these are extensions of general therapeutic practices to the old-old, such as ensuring therapeutic alliance and using its power, or the utility of cognitive behavior therapy with the old-old. Other principles, though often applicable to other age groups, have a special significance in the treatment of the old-old. These include, first, maximizing the physical and social environment to enhance comfort and meaning and minimize risks. The environment can be a tool for enhancing well-being, a means to boost therapeutic activities, or part of the problem that interferes with well-being, and its modification can have direct therapeutic results. Second is incorporating individual differences in health, unmet needs, personality, competencies, as well as personal, social, and environmental resources into the care plan. An understanding of this complex architecture of resources and needs calls for personalized interventions and for coordination and linking with other services and family members. Third is maximizing strengths, positive traits, and self-identity. Fourth is using placebo as a treatment that induces hope, thus allowing for other advances.

The actual range of interventions to enhance well-being in the old-old is much broader than what could be included in this volume. The tremendous range of interventions reflects the extreme heterogeneity in function that epitomizes the old-old. On the one extreme, interventions include home- and community-based services that allow the old-old to remain at home, such as those associated with naturally occurring retirement communities. On the other functional extreme are those who have lost the ability to take care of their activities of daily living. In those cases, interventions to provide those in the most pleasant and individualized manner are part of well-being treatments. In between are myriad other services and interventions, such as adult day care, intergenerational programs, and games.

Future Directions

Each chapter and each section of this chapter raised many areas for future analysis, both theoretical and experimental. Three of those we would still like to highlight stem from contrasting the analyses presented in this book:

- The impact of trauma and other distal effects needs to be clarified as to when and how it affects well-being and whether extreme trauma sets an upper limit or shifts the customary level of well-being. Also to be examined is the distinction between distal trauma, whose effects linger all along the subsequent life phases, and distal trauma that is reactivated in the particular life circumstances of old-old age. Similarly, discerning the differential impact of actual trauma from its memory, meaning, and interpretation in later years is an important research area to pursue.
- The optimal levels of resources need clarification. This includes the nature and levels of social contact needed by older persons. What is it about the social contact that matters: receiving, giving, having

contact, quality of contact? Does it differ by person? Is vicarious contact adequate? It is also crucial to better understand the resources needed in terms of leisure or everyday life activities, with which many old-old persons, especially those with cognitive impairment, need guidance and support to fill this essential part of everyday life. The role and limitations of technology to fulfill some of these needs has to be clarified. Similarly, whereas we identified that economic resources are necessary, additional guidance is needed to clarify, for example, what types of economic resources are necessary to ensure well-being among the old-old with a given level of cognitive impairment.
- The relative importance of transient changes in function and resources as presented in the shifting baseline theory needs to be compared with the explanatory power of more traditional models that examine resources and challenges at a point of time, such as the Developmental Adaptation Model.

Many other areas need to be studied and examined in future research. These include the study of global, cultural processes in a postmodern epoch, which might change the contours and qualities of the category of the old-old. Well-being could be a function of diverse factors such as labor migration, the economics of prolonged longevity, advances in medical technologies, blurring of age boundaries, and the new imagery of aging as a reversible state and of old age as a transient state. An examination of the role of diverse cultures on the manifestation of old-old age, the associated needs, and the ways to fulfill them could bring about new understandings and opportunities for enhancing the last stage of life. Other areas that are central to old-old populations need to include the topics of dementia, as well as its progression and processes that affect well-being in each stage. Topics regarding the dying process, preparation for it, options regarding death, and the impact of distance from death are also crucial areas for further research. Finally, services and policies for the old-old need to be described and enhanced, and the positive aspects of old-old age require further exploration, with emphasis on potential gains in old-old age, such as grandparenthood, life review, a long-term perspective on everyday life, and wisdom.

The study of the old-old is the interplay between the learner and its subject. There is tension between the will to understand the lived experience of the old-old from the individual's point of view, the wish to help and console, and the burden of one's own hopes and fears for what awaits. Those are not easy to disentangle. We juggle many images of the old-old, which are reflected not only in our research findings but also in our cultural heritage. In the well-documented heterogeneity of old-old, we include the one who, despite physical health, cognitive decline, and loss of friends and roles, maintains a level of well-being that is comparable to that of other ages, reflected already in the 25-century-old poem "Age," by Anacreon (c. 572–488 BC):

OFT am I by the women told,
"Poor Anacreon! thou growest old;
Look; how thy hairs are falling all;
Poor Anacreon, how they fall!" –
Whether I grow old or no,
By the effects I do not know;
But this I know, without being told,
'Tis time to live, if I grow old;
'Tis time short pleasures now to take,
Of little life the best to make,
And manage wisely the last stake.

The contrasted image is that of despair, such as the one of those who are suffering, in physical pain, or isolated through cognitive deterioration. Such despair is reflected in "Growing Old," by Matthew Arnold (1822–1888):

What is it to grow old?
Is it to lose the glory of the form,
The lustre of the eye?
Is it for beauty to forego her wreath?
Yes, but not for this alone.

. . .
It is to suffer this,
And feel but half, and feebly, what we feel:
Deep in our hidden heart
Festers the dull remembrance of a change,
But no emotion – none.
It is – last stage of all –
When we are frozen up within, and quite
The phantom of ourselves,
To hear the world applaud the hollow ghost
Which blamed the living man.

And yet there is the hope ("Rabbi Ben Ezra," by Robert Browning, 1812–1889):

Grow old along with me!
The best is yet to be,

The last of life, for which the first was made:
Our times are in His hand
Who saith, "A whole I planned,
Youth shows but half; trust God: see all, nor be afraid!"

And the mystery ("Nature," by Henry Wadsworth Longfellow, 1807–1882):

So Nature deals with us, and takes away
Our playthings one by one, and by the hand
Leads us to rest so gently, that we go
Scarce knowing if we wish to go or stay,
Being too full of sleep to understand
How far the unknown transcends the what we know.

REFERENCES

Cohen-Mansfield, J., & Parpura-Gill, A. (2007). Loneliness in elderly persons: A theoretical model and empirical findings. *International Psychogeriatrics, 19*, 279–294.

Cohen-Mansfield, J., Thein, K., Dakheel-Ali, M., & Marx, M. S. (2010). The underlying meaning of stimuli: The impact on engagement of persons with dementia. *Psychiatry Research*, 15;177(1–2):216–222.

Ebly, E. M, Parhad, I. M, Hogan, D. B, & Fung, T. S. (1994). Prevalence and types of dementia in the very old: Results from the Canadian Study of Health and Aging. *Neurology, 44*, 1593–1600.

Farrer, S., & Cahan, V., (2007, October 30). One in Seven Americans Age 71 and Older Has Some Type of Dementia, NIH-Funded Study Estimates. Retrieved from: http://www.nia.nih.gov/NewsAndEvents/PressReleases/PR20071030ADAMS.htm

Marx, M. S., Hubbard, P., Cohen-Mansfield, J., Dakheel-Ali, M., & Thein, K. (2005). Community-service activities versus traditional activities in an intergenerational visiting program. *Educational Gerontology, 31*, 263–271.

Montross, L. P., Depp, C., Daly, J., Reichstadt, J., Golshan, S., Moore, D., et al. (2006). Correlates of self-rated successful aging among community-dwelling older adults. *American Journal of Geriatric Psychiatry, 14*, 43–51.

INDEX